Exploring History
1400–1900

Exploring History
1400–1900

An anthology of primary sources

edited by
Rachel C. Gibbons

Manchester University Press
Manchester and New York
distributed exclusively in the USA by Palgrave
Published in association with

Published by Manchester University Press
Oxford Road, Manchester M13 9NR, UK
and Room 400, 175 Fifth Avenue, New York, NY 10010, USA
www.manchesteruniversitypress.co.uk

in association with The Open University

First published 2007

Distributed exclusively in the USA by
Palgrave, 175 Fifth Avenue, New York, NY 10010, USA

Distributed exclusively in Canada by
UBC Press, University of British Columbia, 2029 West Mall, Vancouver, BC, Canada V6T 1Z2

British Library Cataloguing-in-Publication Data
A catalogue record for this book is available from the British Library

Library of Congress Cataloging-in-Publication Data applied for

Typeset by SNP Best-set Typesetter Ltd, Hong Kong

Printed and bound in the United Kingdom by Biddles Ltd, King's Lynn

This book forms part of an Open University course A200 *Exploring History: Medieval to Modern, 1400–1900*. Details of this and other Open University courses can be obtained from the Student Registration and Enquiry Service, The Open University, PO Box 197, Milton Keynes, MK7 6BJ, United Kingdom:
tel. +44 (0)870 333 4340, email general-enquiries@open.ac.uk

http://www.open.ac.uk

ISBN-10 0 7190 7587 4 *hardback*
ISBN-13 978 0 7190 7587 2 *hardback*

ISBN-10 0 7190 7588 2 *paperback*
ISBN-13 978 0 7190 7588 9 *paperback*

16 15 14 13 12 11 10 09 08 07   10 9 8 7 6 5 4 3 2 1

Contents

Contents

List of illustrations

Acknowledgements

The editor and publisher would like to thank all the academic and support staff of the A200 Course Team for their contribution to *Exploring History*.

The editor and publisher would also like to thank the following for permission to publish the enclosed documents: The Bourgeois of Paris (1968) *Journal of a Citizen of Paris*, ed. & trans. J. Shirley, Oxford: Clarendon Press, reprinted with the permission of the translator. R. Vaughan ([1973] 2002), *Charles the Bold*, with an introduction by W. Paravicini, 2nd edn., Woodbridge: Boydell, reprinted with the permission of the publisher. S. Dünnebeil (2002–3) *Die Protokollbucher des Ordens vom Goldenen Vlies*, Stuttgart: Thorbecke, 2 vols., vol. 1, reprinted with the permission of the publisher. N. Davis (ed.) (1999) *The Paston Letters: A Selection in Modern Spelling*, Oxford: Oxford Paperbacks, reprinted with the permission of the publisher. S. McSheffrey & N. Tanner (eds) (2003) *Lollards of Coventry, 1486–1522*, Camden 5th Series, vol. 23, Cambridge: Cambridge University Press for the Royal Historical Society, reprinted with the permission of the Royal Historical Society and Cambridge University Press. Clive Burgess (ed.) (1995) *The Pre-reformation records of All Saints Bristol, Part 1*, Bristol Record Society Publications, Vol. 46, Bristol, Bristol Record Society, reprinted with the permission of the Bristol Record Society. Erasmus of Rotterdam (1971) *Praise of Folly and Letter to Martin Dorp, 1515*, trans. B. Radice, introd. & notes A.H.T. Levi, Harmondsworth: Penguin. Translation copyright © Betty Radice, 1971. Introduction © A.H.T. Levi, 1971. Reproduced by permission of Penguin Books Ltd. C.M. Jacobs & J. Atkinson (trans.) 'To the Christian Nobility Concerning the Reform of the Christian Estate' reprinted from in H.T. Lehmann (ed.) *Luther's Works*, vol. 44, copyright © 1966, *The Christian Society*, Philadelphia: Fortress Press. Used by permission of Augsburg Fortress. C. Lindberg (ed.) (2000) *The European Reformation Sourcebook*, Oxford: Blackwell, reprinted with the permission of the publisher. T. Scott & B. Scribner (eds. & trans.) (1991) *The German Peasants' War: A History in Documents*, New Jersey: Humanities Press International, Amherst, NY, Humanity Books. Copyright © 1991 by Tom Scott and Bob Scribner. Reprinted with permission of the publisher, Prometheus Books. A. Duke, G. Lewis & A. Pettigree (eds.) (1992) *Calvinism in Europe, 1540–1610: A collection of documents*, Manchester: Manchester University Press, reprinted with the permission of the publisher. G.R. Elton (ed.) (1960) *The Tudor Constitution*, Cambridge: Cambridge University Press, ©

Cambridge University Press, reproduced with permission from the publisher and the Royal Historical Society. Aberystwyth, National Library of Wales MS 4919D; extracts published in R. O'Day & J. Berrlatsky (eds.) (1979) *Camden Miscellany XXVII*, London: Royal Historical Society, reproduced with the permission of the Royal Historical Society. E. Donnan (ed.) (1931) *From Documents Illustrative of the History of the Slave Trade to America*, Washington D.C.: Carnegie Institute, reprinted with the permission of the publisher. A. Smith ([1776] 1991) *The Wealth of Nations*, ed. & introd. D.D. Raphael, Everyman's Library Classics, London: Everyman, JM Dent, a division of The Orion Publishing Group, reprinted with their permission. J. Breuilly (2002) *Austria, Prussia and Germany 1806–1871*, London: Longman, reprinted with the permission of the publisher. C. Emsley (2003) *Napoleon: Conquest, Reform and Reorganisation*, Harlow: Longman, reprinted with the permission of the publisher. M. Traugott (ed.) (1933) *The French Worker: Autobiographies from the Early Industrial Era*, Berkeley: University of California Press, reprinted with the permission of the publisher. D. Moon (2002) *The Abolition of Serfdom in Russia*, 1762–1907, London: Longman, reprinted with the permission of the publisher. E. Renan (1996) *Qu'est ce qu'une nation/What is a nation?*, introd. C. Taylor; trans. W.R. Taylor, Toronto: Tapir Press, reprinted with the permission of the publisher and translator. C. Hayes (1930) *France – A Nation of Patriots*, New York: Columbia University Press, reprinted with the permission of the publisher. J. Michelet ([1847–53] 1967) *History of the French Revolution*, trans. Charles Cocks, 7 vols., Chicago: University of Chicago Press, reprinted with the permission of the publisher. J.A. Hobson ([1902] 1988) *Imperialism: A Study*, 3rd edn., introd. J. Townshend, London: Unwin Hyman. Reproduced by permission of Taylor & Francis Books UK. Harlow & M. Carter (eds.) (2003) *Archives of Empire. Vol. II: The Scramble for Africa*, Durham, NC: Duke University Press, © Duke University Press, 2003, reprinted with the permission of the publisher.

All attempts have been made to trace the correct copyright holders of the enclosed documents. Please do not hesitate to contact the publisher with any queries you have regarding the permissions and copyright of the documents.

General introduction

This Anthology has been designed and produced as a set book for the Open University course A200, *Exploring History: Medieval to Modern, 1400–1900*. Documents and texts have been chosen and presented primarily with the demands of this course and its assessment in mind. However, we hope that the documents will have a wider use, as sources that illuminate the development of the institutions and mentalities of western Europe and its global outlook during the five centuries covered by the Anthology. This collection will allow readers to engage in a personal and very accessible way with the past and its peoples, and to develop historical skills in the use and assessment of primary source evidence.

Providing a solid introduction to historical study through presentation of a varied collection of sources covering a wide chronological span is, then, the key aim of this Anthology. Documents have been included that were written by people who directed the events of nation states and by those affected by those decisions; by people conforming to the mores of their society and by people rejecting them. There are documents on life at court, in towns and on plantations, on gentry and on peasant life, on the experiences and opinions of men and of women. The aim is to provide a sense of cohesion between the different periods, places and subject matters covered in the six chapters by identifying three underlying historical themes and enabling readers, if they choose, to track developments in any one theme across a full five centuries. This Anthology, then, functions as a coherent collection for either political or religious/ideological or socio-economic history, as well as a means of examining six case study topics in depth.

Primary source materials have become generally more readily available than in the past, with the digitisation of printed collections such as Early English Books Online, Eighteenth Century Collections Online and the publishing on the internet of, for instance, archive newspapers and document extracts. However, for students at the beginning of their historical careers, these still can be difficult to work with, given hard-to-decipher handwriting or typefaces, and the fact that they are sometimes unpaginated, and with unfamiliar spellings, names and terminology that are never explained. Any historical account depends on the contemporary sources, so it is vital that students get the opportunity to read them for themselves. We made a conscious decision as a Course Team, therefore, to devote almost half of the Anthology to Chapters 1 and 2, and material prior to the year 1600, which remains the least accessible elsewhere, both in terms of ease of use and in the quantities of material published.

A great many of the documents and source extracts are published here in an accessible format for students and general readers for the first time. The majority of documents from Chapter 1 and a fair proportion of those from Chapters 2, 5 and 6 have been translated into English specifically for this Anthology by authors of the chapters or Open University translators. Several documents have been transcribed from the original manuscripts; these, and extracts from a number of sixteenth and seventeenth-century publications, have been edited into modern English and punctuated for comprehension by chapter authors.

Each chapter of the Anthology begins with a short introduction written by one or two of the members of the Course Team responsible for selecting the documents and texts of that chapter. These chapter introductions present the particular demands of the historical topic concerned, describe the kinds of documents selected for the chapter, and discuss how they relate to the three underlying themes of the Anthology as a collection. In addition to chapter introductions, each document commences with a head note, providing some background information on its creation and historical context, and is annotated as appropriate with definitions, explanation or commentary through glossing and footnoting. Where a document has been edited or extracted, omissions are marked with ellipses for short cuts and ellipses in square brackets for cuts of several sentences or more.

The choice of documents

Documents are selected to illuminate the six historical periods which we have chosen as case studies to mark the transition from medieval to modern society in Europe and the North Atlantic world, one of which forms the basis for each chapter. Within the six historical periods we have given prominence to three themes. Two further criteria have informed the selection of documents: to provide examples of a range of written sources, and to give readers the opportunity of working with many distinct kinds of evidence from both public and private spheres. Different types of sources have different potential uses, and historians therefore learn to read each of them in different ways in order to understand what individual documents are saying and, sometimes, what they are *not* saying.

The historical periods

The six chapters of this Anthology correspond to six blocks of A200 course material, chosen because each embodies significant features of western European history and of the influence of western Europe on the Atlantic world of the eighteenth century and of the European empires of the nineteenth century, and through which we may mark the transition from medieval to modern society. Chapters address:

1. France, Burgundy and England in the Fifteenth century;
2. The European Reformation, 1500–1600 (including the English Reformation);
3. The Wars of the Three Kingdoms, 1640–90, examining the British Isles during the period of the civil wars;
4. Slavery and Freedom, relating to trans-Atlantic slavery and the emancipation movements, c. 1760–1840;
5. Creating Nations, 1789–1871, providing a sweep of Europe in a time of revolutionary change;
6. Nations and Empire, 1870–1914, focusing on European expansion into Africa.

The themes

Three themes have been highlighted to give a sense of coherence and to measure change across the six diverse historical periods:

(i)   state formation
(ii) beliefs and ideologies
(iii) consumers and producers.

Individual chapters address the themes with differing levels of emphasis, dependent of the topic and subject matter that they are addressing. For instance, Chapter 2 on the Reformation in Europe is primarily concerned with the challenge to longstanding religious structures and practices posed by Protestant evangelicalism and includes many documents and texts discussing beliefs and ideologies. However, the creation of the Dutch Republic after a revolt against their Catholic king, Philip II of Spain, demonstrates that faith and state formation were inextricably linked in this period – as does the gradual Reformation in England. Connections between beliefs and ideologies and producers and consumers are explored in Chapter 4 in documents examining the slave economy, whilst the case study of Dundee in Chapter 6 discusses the relationship between state formation and producers and consumers in the economics of empire. In each chapter, though, documents can be found on all three themes, from the conspicuous and highly political consumption at the Burgundian court in Chapter 1, to the importance of confessional differences in the breakdown of the relationship between king and people in the three kingdoms of the British Isles in Chapter 3, to the use of historical writing in nation building and state development in Chapter 5.

Studying historical documents

Whatever period of history is being studied, certain basic questions need to be asked of any primary source. Readers will want to consider questions of:

(i) creation or authorship – who wrote the document, and why?;
(ii) circumstance – when was the document written and on what basis (as an eye-witness, from gathered evidence or from hearsay)?
(iii) the nature of the evidence – does it offer fact or interpretation? What is the source's intent, the value judgements that it presents or that we bring to it, its credibility, reliability and objectivity compared with other sources that we have of the period?
(iv) purpose – what type of source is it, and whom was its intended audience?

In this Anthology, information about the authorship and contextual circumstance of each document – the basic knowledge of names and dates – usually can be found in the title or head note. Answers to the other two sets of questions might be discovered only after careful reading of the document itself, and hence merit some additional reflection here.

A common distinction used by historians in looking at the primary evidence of the past is to ask whether it was created for public or private purposes, whether it was intended to be read by or in the domain of large numbers of people, or was generated for personal reflection or for the use of certain specified persons. This is not because one type of document invariably is more reliable than another. Governments and individuals equally can mislead, deliberately (by recording some pieces of evidence and events but not others to suit their own purposes), or innocently (through a sincere belief that something was true when, in fact, it was not). Similarly, it does not necessarily follow that documents produced by and for private individuals are less 'neutral' than official papers produced in the public domain and circulated widely. Extracts from King Henry VIII's Act in Restraint of Appeals to Rome (document 2.13) and the Napoleonic Code (document 5.3) both demonstrate that partiality can enter the most formal of state documentation. These two documents also remind us of the need to separate aspiration from reality. Just because laws were imposed does not mean that people followed them, so we need to ensure not to take *prescriptive* evidence as the full facts, but to seek out *descriptive* evidence to test the actual result. A good example of how to do this is provided by Episcopal reports of the 1630s (documents 3.5(a) to (d)), when bishops or their agents inspected parishes in their dioceses to see whether the clergy and parishioners of each church were following prescribed standards and practices laid down by the governing body of the Church of England. These documents tell us what people *should* have been doing, from the questions they were asked, and what they actually *were* doing, from their answers.

The distinction between public and private evidence can appear more blurred in the medieval and early modern periods when, with less of a permanent civil-service framework, ministers of state frequently regarded their official papers as personal property. We should also take into account the tone and purpose of official correspondences intended originally as confidential and private that were deposited as public records. The letters of Major-General Thomas Kelsey (documents 3.19(a) and (b)) and General Leclerc (document 4.7) are good examples of primary sources that seem to be both public and private evidence, written in a public (official) capacity but for a limited (private) audience. Amongst the documents reproduced in this Anthology, however, incontestably public documents are proceedings of courts of law (the trial of the Coventry Lollards in 1511–12 before an ecclesiastical court (document 1.28), for instance), of state assemblies (decrees of the French Provincial government (document 5.17)), and speeches by heads of state and public figures (speeches of Leopold II, king of the Belgians (documents 6.12(a) and (b)). Sources such as the diaries of Isabella and Roger Twysden (documents 3.16(a) and (b)) and personal letters between members of the Stonor family (documents 1.25(a) to (e)) clearly are private evidence.

Several categories of evidence and kinds of document have already been mentioned – legal proceedings, Acts of Parliament, official 'public' letters, family 'private' letters, and diaries. A further distinction for historians to make when considering different types of evidence is between documents of record and discursive sources. A document of record is one that, in itself, proves that an event took place – it embodies the event or, even, *is* it. Prime examples are the Treaty of Troyes between England and France (document 1.2) and the Scottish National Covenant (document 3.6). Discursive sources – somebody's description of an event or a discussion of its merits, faults or consequences – also have a place in enabling historians to build up a fuller picture. Accounts of the Weavers' Rising in Silesia (document 5.11) or the British acquisition of Egypt (document 6.4) are good examples of this kind of primary source, and both also illustrate the importance of knowing about and taking into account the attitude of the document's creator to events that he or she is describing. Questions of bias (positive or negative) or objectivity are important in all kinds of texts, particularly those produced with an expectation of reaching a large audience, such as popular ballads (document 5.8(b)), historical chronicles (document 1.4(b)), newspapers (documents 3.11(a) to (c)), academic publishing (document 6.1), religious treatises (document 2.2), political pamphleteering (document 4.9) or published memoirs (documents 6.16(a) to (c)).

This leads discussion neatly onto questions about the nature of evidence, and how it is used by historians in their work. It is a rare primary source that can be used totally in isolation, without a considerable understanding of its context – the historical events of the time that it is describing and in which it is being written, but also the society and cultural mores surrounding the source's creator, and what he or she is intending to communicate thorough it. Certainly when a source is describing events which were contentious or might encourage a partisan account, it is important, if possible, to weigh it up against others of the same period. For instance, one might compare the opinions of the Bourgeois of Paris (document 1.1) and Thomas Basin (document 1.4(a)) on whom was most to blame for the violence and instability in fifteenth-century France. Similarly, the fact that both John Rushworth (document 3.1) and John Nalson (document 3.2) state such strong opinions in the preface to their histories of the civil wars might cause a modern reader to question, at least in part, the credibility of both.

It is not always the veracity of documents and texts that is important – in some cases, historians might never prove whether or not they are accurate or reliable – but the use to which the individual historian puts them. A good example of this is the selection of extracts from nineteenth-century French schoolbooks reproduced in this Anthology (documents 5.24(a), (b) and (c)) which, arguably, do not present a wholly truthful historical account of French history, but are important sources of how the government of the Third Republic would like to *imagine* France's past and, therefore, how the government regarded her present and future. What primary sources *do not* say, therefore, can sometimes be as important for historians to know as what they *do* say. For instance, the brief mention of Calcutta in the extract from the report of the British Tariff Commission (document 6.6) does not really communicate the nature and extent of the perceived threat from the subcontinent to Dundee textile merchants. Equally, the absence of previously common rituals from the 1552 edition of the Book of Common Prayer (document 2.22(b)) suggests to historians that the Anglican Church was becoming increasingly removed from Catholic practice.

The example of the prayer book also serves as a reminder that historians commonly use texts and documents for purposes other than those for which they were originally intended. This might be in terms of philosophy, such as John Matthews' letters (document 4.2), which present almost an apologist case for the slave trade but tend to be used by historians to argue the complete opposite, or in terms of purpose. A good example is the use made in this Anthology of the accounts and inventories of late medieval churchwardens (documents 1.30(a) to (d)) to glean information about the involvement of ordinary parishioners in the upkeep and supply of their local church. Statistical records can appear quite complicated, but provide historians with a wealth of information, such as, to take another example, the accounts of the Parliamentarian garrison at Great Chalfield (document 3.15), so it is worth taking the time to gain confidence in using them – or even in creating them from raw data. Statistics do not always appear in neat tables or accounts sheets in primary sources: sometimes information occurs in narrative form from which the historian themselves has to extract the data, put it into a table and compile results to draw a conclusion on the evidence, such as in document 6.8.

A final general point to consider on the nature of primary source evidence is the question of presupposition, and what twenty-first-century values and preconceptions a modern reader might bring to bear on a document. In the same way that there is rarely a neutral document, historians cannot be expected to be completely neutral either: our own life experiences, values and beliefs are likely to be brought to what we read and study. The important thing is not to try to suppress this or pretend that subjectivity does not exist, but to be aware of it when approaching a document emanating from a society with, potentially, very different social norms and prejudices, and to take into account that such a disparity may influence the way in which one is able to use and interpret the source. Material in Chapter 4 provides several examples towards which readers need to bear in mind that what is now abhorrent was once considered acceptable, with a good example being Edward Long's *History of Jamaica* (document 4.1) in which he argues that black Africans were fit only for slavery. However, this Anthology also includes examples of nineteenth-century colonial aggressive 'paternalism' (document 6.18(c)) and seventeenth-century anti-Irish prejudice (document 3.8) around which modern readers need to be prepared to work when using these sources in order to broaden their understanding of periods in history separated from today's society by more than mere time.

Note on dates and money

Dates

In the later Middle Ages, the first day of a new calendar year was most commonly taken as 25 March, the Feast Day of the Annunciation to the Virgin Mary, technically Christ's first appearance in the world with the announcement of his conception. With the introduction of a new calendar by Pope Gregory XIII (the Gregorian calendar in use in the West today) in 1582, miscalculations between solar years and calendar years were corrected by skipping ten days, and the first day of the year was set at 1 January. However, states adopted the Gregorian calendar in a piecemeal fashion, broadly speaking, with Catholic states doing so in the sixteenth century, Protestant states gradually over the eighteenth century (with England not doing so until 1752), and Greek and Russian Orthodox states not until the twentieth century. Therefore, for documents created between 1582 and the late eighteenth century, dates occurring between 1 January and 25 March may be expressed in the form 1560/1 or 1732/3. For documents using the French Revolutionary calendar (Chapters 4 and 5), the date in modern Gregorian calendar reckoning is provided as part of the annotation.

Money

Prior to the nineteenth century, the majority of European states used Roman methods of accountancy. Sums of money were recorded as pounds, shillings and pence (£, s, d). Documents 1.30 and 3.15 are good examples of record-keeping under such a system, with 12d to a shilling and 20s to the pound, even if there was not, at that point, any £1 or one shilling coinage in circulation. The actual coins minted in each country had their own names, as was the case in the United Kingdom prior to 'decimal day' in 1971, and, where any specific coins are mentioned in the text, they have been footnoted.

*   *   *

Production of this Anthology has been very much a team effort, and thanks are due to a great number of people. First and foremost, to the A200 Course Team for searching out such a wide and thought-provoking selection of sources, and responding swiftly to any additional demands of mine – in chronological chapter order, Kathleen Daly, Rosemary O'Day, Ole Peter Grell, Anne Laurence, Bernard Waites, Clive Emsley, Paul Lawrence, Donna Loftus, Robin Mackie and Annika Mombauer. For assisting with translating work, we would all like to thank Dario Tessicini, Susanne Meurer, Fabienne Evans, Tim Benton and John Breuilly. Margrit Bass in the Open University's Co-Publishing unit has been invaluable as a point of liaison between production and publication, and the support provided by both her and Alison Welsby and her team at Manchester University Press has been much appreciated. From the Course Management Team of A200, Jackie Rossi and Marion Wildey have been efficient and cheerful in provision of administrative and secretarial support, whilst my greatest debt of thanks is to Roberta Wood, for her expertise and endless patience in the tasks of copy editing and assisting me with the collection of material and preparation of the final manuscript.

Rachel C. Gibbons

Chapter 1

England, France and Burgundy in the fifteenth century

Introduction

Historians of Europe in the later Middle Ages use a wide variety of sources, ranging from the visual, such as paintings, stained glass, illuminated manuscripts and both ecclesiastical and secular architecture, to the written, both official and unofficial. The documents in this chapter have been chosen to give some flavour of the range of written sources available to the historian of fifteenth-century Burgundy, France and England. The choice of documents has been further informed by the themes of state formation; beliefs and ideologies; and producers and consumers.

Prominent in the collection are documents pertaining to state formation and the political crisis in France, c. 1415–61. These sources range from the Treaty of Troyes of 1420 (document 1.2), designed to repair the 'great and irreparable evils' caused by the dissensions between England and France, through a contemporary description of the jubilant entry of King Henry VI into Paris in 1431 (1.3), and several documents concerning English rule in Normandy, to a further group dealing with French resistance to this situation.

The nature of the Burgundian state, c. 1440–70, forms the basis of a further group of documents. The Treaty of Arras in 1435 (1.12) indicates the nature of the official relationship between the duke of Burgundy and the French king. Other documents supply descriptions of the Burgundian court and the household, which imply the development of Burgundy as an independent state.

1.1 Depiction of the State Opening of Parliament, 1523, by Henry VIII, in a ceremony unchanged since medieval times. Seated on the left of the picture are the clergy (Wolsey under the red cardinal's hat), to the centre and right, the Lords and, standing, behind the king's dais, are members of the Commons.

Especially illuminating are the writings of Georges Chastelain, and the statutes of the Order of the Golden Fleece.

The writings of the lawyer Sir John Fortescue, the premier fifteenth-century English political theorist, are represented here by 1.22. They provide a penetrating contemporary diagnosis of the nature of the English crisis in government. Considerable runs of English family correspondence (as opposed to stray letters) survive for the first time in the fifteenth century. Extracts from the Paston and Stonor correspondence (1.24 and 1.25) throw some light on the society of hierarchy and deference. Indentures of life service (1.23) and descriptions of dining and seating arrangements at the funeral of Thomas Stonor (1.27) further illuminate divisions within society and relationships between lords, clergy and servants. The Stonor and Paston letters also indicate the variable effect that the Wars of the Roses had upon gentry families.

The collection concludes with a group of documents relating to beliefs and ideologies current in fifteenth- and early sixteenth-century Catholic Europe. These include a contemporary creed (statement of belief) in 1.26. Churchwardens' accounts and inventories of church goods provide evidence of styles of worship and of community involvement in the life of the church (1.30). Depositions from the Coventry Lollards may be used to indicate their beliefs but also suggest the socio-economic reach and vigour of this heretical movement in the English Midlands prior to the Reformations (1.28 and 1.29).

Rosemary O'Day

1.1

The Armagnac-Burgundian dispute
(Journal of a Citizen of Paris)

The Bourgeois of Paris (1968) *Journal of a Citizen of Paris*, ed. & trans. J. Shirley, Oxford: Clarendon Press, pp. 146–7.

This work is a major source on events in Paris between 1405 and 1449. The anonymous author was probably a cleric, shown by his interest in ecclesiastical affairs, church processions and his grasp of the complex calendar of feasts in the liturgical year. A few references in the text suggest that he may have been a member of the University of Paris, with connections to the cathedral chapter of Notre-Dame, but the evidence is inconclusive. In this extract, the author gives his views on the impact on France of the conflict between the Armagnacs and Burgundians, the rival factions that were competing to control royal government.

[1419] . . . I do not think that anyone, not the most brilliant, could enumerate all the unhappy, appalling, monstrous and damnable sins that have been committed since the disastrous and damnable appearance in France of Bernard, Count of Armagnac, Constable of France [1360–1418]. Ever since France first heard the names of 'Burgundian' and 'Armagnac', every crime that can be thought or spoken of has been done in the kingdom of France, so that innocent blood cries for vengeance before God. It is my sincere opinion that this Count of Armagnac was a devil in the shape of a man, because I cannot see that anyone who belongs to him or who holds by him or who wears his sash[1] ever obeys the law or the Christian faith. On the contrary, they behave towards all those over whom they have power like men who have denied their creator, as is perfectly plain throughout the kingdom of France. I am sure that the King of England [Henry V][2] would never have dared to set foot in France in the way of war but for the dissensions which sprang from this unhappy name. Normandy would still have been French, the noble blood of France would not have been spilt nor the lords of the kingdom taken away into exile, nor the battle lost, nor would so many good men have been killed on that dreadful day of Agincourt[3] when the king [Charles VI][4] lost so many of his true and loyal friends, had it not been for the pride of this wretched name, Armagnac. Alas! Nothing will be left to them of all their wickedness except the guilt. If they do not amend during this poor bodily life they will be for ever damned in great pain and grief, for certainly no one can hide anything from God. He, full of mercy, knows everything, so let no one put his trust in that nor in long life nor any other foolish

[1] To show their political allegiance, supporters of the Armagnac party wore a white sash: their Burgundian opponents wore a St Andrew's cross (like an X).

[2] Henry V (1386/7–1422), king of England (1413–22).

[3] The battle of Agincourt took place on 25 October 1415 on Henry V's first expedition to France. Many leading French nobles were killed, others were taken prisoner by the English. Henry V took Normandy on his second expedition to France, between 1417 and 1419.

[4] Charles VI (1368–1422), king of France (1380–1422).

hope or vainglory. He will indeed render to everyone according to his deserts. Alas, never, I think, since the days of Clovis the first Christian King,[5] has France been as desolate and divided as it is today. The Dauphin[6] and his people do nothing day or night but lay waste all his father's land with fire and sword and the English on the other side do as much harm as Saracens.[7] (It is better, though, much better, to be captured by the English than by the Dauphin or his people who call themselves the Armagnacs.) And the poor King and Queen have not moved from Troyes since Pontoise was taken,[8] where they are with their poor retinue like fugitives, exiled by their own child, a dreadful thought for any right-minded person.

1.2
The Treaty of Troyes, 21 May 1420

E. Cosneau (ed.) (1889) *Les Grands Traités de la Guerre de Cent Ans*, Paris: Picard, pp. 102–15. Translation from French by Kathleen Daly.

The Treaty marks a major new departure in Anglo-French relations. It was intended to bring peace to the two countries by uniting them under a single ruler. The Treaty maintained the independence of each kingdom. It made provisions for them to keep their separate customs and laws, and for Charles VI, king of France, to keep his throne until his death. However, it was also the outcome of French weakness and Henry V's military and diplomatic success. It was not accepted south of the Loire, which was largely loyal to Charles VI's son, the dauphin. These extracts are taken from the French version of the Treaty (the corresponding copy for the English was written in Latin).

---

[5] Clovis (c. 466–511), king of the Franks, who was converted following a battlefield vision in 496 CE and came to be seen as the first Christian king of France.

[6] The future Charles VII (1403–61).

[7] That is, Moslems, regarded as mortal enemies of Christendom.

[8] Pontoise, a key strategic point between Paris and Rouen, fell to the English at the end of July 1419.

Charles by the grace of God, king of France, in perpetual memory. Whereas several notable and divers treaties . . . have been made in time past between our noble [p]rogenitors of good memory and those of the very noble prince our very dear son Henry king of England, heir of France, and between us and our said son, in order to restore peace and remove dissensions between the kingdoms of France and England, but which have not brought the desired fruit of peace: Let it be known to everyone now and in future, that having considered and weighed in our heart how many great and irreparable evils, what enormities and what a pitiful universal and incurable wound the aforesaid division of the two kingdoms has brought, not just to those kingdoms, but to the whole Church Militant, we have recently made a treaty of peace with our said son Henry once again, which . . . is concluded and agreed in the following manner.

1. First, because by the marriage alliance, for the good of the said peace, between our said son King Henry and our dear and much loved daughter Katherine, he has become our son and that of our most dear and most beloved wife, the queen, our son will hold and honour us and our said queen like a father and mother, and as such a great prince and princess should be honoured, before all lay persons in the world.

2. Item, that our said son, King Henry, will not disturb or prevent us, as long as we shall live, from holding, as we hold at present, the crown and royal dignity of France and its revenues, fruits and provisions, to support our royal state and the burdens of the kingdom, and that during her lifetime, our wife shall also keep her state and dignity, according to the custom of the kingdom, with an appropriate part of the rents and income.

[. . .]

6. Item, it is agreed that immediately after our death and from that time forward, the crown and kingdom of France, with all their rights and possessions, will belong forever to our son King Henry and his heirs.

7. Item, as we are frequently prevented from understanding and dealing with the affairs of our kingdom, the power and practice of governing and ordering the government of our kingdom shall be and remain with our said son Henry during our lifetime, with the counsel of noble, wise men obedient to us, who desire the profit and honour of the kingdom, so that from now onwards, he may rule and govern by himself and through others whom he deputes.

[. . .]

12. Item, that our son will work with all his power, and as soon as he can, to bring into our obedience all and every city, town, castle,

place and person in our kingdom that disobeys and rebels against us, following, or being in what is commonly called the dauphin's or Armagnac's party.

13. Item, in order for our son to carry out and accomplish these things effectively, surely and freely, it is agreed that the great lords, barons and nobles and the Estates of the kingdom, spiritual and temporal, the cities and major communities, citizens and burgesses in the towns in the kingdom currently obedient to us, will swear the oaths which follow:

First they will humbly obey our son King Henry [. . .] in all things concerning the government of the kingdom.

[. . .]

Item, that from the time of our death, they will be faithful liege men to our son and his heirs, and will receive our said son for their liege lord and sovereign and true king of France, with no opposition, contradiction or difficulty, and obey him as such, and that after these things, they will never obey another apart from us, except our son Henry and his heirs, as king or regent of the kingdom of France . . .

14. Item, it is agreed that all and every one of the conquests which will be made by our said son, King Henry, in the kingdom of France outside the duchy of Normandy, against the rebels mentioned above, will be for our profit, and that our said son on his authority will restore all and every land and lordship in the places which are to be conquered to those owners who are currently in our obedience, and who swear to keep this [treaty].

15. Item, it is agreed that every cleric with a benefice in the duchy of Normandy or elsewhere in the kingdom of France, in places subject to our said son, obedient to us and favouring the party of our said very dear and very beloved son the duke of Burgundy, who swear to keep this treaty, will have peaceful enjoyment of their ecclesiastical benefices in the said duchy of Normandy or elsewhere as specified above.

[. . .]

18. Item, and when our said son King Henry succeeds to the crown of France, the duchy of Normandy and each and every other place conquered by him, will be under the jurisdiction, obedience and monarchy of the said crown of France.

19. Item, it is agreed that our said son King Henry, by his power will strive and see that those who are obedient to us or to the party known as the Burgundians, and to whom various lordships, lands revenues, or possessions in the duchy of Normandy or elsewhere in the kingdom

of France, and which have been conquered and given away by our said son King Henry, shall be compensated by us, without diminishing the Crown, in those lands which have been, or will be, taken from the rebels who are disobedient to us. And if within our lifetime these [obedient persons] have not been recompensed, our said son Henry will do this from the lands and possessions [conquered from the rebels] when he succeeds to the crown of France. But if the said lands, lordships, rents or possessions belonging to those [obedient] persons in the said duchy or elsewhere, have not been granted out [to others] by our said son, they shall be restored to those [obedient] persons without delay.

[...]

21. Item, that during our lifetime, our said son, King Henry, will not call himself or write of himself, or cause himself to be called or written of, as King of France, but will abstain from using this title in every point, as long as we live.

22. Item, it is agreed that in our lifetime, we shall name, call and write of our son King Henry, in the French language as 'Our very dear son Henry, King of England, heir of France' and in the Latin Language in [the same] manner . . . [the Latin title is given here].

23. Item, that our said son will not impose or have imposed, any imposition or exaction [tax] on our subjects, without necessity and good reason, nor otherwise than for the good of our kingdom and as ordained and required by the reasonable and approved customs of the kingdom.

24. Item, so that concord, peace and tranquillity may be observed for all time between the kingdoms of France and England . . . it is agreed that our said son will use his power, with the advice and agreement of the Three Estates of both kingdoms[1] [...] so that it shall be agreed that when our said son, or one of his heirs, succeeds to the crown of France, the two crowns of England and France shall be perpetually joined together in the same person, that is to say, in the person of our son, King Henry while he lives, and thereafter in the persons of his heirs who will rule successively one after another, and from the time of our son or one of his heirs the said two kingdoms shall not be governed separately under different Kings, at the same time, but under the same person, who will be King and sovereign lord of one and the other kingdom [i.e. both], as we have said, nonetheless,

---

[1] In the case of England, this would be the English Parliament (the Lords, including the bishops, and Commons); in the case of France, the Three Estates (nobility, clergy and third estate).

maintaining in each kingdom its rights, liberties or customs, usages and laws in every other thing, not in any way submitting one kingdom to the other, nor its laws, rights, customs or usages to those of the other [kingdom].

[. . .]

27. Item, it is agreed that our son King Henry with the advice of our very dear son, Philip, duke of Burgundy,[2] and other nobles in the kingdom who shall be summoned for this purpose, will provide for the guard of our person, honestly and appropriately, according to the requirements of our status and royal dignity, in such a way that it will honour God and ourself, and the kingdom of France and its subjects; and that all persons, nobles or otherwise, in our personal and domestic service, both in offices and other functions, shall be born in the kingdom of France, or French-speaking areas, and be good, wise, loyal and qualified for such service.

28. Item, that we shall live and reside in an important place in our obedience, and not elsewhere.

29. Item, considering the horrible and enormous crimes carried out in the kingdom of France by Charles, calling himself the dauphin of Viennois, it is agreed that neither we, nor our son King Henry, nor our dear son Philip duke of Burgundy, will negotiate any peace or agreement with the said Charles, nor shall we, without taking counsel and agreeing amongst our three selves, and likewise with the three estates of the two kingdoms.

[. . .]

1.3

Henry VI's entry into Paris, 2 December 1431

B. Guenée & F. Lehoux (eds.) (1968) *Les entrées royales de 1328 à 1515*, Paris: Éditions du Centre national de la recherche scientifique, pp. 62–70. Translation from French by Kathleen Daly.

Royal entry ceremonies provided an opportunity for the king to meet his people. According to this anonymous account of Henry

[2] Philip was also Charles VI's son-in-law, through his marriage to the king's daughter, Michelle (1395–1422).

VI's entry, the procession passed some of the major landmarks of the city, and the principal royal and municipal officials came to greet the king. The themes chosen for the 'mysteries' or 'scenes' promoted the town's interests as well as those of the ruler. The ceremony blended religious and political symbolism, but also entertained the onlookers.

The year of Grace 1431, Sunday 2 December, first day of Advent, Henry [VI (1422–71)], by the grace of God king of France and England, came and made his entry into the town of Paris. Son of the late Henry, formerly king of England, during his lifetime heir and regent of France, and of Katherine, daughter of the late Charles of Valois, during his life king of France, VIth of this name, the said Henry being ten years less five days, accompanied by my lord the cardinal of England,[1] my lord the bishop of Thérouanne, chancellor of France[2] . . . and numerous other prelates of Holy Church, and by the very great and excellent princes the duke of Bedford his uncle,[3] the duke of York[4], the earl of Warwick,[5] . . . and several others, as many from the country of France as from England.

[. . .]

[The king first made his entry into the town of Saint Denis and the abbey, closely associated with the monarchy as most French kings were buried there, where he was met by civic officials and citizens of Paris. Then on his way to the city, he passed a scene representing the Nine Worthies.[6] He was then escorted into Paris by groups of royal officers including the Parlement].[7]

And in the fortress of Saint Denis, above the drawbridge, there was a great coat of arms of the said town [of Paris] covering all the façade,

---

[1] Cardinal Henry Beaufort (c. 1375–1447) was an illegitimate son of John of Gaunt, Henry V's grandfather, and was thus related to Henry VI.

[2] Louis de Luxembourg (died 1443), bishop of Thérouanne from 1415, chancellor of France under the Anglo-Burgundian regime, from 1424.

[3] John, duke of Bedford (1389–1435), brother of Henry V, had been regent in France until the arrival of Henry VI and his Council – there was no need for a regent when the king himself was present. Bedford resumed his regency after their departure in February 1432.

[4] Richard, duke of York (1411–60).

[5] Richard Beauchamp, earl of Warwick (1382–1439).

[6] Nine famous heroes, three from the Bible (Joshua, David, Judas Maccabeus), three from Antiquity (Hector of Troy, Alexander the Great and Julius Caesar), and three from the Christian era (King Arthur of Britain, the Emperor Charlemagne and Godefroy de Bouillon, a hero of the First Crusade in 1099 CE).

[7] At this date, the Parlement of Paris was the supreme law court for that part of France acknowledging Henry VI as king of France. It was a legal, not a representative, body.

on which, as was proper, there was a silver ship so big that there were twelve people in it, divided among the three estates, representing the three estates of the town, who held out three hearts towards the king, which opened when he looked at them; from one came two white doves, from another, flying birds, from another, violets and sweet greenery, as a sign that the hearts of the estates of the town opened with joy at the coming of their prince and lord. And under the coat of arms there was written in very large letters on a tablet:

> The estates of this city
> Offer you, with one accord
> Their hearts, in true humility.
> Receive them kindly.

And when the king had entered the town, and he had passed the said fortress, the aforesaid aldermen and clerk of the said town carried above the head of the king a canopy, which was made of a very rich cloth of gold with blue satin drapes covered in gold fleurs de lys; and the lining of that canopy was of fine blue silk cloth, on which was a moon and a gold sun, scattered with gold stars. That canopy was carried by these and other citizens of the town[8] . . .

[The king passed a group of wild men and women playing in a wood, with a fountain surmounted by a fleur de lis, with three sirens, the fountain spouts wine and water. He passed a scene of the Nativity of Christ.]

And at the old gate of Saint Denis there was a stage . . . very richly draped with tapestry, on which there were also real people, showing by their appearance and without moving, three stories from the life of Saint Denis, that is: how he preached the [Christian] faith in France; how he was led before the provost Livius, who had him martyred; and the next how, while he was in prison, Our Lord visited him and gave him his very precious Body.[9] And over each story there was written in large script on a tablet:

> To increase our faith
> Saint Denis came from Greece to France,
> And wished to announce it by preaching:
> Here is the proof.

---

[8] The canopy was probably originally a religious symbol: it was carried over the Eucharist during Corpus Christi processions.

[9] The Eucharist, or consecrated bread.

[. . .]
If the French kings Most Christian,
Are called to protect the faith,
Protect it, young king,
As the kings of old have done.

[The king passed members of the clergy from local churches, holding crosses, holy water and reliquaries; at the church of the Holy Sepulchre, the relic of the arm of Saint George is brought out for the young king Henry to kiss.]

At the fountain of the Holy Innocents, there was a wood, with hunters and dogs; and when the king arrived there, they began to blow their horns, and the dogs began to yelp; and then a stag leapt out, running across the street towards the king, with the dogs following; and then [it] went back into the wood and was taken.

By the Châtelet in Paris,[10] there were high platforms, very finely decorated and draped with rich tapestry, and there was a child, representing the king, sitting on a faldstool,[11] and behind and above him was a dais and backcloth of satin with the arms of France and England, and at each side of him were two shields, on the right, the arms of France, and on the left, the arms of England. And above them, two crowns in the air, and on the right were figures representing my lord the duke of Burgundy,[12] [his cousins] the counts of Nevers and Rethel, the bishop of Thérouanne, chancellor of France, my lord John of Luxembourg and several other important [Burgundian] lords, in sufficient numbers for the place; and by their stance all were supporting the coat of arms and crown of France. And on the other side were represented images of the duke of Bedford, my lord the cardinal, my lord the duke of York, the earls of Warwick, Stafford, Salisbury, the count of Mortain, the earl of Arundel,[13] and other notable lords, in

---

[10] The Châtelet was the royal court with jurisdiction over Paris, situated on the right bank of the Seine (the modern Place du Châtelet).

[11] A ceremonial, backless folding seat.

[12] Philip the Good, duke of Burgundy (1396–1467) was actually absent from the procession, and from Henry's coronation nine days later.

[13] These were all important English noblemen: Humphrey, earl of Stafford, (later 1st duke of Buckingham (1402–60) who was constable of France; Richard Neville, 5th earl of Salisbury (c. 1400–60), whose son, Warwick 'the Kingmaker' married Anne, the daughter of Richard Beauchamp; Edmund Beaufort (c. 1406–55), earl of Dorset from 1442, and count of Mortain (in France) from 1427, later becoming duke of Somerset; and John Fitz-Allan, 7th earl of Arundel (c. 1408–35).

number suitable for the space all armed and wearing their coats of arms; and all by their stance seemed to support the two crowned shields.

And on the other platform which was also richly draped with tapestry – but was a little lower than the platform mentioned previously – was represented the provost of Paris,[14] holding a piece of writing in his hand, and he presented it to the king as if it were a petition; and with the other hand he showed those who were behind him, in great number, representing the estates of the college of the Châtelet;[15] and there were many others, representing the provost of merchants,[16] aldermen, burgesses, labourers, artisans and inhabitants of the town, all gazing at the king, and looking to his honour and gain. And all these people were still as if they were images, and above each scene the following was written:

> Your true French subjects
> have protected the crown for you,
> And at the wish of the King of Kings,
> It will be preserved for you by them.
> [. . .]
> We who administer justice
> Pray to you that it will be protected
> Which will be of benefit to you.
> Through her [justice], kingdoms have endured.
>
> The people with all its power
> Has struggled to maintain
> The town in your obedience
> If you wish to call it to mind.

And at the entry to the great bridge the butchers of the town presented a living stag, with eight tines[17] draped in the arms of France and England, and led it as far as the Hôtel des Tournelles . . .[18]

---

[14] The provost of Paris administered French royal justice in Paris.

[15] That is, the various officers of the Châtelet.

[16] The provost of merchants, the equivalent of mayor in Paris, governed the city from the town hall (Hôtel de Ville) on the right bank of the Seine. With the aldermen (*échevins*), he represented the municipal government.

[17] Spurs of the antler.

[18] The Palace of the Tournelles, near the royal fortress of the Bastille, was Bedford's chief residence in Paris.

1.4
Normandy under the English occupation

Thomas Basin (1412–89) was born in Caudebec-en-Caux, in the duchy of Normandy, into a prosperous merchant family. He became bishop of Lisieux in 1447, during the English occupation, but retained his bishopric when Charles VII conquered the duchy in 1449–50. He fell into disfavour under Louis XI, was exiled from his bishopric, then left the kingdom permanently in 1468. He composed a *History of Charles VII* (1471–2), a *History of Louis XI* (in stages between 1472–84), and in 1488, a *Breviloquium*, or short discourse on his life. Basin is one of the major historians of the fifteenth century. He appears to have relied less on documents than on his personal experiences and the accounts of events given to him by people he had met.

(a) The unfortunate experiences of the Basin family

T. Basin (1855–9) 'Breviloquium', in *Histoire des règnes de Charles VII et Louis XI*, ed. J. Quicherat, Paris: Renouard, 4 vols., vol. 4, pp. 9–12. Translation from original Latin text by Dario Tessicini and Kathleen Daly.

Here I tell the story of my itinerant and unsteady life, the wanderings and travels through different regions, cities, and stages, starting from my childhood and youth.

Three years after I was born in 1412 in the village of . . . Caudebec . . . , which is located on the bank of the River Seine, seven French leagues from the city of Rouen in the direction of the sea, the English king Henry of Lancaster set up camp and put Harfleur under heavy siege. Since both its inhabitants and the soldiers who were there to defend the city suffered from famine and deprivations, the town decided to capitulate of its own free will and according to laws and agreements that they decided to set when under siege.[1]

---

[1] Harfleur was a key strategic point on the French coast, and the mouth of the river Seine (and thus the approaches to Rouen and Paris). The English siege of Harfleur lasted from mid-August to 22 September 1415.

I. As soon as the garrisons were removed and the French armies left the aforesaid town where I was born, my parents decided to leave that place in order to avoid the violence, offences and misdemeanours of the troops. Thus, they went to Rouen, in the hope of living there, with family, valuables, and taking me with them wherever they went.

II. After a few months, the inhabitants left the land, since the armies of England, on the one side, and those of France, on the other, raided the entire region of Caux, and sacked everything. A dreary countryside was left, deprived of farmers, of which a substantial part, for fear of the English, found refuge in the fortified town of Rouen in which plague and famine started to spread fiercely. My parents did not want to linger there, because of the dangers of a violent epidemic. Instead, they moved once again to the town of Vernon, which seemed to be a safer place. I went with them as always.

III. After they had spent a few months in that place and since it was said that the plague had to some extent left Rouen, they went back there again.

IV. Then, day after day the rumour grew stronger that the said King Henry of England was preparing many more ships and troops, with all sorts of war machines that had been previously made in England, in order to attack Normandy and the French realm. Almost everybody believed that these would have to pass on the side of the River Seine where the town of Harfleur, which he had already conquered, was situated, and from there, once the armies had landed and spread, he would have to attack Rouen, the capital and main city of Normandy. My parents did not want to wait for the danger there, but they preferred to hide in some safe place until the storm of the incoming war had calmed down. At their friends' suggestion, they fled with their family and valuables to the stronghold of Falaise, taking me, who at the time was a little more than four years old, with them.

V. After they had stayed in that place for a few months, waiting to see which direction the war would take, suddenly the word spread through the entire area that the English king with his army and fleet had not crossed from the bank of the River Seine on which he had taken Harfleur, as was generally thought, but had positioned his troops in another place, near the town of Touques towards Lower Normandy, from which he could first attack Caen and Lower Normandy.[2] My

---

[2] Henry V and his army landed at Touques (Calvados, Normandy) on 1 August 1417.

parents swiftly decided to leave [for] Brittany. Having left Falaise in a hurry, they started their trip [to] Brittany and at first they stopped near the border between Normandy and Brittany, in a town which bears the name of . . . Saint James.

VI. Having left that place as soon as they learned that the English were spreading throughout Lower Normandy, [my parents] travelled towards the town of Rennes [Brittany], taking me with them wherever they went. Once they arrived there, they stayed for almost a year.

VII. Afterwards the English troops, who had conquered almost all of Lower Normandy, raided and plundered the area up to the borders of Brittany, not far from the town of Rennes. My parents, wishing to flee [to] a fortified place and having left Rennes, went to the town of Nantes [Brittany], which is on the banks of the River Loire, not far from the place where it flows into the ocean. They stayed in that city for more than a year.

VIII. In the meantime, the English king first subjugated Lower Normandy, then, after a long siege, forced the town of Rouen to capitulate,[3] and he had under his rule almost all of Normandy. Thus, some sort of peace being restored, my parents decided to return to their home. And so, not long after, they were back in their fields and home, that is, in the aforesaid village of Caudebec, when I was almost seven years old.[4]

IX. There I stayed until I had almost completed my twelfth year of age. Since I was inclined to letters, and my parents did not want to curb my enthusiasm, they sent me to the renowned university of Paris, where, under the supervision of a tutor, I studied logic and philosophy for a little more than five years. After I had been granted an exemption for my age, since I was not yet eighteen, I obtained the degree of Master of Arts, according to the regulations of that university.

X. Then, since a new university had opened in Louvain, a town in Brabant, I went there to study civil law, on my parents' orders.[5]

[3] Rouen surrendered in January 1419, after a six-month siege by the English.

[4] The Basin family thus returned home once the English occupation of Normandy was secure, and the duchy was shielded from the direct effects of warfare.

[5] Civil or Roman law was based on the sixth-century legislation of the emperor Justinian, interpreted to apply to contemporary and practical legal problems. The University of Paris did not provide instruction in civil law.

+ footnote: p. 20

(b) On the pillages and plundering deplorably carried out throughout France

T. Basin (1933) *Histoire de Charles VII*, ed. & trans.
C. Samaran, Paris: Les Belles Lettres, 2 vols., vol. 1,
pp. 106–9.[6] Translation from original Latin text by Dario
Tessicini and Kathleen Daly.

Besides those who claimed to serve under the French army, although most of them did not have a rank or receive a salary[7] but lived and sheltered themselves and their booty in the towns and the castles controlled by the French, there was also a great number of desperate and scattered men, who either because of weak-mindedness, or hatred for the English, or for the pleasure of stealing others' possessions, or forced to escape the nooses of Justice because they were conscious of their crimes, had left their fields and houses but did not live in the French towns and castles, or serve in their army.[8] Rather, like wild beasts or wolves, they inhabited the thickest and most inaccessible forests, from which, deprived of food and driven mad by starvation, they usually sortied out at night, under the cover of darkness, and sometimes, more rarely, by day, breaking into the houses of the peasants, robbing and abducting them to their secret hiding-places in the woods. There, they abused [the prisoners] with all manner of hardship and starvation, and forced them to bring at a fixed time and place large sums of money, along with everything else they deemed necessary and useful, for their ransom and freedom. And if they failed to do so, either the hostages, or those who had left them, were dealt with in the most cruel way, or they themselves were killed, if the robbers could come again to catch them, or their houses would burn, stealthily set on fire at night.

This kind of villain, commonly known as 'brigands', grew extraordinarily strong in Normandy and the neighbouring provinces and regions occupied by the English, tyrannising the inhabitants and infesting the countryside.

And although the English leaders and captains took great care and were usually thorough in cleansing the region from this kind of noxious beast, instantly hanging from gallows and gibbets all of those they could seize – on which account the English themselves were killed

---

[6] This passage occurs after a reference to the battle of Verneuil (1424) and before an allusion to the siege of Orleans, 1429. However, the content, going up to the departure of the English, may suggest Basin had the whole period of the English occupation in mind.

[7] That is, they did not have a rank or regular salary.

[8] That is, the places and troops loyal to Charles VII.

without mercy every time they were caught –, nonetheless their zeal and skill never succeeded in exterminating this evil seed as long as they lived in and held Normandy. Yet, experience showed clearly the value of the advice given to the English by a certain Norman priest who happened to dine with them.[9] In fact, while they were discussing the brigands amongst each other, during the conversation each of those attending the dinner was required to speak his mind on a possible way or strategy to rid the country of this wicked kind of men. When each [of the] English had expressed his own personal opinion, it was the turn of that worthy priest who, required to give his view, set forth many excuses and asked whether he could be excused, since he was ignorant and inexperienced in such matters, it being inappropriate for the priestly office to discuss the punishment of these criminals. When nevertheless he was urged to express an opinion, having first asked and requested that, if he said something foolish, his ignorance would be forgiven – this being immediately granted by those present –, he said that it seemed to him that it was possible to devise one, and only one remedy, that is, that all the English should leave France and go back to England, their native country, for, when they left, the brigands would also stop living on the region [of Normandy]. Indeed, nothing was more true as was later acknowledged. For as soon as the English were chased out of Normandy and were forced to go back to their own country, this region [of Normandy] was also freed of that pestilential nuisance.

1.5

Letter of remission granted by Henry VI as king of France to one of his Norman subjects

P. Le Cacheux (ed.) (1907) *Actes de la Chancellerie d'Henri VI concernant la Normandie sous la domination anglaise (1422–35)*, Paris: Picard, 2 vols., vol. 1, pp. 106–8. Translation from French by Kathleen Daly.

A letter of remission was an 'act issued by the [French royal] chancellery by which the king gave his pardon for a crime or

---

[9] It is possible that this priest was actually Basin himself.

offence, so stopping the ordinary course of justice, whether royal, seigniorial, urban or ecclesiastical. In addition to the remission of the penalty, the accused was fully restored to his possessions and good reputation, while maintaining the interests of the opposing party'.[1] The beneficiary or his/her friends had to petition the king for the letters, and pay a fee to the royal chancellery, so the very poor were unlikely to get letters. The letters had to be convincing, as they might be scrutinised by the royal *Parlement*, hence the emphasis on factors mitigating the crime.[2] With these precautions, they can give a valuable insight into how individuals adapted, where the uncertainties of war, pillage and competing allegiances were a fact of life.

Henry, etc. We make known, etc. that we have received the humble supplication of Jean Manourry, a poor young man aged 25 or so years,[3] burdened with a young wife, living at Saint-Pierre-sur-Dives, containing how two years or so ago, he was accused at law by some who hated him, or otherwise, of having sold a horse to the brigands or Armagnacs, our enemies, and on this pretext he was taken by the *vicomte*[4] of Falaise, or his lieutenant, and put in prison in [Falaise]; and he was held prisoner in those prisons for six weeks or so, in great poverty and hardship where he paid out and spent all his own, and a large part of his friends', livelihood and what is more, he was tortured, so that he could never again have the use of his body; such that the supplicant was brought before the local court by which he was found pure and innocent of the said crime, and afterwards he was released on bail to appear on the days assigned by the *vicomte* or his lieutenant.

While he was on bail, the said supplicant married the wife he has at present, and because of this forgot to return to court on the day assigned to him, so that he feared that he, together with those who had given their guarantees [for his appearance] would be pursued or be held accountable for his failure to answer the summons to court . . . [and] his guarantors have been imprisoned for these non-appearances and since then have been freed by the *bailli*[5] of Caen, or

---

[1] C. Gauvard (1991), *Crime, état et société à la fin du Moyen Age*, Paris: Publications de la Sorbonne, Paris (1991), 2 vols., vol. 1, p. 63.

[2] Gauvard (1991), 1, pp. 60–85, 136–42, 163–70.

[3] On 22 December 1421, Henry V confirmed a Jean Manourry and his wife Gervaise as owners of their goods in the vicomté of Auge. This letter may refer to the same couple.

[4] The *vicomte* was a local royal official, subordinate to the *bailli*. He was responsible for administering justice in the king's own lands, or royal domain.

[5] The *bailli* or bailiff (frequently of noble birth) exercised judicial and military functions on behalf of the French crown within an administrative district (the *bailliage*).

his lieutenant, to appear before the second assizes to be held by the said *bailli* or his lieutenant.

And it so happened that before they were freed, while the said supplicant was in the town of Bayeux, in an inn where he was drinking, a herald or pursuivant at arms arrived, and the said supplicant asked where he was from. This pursuivant replied that he came from Brittany, claiming to be of the duke of Alençon's party.[6] And after a few words, the said supplicant said the following, or the gist of it: 'God keep the crown of France and give the duke of Alençon long life and give us a good peace!' without saying anything else. And soon after, the said pursuivant went to Caen, to the *bailli* and said and recalled the words that the supplicant said to him; and in fact the *bailli* sent a sergeant to the house of [the supplicant's] father in law, to find him and put him in prison.

The said supplicant, remembering the harsh imprisonment where he had been for a long time previously, as aforesaid, and through fear of being put back there, and of the rigour of justice, left the region. So we order our *bailli* of Caen, *vicomte* of Falaise etc. [not to pursue the supplicant].

Paris, in the month of September, the year of Grace 1424, and second of our reign. So signed, by the King, at the report of (his) Council. [Signed] G. DE MARC (Secretary)

1.6

Joan of Arc's letter to Philip, duke of Burgundy, 17 July 1429

J. Quicherat (1841–9) *Procès de condamnation et de réhabilitation de Jeanne d'Arc dite la Pucelle*, Paris: Société de l'Histoire de France, 5 vols., vol. 5, pp. 126–7. Translation from French by Kathleen Daly.

Joan of Arc (1412–31) appeared at Charles VII's palace of Chinon in February 1429. She told the king and his advisers

---

[6] Jean II, duke of Alençon, was a leading Norman nobleman and follower of Charles VII, and therefore an enemy of Henry VI. He served with Joan of Arc, but in 1456 was arrested for treason and condemned to life imprisonment on 10 October 1458 (an event commemorated in a miniature by Jean Fouquet).

that she could relieve the siege of the key town of Orleans, which had been besieged by the English since October 1428, and lead the king to his coronation at Rheims. After the successful relief of Orleans (8 May 1429), and the king's arrival at Rheims (recaptured from the English), she wrote this letter to Philip, duke of Burgundy on 17 July 1429, the day of Charles VII's coronation at Rheims. As a peer of France, Philip should have played a particularly important ceremonial role at the coronation of Charles VII. He attended neither this event, nor the coronation of Henry VI, in Paris, in 1431.

+ [sign of the cross] Jesus, Mary

Mighty and feared prince, duke of Burgundy, Joan the Maid requires you on the part of the King of Heaven, my rightful and sovereign lord, that the king of France and you make a good firm peace, which will last a long time. Pardon each other with a good heart, completely, as faithful Christians should do; and if you want to fight, go against the Saracens. Prince of Burgundy, I ask, beg and require you as humbly as I can, that you will no longer fight against the holy kingdom of France, and that you withdraw your people at once, and quickly, from places and fortresses in the said holy kingdom; and the gentle lord of France on his part is ready to make peace with you, saving his honour; so it rests with you. And I tell you from the King of Heaven, my rightful lord, for your good, honour and life, that you will never win a battle against our loyal Frenchmen, and that all those who fight against the holy kingdom of France fight against the lord Jesus, king of Heaven and of the whole world, my rightful and sovereign lord. And I pray you and ask you with my hands joined [in prayer] that you do not join battle or fight against us, neither you, nor your subjects, and be certain, however many you lead against us, they will never win, and it will be a pity [to see] the great battle and blood shed by those who come against us. And it is three weeks since I wrote to you and sent fine letters by a herald, summoning you to the coronation of the king [Charles VII] which is taking place today, Sunday, 17th day of the present month of July, in the city of Rheims, but I have had no response, nor heard any news of that herald. I commend you to God and may you be protected, if you please, and I pray God to bring peace. Written in the place of Rheims, the said 17th day of July.

1.7

Charles VII institutes a commemoration of the fall of Cherbourg and recovery of Normandy

G. du Fresne de Beaucourt (1881–91) *Histoire de Charles VII*, Paris: Picard, 6 vols., vol. 4, pp. 447–8. Translation from French by Kathleen Daly.

These letters record what was intended to be a national celebration of the reconquest, in the form of a religious feast. The king sent these letters to the cathedrals and all the major towns in the kingdom. Surviving evidence of the celebration of the feast day in Rouen, Poitiers and Paris indicates that it involved processions around the major urban religious sites or town ramparts, and probably involved the delivery of a sermon commemorating the recovery of the duchy. In rural parishes in Normandy, the recovery was celebrated until the French Revolution.[1]

The king [Charles VII] to his bishops, cathedral chapters and towns.

Our beloved, very dear and loyal friends, you know of the grace which it has pleased God to show us, concerning the recovery and complete return to our obedience of our country and duchy of Normandy, a thing that was completed and accomplished the twelfth day of the present month of August, when the place of Cherbourg, which was the last one held and occupied by our enemies in our country of Normandy, was regained and brought back into our obedience. When we consider the short time taken to carry out this recovery and reduction, and the manner in which it was done, in which one can see no cruelty or inhumanity, nor the terrible evils that often happen during warfare, it seems the more credible that this is a divine and miraculous work.

For this reason, with the advice and opinion of our Council, it has seemed to us that it would be good and reasonable, in order to thank our Creator, to whom above all one should attribute the honour and glory [for this deed], that general processions and solemn masses should take place in our kingdom on the fourteenth day of the month of October next, and that in the future, similar processions and masses should take place in all the metropolitan and canonical[2] churches of

[1] C. Beaune (1985) *Naissance de la nation France*, Paris: Gallimard, pp. 182–6.
[2] That is, cathedral churches.

our kingdom, on the day that this recovery took place, that is, the twelfth day of August for the eternal praise of our said Creator, in everlasting acknowledgement of the grace which He has given us.

So we ask you for your part to do this, and to officially record the solemnisation of this 12th of August in your papers and registers, so that this event will not be forgotten in the future. In doing these things, we hope that God will be pleased, and for our part we shall be grateful to you.

Given at Maillé, the last day [31] of August [1450].

[Signed] Charles *(Authorised)*

(Secretary) Froment.

official Document

1.8

The Juvénal family

P.S. Lewis (ed.) (1978–92) *Écrits politiques de Jean Juvénal des Ursins*, Paris: Société de l'Histoire de France, 3 vols., vol. 3, pp. 241–4. Translation from French by Kathleen Daly.

On 14 June 1443, Jean Juvénal (II), Guillaume, Jacques, Michel and their mother Michelle de Vitry obtained permission from the cathedral chapter to set up in Notre Dame, Paris, in the chapel of St Rémy, a tomb depicting Jean Juvénal I des Ursins and Michelle de Vitry, 'and to have the wall painted as they wish and to change the stained glass . . . as they think fit'. This extract is from a seventeenth-century description of the tomb and chapel.

[A] tomb with a praying figure in armour, and around the tomb is written: Here lies the noble and wise man, my lord Jean Juvénal des Ursins, knight and lord of Traînel and counsellor of our lord the king, who died at Poitiers the year of grace 1431, the first day of April, Easter day, and the lady Michelle de Vitry his wife, who died the year of grace 1456 the 12th day of July. Pray God (for them etc).

Above the tomb is a painting, of those who follow below, at the beginning of which is written: Here are the images of noble persons my lord Jean Juvénal des Ursins, knight, lord and baron of Traînel, counsellor of the king, and of dame Michelle de Vitry his wife, and their children.

Reverend father in God my lord Jean Juvénal, doctor in canon and civil law, in his time bishop and count of Beauvais, and since then bishop and duke of Laon, count of Ainizy, peer of France, counsellor of the king.[1]

Jeanne Juvénal des Ursins, who was married to noble man Master Nicole Contalart, counsellor of the king.

My lord Louis Juvénal des Ursins, knight, counsellor, chamberlain of the king and bailiff[2] of Troyes.

The lady Jeanne Juvénal des Ursins, who was married to Pierre de Chailly, squire, and since to my lord Guichart, lord of Pelvoisin, knight.

Demoiselle Eude Juvénal des Ursins, who was married to Denis des Marés, squire, lord of Doué.

Denis Juvénal des Ursins, squire, cupbearer of my lord Louis, dauphin of Viennois and duke of Guyenne.

Sister Marie Juvénal des Ursins, nun at Poissy.

My lord Guillaume Juvénal des Ursins, knight and baron of Traînel, in his time counsellor of the king, bailiff of Sens and since chancellor of France.

Pierre Juvénal des Ursins, squire.

Michel Juvénal des Ursins, squire and lord of La Chapelle-Gautier-en-Brye.

The very reverend father in God my lord Jacques Juvénal des Ursins, archbishop and duke of Rheims, the first peer of France, counsellor of the king and president in his chamber of accounts.[3]

Item, a copper tablet, on the left hand side, below the altar, inscribed:

Here lies nobleman my lord Guillaume Juvénal des Ursins, knight, lord and baron of Traînel, who in his time was counsellor in the court of Parlement of the very wise and very victorious king of France, Charles, VII of this name, and since then a knight on his coronation march, and captain of men at arms, then lieutenant of the Dauphiné, and after bailiff of Sens, and finally Chancellor of France from the year [1]445, who died the 24th day of June the year 1472, God keep his soul.

And there are several complete coats of arms of the des Ursins, impaled with those of Vitry, in the window of the said chapel, and also around the tomb, which is in black marble.

---

[1] The bishop of Laon also held secular lordships. Ainizy-le-Chateau is near Laon.

[2] See Anthology document 1.5, note 5.

[3] The royal *chambre des comptes* in Paris that controlled the income and expenditure from the royal domain.

1.9

The rise and fall of Jacques Coeur

T. Basin (1933) *Histoire de Charles VII*, ed. & trans.
C. Samaran, Paris: Les Belles Lettres, 2 vols., vol. 2,
pp. 150–5, 282–7. Translation from Latin by Dario Tessicini
and Kathleen Daly.

Jacques Coeur (c. 1395–1456) was the son of a wealthy merchant of furs in Bourges and built up a considerable fortune through commerce. In 1438, Charles VII appointed him his *argentier*, the officer responsible for supplying the royal household with luxury goods and clothing. He was also a royal commissioner on finances, which meant that he was responsible for farming out royal revenues in the Languedoc to lessees, in exchange for a lump sum. Coeur's wealth allowed him to lend large sums to the king and to courtiers. In 1451, he was arrested on a variety of charges, and his property was confiscated. Sentence was passed against him on 29 May 1453. He escaped from prison and ended his life organising a crusade against the Turks on behalf of the pope.

Though Basin's account was written in 1471–2, it reflects Coeur's reputation among his contemporaries, of whom Basin was one.[1]

(a) Portrait of Jacques Coeur

At that time [1449], an industrious and shrewd man, Jacques Coeur from Bourges, of lowly origin[2] but of great and lively intelligence, and with vast expertise in all worldly affairs, served in the administration of the royal household. He was the king's household treasurer (*argentier*) and the commercial business which occupied him incessantly had made him extremely rich and famous. In fact he was the first Frenchman of his time to equip and arm galleys which, loaded with woollen cloth and other French products, roamed the shores of Africa and the East as far as Alexandria in Egypt, and brought back up the Rhone silk cloths and all types of spices and other goods, which, spread not only through France but to Catalonia and neighbouring regions, could be useful to those countries. Before him, such trade had

---

[1] For Basin, see the headnote to document 1.4.
[2] In fact, Coeur's father was one of the wealthiest merchants in Bourges.

25

been exceptional for many years and it was only through the efforts of other peoples – Venetians, Genoese, Catalans – that such goods were brought to France. Jacques Coeur therefore became wealthy and exalted, thanks to this sea-trade. The magnificent dwelling that he had built in his town of Bourges is the clearest testimony of this [wealth]: it is so fine, decorated so lavishly, that, in all France, it would be hard to find a more magnificent dwelling belonging, not just to the middling nobility but even, because of its vast size, to the king himself.

Since he had plenty of riches and resources, inspired with zeal for the king's honour and the good of the kingdom, he did not fail in his duty to the public good.[3] While certain great lords, overwhelmed with goods by royal generosity, excused themselves [from helping the king] on absurd pretexts, he spontaneously offered to lend the king a mass of gold and gave him a sum amounting, so they say, to 100,000 gold écus,[4] to use for this great and necessary work [the reconquest of Normandy]. It was thanks to his powerful assistance that the castles of Falaise, then Domfront and finally Cherbourg, were besieged . . .

(b) The arrest and condemnation of Jacques Coeur

[1]
Seeing that she [Agnès Sorel the king's mistress (c. 1422–50)] had died by poison, his rivals plotted so that the royal treasurer Jacques Coeur was held as a suspect (although in fact many thought him innocent of this crime). After most of Normandy had been completely recovered, to which the advice and work of the treasurer had greatly contributed, as we have said above, he was formally accused of poisoning, then imprisoned and long detained in the castle of Lusignan in Poitou. There the king gathered a large assembly [May 1453] (which some used to call the seat, bed or throne of justice) to judge and condemn him, where the witnesses accused him of smuggling weapons and forbidden goods to the Infidels on his ships. At the same time he was also accused of extortion, having illicitly and surreptitiously stolen money from the inhabitants of the Languedoc region, where he

---

[3] The original Latin gives the term 'res publica' which can also mean the kingdom, common good, or affairs of state, or even what we would call the 'state'.

[4] An écu was an actual coin, worth a *livre tournois*, or pound of the city of Tours (a measure of value).

held important offices. He was condemned because of these and several other charges that many believed had been invented by his rivals, rather than being true (while the aforesaid accusation of poisoning was passed over in silence).

[2]

For a long time he was prisoner in the castle of Lusignan. He finally managed to bribe his guards and escaped. He was given sanctuary in churches in various parts of the kingdom, until he arrived at a convent of the Minorites in Beaucaire-sur-Rhone. There he was imprisoned and put in chains. He had a very loyal servant, called Guillaume de Varye,[5] a native of Bourges like himself. This man arrived one night with one or two brigantines (which are commonly called light galleys or cutters),[6] and with the help of his attendants took Jacques Coeur from the convent of the Friars Minor [at Beaucaire-sur-Rhone], carried him onto the brigantine, took off his chains and gave him back his freedom. Later, when Pope Nicholas [Nicholas V (1397–1455)] gave Coeur command of several galleys to fight the Infidel, he spent some time carrying out his new duties. He fell ill and finally passed from this life to a happier one. This was an uncultivated man, but very intelligent, shrewd and able in all worldly affairs.

[3]

Who would have believed that King Charles, whom he had served with such zeal and loyalty, and whose trust, and even friendship (so they say) he had gained, could one day treat him with such harshness? Yet, without doubt, whatever the crime that was used as an excuse to demand his sentence, under the banner of justice, the king's acrimony was mainly instigated by what wicked informers whispered in his ears and wrongly claimed, that [Jacques] had poisoned the beautiful Agnes. They say that while his life was coming to an end, he exculpated himself from this and many other crimes in front of many people, pardoned the king and his accusers, and invoked God Almighty to absolve all the offences committed against him. Such is often the fate of those who try to become confidants of kings and princes. Once they have, they believe themselves to be happy. We find such cases often in almost all kingdoms and peoples; ancient annals and more recent history are teeming with such examples.

---

[5] The rescue was carried out not by Guillaume de Varye, but by Jean de Village, another of Coeur's agents or factors.

[6] Types of ship.

1.10

Journal of Jean Dauvet, royal proctor: investigations at Bourges (1453)

M. Mollet (1952) *Les affaires de Jacques Coeur. Journal du Procureur Dauvet*, Paris: Armand Colin, 2 vols., vol. 1, pp. 149–54. Translation from French by Kathleen Daly. Paragraph numbers added.

Jean Dauvet (c. 1400–71) was a senior law officer (known as the *procureur général*) in the *Parlement* of Paris. A large fine was imposed on Jacques Coeur after his trial, to be met by the confiscation and sale of his possessions. Charles VII commissioned Dauvet to oversee this task, from 2 June 1453 to 5 July 1457. This extract is taken from one of the many interrogations of witnesses preserved by Dauvet in his 'Journal', a detailed record (often written day by day) of his attempt to trace Coeur's goods, in this case, from the mansion in Bourges.

Wednesday 5th day of December [1453]

1. Guillot Trépant, whom I had ordered to come to me, came and appeared and I questioned him about the goods belonging to Jacques Coeur. And after taking the oath to tell the truth, he said and deposed as follows: that is, that he came to live with the said Coeur 15 years or so [ago] and began to serve him in his office [of *argentier*] for his expenditure and several other matters, and rode out with him and used to serve him in the aforesaid manner, until the time the king was at Nancy [1444] where the said Coeur left him and ordered him, together with Guillaume Varye, to deal with the expenditure of the *argenterie*,[1] made by Guillaume and other servants in the said *argenterie*, and not to get involved with merchandise or with the paperwork in the said *argenterie*, except occasionally when he helped load and unload and wrap up the cloth and take it to wherever the king went.

2. And he stayed in this condition for three years or so, and said that since then, that is, in the year 1447, while the king was in this town of Bourges, the said Coeur, his master, who was having his great house built, ordered he who speaks [Trépant] to stay in that house

---

[1] Treasury of the royal household.

1.2 Nineteenth-century engraving, depicting the arrival of Charles VII and his retinue at the home of Jacques Coeur in Bourges.

with the late wife[2] of the said Coeur, and ordered him to look after the supplies and the expenditure of the household and supervise the work [on the house] with Jacques Culon; and since then [Trépant] continuously stayed in the mansion and served [in the above capacity] until Coeur was arrested.

3. And said that about a year before Coeur was arrested, Coeur married him off to the daughter of Estienne Mery, who was related to the late bishop of Luçon, Coeur's brother, and after their marriage [Trépant] and his wife lived with Coeur's late wife for a year or so after Coeur's arrest, at which time the archbishop of Bourges[3] and other relatives and friends of Coeur considered that they should reduce some of the expense of the house and the people in it. [. . .] And [Trépant] said that, when Coeur married him off to [Estienne Mery's daughter], Coeur promised to pay him 500 écus and pay all his salary for his services and provide for his estate and employment, so that he could live well and honourably, but he never received that, nor recovered a single penny, and he is a poor man and is in a miserable condition and, if his friends had not helped him, he would have had nothing to live on.

4. Asked what goods of Coeur's he looked after while he stayed in Coeur's house, [he] said that he did not look after the household goods and utensils, as Coeur's wife took charge of them and had the keys. [. . .] However, he said that, after the feast for the entry of my lord the archbishop of Bourges, which took place in September 1450 in this town, Coeur left in the lower counter[4] of his house, near the hall, a large image of the Magdalene,[5] and he did not know whether it was of gold or silver-gilt, and cannot remember whether there were jewels on it or not. Also [Coeur] left three or four gold salts[6] in the shape of men and women, and there was another in the form of a stag and a cross decorated with jewels . . . which Coeur left in his keeping, and gave and left him the key of the counter where they were kept and told him to keep them securely without showing them to anyone else at all until [Trépant] heard from [Coeur] and he kept them for three months

---

[2] Macée de Léodepart.

[3] Jean Coeur, Jacques' son.

[4] This reference to a 'counter' shows that, although Coeur had been ennobled, he also used his mansion in Bourges for business. Nobles were supposed to pursue a 'noble' lifestyle, generally the pursuit of arms, and not commerce, if they wanted to maintain their noble status.

[5] Saint Mary Magdalene.

[6] A salt, as its name suggests, held salt; however, it was often made of precious metal and could be extremely elaborate and costly.

or so, until Coeur and Guillaume de Varye wrote to him to give the goods to Martin Anjorrant and Colas de Manne, who would take them to Tours, where the king was then, and he who speaks handed them over.[7] And he does not know what became of those valuables afterwards.

5. Asked what other valuables, gold and silver plate, tapestries, chambers,[8] linen and other goods were in Coeur's house at the time of his arrest . . . he said he did not know about valuables and gold plate . . . and had never seen anything else. But [Coeur's] wife had hats, belts and pearl purses, and other bridal clothes that were not very valuable, as he thought, but he could not assign a value to them, for he did not really take careful note. [. . .] And as for tapestry, there were several pieces with the arms and device of the king and other pieces with Coeur's arms and device . . . but he could not specify how many. [. . .] And concerning the chambers of tapestry . . . , there was a chamber of damask embroidered with figures from [the story] of Nebuchadnezzar . . . and there were two wall hangings embroidered with twigs, as he thought, . . . and another chamber set of green and white . . .

[. . .]

6. As for kitchen vessels . . . he said that the kitchen was so poorly furnished that, when Coeur came and put on dinners and feasts, they hired goods from a tinsmith called Gieffroy Pischart and they borrowed pans and other things. Furthermore he said, as the house was not complete, it had not been properly furnished yet, and Coeur was waiting until it was finished before furnishing it, as the workmen coming through the house would have ruined everything, and a lot would have gone missing. Also he said Coeur's late wife spent and wasted all she had in her hands, and for this reason Coeur left the bare minimum in his house.

[. . .]

7. When asked what had become of a chamber of red taffeta embroidered with 'R.G.' and little angels,[9] he said that formerly he had seen

---

[7] This information suggests that the goods mentioned here were intended for the king, and Jacques had acquired them in his role as treasurer of the royal household, rather than for his own use.

[8] A 'chamber' was a complete set of tapestries and hangings to furnish a room.

[9] The letters, probably signifying 'real guerdon', royal reward or protection, are sculpted into the stonework on the façade of Jacques Coeur's mansion, with his motto: 'A vaillans [Cuers] riens inpossible. RG' (to the valiant [heart], nothing [is] impossible). Angels also feature in the sculpted decoration, for example in the *Chambre du Trésor*, and supporting coats of arms in the chapel.

it in Coeur's house, and it had been taken to Rome when Coeur went there, and since had been brought back to the house and had been hung up for the wedding of master Jean Thierry in the Galley chamber and had since been hung up on the orders of Coeur's late wife, according to what other servants in the household told him, and he does not know what became of the said chamber since, nor what had been done with it.

[. . .]

1.11

Jacques Coeur's mansion: evidence from the seventeenth century

A. Gandilhon (1931) 'Un état des lieux de l'hôtel Jacques-Coeur à Bourges dressé en 1636', in *Bulletin historique du comité des travaux historiques*, pp. 153–64. Translation from French by Kathleen Daly.

From 1629–36, Henri de Bourbon, Prince of Condé, rented the Coeur mansion in Bourges to house his son Louis, who was attending the Jesuit college in Bourges as a pupil. While the young prince was in residence, the stained glass windows of the Galley Chamber (*Chambre des Galées*), the great hall on the ground floor, and the great hall on the first floor were taken down and kept in the Treasure Chamber (*Chambre du Trésor*).

(a)

On 8 Feb. 1636 the glass maker Jacques Barbellion was commissioned to return the windows to their original position: –

In the room where [Louis of Bourbon] lodged, it is necessary to put back the six large painted glass panes, which represented several galleys, which were taken down when the said lord moved in, and if any part of the said panes is missing, to put back similar painted glass in the colour of that which was lost or broken, so that there shall be no distortion afterwards in what is depicted in the panels; [and] to clean them and fix them properly. Also to put up and affix in the lower and upper great halls all the other painted glass panes which have been taken down . . . put in new lead, . . . and replace all the missing pieces in the panes in the same colour, and representing the same things as those that were lost, so everything depicted in those panes matches.

(b)

On 26 February 1636, at the end of the lease, the owner (Charles de l'Aubespine, marquis of Chateauneuf) instructed a notary, Yves Dugué, to visit the house to check that it was in good condition, that any damage during the lease had been repaired, and that Condé had made good any changes that they had made while renting it: –

[2] In the little corridor . . . leading to the lower hall were found two windows with complete stained glass with the arms of Jacques Coeur.

[. . .]

[3] In the said hall were found thirty complete and painted panes where the 12 peers of France are depicted, and several Christian kings, all in fine painted glass . . .[1]

[. . .]

[14] In the great upper chamber were found sixteen glass windows . . . where are represented the arms of Jacques Coeur and those with whom he had family connections . . . There are four doors into the said [chamber].

[. . .]

[16] In a chamber known as the Galley chamber . . . there are six great windows where there are galleys and ships very finely painted.

[. . .]

[25] In the gallery leading to the chapel there was no furniture, and the windows are decorated with 32 panes of glass, that is, 24 on the courtyard side in which are depicted the 12 months of the year and the arms of several ancient families of Berry, and 8 on the street side, some of which have recently been re-leaded, the others newly made and others repaired. The [floor of the] gallery is well and properly tiled.

[1] Gandilhon (p. 155) identifies these as the Nine Worthies. See document 1.3, note 6.

[26] In the chapel there was nothing but a painting, with its shutter painted inside as well, which is in front of the chapel altar, and as for the windows, they have been restored and are complete.

[. . .]

1.12

The Treaty of Arras, 1435

E. Cosneau (ed.) (1889) *Les Grands Traités de la Guerre de Cent Ans*, Paris: Picard, p. 143. Translation from French by Kathleen Daly.

The Congress of Arras was intended to arrive at a lasting peace between the two claimants to the French throne, Henry VI and Charles VII. Efforts to reconcile the English and French foundered, because the English refused to abandon the terms of the Treaty of Troyes (see document 1.2). However, the Congress had an important outcome: peace between Charles VII and Philip duke of Burgundy, and their Armagnac and Burgundian supporters. Philip also obtained important territorial concessions. Furthermore, the clause translated here marked an important change in the feudal relationship between the duke and the king in Philip's French lands.

28. Item, [it is agreed that] my said lord of Burgundy will not be required to do faith, nor homage, nor service to the king for lands and lordships which he currently holds in the kingdom of France, nor for those that he should receive through this present treaty, and similarly for those which may come to him afterwards, by succession, in the said kingdom; but he will be exempt in his personal capacity, in every case, from subjection, homage, right to take appeals, sovereignty and other [rights] of the king, during [Charles VII's] lifetime; but after his death, my said lord of Burgundy shall pay to his son and successor the appropriate homages, fealties and services; and, if my lord of Burgundy dies before the king, his heirs and claimants will perform the appropriate homages, fealty and services to the king.

1.13
Ordinance of Thionville, Luxemburg, December, 1473

PART 2

R. Vaughan ([1973] 2002), *Charles the Bold*, with an introduction by W. Paravicini, 2nd edn., Woodbridge: Boydell, p. 186.

In December 1473, Charles the Bold (1443–77) made a major series of ordinances setting up new central institutions for his northern land. This extract, translated by Vaughan, is taken from the preamble of an ordinance setting up the Parlement of Malines: the new Parlement was intended to supplant the judicial role of the Parlement of Paris and imperial courts.

By divine bounty and providence, which directs and governs all terrestrial affairs, princes have been instituted and ordained to rule principalities and lordships, in particular so that the regions, provinces and peoples are joined together and organized in union, concord and loyal discipline by them, in the place of God our creator. This union and public order can only be maintained by justice, which is the soul and spirit of the public weal. Because of this we, desiring with all our heart and power in doing our duty to God the all powerful and to the lands, principalities and lordships which, by his esteemed bounty he has submitted to us, and following the example of our most noble progenitors, to fulfil, improve, maintain and defend the union, concord and public order of our said principalities and lordships, we have from our infancy taken, chosen and selected, as our principal shield and means to achieve this, true and thorough zeal for and observance of justice, without which the regions and provinces would more truthfully be described as assemblies of wicked men than as kingdoms or principalities. We believe that it is because of this zeal, care, solicitude and labour which we have undertaken, voluntarily and with a good heart, for the observance and maintenance of good justice in our lands and lordships, more than through any other power or merit in us, that we have enjoyed the victories which, in defending our said lands and lordships, in reducing to union with our holy mother church those who by prolonged obstinacy and contempt of her leaders and censures have been alienated from her and also in reducing to our obedience what justly has belonged and does belong to us, God our creator, who is the sole author of victories, has in a short time given us several times in the lands of France, Liège and Guelders, for which we render him most humble and infinite thanks.

1.14
Charles the Bold's jewelled hat

R. Vaughan ([1973] 2002), *Charles the Bold*, with an introduction by W. Paravicini, 2nd edn., Woodbridge: Boydell, p. 169.

As medieval jewellery and costumes only rarely survive to the present day, we are often dependent for our knowledge of them on descriptions in financial accounts, or in inventories. This document gives a description of one of the elaborate hats created for Charles the Bold, by his goldsmith, Gérard Loyet.

To Gérard Loyet, goldsmith and *valet de chambre*,[1] the sum of £484 which was owing to him for certain pieces of workmanship, which by the duke's command he made and delivered last February, 1471, as follows: Firstly, for having made and lined a hat of steel and covered it with a ducal hat in gold garnished with eighteen large balas-rubies[2] and forty great pearls, with large raised open-work leaves around the rubies and several other settings of leaves, to go round the said pearls, £105. Also for making for this hat an ornament of three great guns arranged in a triangle and adorned with three large balas-rubies in lieu of flints, with great flames of gold shooting outwards all round like a sun and, above the said ornament, a large flower enamelled in white with a very large balas set in it, £15. Also, for making gold buttons to go round the rim of the said hat and on the strap which does up under the neck, £3 [. . .].

---

[1] Officer in the ducal household, often an honorary appointment.
[2] That is spinel rubies, rose-red precious stones.

1.3 Seventeenth-century engraving of one of several magnificent jewelled hats (now sadly lost) known to have been owned by Charles the Bold.

1.15
Court protocol in France and Burgundy

J. Paviot (1998) 'Éléanore de Poitiers, *Les États de France
(Les Honneurs de la Cour)*, in *Annuaire – bulletin de la
Société de l'Histoire de France*, année 1996, pp. 75–137.
Translation from French by Kathleen Daly.

Éléanore (or Aliénor) de Poitiers (c. 1444/6–1509) lived at the
Burgundian court from the age of seven. Her mother was a
Portuguese noblewoman who came to Burgundy with Philip the
Good's bride, Isabel of Portugal (1397–1471). From 1458, she was
lady in waiting to three generations of Burgundian wives.
Éléanore wrote this treatise in July 1484 and August 1487. The
text is only known through two later copies, as the original has
not survived.

(a) Charles VII of France and his queen Marie of Anjou visit Duchess Isabel at Chalons in 1445

My lady the duchess [of Burgundy] . . . came with all her company, on
horses and in carriages, to the place where the king and the queen
were. And my lady the duchess got out and her first maid of honour
took her train; and my lord [Jean de] Bourbon[1] escorted her on his
right hand.

[. . .]

[The queen is notified of the duchess's arrival, and agrees to see
her].

My lady the duchess went to the threshold of the chamber where
the queen was. All the knights and gentlemen accompanying [the
duchess] went in. Then when my lady [the duchess] came to the
threshold, she took the train of her dress in her hand, and took it away
from the lady who was carrying it. And when she stepped over the
threshold, she let her train drop and kneeled right down to the ground.
And then she walked to the middle of the room where she paid the
same honour.[2] And then she began to walk towards the queen who
was straight ahead, and my lady [the duchess] found herself next to

[1] Duchess Isabel's nephew, Jean de Bourbon, son of the duke of Bourbon.
[2] That is, she kneeled again.

the head of her bed.[3] And when my lady began to curtsey for a third time, the queen stepped forward two or three feet, and my lady kneeled. The queen put one of her hands on [the duchess's] shoulder, and embraced her, and kissed her, and made her rise up.

After my lady had risen, she kneeled down again very low and then came to my lady the dauphine,[4] who was five or six feet from the queen. And my lady got down on her knees again; and like the queen, my lady the dauphine kissed my lady the duchess. But it seemed, to see the dauphine's attitude, that she wished to stop my lady the duchess from kneeling completely on the ground. But my lady wanted to do it, so said my mother, who had seen all these things.

From there my lady the duchess went to greet the queen of Sicily, who was two or three feet from the dauphine.[5] And my lady paid no more honour to the queen of Sicily than that lady did to her.[6] And as my lady mother said, neither lady put herself out trying to kneel.[7]

[. . .]

My lady the duchess kissed all the ladies [in waiting] of the queen [of France] and the dauphine; but she didn't kiss any more of the Queen of Sicily's ladies than that queen did of hers.

And my lady the duchess [of Burgundy] Isabel wished on no account to go after the Queen of Sicily, for she said that my lord the Duke was nearer to the crown of France than was the king of Sicily. . . . [W]hen they were in the Queen [of France]'s Chamber, one stood on one side and the other on the other (side); and it seemed that the King and Queen and my lord the dauphin and my lady the dauphine had a greater desire to honour my lady the duchess than the Queen of Sicily, and so had all the princesses of the kingdom.

[. . .]

(b) The birth of Mary of Burgundy   *1457*

In that chamber [where Mary of Burgundy was born] there was a great dresser, on which were four fine steps, as long as the dresser was wide,

---

[3] In the fifteenth century, beds were not just for sleeping in. In a ruler's or noble's chamber, the bed was comparable to a throne and, like a throne, might have a canopy. An elaborate bed with a canopy and curtains made out of expensive fabrics also showed the owner's wealth and status.

[4] The title given to the wife of the heir apparent to the French throne, the dauphin.

[5] Isabel of Lorraine, queen of Sicily, wife of René of Anjou, king of Sicily, brother-in-law and cousin of King Charles VII of France.

[6] That is, the duchess of Burgundy was careful to avoid showing more attention to the queen of Sicily than the queen of Sicily paid to her.

[7] The original French phrase is 'neither lady burst the fastenings [of her bodice] by kneeling'.

and all covered with cloths. The said dresser and the steps were all loaded with crystal vessels decorated with gold and precious stones and the gold was fine, for all the richest plate of Duke Philip was there, all the pots, as well as cups of fine gold, and other vessels and basins, which were only put out on such occasions. Among the other vessels, there were on the dresser two sweet dishes of gold and stones, one of which was estimated to be worth about 40,000 écus, and the other 30,000.

(c) The arrangements to be observed in the houses of princes or lords

[I]t should be known that when kings, queens, dukes, duchesses [and] princesses have relatives – nieces, first cousins and others of high lineage – because they are of royal blood, they should be called 'dear nephews', 'dear nieces', 'dear cousins', 'dear aunts', and this word 'dear' should be used by one or the other when writing, as long as they are of the same degree and nobility.

(d) The arrangements to be observed in households of lower status

The above mentioned things should not be done in houses of lower degree, for example, of countesses, viscountesses, baronesses.

[. . .]

In such households, no one should taste the wine and meat [before serving], nor should items given to [that] lord or lady be kissed, nor should they have a canopy, nor call their children my lord like the aforesaid princes and it is not appropriate either for them to call their relatives 'dear cousin . . .', only 'my cousin'; and whoever does otherwise than stated here, it should be notorious to all that it is done through vainglory and presumption and should be regarded as worthless, because these are wilful, disorderly and unreasonable, for no one should be allowed to take more precedence or more ceremony than is due to him and which has not been customarily granted and established for a long time.

It is not appropriate either for them to place hats nor golden circlets on their coats of arms with fleurons[8] that pass the border, nor

---

[8] The projection resembling a *fleur de lis* rising from the circlet of the crown.

to wear ermines, ... except those descended from the stock and coats of arms of kings and dukes and princes in direct line, and such countesses and baronesses [of lower rank] should not go in the same rank nor holding the hand of daughters of kings, duchesses, princesses nor of their children, and should show [these] every honour and respect.

Nor should they wear robes or garments of brushed cloth of gold or richer,[9] for such clothes of gold and ornaments are reserved for kings and the others before mentioned, but it should be enough for them to wear less costly cloth of gold, otherwise there would be no difference between [them] and the garments of kings and princes.

[...]

Nor should they be served at table by any gentlemen who have a napkin over their shoulder, or anywhere other than around their arm, and their bread should not be broken at the table, but only put on the table with the knives, and covered by an open napkin, unfolded.

Neither should their masters of the household carry rods [of office], nor should they be served at table with double table cloths, nor should the train of their dresses be carried by ladies of honour, only by a gentleman or page.

Nor should they have in their household gentlemen without number, nor horses without number, but only what belongs to their condition.

These are the honours ordained, preserved and kept in Germany.... [and] in the kingdom of France.

[...]

And we should not take account of those who allege that the aforesaid matters were done in the past, and that now there is another world: such claims do not justify breaking with former and well-ordered things.

---

[9] In French, *drap d'or frizé*.

1.16

Olivier de La Marche: the estate of the household of Charles duke of Burgundy

O. de La Marche (1888), *Mémoires d'Olivier de la Marche*,
ed. H. Beaune & J. d'Arbaumont, Paris, Société de l'Histoire
de France, 4 vols. (1883–8), vol. 4, pp. 1–2, 31,
85–6, 93. Translation from French by Kathleen Daly.

Olivier de la Marche (c. 1425–1502) was successively a page, squire-pantler[1] of the count of Charolais (the future Charles the Bold), and, from 1461, grand master of the household (*maître d'hôtel*) of the dukes of Burgundy. When La Marche sent a copy of his treatise on Charles the Bold's household to the emperor Maximilian in 1500, he explained that he had originally composed it 'at the request of King Edward [IV] of England . . . because . . . he wished to land in France with armed might and show himself to be a great and powerful king'. Maximilian himself wanted suitable advice on who should be appointed to the household of his son, Philip the Fair, who had just become prince of Castile and potentially the future king of Spain. The treatise's influence grew in 1548, when the Hapsburg court of Philip II, king of Spain (Philip the Fair's grandson), adopted what it termed the 'Burgundian' form of court ceremonial, apparently following the *Estate*.[2]

In accomplishing [this] at your request, my lord Victualler of Calais,[3] I have put briefly what I have understood about the estate and household of duke Charles of Burgundy, my very sovereign lord, together with his ordinances of war. And we will begin with the state of his household, and with the service of God and his chapel, which must be the beginning of all things.

[. . .]

Now we must talk of the second estate, who are the cup bearers [*échansons*] which are the second estate according to the ancient order

---

[1] An honorary office in the count's household whose duties included the task of serving bread to the count at table.

[2] W. Paravicini (2003) 'La Cour de Bourgogne selon Olivier de La Marche', *Publication du Centre Européen d'Études Bourguignonnes*, 43, p. 118–24.

[3] William Ross, lieutenant of William, Lord Hastings who was then governor of Calais, contacted La Marche at the request of Edward IV.

as I find it written down; and the reason for this is, because the cup-bearer serves the wine where is consecrated the precious blood and body of Our Lord Jesus Christ . . . and this is a good reason that the service of bread and wine should take precedence before all things.

[. . .]

Charles the Bold appoints new captains [*conducteurs*] of his ordinance companies annually.

The duke has the captains that he has chosen for the year addressed, and has the ordinances regulating the conduct of war read to them; and after they have been read, he has each captain called before him individually, one after the other, and in public, gives to each two things, first the book of his ordinances richly made and written, covered in velvet, in a very worthy volume, sealed with his great seal in green wax, with silk threads, and giving it [to the captain] the duke himself speaks, and says 'You [name of captain] I make you captain for the year, of such and such a company of a hundred lances[4] of my men at arms. And in order that you should know, listen, and cannot be ignorant of the manner in which I intend my men at arms and wars to be conducted and organised, I give you the ordinances that I have had made and ordained on this matter, and I command you to keep and follow them strictly, in accordance with their content'. And then the duke takes a baton called the captain's baton,[5] and this baton is covered with blue and twisted white silk which are the prince's colours, and gives the baton to the captain and says to him, 'In order that you should be obeyed, and more powerful over those over whom I have appointed you, and so that you can keep, and enforce, my ordinances, I give you this baton to give you power over your men, the same authority and power that I have myself'. And at that, he receives the oath of the captain that he will carry out and maintain the prince's ordinances; so one after the other, the duke of Burgundy creates his captains, and they are obliged to return [the copy of] these ordinances and the baton [of office] at the end of the year, so that they can be given to those whom the duke appoints [next], then each goes to his own company.

[. . .]

And in order that it be clear that I want everyone to know that what is given in this writing is given by a man who knows his subject well, I have put my name in writing after this present letter, commending myself to you, which letter I have made and compiled at the siege of Neuss in Germany in the month of November 1474.

---

[4] A unit of six mounted men, including a man at arms and three archers.
[5] Rod of office.

Truly, your Olivier de La Marche, knight, counsellor and maitre d'hôtel of my lord the duke of Burgundy, captain of his guard . . .

1.17
Georges Chastelain, *Chronique*

D. Regnier-Bohier (ed.) (1995), *Splendeurs de la Cour de Bourgogne: récits et chroniques*, Paris: Robert Laffont, pp. 765–6, 831–2, 932–5. Translation from French by Kathleen Daly.

Chastelain (c. 1414/15–75) was the son of a Ghent shipper, though his mother may have been noble. He spent time at the French and Burgundian courts, and entered ducal service around 1445. On 25 June 1455 he was made Philip's official historiographer. From 1455–64, he was in regular attendance on the duke, though probably never intimate with him, and knew other leading political figures such as the Croys, and men of letters such as Olivier de La Marche. From 1464, he was less regularly at court, and became resident at Valenciennes, although he was given the title of knight (but not membership of the Order of the Golden Fleece) by Charles the Bold. Although he kept in touch with events at the court, he is probably less reliable as a source for the last years of his life.[1]

(a) Prologue

I, George Chastelain, pantler of the very noble, very powerful and very famous prince, my most feared and sovereign lord, my lord the duke Philip of Burgundy, son of John [was] born in the imperial county of Alost in Flanders, descending from the house of Gavre and of Mammynes, soberly educated in letters, brought up in arms in the flower of my youth, and by frequenting royal courts and nobles, above all the French, toughened in arms and for a long time fighting against hard, contrary fortunes, I have sufficiently observed and remembered the events and the true report of them that I heard, [. . .] for the plea-

[1] G. Small (1997) *George Chastelain and the Shaping of Valois Burgundy: Political and Historical Culture at Court in the Fifteenth Century*, London: Boydell, pp. 13, 26, 45, 49, 66–84.

sure of my sovereign lord, who does not seek his own personal glory but that of the holy House of France from which he comes, and of which he has taken all his pride and splendour . . .

[. . .]

I require and beg my readers, from whatever party they come, French, Burgundian or English, not to regard me with any partiality, suspicion or favour, but to judge me as I describe myself: a loyal Frenchman with my prince, daring to pronounce the truth against my master where necessary, and without dissimulation towards the French or the English, whose glory must not be extinguished on one part or the other, but giving each his due according to the course of events.

(b) Competition for office

One Monday, on Saint Anthony's day [17 January 1457], after mass, the duke, wanting his household to be peaceful and without discord between his servants, and to see his son [Charles] act according to his counsel and his wishes, after having said a large part of his Hours, when the chapel was empty, the duke called his son and said gently:

– Charles, about the conflict between the lords of Sempy and Aymeries concerning the position of chamberlain,[2] I want you to end it – the lord of Sempy should have the position.

Then the count [of Charolais] said:

– My lord, you have given me your list already, which did not contain the lord of Sempy, and so please, my lord, I ask you to stand by it.

– The Devil! said the duke, do not concern yourself with lists! It is for me to increase or decrease it! I want the lord of Sempy to be installed in the position.

– What a mistake! said the count (for he always swore like that). My lord, please, forgive me, but I cannot do that: I'll keep to what you ordered me. It is the lord of Croy[3] who has schemed against me in this, as I can clearly see.

– What? said the duke, would you disobey me? Will you not do what I wish?

– My lord, I will willingly obey you, but that I won't do.

---

[2] Philippe de Croy, lord of Sempy, son of Jean de Croy, high bailiff of Hainault, and Anthoine Rolin, son of Nicolas Rolin, the Chancellor of Burgundy.

[3] Anthoine de Croy, governor of Luxembourg, Namur and Boulogne, and his brother, Jean, enjoyed the favour of duke Philip and had aroused the hostility of Charles count of Charolais, who supported the Rolins.

At these words, the duke was seized by violent anger, and replied.

– Ha, you scamp, will you disobey my wishes? Get out of my sight!

And the blood rushed to his heart at these words, and he went pale, and then all at once so inflamed and terrible in his expression – as I heard it told by the clerk of the chapel, who was alone with him – that he was awful to see.

(c) Charles the Bold as duke

[T]his duke, seeing his glorious beginnings at his coming to power, proposed to restore his household, which would not have its equal in France. He saw that he had enough power and resources to realise this. Nothing was missing but regulation and order, and setting to work to distribute everything properly. This was a man and a prince who could work very hard and wanted to know his situation and know how much power and resources he had, and what was coming in and what was laid out: he was thus perfectly able to carry all this out. And in fact, he set to, he reviewed and studied his finances and all that he had in rents and domains in his different lands, and above all what he owed at his father's death, and what could harm his domains.

[. . .]

It was said not to be suitable for such a prince to consecrate himself to this domestic labour. However, he acted like a wise man, and better advised than not to busy himself with this; for his good and noble father [Philip the Good], through being too benevolent, had let many things go. His son realised this and intended to do better himself, and not put himself in the power of another, as his father had. So, in spite of what was said to him, he would not give up, but watched over it and worked at it day and night, and kept his financial officers very hard at work – to which they were not accustomed – by his own too painstaking work. He sat with them, counting and discounting and calculating and ordering until all was done . . . He established himself on this basis, and on that he built up his estate.

[. . .]

But if he wished to do this for avarice and to take pleasure in great heaps of gold, for which some reproached him, his glory is the lesser. [. . .] The devil! It is estimable for a man who wants possessions in order to carry out his duty, and looks after his affairs, and who knows how to balance his liberality in proportion to his power . . . and who likes to save to provide for unexpected events: certainly he is to be praised. But to give oneself over to unsuitable love and an idolatrous passion [for money] that is a damnable and despicable thing in a prince, and an incurable wound to the public good.

[. . .]

To speak truly, and his deeds bore this out – he loved glory and grandeur; because you can tell a man from his manners, it is a good idea to follow him and please him in what he desires, at his own expense; and there is no shame in having oneself served assiduously, and to surround oneself with a multitude of lords and nobles, which no garment of gold or silver, no other worldly wealth can rival. He also brought order and regulation into his counsel and all that depended on it taking appropriate measures. He did the same for his archers, all with the aim of organising his household.

1.18

Statutes of the Order of the Golden Fleece

S. Dünnebeil (2002–3) *Die Protokollbucher des Ordens vom Goldenen Vlies*, Stuttgart: Thorbecke, 2 vols., vol. 1, p. 196. Translation from French by Kathleen Daly.

Philip the Good founded the Order of the Golden Fleece on 10 January 1430, during the celebrations for his marriage to Isabel, daughter of the king of Portugal. The original statutes drawn up in 1430 were revised in the winter of 1445–6. This translation retains the numbering of the original statutes, as followed by Dünnebeil's edition.

Philip by the grace of God duke of Burgundy, of Lotharingia, of Brabant and of Limburg, count of Flanders, of Artois, of palatine Burgundy[1] and of Namur, marquis of the Holy Empire, lord of Salins and of Malines, make known to all, present and future – that for the very great and perfect love that we have for the noble estate and order of chivalry, of which, with very ardent and special affection, we desire the honour and growth, by which the true catholic faith, the estate of our mother Holy Church and the tranquillity and prosperity of the public weal are, as they may be, protected, guarded and maintained – we, to the honour and glory of the All Powerful [God], our Creator and Redeemer, in reverence to his holy mother and in honour of Monseigneur Saint Andrew, glorious apostle and martyr, for the exaltation of the

---

[1] The county of Burgundy, or Franche-Comté.

faith and of Holy Church and to encourage virtue and good morality the tenth day of January in the year of Our Lord [1430] which was the day of the solemnisation of the marriage of ourself and our very dear and much loved wife Elizabeth [Isabel of Portugal] in our town of Bruges, have created and ordained, and by these presents take, create and ordain an order and brotherhood of chivalry or loving company of a certain number of knights whom we wish should be called the order of the Golden Fleece, according to the form, condition, statutes, manner and articles which follow:

[1] First we ordain that the aforesaid order will have thirty one knights, gentlemen in name and arms and above reproach, among whom we, in our [life]time, will be one, head and sovereign, and after us, our successors [as] dukes of Burgundy.

[2] Item, that the brothers and knights of the said order at their entry into it must leave and will leave other orders if they have any, whether of a prince or a company [of knights] (except for emperors, kings or dukes who, with this Order, may wear the order of which they are the head; as long as this is with the agreement of ourself and our sovereign successors, and the brothers of the Order, agreed in their chapter and not otherwise. And similarly, we and our sovereign successors of this present Order, in similar cases may, if we wish, wear the order of the aforesaid emperors, kings and dukes, with our own, as a sign of our true and brotherly love for one another and for the good which may come from it).[2]

[3] Item, in order to recognise the said Order and the knights who will be part of it, we shall give, once, to each of the knights of this said Order, a gold collar with our device, that is: pieces in the form of flints striking stones from which come burning sparks, and at the end of the collar, the image of a golden fleece. [That] collar will belong and must remain [the property of] the Order [and] we and our sovereign successors and each of the said knights of the said Order are obliged to wear [it] visibly each day round the neck, on pain of having to have a mass worth 4 sols [shillings] said, and of giving 4 sols to God, which each must give according to his conscience for each day that he should have worn it, unless in armour, when it will be sufficient to wear the fleece without the collar.

[. . .]

This collar must not be enriched with jewels nor anything else and the knights must not give, sell, pawn or alienate it, for whatever need or cause, or in any manner whatever.

---

[2] The section in brackets was added to the statutes after 1440.

[4] Item, to have friendship in this Order, all its knights are obliged, and will promise when entering, to have real and true love for us [and] our successors, sovereigns of the said order, and towards each other [as] we [shall] towards them, and [will] desire to pursue and advance as far as they can the honour and profit, and avoid the dishonour and harm, of those in the said order.

[. . .]

[5] Item, the said knights will promise that, if anyone tries to injure or harm us and our successors, heads and sovereigns of this order, or our lands, lordships, vassals and subjects; or that we or our sovereign successors should take up arms or enterprises for the defence of the Holy Christian Faith, or to defend, maintain and restore the dignity, estate and liberty of our mother Holy Church and of the holy Apostolic See of Rome [the Papacy], if this happens, the knights of this order who are able must serve us in person, and those who cannot, must provide a substitute for reasonable payment, unless they have a real excuse or impediment, in which case they can excuse themselves to the sovereign.

[6] Item, for this reason and for our great love and trust in our brothers and knights of this order, we, on our behalf and on that of our successors, heads and sovereigns, we determine that we and our successors shall undertake no wars or other lofty and serious matters until we have made them known to the greater part of our brother knights, to have their views and counsel on these, excepting secret or urgent matters, where revealing them might prejudice or harm these undertakings.

1.19

Criticism of Charles the Bold

R. Vaughan ([1973] 2002), *Charles the Bold*, with an
introduction by W. Paravicini, 2nd edn., Woodbridge: Boydell,
pp. 172–3, 177–8.

The statutes of the Order of the Golden Fleece made it clear that the duke, like other members, had to submit himself to the scrutiny of his fellow knights. Extract (a) gives details of some of the criticisms levelled at Charles the Bold, at a meeting of the Chapter (assembly) of the Order held at Bruges in 1468. They were repeated at another Chapter held at Valenciennes in 1473; extract (b) gives

49

part of Charles' lengthy response. Together, these extracts give us some insight into Charles' ideas of his role as a prince, the friction caused by the duke's character and method of government, and the difficulties faced by a prince when trying to govern his state.

(a) Mention was made of the points, remonstrances and requests which, in all humility and obedience, had been made to my lord the sovereign [Duke Charles] at the last chapter-general of the Order, held in the town of Bruges in the year [1468] and included in the acts of the said chapter. These were, in effect:

1. That my lord sometimes speaks a little sharply to his servants.
2. That he becomes emotional sometimes when talking about [other] princes.
3. That he works too hard so that it is doubtful if he will live when he is older.
4. That, when he mobilizes his armies, he should make provision to ensure that his subjects are not oppressed as they have been.
5. That it please him to be benign and moderate, and keep his lands in good justice.
6. That he be pleased to comply with what he has agreed to, and keep his word.
7. That he involves his people in war as late as possible and not without good and mature counsel.

(b) On the sixth point, concerning things which my lord agrees to and promises, that he should accomplish them and keep his word, my lord replied that he has always wanted and tried to keep his word and he would be glad to know if anyone could show that he had done the contrary in whatever matter except when he had beforehand agreed to, promised and disposed something in one way which afterwards, through inadvertence, he had done or promised [in another way] and not kept [to]. For numerous people make requests to him at different times, and sometimes people ask or demand things which are not ready to be dealt with without inconvenience. Others ask him for estates or offices when at the time, for certain reasons, he is undecided to whom to give or commit them. He suffers importunate requests to which he replies sometimes either that he will do what he can about it or that he will take advice about it or that he will see to it, reserving nonetheless to himself his freedom of conclusion and the interpretation of his words or replies. But the applicants choose to interpret or understand them to their advantage, blinded by their affection for their own ends. Nonetheless it will certainly not be found that my lord has agreed to or promised something affirmatively which he has not kept to except when he had already promised it beforehand to someone else and not been told or advised about this at the time of his second promise or agreement.

1.20

The submission of Ghent to Charles the Bold, 1469

R. Vaughan ([1973] 2002), *Charles the Bold*, with an introduction by W. Paravicini, 2nd edn., Woodbridge: Boydell, pp. 7–9.

Charles the Bold made his solemn entry into Ghent and was inaugurated as the new count of Flanders on 28 June 1467. The following day a riot broke out in the city and Ghenters demolished a tax-collection booth when bringing back the relics of the local saint, St Lievin, after a procession. They went on to demand the repeal of the harsh measures imposed on the city by Philip the Good, after his victory at the battle of Gavere (1453). Charles had to promise concessions, before he and his daughter Mary could flee the city on 1 July, and on 28 July Charles had to restore banners to the craft guilds. Fear of ducal vengeance persuaded the city authorities to submit to Charles and give up Ghent's privileges, in the formal ceremony described in this extract, in Brussels on 29 January 1469.

First, the said hall was adorned and hung round with very fine tapestries of the great king Alexander, of Hannibal and of other ancient worthies, and on a dais at the head of the hall my lord the duke was seated on a superb throne most nobly decorated and hung round with cloth of gold. Seated similarly, on the lowest of some steps leading up to the throne, was the most high and mighty prince my lord Anthony, bastard of Burgundy, count of la Roche, lord of Beveren and of Beuvry, who, as first chamberlain of my lord the duke, had on this occasion the cognizance of and responsibility for what followed.

Near the said throne of my lord the duke was another very fine and richly decorated bench, on which were seated first, my lord the bishop of Liège, duke of Bouillon and count of Looz; Messire Philip of Savoy, brother of the most noble and excellent lady my lady the queen of France; and the most high and mighty prince my lord Adolf of Cleves, count of la Mark and lord of Ravenstein. After them, in very fine seats, were the most high and mighty lords Messieurs of the noble Golden Fleece and, after them the other nobles. . . . Also present in this enclosure were a number of foreign ambassadors, including those of France, England, Hungary, Bohemia, Naples, Aragon, Sicily, Cyprus, Norway, Poland, Denmark, Russia, Livonia, Prussia, Austria, Milan, Lombardy and others: a wonderful sight indeed.

Next, my lord the duke's lesser court officials took their places on benches erected for them along the hall, each in order according to his status and office. There was a beautifully carpentered passage-way in the hall made like a street for those coming, passing and staying; and the duke's officials made their way along this to their seats, each in order and according to the dignity of his office as has been said. . . .

Monsieur Olivier de la Marche, knight, and Pierre Bladelin, called Leestmakere, *maîtres d'hôtel* of my said lord the duke, deputed for this purpose . . . , went . . . to the square called Coudenberg, in front of the palace, where the Ghenters, that is to say, the magistrates, the fifty-two deans of the craft gilds and the jurors of the town of Ghent, who had come from the town hall of Brussels, were assembled. They led them most graciously from the said square into the courtyard, each dean having before him the banner of his gild unfurled on a lance, where they waited in the snow more than an hour and a half. When they came and entered the hall as a result of the intercession of their guides, each of them knelt down most humbly on the ground three times with his banner before entering the said enclosure, where each placed his banner at the feet of my lord the bastard of Burgundy and they all cried 'Mercy!' together very humbly, which was piteous to see and hear.

Immediately after this the Great Privilege of Ghent was read out in full, particularly the passage concerning the renewal of the magistrature etc. This done, the reading over, Messire Pierre, lord of Goux and of Wedergrate, chancellor of Burgundy, asked my lord the duke what was his pleasure. He replied straight away that the whole of the said privilege should be annulled. Hearing this, Master Jehan le Gros, first secretary and *audiencier*, took a knife or quill-cutter and lacerated the privilege in front of everyone.

This done, my said lord the duke began to speak about the recent wars in Flanders, complaining in detail of the offences and misdeeds [of the Ghenters] and of their behaviour towards the most high and noble person of the late mighty duke Philip his father, whom God pardon. He also explained and demonstrated how he had always supported them to the utmost, even speaking on their behalf to his said most noble father. Among other things, he complained that, when he wanted to have his most noble daughter with him in Brussels they were unwilling to let her leave [Ghent], showing well enough by this that they had offended most against him when he trusted them most. What is more, when he wanted to enter into possession of his land of Flanders and to swear to maintain and respect its privileges etc., they had offended even more vilainously, and vented all their spleen etc. He then outlined how, in reparation, they had agreed first, at his request to close the gates; second, they had brought their banners, as above-mentioned; third, they had very humbly cried mercy for the heinous crime of lese-majesty which they had perpetrated; fourth, they had brought their privileges, also noted above.

'By means of these obeisances, if you keep your promises to be our good people and children as you ought to be you may obtain our grace, and we shall be a good prince and archimandrite'. And he concluded by asking them if entire satisfaction could have been made for their said offence and vilainous disobedience, to which, as might be expected, they did not reply a word.

1.21

Contracts for making the tomb of Richard Beauchamp, earl of Warwick, 1447–54

A.R. Myers (ed.) (1969) *English Historical Documents*, vol. 4: *1327–1485*, London: Eyre & Spottiswoode, pp. 1161–5.

Richard Beauchamp (1382–1439), earl of Warwick, was one of the richest noblemen in England. He played a leading role in the wars in France, and was made lieutenant of France and Normandy in 1437, dying at Rouen in 1439. He left instructions in his will for the building of a chantry chapel attached to St Mary's Church, Warwick, which cost £2,481 4s and $7^{1}/_{2}$d. It was begun in 1443, and the structure had been completed by 1449, although it was not consecrated until 1475. The contracts for the earl's fine tomb, and the decoration of the chapel, from which extracts are given here, were drawn up from 1447–54. These extracts supply important information about the craftsmen involved and the directions given by the executors, which can be compared to what is visible in the chapel today (after successive restorations). The original document has not survived. These extracts are taken from a nineteenth-century copy in collections on Warwickshire history compiled by Robert Bell Wheeler (now British Library, Additional MS 28,546).

1 *The contract for the construction of the marble base of the tomb*

A covenant by indenture bearing date the 16th day of May in the 25th year of King Henry VI [1447] between Thomas Huggeford, Esq., Nicholas Rodye, gentleman, and William Brackeswell, priest, executors of the last will and testament of the said lord Richard Beauchamp, late Earl of Warwick, whom God absolve, on the one hand, and John Bourde of Croft Castle in the County of Dorset, marbler, on the other hand, whereby the said John Bourde covenants to make a tomb of marble to be set on the said earl's grave. The same tomb to be made well clean and sufficiently of a good fine marble and as well coloured as may be in England. The upper stone of the tomb and the base thereof shall contain in length 9 foot of the standard, in breadth 4 foot, and in thickness 7 inches. The course of the tomb to be of good and due proportion to answer the length and breadth of the uppermost stone. And a pace to be made round about the tomb of like good marble to stand on the ground, which pace shall contain in thickness 6 inches and in breadth 18 inches. The tomb to bear in height from the pace 4 foot and a half, and in and about the same tomb he shall make the principal housings and 36 small housings, and under every principal housing a goodly quarter for an escutcheon of copper and gilt to be set, and to do all the work and workmanship about the tomb to the carving, according to the portraiture delivered to him. . . . The carving to be at the executors' charge, after which the said marbler shall polish and clean the said tomb in workmanlike fashion. And for all the said marble, carriage, and work he shall have in sterling money – £45.

[. . .]

2 *The contract for the glazing of the chapel*

A covenant by indenture bearing date the 23rd June, 25 Henry VI, between Thomas Huggeford, Nicholas Rodye, and William Brakeswell, executors, on the one hand, and John Prudde of the town of Westminster, on the other hand, wherein the said John Prudde covenants to glaze all the windows in the new chapel in Warwick with glass [made] beyond the seas, and with no glass of England, and that in the finest wise with the best, cleanest, and strongest glass of beyond the sea that may be had in England, and of the finest colours of blue, yellow, red, purple, sanguine, violet, and of all other colours that shall be most necessary and best to make rich and embellish the matters, images, and stories that shall be delivered and appointed by the said executors by patterns in paper afterward to be newly traced and pictured by another painter in rich colour at the charges of the said glaziers. All these proportions the said John Prudde must make perfectly to fine glass, anneal it, and finely and strongly set it in lead, and solder it as well as any glass that is in England. Of white, green, and black glass he shall put in as little as shall be needful for the showing and setting forth of the . . . matters of images and stories. And the said glazier shall take charge of the same glass wrought and to be brought to Warwick and set up there in the windows of the said chapel, the executors paying to the said glazier for every foot of glass 2d, and for the whole, £93 1s 10d.

[. . .]

3 *The contract for the preparation and polishing of the image ready for gilding*

[Bartholomew Lambespringe, 'Dutchman'[1] and goldsmith of London, was paid £23 to prepare and polish and perfect for gilding the image of latten[2] of a man armed and all the apparel belonging to it, as helm, crest, sword, etc. and beasts. Contract dated 24th May, 27th Henry VI.]

4 *The contract for the making of the effigy*

A covenant by indenture, bearing date 11th February 28 Henry VI [1450] [between Hugford, Rodye, and Brakeswell] and William Austen, citizen and founder of London, whereby Austen covenants to cast and make an image of a man armed, of fine latten, garnished with certain ornaments, viz., with sword, dagger, garter, helm, crest under his head, at his feet a bear muzzled and a gryphon, perfectly made of the finest latten, according to the patterns, all which are to be brought to Warwick and laid on the tomb at the risk of the said Austen.

[Total cost £40]

[. . .]

6 *The contract for painting the Last Judgement on the west wall of the chapel*

A covenant by indenture, bearing date 12th February 28 Henry VI between John Brentwood, citizen and stainer of London [and the exec-

[1] German.
[2] Metal beaten into thin plates.

utors], wherein the said John Brentwood covenants to paint, finely and skilfully, at Warwick on the west wall of the new chapel there the doom of Our Lord God Jesus, and all manner of devices and imagery belonging thereto, of fair and sightly proportion as the place should serve for, with the finest colours and fine gold. The said Brentwood shall find all manner of stuff thereto at his charge, the said executor paying him therefor, £13 6s 8d.

7 *The contract for making the images to stand round the tomb*
A covenant by indenture bearing date 14th March, 30 Henry VI [1452] [between the executors] and William Austen, citizen and founder of London, whereby the said William Austen covenants to cast, work, and perfectly make of the finest latten, to be gilded, that may be found, 14 images, embossed, of lords and ladies in diverse vestures, called weepers, to stand in housings made about the tomb, those images to be made in breadth, length, thickness, etc., to 14 patterns made of timber. Also he shall make 18 lesser images of angels to stand in other housing as shall be appointed by patterns, whereof nine shall be on one side, and nine on the other. Also he must make a hearse to stand on the tomb, above and about the principal image that shall lie on the tomb according to a pattern. The stuff and workmanship to the making to be at the charge of the said William Austen. And the executors shall pay for every image that shall lie on the tomb, of weepers so made in latten 13s 4d for every image of angels so made 5s, and for every pound of latten that shall be in the hearse, 10s, and shall pay and bear the costs of the said Austen for setting the said images and hearse, £18 16s 8d.

8 *The contract for making the escutcheons for the fourteen weepers round the tomb*
[An indenture dated 6th July, 30 Henry VI, between the executors and Bartholomew Lambespringe for the making of escutcheons of the finest latten to place under the 14 images, according to the 'patterns', for the gilding, enamelling, polishing, and fixing of these escutcheons, with the cost of the materials, at 25s each. Total, £10 10s 0d.]

9 *The contract for gilding the faces and hands of the weepers and angels round the tomb*
A covenant bearing date 20th July, 31 Henry VI [1453], between [the executors] and Bartholomew Lambespringe, goldsmith, wherein the said Bartholomew covenants to gild, polish, and burnish 32 images, whereof 14 mourners and 18 angels are to be set round the tomb. And he is to make all the faces, hands and all other bare flesh of all the

said images in most lively and fair manner, and to save the gold as much as may be without spoiling, and to find all the materials, except the gold. The said executors are to find all the gold that shall be used in this work, and to pay him for his other charges and labours, either £40 or else so much as two honest and skilful goldsmiths shall say upon the view of the work, what it is worth, apart from the gold and his labour. And the executors are to deliver money from time to time as the work goes forward, whereof they pay £51 8s 4d.

10 *The contract for the gilding of the effigy of the earl*
[A similar contract, dated 3rd March 32 Henry VI [1454], with Bartholomew Lambespringe, for gilding, burnishing, and polishing the great effigy of laten to be laid on the tomb, with the helm, crest, bear, and gryphon. Bartholomew to provide all the workmanship and all materials, except gold. The work to be viewed by two honest and skilful goldsmiths, as before. Some of the money to be paid for the board of the workmen as the work proceeds, whereof they pay £95 2s 8d.]

[. . .]

12 *The contract for the latten plates to go under the effigy and round the edges of the tomb, and for the latten hearse over the effigy*
[An indenture dated 13th June, 32 Henry VI, between the executors and John Essex, marbler of London, William Austen, founder of London, and Thomas Stevenyes, coppersmith of London, for the three latter to make a large latten plate (8 ft by 3 ft) to be on the tomb, and a hearse of latten, to be made according to a design of a hearse in timber. The long plates and hearse were to be inscribed with lettering and set with escutcheons. All the plates and the latten were to be gilded. For the materials and the making they are to have £125.]

13 *The contract for the painting of four images for the chapel*
A covenant by indenture dated 13th June, 32 Henry VI, between [the executors] and Kirstian Colebourne painter dwelling in London wherein the said Kirstian covenants to paint in the finest, fairest, and most skilful manner four images of stone ordained for the new chapel in Warwick, whereof two shall be principal images, the one of Our Lady, the other of St Gabriel the angel, and two shall be lesser images, one of St Anne, the other of St George. These four are to be painted with the finest oil colours in the richest, finest, and freshest garments that may be devised, of fine gold, of fine azure, of fine purple, of fine

white and other finest colours that are necessary, garnished, bordered, powdered in the finest and most skilful fashion.

1.22

Sir John Fortescue, *The Governance of England*, 1470s

S. Lockwood (ed.) (1997) *Sir John Fortescue, On the Laws and Governance of England*, Cambridge Texts in the History of Political Thought, Cambridge: Cambridge University Press, pp. 92–3, 100–3.

Sir John Fortescue (c. 1395–c. 1477) is widely acknowledged as the principal English political theorist of the fifteenth century. His vision of England as 'a dominion political and royal', governed by the common law, was distinctive. Above all, it developed in response to a real crisis of English governance in the mid century. The council was torn apart by faction; the king's household was deeply in debt and clearly the king was not living 'of his own'; abuses associated with bastard feudalism were on the increase. Coupled with weakness in the king himself, this spelt disaster for government. Fortescue's writings provided a remedy, which rested squarely on the supremacy of ideas of justice and the public interest in the ordering of the state.

Chapter 5: The harm that comes of a king's poverty.

First, if a king is poor, he shall by necessity make his expenses, and buy all that is necessary to his estate by credit and borrowing; wherefore his creditors will win upon him the fourth or the fifth penny of all that he spends. And so he shall lose, when he pays, the fourth or the fifth penny of his revenues, and thus be thereby ever poorer and poorer, as usury . . . increases the poverty of he who borrows. His creditors shall always grumble for lack of their payment, and defame his highness of misgovernance, and default of keeping of payment days; which if he keeps, he must borrow as much at the payment days, as he did first; for he shall then be poorer than he was by the value of the fourth or fifth part of his first expenses, and so be ever poorer and poorer, until the time when he is the poorest lord of his land. For such manner of borrowing makes the great lords to be poorer than their tenants.

What dishonour this is, and abating of the glory of a king. But yet it is most to his insecurity. For his subjects will rather go with a lord who is rich, and may pay their wages and expenses, than with their king who has nothing in his purse, such that they must serve him, if they want to do so, at their own expense.

[. . .]

But the greatest harm that comes of a king's poverty is that he shall by necessity be compelled to find extreme means of getting goods; such as to accuse some of his subjects who are innocent, and upon the rich men more than the poor, so that he may better pay; and to show rigour where favour ought to be shown, and favour where rigour should be shown, to perversion of justice, and perturbation of the peace and quiet of the realm. For, as the Philosopher says in his *Ethics*, 'It is impossible to do good works without resources.'[1]

[. . .]

But we must hold it to be undoubted, that no realm may prosper, nor be worshipful, under a poor king.

[. . .]

Chapter 9: Here he shows the perils that may come to the King by over-mighty subjects

[. . .] Then it is necessary that the king's livelihood over and above such revenues as shall be assigned for his ordinary charges, are greater than the livelihood of the greatest lord in England.

And perhaps, when livelihood sufficient for the king's ordinary charges is limited and assigned thereto, it shall appear that divers lords of England have as much livelihood of their own, as shall then remain in the king's hands for his extraordinary charges. This would be improper, and very dangerous to the king. For then such a lord may spend more than the king, considering that he is charged with no such charges, extraordinary or ordinary, as is the king, except a household, which is but little in comparison of the king's house.

[. . .]

Whereof it has happened that often, when a subject has had as great a livelihood as his prince, he has before long aspired to the estate of his prince, which may soon be got by such a man. For the rest of the subjects of such a prince, seeing that if so mighty a subject might obtain the estate of their prince, they should then be under a prince twice as mighty as was their old prince . . . will therefore be very glad

---

[1] Aristotle, *Ethics*, i.viii.15. Aristotle (384–322BCE) was one of the most influential Greek philosophers, also producing works in an astonishing range of fields in science and literature.

to help such a subject in his rebellion. And also such an enterprise is the more feasible, when such a rebel has more riches than his sovereign lord. For the people will go with him who may best sustain and reward them. This manner of doing has been so often practised in almost every realm, that their chronicles are full of it.

[. . .]

We have also seen recently in our own realm, some of the king's subjects give him battle, by occasion that their livelihood and offices were the greatest of the land, and otherwise would not have done so.[2] The earls of Leicester and Gloucester, who were the greatest lords of England, rose against their king Henry III [1207–72], and took him and his son prisoners in the field.[3]

[. . .]

And also it may not be eschewed, but that the great lords of the land by reason of new descents falling unto them, and also of marriages, purchases, and other titles, shall often grow to be greater than they are now, and perhaps some of them to be of livelihood and power like a king, which shall be very good for the land so long as they aspire to none higher estate.[4] For such was the duke of Lancaster,[5] who made war upon the king of Spain, one of the mightiest kings of Christendom, in his own realm.

But this is written only to the intent that it is well understood how necessary it is that the king has great possessions and peculiar livelihood for his own safety, above all, when any of his lords shall happen to be so excessively great, as there might thereby grow peril to his estate. For certainly there may no greater peril grow to a prince, than to have a subject of equal power to himself.

[. . .]

Chapter 15: How the king's council may be chosen and established.

The king's council used to be chosen from great princes, and from the greatest lords of the land, both spiritual and temporal, and also other men that were in great authority and offices, which lords and officers had almost as many matters of their own to be treated in the council, as had the king. Wherefore, when they came together, they were so occupied with their own matters, and with the matters of their

---

[2] A reference probably to the rebellion against Edward IV (1442–83) of his brother, George, duke of Clarence (1449–78) and Richard Neville, earl of Warwick (1428–71), but their respective fathers, Richard, duke of York (1411–60) and Richard Neville, earl of Salisbury (1400–60) also are possibilities.

[3] Simon de Montfort, earl of Leicester (1208–65) and Gilbert de Clare, earl of Gloucester (1243–95), captors of the king at the Battle of Lewes, 14 May 1264.

[4] Reference to the earl of Warwick.

[5] John of Gaunt (1340–99), duke of Lancaster – son of Edward III.

kin, servants and tenants, that they intended but little, and other times not at all, to the king's matters.

And also there were few matters of the king which did not also touch the said counsellors, their cousins, servants, tenants, or such other as they owed favour to. And what lower man was there sitting in that council, who dared speak against the opinion of any of the great lords? And why, then, might not some men corrupt some of the servants and counsellors of some of the lords in order to move the lords to partiality, and to make them as favourable and partial as were the same servants?

[. . .]

Then no matter treated in the council could be kept secret. [. . .] How may the king be counselled by such great lords to restrain the giving away of his land and the giving of offices . . . to other men's servants, since they most desire such gifts for themselves, and their servants?

Which things considered, [. . .] it is thought good, that the king should have a council chosen and established in the following form

[. . .]

First, that there should be chosen twelve spiritual men and twelve temporal men, from the wisest and best disposed men that can be found in all the parts of this land; and that they shall be sworn to counsel the king after a form to be devised for their oath. And in particular, that they shall take no fee, nor clothing, nor rewards from any man, except only from the king; just as the justices of the King's Bench, and of the Common Pleas are sworn,[6] when they take their offices. And that these twenty-four shall always be councillors, unless any fault is found in them, or unless the king wishes, by the advice of the majority of them, to change any of them.

[. . .]

[and each year the king shall add four spiritual and four temporal counsellors to their number to serve for just one year]

And that they shall have a head . . . to rule the council, one of the said twenty-four, and chosen by the king, having his office at the king's pleasure.

[. . .]

And though the wages of the said twenty-four councillors seem to be a new and a great charge to the king, yet when it is considered what great wages the great lords and other men, who were of the king's council in times past [took, when the council was nothing like so useful, these wages] shall appear no great charge to the king. . . .

---

[6] The two principal Westminster Courts where common law was enforced.

[. . .]

These councillors are able continually . . . to consult and deliberate upon matters of difficulty which appertain to the king, and then upon matters of the policy of the realm, as how the export of the money may be restrained [. . . etc]. And also how the prices of merchandise grown in this land may be sustained and increased, and the prices of merchandise brought into this land abated, Also, how our navy may be maintained and augmented. [. . .] How also the laws may be amended in such things as they need reformation in, wherefore the parliaments shall be able to do more good in a month to the mending of the law, than they shall be able to do in a year, if the amending thereof be not debated, and by such council ripened to their hands.

There may be of this council . . . the great officers of the land, such as chancellor, treasurer, and privy seal, of which the chancellor, when he is present, may be president, and have the supreme rule of all the council. Also the judges, the barons of the exchequer, the clerk of the rolls . . . may be of this council when they be so desired, and otherwise not.

All other matters which shall concern this council, such as when a councillor dies how a new councillor shall be chosen, how many hours of the day this council shall sit [. . . etc] can be conceived at leisure, and put in a book, and that book kept in this council as a register or an ordinary of how they shall act in all things.

1.23

Private indentures for life service in peace and war

M. Jones & S. Walker (eds.) (1994) *Private Indentures for Life Service in Peace and War, 1278–1476*, Camden Miscellany XXXII, Camden 5th Series, vol. 3, London: Royal Historical Society, pp. 172, 173–4. Additional editing and modernisation of spelling by Rosemary O'Day.

Indentures of retainer for life in peace and war were non-feudal contracts used to regulate relations between lords and their men, which bound men to service and loyalty in return for a money fee and favour, and sometimes included residence in the lord's house.

These indentures replaced the feudal grants of land in exchange for service. They probably originated because available land was in increasingly short supply. There were, however, other ways of securing the loyalty of servants, including the exercise of patronage (appointing loyal servants to important posts in household and estate) and short-term contracts for service during particular campaigns. Carole Rawcliffe has shown, for example, that of Humphrey Stafford, Duke of Buckingham's 141 recipients of annuities only 31 were bound by indentures such as these below.[1] Where indentures of this kind were used, each of the parties would be provided with an identical copy of the deed, with each of the contracting parties sealing the part of the deed held by the other party. By the fifteenth century, indentures rarely contained details of the privileges and favours granted to the servant, and livery robes tended to be given only to those of lower social status. At this time the most important part of the contract was the retaining fee (usually either £20 or 20 marks for a knight and £10 or 10 marks for an esquire and considerably less for those of low social status) normally paid as a rent-charge (from specified land belonging to the lord) in two annual instalments. There were attempts to limit the practice of retaining by indenture from the 1330s onwards but it was not until 1468 that Edward IV restricted retaining to household servants, officers and councillors, and annulled existing contracts providing livery and maintenance. Indentures for life service had already outlived their usefulness by 1468 and were fast disappearing. The war with France was over and lords had no need to raise troops. For services at home a system of annuities for services rendered was perfectly satisfactory.[2] Both of these examples come from the end of the period during which such indentures were common.

(a) Richard Neville, earl of Warwick and Salisbury and Robert Cuny, esquire, 25 September 1467[3]

This indenture made between Richard earl of Warwick and Salisbury one the one part, and Robert Cuny[4] squire on the other beareth witness

---

[1] C. Rawcliffe (1978) *The Staffords, Earls of Stafford and Dukes of Buckingham, 1394–1521*, Cambridge: Cambridge University Press, pp. 232–40.

[2] Jones & Walker (1994), p. 32.

[3] This document is taken from Oxford, Bodleian Library, MS Dugdale 15, p. 8, after the original at Stafford Castle in 1638.

[4] Of Weston Coyney, Staffs. He was appointed to the official position of escheator of Staffordshire in November 1560.

that said Robert is withholden and belest[5] with and toward the said Earl against all persons his allegiance except, and the same Robert well and covenably horsed, armed and arrayed shall be ready to ride, come and go with, toward and for the said Earl at all times and into all places upon reasonable warning to be given unto him on the behalf of the said Earl at his costs or reasonable reward, the said Robert taking for his fee yearly to term of his life an hundred shillings sterling to be perceived and had of the issues of Yardeley[6] within the county of Warwick etc.

And the said Earl shall have the thirds of all winnings at war won or gotten by the same Robert and the third of thirds of all his servants[7] that he shall have at the wages and cost of the said Earl. And if any captain or man of estate be by the said Robert or any of his servants taken the said Earl shall have him doing to the taker reasonable reward for him.

(b) Thomas Sandforth of Askham, esquire, and William Bradley of Knipe, yeoman, 17 January 1468[8]

This indenture made at Ascom the 17th day of January, the year of the reign of King Edward the fourth after the conquest of England the vii, betwixt Thomas of Sandiforth of Ascom,[9] esquire[10] on the one part and William Bradle of Knipe in the County of Westmorland yeoman on the other part bears witness that the said William Bradle is withholden, believed and become the said Thomas's man for term of life and the said William, his friends and all that he may cause and strain, shall take true and faithful part with the said Thomas as oft as he make the said William sufficient warning against all manner of men except the sovereign lord the King, for the which withhold, belief and service the said Thomas shall be to the said William good and tender master and the said Thomas shall pay or make to be paid to the said William during the said term yearly at Whitsunday and Martinmas by

---

[5] Held.

[6] Yardley, Worcestershire.

[7] This indicates that Robert Cuny would have similar contracts with his own servants, whereby a third of all their winnings were Cuny's. By this indenture, the earl of Warwick levied a third of Cuny's profits from this source.

[8] The original is in Carlisle, Cumbria Record Office, D Lons/L/MD/AS 63.

[9] Askham, Westmorland.

[10] Sandforth had himself been a retainer of the earl of Warwick since 1462.

even portions 13s. 4d., the which shall be received of the said Thomas Graves within the parish of Bampton, who so ever happens to be for the time. And at all these these premises and conditions above said shall be truly kept and fulfilled either party of these indentures to other are assured. In witness whereof to the other party of this indenture that is remaining with the said William Bradley the said Thomas Sandforth has set to his seal.[11] Given the place, day and year above said.

1.24

The Paston correspondence

N. Davis (ed.) (1999) *The Paston Letters: A Selection in Modern Spelling*, Oxford: Oxford Paperbacks, Letters 40, 50, 73, 93, 94 and 95, pp. 77–9, 97–9, 152–5, 168–70, 194–9.

The Pastons are well known both because their voluminous correspondence survived and because modern editions of this correspondence have been printed. The letters are a major source for English society below the nobility during the period from about 1420 until the early sixteenth century. The small selection presented here shows the culture of lordship and patronage in which the family, men and women, participated. This is evidenced both by the obeisance paid by the writers to the addressees of the individual letters and by the content of the letters themselves, with their frequent references to good mastership, to favours done and promised, to requests for place and for recompense for services rendered. Note that writers 'groom' the recipients of their letters. When they seek favours, writers make it clear that, lowly though they be, they can offer the master or mistress something in return, in the form of loyal service and of prayer. To be powerful a lord needed humble followers. The letters also point to some of the other purposes of correspondence – convey-

---

[11] It was this process of sealing that gave the indenture its legal validity.

ing important news or 'tidings', both familial and local or national in import; expressing love, reassurance or doubt, making clear the reasons why an individual deserves patronage.

(a) Clement Paston to John Paston I, 25 August 1461

Right reverend and worshipful brother, I recommend me to your good brotherhood, desiring to hear of your welfare and good prosperity, the which I pray God increase to his pleasure and your heart's ease.

[. . .]

Also I understand by W. Pecock that my nephew had knowledge thereof also upon Saturday next before Saint Bartholomew in the King's house. Notwithstanding upon the same day Playter and I writ letters unto him rehearsing all the matter.

[. . .]

I feel by W. Pecock that my nephew is not yet verily acquainted in the King's house, nor with the officers of the King's house. He is not taken as none of that house, for the cooks be not charged to serve him nor the sewer to give him no dish; for the sewer will not take no men no dishes till they be commanded by the comptroller. Also he is not acquainted with nobly but with Wykes, and Wykes had told him that he would bring him to the King, but he hath not yet do so. Wherefore it were best for him to take his leave and come home till you had spoke with somebody to help him forth, for he is not bold enough to put forth himself.

But then I considered that if he should now come home, the King would think that when he should do him any service somewhere that then you would have him home, the which should cause him not to be had in favour; and also men would think that he were put out of service. Also, W. Pecock telleth me that his money is spent, and not riotously but wisely and discreetly, for the costs is greater in the King's house when he rideth than you weened it had be[en]. [. . .] And there we must get him 100s at the least . . . and yet that will be too little.

[. . .]

If I knew verily your intent were that he should come home, I would send him none. There I will do as me thinketh you should be best pleased; and that methinketh is to send him the silver. [. . .] I pray you send me it as hastily as you may, for I shall leave myself right bare; and I pray you send me a letter how you will that he shall be demeaned.

[. . .]

Christus vos observet.[1]

(b) John Paston III to John Paston I, 1 November 1462

Right reverend and worshipful father, I recommend me unto you, beseeching you lowly of your blessing. Please it you to have knowledge that my lord[2] is purposed to send for my lady, and is like to keep his Christmas here in Wales, for the King hath desired him to do the same. Wherefore I beseech you that you will vouchsafe to send me some money. [. . .] The bearer hereof should buy me a gown with part of the money . . . for I have but one gown at Framlingham[3] and another here, and that is my livery gown and we must wear them every day for the most part,[4] and one gown without change will soon be done.

As for tidings, my Lord of Warwick yede [rode] forward into Scotland on Saturday last past,[5] with twenty thousand men, and Sir William Tunstall[6] is take with the garrison of Bamburgh, and is like to be headed,[7] by the means of Sir Richard Tunstall, his own brother.

[. . .]

Written in haste at the castle of the Holt[8] upon Hallowmass Day.
Your son and lowly servant,
John Paston, junior.

(c) J. Payn to John Paston I, 1465

Right honourable and my right entirely beloved master, I recommend me unto you with all manner of due reverence in the most lowly wise, as me ought to do, evermore desiring to hear of your worshipful state,

---

[1] Christ protect you.

[2] John Mowbray, 4th duke of Norfolk, 1461–76, who was at this date just 18 years of age (the same age as John III) and was married to Elizabeth Talbot, daughter of the earl of Shrewsbury.

[3] Residence of the duke of Norfolk.

[4] Effectively a uniform in Mowbray's colours.

[5] 30 October 1462.

[6] Of Northstead, near Scarborough.

[7] Beheaded.

[8] Holt castle, Denbighshire, 5 miles north-east of Wrexham.

prosperity, and welfare, the which I beseech God of his abundant grace increase and maintain to his most pleasance and to your heart's desire.

Pleaseth it your good and gracious mastership tenderly to consider the great losses and hurts that your poor petitioner hath and hath had ever since the commons of Kent came to the Black Heath,[9] and that is at fifteen year past, whereas my master Sir John Fastolf, knight, . . . [commanded me] to take a man, and two of the best horse that were in his stable, with him to ride to the commons of Kent to get the articles[10] that they came for. And so I did . . . [and was taken captive by the Captain of Kent and asked what his business was].

And I said that I came thither to cheer with my wife's brethren and other that were mine allies and gossips of mine that were present there. And then was there one . . . said to the captain that I was one of Sir John Fastolf's men [. . .] and then the captain let cry treason upon me throughout all the field, and brought me at four parts of the field with a herald of the Duke of Ex[e]ter before me in the Duke's coat of arms [. . .] proclaiming openly by the said herald that I was sent thither for to espy their puissance and their habiliments of war, for the greatest traitor that was in England or in France, [. . .] for one Sir John Fastolf knight, the which minished all the garrisons of Normandy and Mans and Maine, the which was the causing of the losing of all the king's title and right of an inheritance that he had beyond sea.

[And that Sir John] had furnished his place . . . to destroy the commons of Kent when they came to Southwark. [. . .] And therefore he said plainly that I should lose my head.

[. . .]

[Payn was saved by the interventions of some of Cade's men and sent to persuade Fastolf to desist.]

And had I not been, the commons would have burned his [Fastolf's] place and all his tenantries.

[Payn had to pay the rebels for his freedom and the Captain commanded Lovelace] to despoil me out of my array, and so he did; and there he took a fine gown . . . furred with fine beavers, and a pair of brigandines covered with blue velvet and gilt nail, with leg harness, the value of the gown and the brigandines £8.

Item the captain sent certain of his men . . . and there brake up my chest and took away an obligation of mine that was due unto me of

---

[9] A reference to Jack Cade's rebellion, which began at the end of May 1450. The rebels camped on Black Heath from 11–18 June 1450 and regrouped there by 29 June 1450.

[10] Complaints of the rebels.

£36 by a priest of Paul's, and another obligation of a knight of £10, and my purse with five rings of gold and 17s 6d and [various other items of value].

[. . .]

[The rebels stole goods from Payn's wife, who lived in Kent, and she and the children were threatened with hanging. Payn was arrested and thrown into the Marchalsea prison and threatened with death if he did not accuse Fastolf of treason. Because he would not provide evidence against Fastolf he was threatened with even more dire imprisonment.]

[. . .] but my wife's and a cousin of mine own that were yeomen of the Crown,[11] they went to the King and got grace and a charter of pardon.

By your man, Payne

(d) William Ebsham to John Paston II, summer or early autumn 1468

My most worshipful and most special master, with all my service most lowly I recommend [me] unto your good mastership, beseeching you most tenderly to see me somewhat rewarded for my labour in the great book which I write unto your good mastership.[12] I have often times written to Pamping . . . to inform you how I have laboured in writings for you; and I see well he speaks not to your mastership of it, and God knoweth I lie in sanctuary at great cost and amongst right unreasonable askers. I moved this matter to Sir Thomas[13] late, and he told me he would move your mastership therein; which Sir Thomas desired me to remember well what I have had in money at sundry times of him, which parcels here ensue:

First I had for half the writing of the privy seal with Pamping 8d
[There follows a page of items of account.]

And in especial I beseech you to send me for alms one of your old gowns. [. . .] And I shall be yours while I live and at your command-

---

[11] Officials of the royal household, first mentioned in the records in 1450.

[12] This 'great book' contained treatises on the coronation, knighthood, war, challenges and acts of arms plus a verse rendering (*De Regimine Principum*) of the pseudo Aristotelian *Secreta Secretorum*. It survives partially as London, British Library, MS Lansdowne 285.

[13] Thomas Lyndes, priest under Paston patronage from 1466 until his death. It was customary to address non-graduate priests as Sir.

ment. I have great mister of it, God knows, whom I beseech preserve you from all adversity. I am somewhat acquainted with it.

Your very man, W. Ebsham.

(e) John Paston III to Margaret Paston, 12 October 1470

After humble and most due recommendation, as lowly as I can I beseech you of your blessing. Please it you to wit that, blessed be God, my brother and I be in good heal and I trust that we shall do right well in all our matters hastily. For my Lady of Norfolk hath promised to be ruled by my Lord of Oxford in all such matters as belong to my brother and to me; and as for my Lord of Oxford,[14] he is better lord to me, by my troth, than I can wish him in many matters. [. . .] The Duke and the Duchess [of Norfolk] sue to him as humbly as ever I did to them, insomuch that my Lord of Oxford shall have the rule of them and theirs by their own desires and great means.

As for the offices that ye wrote to my brother for, and to me, they be for no poor men; but I trust we shall speed of other offices meetly for us, for my master the Earl of Oxford biddeth me ask and have. I trow my brother Sir John shall have the constableship of Norwich Castle with £20 of fee.

[. . .]

Tidings, the Earl of Worcester is like to die this day or tomorrow at the farthest.[15] John Pilkington,[16] Master W. Attcliff[17] and Fowler[18] are

---

[14] John de Vere, 13th earl of Oxford (1442–1513) was a prominent Lancastrian. He was incarcerated in the Tower for a while in 1468, was a leader in the temporary restoration of Henry VI in 1470–71, and went into exile when Edward IV reclaimed the throne. John Paston III became a member of Oxford's council in Henry VII's reign.

[15] John Tiptoft had been constable of England since 1462 and had a reputation for ferocious treatment of prisoners and, especially, for the execution of Oxford's father in 1462. When Oxford became constable on Henry VI's restoration, he quickly condemned Tiptoft to death. Tiptoft was executed on 18 October 1470.

[16] John Pilkington, squire of the king's body since 1461 and sheriff of Lancashire and Justice of the Peace (JP) of Northamptonshire and the west Riding of Yorkshire. He survived to fight and be knighted at the Battle of Tewkesbury in 1471. He later served as Member of Parliament (MP) for Yorkshire and as chamberlain of the exchequer. He died in 1479.

[17] Dr William Hatcliff had been physician to Henry VI and continued as such to Edward IV. He became the king's secretary in 1466. He took part in several diplomatic missions, including the negotiations for the marriage of Edward IV's sister Margaret to the duke of Burgundy in 1468.

[18] Thomas Fowler, a London fishmonger, had been a JP and an Oxford alderman. He later became squire of the body, MP, and sheriff of Buckinghamshire and Bedfordshire. He died in 1496.

taken and in the castle of Pomfret, and are like to die hastily, without they be dead.[19] Sir T. Montgomery and John Donne be taken; what shall befall them I cannot say.

The Queen that was,[20] and the Duchess of Bedford,[21] be in sanctuary at Westminster. The Bishop of Ely[22] with other bishops are in St Martin's. When I hear more I shall send you more

[. . .]

Your son and humble servant, J.P.

(f) John Paston II to Margaret Paston, 18 April 1471

Mother, I recommend me to you, letting you weet [know] that, blessed be God, my brother John is alive and fareth well, and in no peril of death. Nevertheless he is hurt with an arrow on his right arm beneath the elbow, and I have sent him a surgeon . . . and he telleth me that he trusteth that he shall be all whole within right short time. It is so that John Milsent is dead, God have mercy on his soul, and William Milsent is alive, and other servants all be escaped.

[. . .]

Item, as for me, I am in good case . . . and in no jeopardy of my life . . . for I am at my liberty if need be.

Item, my Lord Archbishop is in the Tower.[23] Nevertheless I trust to God that he shall do well enough. He hath a safeguard for him and me both. Nevertheless we have been troubled since, but now I understand that he hath a pardon; and so we hope well.

There was killed upon the field, half a mile from Barnet, on Easter Day, the Earl of Warwick[24], the Marquis Montagu,[25] Sir William Tyrell,[26] Sir Lewis John,[27] and divers other esquires of our country, Godmanston[28] and Booth.[29] And on the King Edward's party, the Lord

---

[19] Paston's prediction was not fulfilled: none of these was put to death.

[20] Elizabeth Woodville (Wydeville), queen of Edward IV.

[21] Mother of Elizabeth Woodville.

[22] William Grey, bishop from 1454–78.

[23] George Neville.

[24] Richard Neville, 16th Earl of Warwick (1428–71), known as 'Warwick the Kingmaker'.

[25] John Neville.

[26] Of Essex; JP, MP frequently between 1443 and 1466; knighted in 1460.

[27] Of Essex; sheriff of Essex and Hertfordshire, 1457–8; MP 1459; JP from 1465.

[28] William Godmanston, esquire, of Frinton, Essex.

[29] Richard Booth, sheriff of Essex and Herts, 1455–6, and of Norfolk and Suffolk, 1456–7.

Cromwell,[30] the Lord Say,[31] Sir Humphrey Bourchier of our country,[32] which is a sore moaned man here, and other people of both parties to the number of more than a thousand.

As for other tidings is understand here that the Queen Margaret[33] is verily landed,[34] and her son, in the west country, and I trow [trust] that as tomorrow or else the next day the King Edward will depart from hence to her ward to drive her out again.

Item, I beseech you that I may be recommended to my cousin Lomnor, and to thank him for his good will to me wards if I had had need. [. . .] And I beseech you . . . to advise him to be well ware of his dealing or language as yet, for the world, I ensure you, is right queasy, as ye shall know within this month. The people here feareth it sore. God hath showed himself marvellously, like him that made all and can undo again when him list; and I can think that by all his likelihood shall how himself as marvellous again, and that in short time

[. . .]

Item it is so that my brother is unpurveyed of money. I have holpen him to my power and above. [. . .] I hope hastily to see you. All this bill must be secret.

Be you not adoubted of the world, for I trust all shall be well. If it thus continue I am not all undone, nor none of us; and if otherwise, then, &c.

(g) John Paston III to Margaret Paston, 30 April 1471

After humble and most due recommendation, in as humble wise as I can beseech you of your blessing, praying God to reward you with as much pleasure as heart's ease as I have lateward caused you to have trouble and thought. And, with God's grace, it shall not be long to ere than my wrongs and other men's shall be redressed, for the world was never so like to be ours as it is now; wherefore I pray you let Lomnor not be too busy as yet.

Mother, I beseech you, an ye may spare any money, that you will do your alms on me and send me some in as hasty wise as is possible, for by my troth my leechcraft and physic and rewards to them that have kept me and condite me to London, hath cost me sith Eastern Day[35]

---

[30] Humphrey, son of Henry Lord Bourchier, had been created Lord Cromwell in 1461.

[31] William Fiennes had served with Warwick at the battle of Northampton in 1460 and had accompanied Edward IV into exile in 1470.

[32] Son of Lord Berners.

[33] Of Anjou, queen of King Henry VI.

[34] At Weymouth 14 April 1471.

[35] Since Easter Day.

more than £5. [I now have no money for food and sustenance] but upon borrowing, and I have essayed my friends so far that they begin to fail now in my gratest need that ever I was in.

[. . .]

And if it please you to have knowledge of our royal person, I thank God I am whole of my sickness, and trust to be clean whole of all my hurts within a seven-night at the farthest, by which time I trust to have other tidings. And those tidings once had, I trust not to be long out of Norfolk, with God's grace, whom I beseech preserve you and your for my part.

[. . .]

The bearer hereof can tell you tidings such as be true for very certain.

Your humblest servant, John of Gel[de]ston.

1.25

The Stonor letters and papers

C. Carpenter (ed.) (1996) *The Stonor Letters and Papers, 1290–1483*, Cambridge, Letters 161, 162, 166, 171, 172, pp. 258–9, 262–3, 268–71. Additional editing and modernisation of spelling by Rosemary O'Day.

Sir William Stonor (d. 1494), who figures in these letters, was well placed to marry, in succession, Elizabeth Rich (d. 1479), Agnes Wydesdale (d. 1481) and Anne Neville (d. 1486). The Stonors are thought to have been more typical than the Pastons in their relative lack of involvement in national affairs and in the tumults of the Wars of the Roses. As these letters suggest, they concentrated instead on family and local affairs and on the pursuit of trade. The letters demonstrate, both in the forms of address used and in the contents of the letters themselves, the relationship of deference between family members, servants and business partners. There was clearly a hierarchy of deference in which everyone, high or low, deferred to someone else. Patronage is shown to have been part of this system. The letters hint at the importance of foreign trade and also of manorial courts to a country gentry family which relied on different sources of income. They indicate the importance of married women in holding together the family business, communicating information and advice, and maintaining the family's status. Above all, perhaps, the letters are evidence of the increasing importance of vernacular lay literacy in the context of the economic and social affairs of gentry families, as individuals of both sexes corresponded about affairs of the heart as well as of the audit.

(a) Thomas Betson to William Stonor, 12 April 1476

Right worshipful sir, I recom[mend] me unto your good mastership, and to my right worshipful mistress your wife, and, if it please your mastership, to my mistress Katherine. And sir, thanked be the good Lord, I understand for certain that our wool shipped be come in . . . best to Calais. I would have kept the tidings till I had come myself, because it is good: but I durst not be so bold, for your mastership now against this good time may be glad and joyful of this tidings, for in troth I am glad and heartily thank God of it. And sir, when I come I shall tell your mastership many things more by mercy of our Lord, who preserve your mastership ever. [. . .] Your servant to my power

Thomas Betson.

To my right worshipful and singular good master Willm Stonor, esquire.

[. . .]

(b) Thomas Betson to William Stonor, 22 April 1476

Right worshipful and my right singular good master I recommend me unto your good mastership. And sir, please it you to wete [understand], this same day I depart to Calais wards through the might of our Lord Jesus be my good speed. And sir with all my heart I thank your mastership ever of your gentle cheer and faithful love, the which always you bear and owe unto me, and of my behalf nothing deserved: [. . .] And sir, for a remembrance I send you be [by] the bringer hereof . . . 2 powdered lampreys, to eat them when it please you, I would they were better. Also sir, you shall receive by the grace of God in John Somers' barge now coming to Henley a pipe [of] red wine from my brother: I trust it shall please your mastership well.

[. . .]

At London . . . be your servant T. Betson.

Sir, I beseech your mastership that this poor writing may have me lowly recommended to my right worshipful mistress your wife, and in likewise to my gentle cousin and kind mistress Katherine Rich,[1] to whom I beseech your mastership ever to be favourable and loving [. . .].

(c) Thomas Betson to Katherine Rich, 1 June 1476

Mine own heartily beloved Cousin Katherine, I recommend me unto you with all the inwardness of my heart. And now lately you shall understand that I received a token from you, the which was and is to me right heartily welcome, and with glad will I received it; and over that I had a letter from Holake, your gentle squire, by the which I understand right well that you be in good health of body, and merry at heart. And I pray God heartily to his pleasure to continue the same: for it is to me very great comfort that you so be

[. . .]

And if you would be a good eater of your meat always, that you might wax and grow fast to be a woman, you should make me the gladdest man of the world, by my troth: for when I remember your favour and your said loving dealing to me wards, forsooth you make me even very glad and joyous in my heart: and the otherside again when I remember your young youth [. . .]. And therefore I pray you, mine own sweet cousin, even as you love me to be merry and to eat your meat like a woman.

[. . .]

I can no more say now, but at my coming home I will tell you much more between you and me and God before. And whereas you, full womanly and like a lover, remember me with manifold recommendation in divers manners, remitting the same to my discretion to depart them there as I love best, for sooth . . . you shall understand that with good heart and good will I receive and take to my self the one half of them, and them will I keep by me; and the other half with heartily love and favour I send them to you, mine own sweet cousin, again, for to keep by you [. . .].

Mine own sweet cousin, it was told me but late that you were at Calais to seek me, but you could not see me nor find me: forsooth you might have come to my counter, and there you should both find me and see me . . . but you sought me in a wrong Calais [. . .].

---

[1] Katherine Rich (born c. 1462 or 3) became Betson's wife in 1478. She was the eldest daughter of Elizabeth Stonor by her first husband, Thomas Rich.

My very faithful cousin, I trust to you that though all I have not remembered my right worshipful mistress your mother afore in this letter that you will of your gentleness recommend me to her mistress-ship as many times as it shall please you, and you may say, if it please you, that in Whitsun week next I intend to [visit]. [. . .] And I trust you will pray for me, for I shall pray for you. [. . .] And almighty Jesus make you a good woman, and send you many good years and long to live in health and virtue to his pleasure. At great Calais on this side on the sea . . . when every man was gone to his dinner, and the clock smote nine, and all our household cried after me and bade me come down: come down to dinner at once! And what answer I gave them you know it of old.

By your faithful cousin and lover Thomas Betson

I sent you this ring for a token.

To my faithful and heartily beloved cousin Katherine Rich at Stonor this letter be delivered in haste.

(d) Henry Dogett to William or to Thomas Stonor,[2] 20 October 1476

Right worshipful and my good and faithful master, I recommend me to you: pleaseth you to wete [know] that I have received the farm of Burghwardescote[3] for Michaelmas last past, and for your mares there 13s. 4d., the which is ready ay your commandment. And for your courts, I will keep them at All Souls' Day at Stonor, and the week following at Watlington, if you command me not to the contrary, with God's leave, who ever preserve you, my good and faithful master. Written at Astun, the Sunday next after Saint Luke's day.

Your old servant Henry Dogett.

(e) Elizabeth Stonor to William Stonor, 22 October 1476

Right entirely and best beloved husband, I recommend me unto you in my most hearty wise, evermore thanking you right heartily of all kindness to me showed at all times, and now for your good venison and

---

[2] Henry Dogett had been in the service of Thomas Stonor as early as 1444–5 and this letter may be addressed to Thomas. However, the letter is placed in the collection as if relating to William Stonor's correspondence for 1476.

[3] Buscot.

coneys,[4] the which you sent me . . . the which is great dainties to have here in London: wherefore I sent the half haunch to my father and a couple of coneys: and they recommend them unto you and thank you right heartily. And sir, you shall understand that I have to be with my Lady of Suffolk as on Thursday last was,[5] and waited upon her to my lady the King's mother and hers by her commandment. And also on Saturday last was I waited upon her there again, and also from thence she waited upon my lady her mother, and brought her to Greenwich to the King's good grace and the Queen's: and there I saw the meeting between the King and my lady his mother. And truly me thought it was a very good sight. And, sir, I was with my lady Suffolk . . . hoping that I might have had her at some leisure that I might a spoken to her for the money, but truly she was very busy to make her ready [. . .] Also I spake with my cousin Fowler[6] . . . and I thanked him as heartily as I could for his great kindness that he showed to you and to me at all times, praying him of his good continuance. . . . And also I spake with my cousin Rokysse[7] . . . for John Matthews' matter, and prayed him to be good master unto him, and he answered me . . . and said that he had little cause, for he saith that he have been the most importune man that might be to himwards. And I answered and said to him, that I could never understand it but that he owed him his service to his power.

And sir, my lady of Suffolk is halfindell[8] displeased because that my sister Barantyne[9] is no better arrayed, and likewise my sister Elizabeth.[10] And she saith without they be otherwise arrayed, she saith, she may not keep them, and she saith that my Mother and yours should say that you have enough to find my sister Elizabeth with all. Also I understand that Sir John Buttelyr[11] hath spoken to my lady to have my sister Barantine with him: what he meaneth therein we wot nere, without that he would have the rule of her husband's livelihood

---

[4] Rabbits.

[5] Elizabeth of York, wife of John de la Pole, 2nd duke of Suffolk.

[6] Possibly Richard Fowler, chancellor of the Duchy of Lancaster, who was influential at court.

[7] Thomas Rokes.

[8] Half-part (partly).

[9] William Stonor's sister Mary was married to John Barantine or Barantyne, who was under age.

[10] This is Elizabeth Stonor's unmarried sister-in-law, William Stonor's third sister, another Elizabeth Stonor.

[11] Sir John Boteler was John Barantyne's stepfather, having married the widowed Elizabeth Barantyne; he died on 14 June 1477.

be [by] that mean. Wherefore my sister would speak with you for that matter to have your counsel in what is best to do

[. . .]

Good sire, let it not be long [bef]or[e] I may see you: for truly me think right long since I see you. You children and mine fare well, blessed be God, and they be to me a great comfort in your absence.

[. . .]

My own cousin I send you a bladder with powder to drink when you go to bed, for it is wholesome for you.

Be [by] your own to my power Elizabeth Stonor.

To my right well-beloved cousin William Stonor, squire, at Stonor, this be delivered.

1.26

The Creed

P.S. Barnwell, C. Cross & A. Rycraft (eds.) (2005), *Mass and Parish in Late Medieval England: The Use of York*, Reading: Spire Books, p. 172.

Christians made a statement of belief during their worship, called the Creed after the Latin for 'I believe'. The Creed (of which there were several versions including the Apostles' Creed and the Nicene Creed) was said or chanted in Latin. The translation offered here is from that in the Diocese of York, which was used just in the north of England but a similar Creed would have been used elsewhere. The parts marked in bold were the rubrics or instructions for the priest.

I believe in one God [said by the priest in a loud voice].

The Father Almighty, maker of heaven and earth, of all things seen and unseen.[1] And in one Lord Jesus Christ, the one and only born Son of God, born of the Father before all ages. God from God, light from light, true God from true God, born, not made, of one substance with the Father, through whom all things were made; who, for us men and for our salvation came down from heaven and was incarnate by the

---

[1] The Godhead is a trinity. The first person of the Trinity is God the Father.

1.4 Parishioners undertaking the Sacrament of Confession during Holy Week (the week before Easter Sunday).

Holy Spirit of the Virgin Mary and was made man.[2] For our sake also he was crucified under Pontius Pilate: he suffered death and was buried.[3] And he rose again on the third day in accordance with the scriptures,[4] and ascended into heaven,[5] and sits at the right hand of the Father, and he shall come again in glory to judge the living and the dead.[6] Of his kingdom there shall be no end. And [I believe] in the Holy Spirit, the Lord and giver of life, who proceeds from the Father

[2] The second person of the trinity is God the Son, in the form of Jesus Christ (Christmas marks the birth of Christ.)

[3] Known as the crucifixion. Good Friday is the holy day associated with this in the Church's calendar.

[4] The resurrection (rising from the dead). Easter Day is the holy day associated with this in the Church's calendar.

[5] The ascension of Christ into Heaven. Ascension Day marks this in the calendar.

[6] This is known as the Second Coming or Parousia.

and the Son; who together with the Father and the Son is worshipped and glorified; who has spoken through the prophets.[7] And [I believe] in one holy, catholic and apostolic church. I acknowledge one baptism for the forgiveness of sins. And I await the resurrection of the dead and the life of the world to come. Amen.

It should be noted that the Creed is said without exception on all Sundays throughout the whole year.

While the Creed is being chanted the subdeacon with the text [of the Gospels] and the acolyte with the censer are to go around the choir.

1.27

The funeral of Thomas Stonor and heirlooms in the chapel and house at Stonor, c. 1474

C. Carpenter (ed.) (1996) *The Stonor Letters and Papers, 1290–1483*, Cambridge: Cambridge University Press, vol. I, Documents 138 and 140, pp. 143–7. Additional editing and modernisation of spelling by Rosemary O'Day.

These are extracts from contemporary inventories. Note the existence of a private chapel (9–10) and the prominence of expensive cloths (velvet, sarsnet, lawn, linen, finest worsted) and colours (black, purple, silver, gold) all indicative of the status of the Stonor family as gentlemen (1–10). Of interest also is the detail of dining arrangements after the funeral (3–8). These indicate the hierarchical divisions between 'poor men' on the one hand and priests and gentlemen on the other. (It was customary for the well-to-do to entertain a specified number of poor people at funerals, and probably the poor of a parish relied considerably for their diet on the funeral, wedding and feast day celebrations of their social superiors.) Note also that the goods of the chapel belonged not to an individual but to the chapel (9). Similarly the contents of the house (with some exceptions) belonged to the house and could not be alienated by the Stonor family. Some of

---

[7] The third person of the trinity was God the Holy Spirit (also referred to in old-fashioned works as the Holy Ghost).

the original spelling has been retained to indicate the difficulties of interpretation facing the medieval historian even when the document in question is legible and in English.

(a) The funeral of Thomas Stonor

1. M[emoran]d[um] to send for the cover with ornaments of the altar and the hearses to be had over. Item, a black cloth for the house [. . .].

2. In Pirton church
First 6 altars. Item the high altar with black ornaments thereto. Item, candlesticks, censers, basins, silver thereto. Item, rectors' choirs suits of vestments black and white &c. Item ornaments for the hearse and for the burial, black cloth to the ground with a white cloth of gold. Item a cross with a foot on the hearse, silver and gilt. Item 4 tapers about the hearse. Item 2 tapers about the burial. Item black hanging about the chancel and church. Item lights for the high altar and other altars beside. Item singing wine, singing bread.

3. Meat for poor men at deriges. Item after deriges bread and cheese for the said poor men. Item for [priests] and gentlemen, sew purtenances of lambs, and veal, roasted mutton, 2 chickens in a dish.

4. On the morrow to breakfasts. For priests and other honest men. Item calves' heads and side beef.

5. At the dinner on the morrow.
For poor men: item, umbels to pottage, side beef, roasted veal in dish together, and roasted pork.

6. The first course for prestes &c. First to potage, browes[1] of capons or &c., capons, motons, gese, custard. The second course. The second potage. Jussell, capons, lambe, pigge, velel, peiouns rosted, baken rabbits, fesauntis, venison, gelie &c. Item. . . .[2]

7. Item spices. First a pound of saunders, an ounce of saffron, 3 lbs pepper, half a pound cloves, half a pound mace, a loaf sugar, 3 lbs raisins currants, 3 lbs dates, half a pound ginger, 1 pound cinnamon, [. . .] Item in almonds 4 lbs.

[1] Possibly 'brace' meaning two (or a couple of).

[2] This paragraph is reproduced with the original spelling to show how difficult it can be to determine meanings. My transliteration into modern spelling would be: The first course for priests &c. First to potage, brace of capons or, &c. capons, muttons, geese [or possibly cheese], custard. The second course. The second potage. Jussell, capons, lamb, pig, veal, pigeons roasted, baked rabbits, pheasants, venison, jelly &c. Item . . . There is still however uncertainty about what foods are meant. What is a 'brow' of capon? What is a jussell? Does 'gese' mean cheese or geese?

8. Item, treen[3] vessel for poor men. Item sitting places for the poor men. Item, pewter vessel for gentlemen.

(b) Heirlooms in the chapel and house at Stonor, c. 1474

9. This be the stuff of the chapel of Stonor the which must be left from year unto year within the manor of Stonor.

10. First the vestments of purple velvet lined with green sarsnet with albe, stole, vanon [fanon], and amice thereto.[4] Item [another vestment] of bawdkin lined with tawney sarsnet, 2 albs of ranus, and 2 amices thereto to the [vestment of] purple velvet. Item [. . .] carpets for the sacrament with a canopy of red tartan. Item 2 copes of purple velvet lined with tawney sarsnet. Item 1 figure of the Trinity of alabaster. Item 1 table of alabaster the stories of the passion of Our Lord, the which table Mistress Jane Stonor[5] has left unto the chapel of Stonor with many other things thereto belonging. Item, 6 lables of purple velvet with crosses. Item 1 old frontal of purple velvet lozenged with gold. Item 1 old vestment of blue bawdkin, with alb, stole, vanon, and amice. Item 1 corperas of rayns and the case therefore of white and blue velvet embroidered with 1 trail of ivy, with 1 bar of red velvet. Item 1 crucifix of silver gilt in a tablet of tree. Item 1 chalice of silver with the patten. Item 1 pair cruets of silver gilt. Item 1 pillow covered with tartan for the sepulchre. Item 1 cellar and 1 tester of white linen for the sepulchre. Item 1 kerchew[6] of umpull for the sacrament. Item 2 narrow kerchiefs of lawn for the sepulchre. Item 3 cloths for to cover the images then lent. Item 1 stained cloth for the rood with 1 crucifix and drops. Item 1 hanging for the altar stained with 1 crucifix, the images of Our Lady and Saint John. Item 2 curtains and another beneath the altar of the same work with 3 images. Item 1 hanging for the chapel of old worsted. Item 2 altar cloths for the altar [. . .].

Item 1 superaltar for the altar. Item 2 pair candlesticks of laton for the altar. Item 2 mass books, one of them is at Pirton, . . . and 1 grail. [. . .] Item 1 sacring bell. Item 1 old frontal of purple sarsnet . . .

---

[3] Wooden.
[4] Alb, stole, fanon and amice are all individual components of religious vestments.
[5] Jane Stonor, widow of Thomas Stonor.
[6] Kerchief?

1.28
Lollards of Coventry, 1486–1522

S. McSheffrey & N. Tanner (eds.) (2003) *Lollards of Coventry, 1486–1522*, Camden 5th Series, vol. 23, Cambridge: Cambridge University Press for the Royal Historical Society, pp. 122–4, 126–7, 129–34, 137–40, 142–3.

Here is a selection of the relatively informal documentation, preserved in the Lichfield Court Book and the Bishop's Register, of the trials of suspected heretics, 1511–12, in the large midland diocese of Coventry and Lichfield.[1] There had been earlier trials of Lollards in that diocese in 1486 and sporadic pursuit of the problem in the intervening period before 1511. Part of the account of the deposition of Margery Locock is given in the original Latin as well as the English translation, purposely to draw attention to the particular difficulties medievalists face in interpreting the sources. The selection demonstrates the types of persons who were involved in Coventry Lollardy and the variety of beliefs and practices of which they were accused. Deponents indicated the existence of a network that stretched beyond Coventry and Warwickshire, and that probably followed trade routes – such as those to Bristol and to Leicester. They also contribute to a discussion of the possible links between Lollardy and early Protestantism (see Document 1.29). While these depositions reveal much of value about Lollards in Coventry they also fascinate because of what they say about ecclesiastical attitudes to heresy and the practice of church discipline at this date.

(a) Margery Locock, 31 October 1511

Ultimo die mensis anno Domini et loco supradictis.

Margeria Locock, uxor Henrici Locock, civittatis Civentr', girdeler, nuper uxor Hugonis Stubbe.

Iurata et examinata, dicit quod non modo temporibus primi mariti sui, videlicet Hugonis antedicti, verum etiam in diebus istius Henrici,

---

[1] See also John Fines (1963) 'Heresy Trials in the diocese of Coventry and Lichfield, 1511–1512', in *Journal of Ecclesiastical History* 44, pp. 160–74; and lmogen Luxton (1971) 'The Lichfield Court Book: a postscript', in *Bulletin of the Institute of Historical Research* 44, pp. 120–5.

conmversabatur cum Landesdale, Silkby et aliis. Et presertim infra annum in doum prefati Rogeri Landesdale, unacum uxore eiusdem Rogeri, lecturam a sepenominato Rogero in libris heresim continentibus audivit et opinions hereticas favebat.

[. . .]

The last day of the month in the year of the Lord and the place given above.

Margery Locock, wife of Henry Locock of Coventry city, girdler, recently the wife of Hugh Stubbe.

Sworn and examined, she says that not only in the time of her first husband, Hugh Stubbe, but also in the time of the said Henry, she conversed with Landesdale, Silkby, and others. Especially within the last year, in the house of the said Roger Landesdale, together with Roger's wife, she heard the oft-mentioned Roger reading heretical books and she favoured heretical opinions.

[. . .]

Then she wholly renounced these beliefs publicly before the bishop.

The bishop, however, fearing she might be repudiated by her husband, deferred ordering her to make a solemn abjuration. While, by way of precaution, binding her under oath to perform the penance that would be imposed, he absolved her etc.

(b) Alice Rowley, 31 October and 5 November 1511

The same day and place, Alice Rowley of Coventry, widow of William Rowley, recently a merchant of the same city, appeared before the bishop accused of certain heretical opinions.

Sworn and examined, first regarding whether she had been summoned in judgement on suspicion of heresy before, she admitted she had been, and especially before the bishop in Coventry.

Asked whether since 1506 she had conversed with Roger Landesdale and others named above, or had heard any of them reading heretical books, or had supported their beliefs, she says no.

(c) Robert Hatchet,[2] 5 November 1511

The same day and place Robert Hatchet of Coventry, tawyer, aged sixty, appeared before the bishop detected of heresy etc.

---

[2] Hatchet was not condemned to death in 1511/12 but he was among eight heretics burned in Coventry a decade later while Blyth was still bishop.

Sworn and examined and first about his contacts with Landesdale, Silkby and others, he admits he was often with them and heard them speaking against the sacrament of the altar,[3] as above.

He says that Matthew Maclyn,[4] fuller in Little Park Street, next to the house of Master [. . .], knows by heart the Gospel,[5] 'In the beginning was the Word'. The said Matthew frequently talked with Landesdale, Silkby and others.

He also admits that Alice Rowley heard Landesdale reading in his presence.

There is also a foreign painter in Leicester who is well instructed and expert in these heretical books, and likewise in the Lord's Prayer. Londesdale knows his name and led him to this deponent.

He says that Robert Peg, painter in Gosford Street,[6] belonged to the same sect with him for the last seven years.

Balthasar Shugborowe is also a heretic; he deposes about him with the others.

He says that Joan, the widow of Padland and now Richard Smyth's wife, is suspect of heresy. For, as he says is rumoured, she had heretical books.

He says that John Spon, butcher, was in Landesdale's house two or three times during the last two years, hearing Landesdale and this deponent reading heretical books etc.

He deposes that Thomas Bownd, his servant, is a heretic. Thomas has now fled.[7]

The wife of Thomas Trussell, hosier, has a book of the Old Testament. She is pregnant and close to giving birth. The book belonged to Thomas Forde.

Thomas Acton, purser of Coventry, near Jordan Well,[8] was one of the first who provoked and drew this deponent to these heresies. He frequently conversed with Alice Rowley.

It was reported, he says, that Doctor Alcock of Ibstock belonged to the sect.[9]

He thinks that Sir Ralph Shor has erroneous books.

He says that Gest senior and junior are suspect. Gest senior had a heretical book. Sir Thomas Gest had the same book with him for a year in his father's house.

[3] The Mass.
[4] i.e., Matthew Marklond.
[5] St John's Gospel.
[6] Gosford Street, Coventry.
[7] In fact, probably in custody at this time.
[8] Name of a street and of a ward in Coventry.
[9] John Alcock, Doctor of Civil Law, and Rector of Ibstock, Leicestershire.

He was asked about the secret saying among them, 'May we drink of the same cup'.

He says his wife knew his secrets and beliefs, but she did not, he says, agree with them.

He says the wife of the said Thomas Acton is a heretic, together with her husband.

Asked why he says that Gest senior belongs to the sect, he replies that he heard the said Gest saying – after he married the wife of John Smyth, recently a tailor of Coventry, who abjured – that his wife drew him to his heretical beliefs, which, he affirmed, she supported.

He says that the wife of Gest junior is wicked in heretical beliefs, and that she was the servant of the said John Smyth's wife [. . .] was in these beliefs etc.

There is another Ralph [. . .] weaver [. . .] of the same sect and belief.

Thomas Clerc, hosier, servant [. . .] belonged to the same sect and read a heretical book to this deponent seven years ago: the book, as he now believes, was taken to Bristol and there burnt.

(d) John Atkinson, 2 November 1511
(a continuation of that on 30 October 1511)

Finally, however, [. . .] John Atkinson, appearing before the bishop, admitted that he had conversed with Robert Silkby and John Davy, painter. They first, he says drew him towards heresies.

Asked about his age when he first came from his country, he says about eight years old. He then came to Sir William Coor, his uncle,[10] and stayed with him for three years. Afterwards he was apprenticed at Coventry with James Reynesford, and he stayed there more than three years. He then returned to the said uncle and remained with him for half a year. From his uncle he went to Warwick, and lived there for a year and a half. From Warwick he moved to Sir Latemer, doctor,[11] and stayed with him for a year. Then he returned to Warwick and remained there a year. From there he came to Stivichall[12] and stayed there for a year. From Stivichall he came to Coventry, where he worked at the sign of the Angel for more than a year.[13] Since then he has lived continuously in Coventry for almost two years.

[10] Vicar of Corby, Northants, or, possibly, of Corby Glen, Lincs.
[11] Possibly Thomas Latimer, Doctor of Theology, prior of Warwick Convent in 1495.
[12] Just outside Coventry.
[13] Probably an inn or tavern of this name in Coventry. There was an inn of this name in Coventry in 1600.

He says he first heard Robert Sylkby and John Davy and believed their teaching when he was working at the sign of the Angel, that is to say for the past three years. He admits that the said Robert and John Davy taught against the sacrament of the altar, pilgrimages etc., as is contained above in the depositions of others, and he believed in their teachings.

He says, moreover, that Abel and, as he remembers, Sylkby told him that William Grevis,[14] skinner of Coventry, was of their beliefs and sect. But [. . .] in this matter they said, and he is unable to state, since not [. . .] with the said William as he says

He heard Thomas Bown [. . .] savouring of heresy [. . .];

He admits he was often in Roger Landesdale's house and heard him reading heretical books.

He admits the article concerning John Davy and Richard Dowcheman, both of whom are heretics, he asserts. The same Richard has a book in his vernacular language.[15]

He says he heard from Thomas Bown that Master Pisford[16] is of the same sect and beliefs.

He says that, three years ago, he was in Thomas Acton's house and he saw there a book of the commandments,[17] which had been brought out of a chest onto a table by the said Thomas etc.

(e) Thomas Bown,[18] 3 November 1511

Thomas Bowne of Coventry, shoemaker, aged forty.

Sworn and examined and first where he was born, he says in Charlbury near Banbury.[19] And from his tenth year he lived continuously in Coventry, [. . .] and there he heard Roger Londesdale reading heretical books and conversed with Robert Hatchet, Robert Silkeby, and others.

He says that Richard Weston, once a servant of Sir John Halse,[20] recently Bishop of Coventry and Lichfield, first attracted and drew him to these heresies.

---

[14] Also known as William Revis.

[15] Possibly a printed German Bible.

[16] The Pisford or Pysford family was a wealthy and politically powerful Coventry family. William Pisford the elder was active in Coventry politics from 1486–1518 and served as mayor in 1501. Henry Pisford, his son, was extremely wealthy.

[17] The Ten Commandments given to Moses.

[18] Among those burned to death in Coventry a decade later.

[19] Perhaps Charlbury, Oxon, although this was 15 to 20 miles from Banbury.

[20] John Hales, bishop of Coventry and Lichfield, 1459–90.

He admits that he heard Roger and others speaking against the sacrament of the altar,

[. . .]

He admits that within the last three years he had . . . a book of St Paul's Letters on loan from Alice Rowley, in Roger Londesdale's name. He immediately brought the book to the said Roger.

. . . [T]he same Alice taught him that at the time of the elevation of the Eucharist he should believe the host was offered spiritually in memory of Christ's passion, and thus he should receive the host spiritually by recalling Christ's passion. Alice also taught him, 'How can a creature fashion God, his creator?' etc., as in other depositions; this within the three years.

A certain Robert Bastell . . . heard her teaching [. . .]: he has now gone away, the deponent knows not where.

Thomas Bown also admits that Thomas Acton of Coventry, purser, Robert Peg, Wrexham, glover, Thomas Clerc, Matthew Marklond, and Ralph the weaver of Allesley, and Gest senior of Birmingham are heretics and share his beliefs.

[. . .]

Gest told him that his wife drew him to these beliefs.

[. . .]

(f) John Spon, 3 November 1511

John Spon of Coventry, butcher, appeared before the bishop . . . aged forty and more, born . . . in Allesley, where and in Coventry he has lived all his life.

[. . .]

Asked about a book that he had from Richard Gest senior, he admits receiving the book and that it was a book of the Old Testament translated into English and that he heard Londesdale reading it. After the solemn reading of the greater sentence in the church . . . [he] confessed his sins to him [Master Bowd,[21] vicar of Holy Trinity, Coventry] especially his keeping of the book.

Asked whether he ever heard Roger Landesdale or anyone else speaking privately or publicly against the sacrament of the altar, the veneration of saints, or pilgrimages etc., he says no.

[. . .]

Asked how often he heard Landesdale reading, he says on five or six occasions.

---

[21] Thomas Bowd, Vicar of Holy Trinity, Coventry, c. 1504–8.

Asked about what was read, he says that . . . was saints' lives and Paul's Letters. He heard nothing in the reading against the veneration of images, the sacrament of the altar, or anything else against the Church's sound teaching,

[. . .]

(g) Thomas Flesshor, 3 November 1511

Finally the same Flesshour . . . recognising the errors [. . .] and spontaneously renouncing every heresy and read the abjuration . . . and submitted himself to the Church's judgement. The bishop, after [. . .] taken by the said Thomas . . . about obeying the Church's law and commandments, absolved him from the sentence of excommunication.

The bishop enjoined him the next Friday he shall go before the general procession in Coventry, carrying a faggot of wood on his shoulders until the procession finishes. And on the following Sunday . . . likewise before the procession in St Michael's parish church, carrying a faggot of wood as above, and shall be present at the sermon there . . . And when the preacher orders I, . . . he shall raise the faggot to his shoulders until the declaration of the articles is finished. The rest of his penance is deferred until the bishop's visitation when he may decide to summon him.

[. . .]

(h) Letter of Geoffrey Blyth,[22] bishop of Coventry and Lichfield, to William Smith, bishop of Lincoln,[23] 3 November 1511

In my most hearty manner I recommend me unto your good lordship.

Please it the same to understand that by the confession of the most noted heretics now found within my diocese I have knowledge that one John Davy painter, late of Coventry now dwelling in Leicester and another Richard Dowcheman of his occupation abiding with the said John, [. . .] hath been and yet be of their damnable opinions as well against the sacrament of the altar as prilgrimages, worshipping of images and other which your lordship at more leisure shall plainly

---

[22] Geoffrey Blyth, bishop of Coventry and Lichfield, 1503–31.
[23] William Smith, bishop of Lincoln, 1496–1514.

understand and have sufficient record to convict them if they will deny.

[. . .]

There is also . . . within your diocese one Sir Rafe Kent priest, executor to one Master William Kent, late parson of Staunton in Leicestershire, which . . . was master of divers heretics and had many books of heresy, which of likelihood should come to . . . Sir Rafe, standing . . . executor. . . . I pray God you may come to the said books, for by such there be many corrupted.

They will not confess but by pain of prisonment. And by such means I have got . . . many damnable books, which shall [an]noy no more by God's grace, . . .

From Maxstock . . .

(i) Joan Smith,[24] 4 November 1511

Joan, aged fifty and more, wife of Richard Smyth, mercer of Coventry, recently the widow of John Padland, capper of Coventry, detected of heresy, appeared before the bishop.

Sworn and examined . . . she admitted she had held heretical beliefs for eleven years and that Richard Landesdale, her first husband, drew her into these heresies three years before his death.

She says that, at the moment of the elevation of the Eucharist, she did not believe the Lord's true body was there, but rather the substance of bread.

She admits she held opinions about pilgrimages.

Asked about heretical books, she says she had various heretical books and she handed some of them over to Roger Landesdale.[25] Asked why she did this, she says so that they would not be found in her keeping.

[. . .]

She acknowledged . . . that various books . . . which the bishop showed her, had once belonged to Richard Londesdale, her husband, and that she had kept these books with her from the time of John's death until three months ago.

Asked whether she heard others saying, 'May a priest make God today and eat him and do likewise tomorrow, etc.' she admits this etc.

She says she delivered a book on Christ's passion and Adam . . . to Master Longland three weeks ago.

[24] Burned to death at Coventry a decade later.
[25] Also burned to death at Coventry a decade later.

She says that when Roger Londesdale read to her, she entered into a hall with the doors closed.

When she lay ill in bed, Alice Rowley visited her [. . .].

She also admits she held opinions against images.

1.29

Foxe's *Book of Martyrs*

John Foxe (1516–87) had, as early as 1559, been commissioned by some of those Protestants exiled during the reign of Mary I (1553–8) to produce an account of the trials and tribulations of evangelicalism and, eventually, the role of Elizabeth I as its saviour. This book was in the tradition of Christian hagiography. Foxe used the trials of the midland Lollards in the 1480s and the early sixteenth century to draw attention to the historical roots (and therefore respectability) of Protestant belief and practices; to the persecution and cruelty of the Catholic bishops and their officers; and to the status of the Lollards as innocent martyrs for the true faith as espoused by Protestants. These extracts show how contemporary English reformers themselves interpreted the English Reformation as in some real sense a direct outgrowth of late medieval Lollardy.

The three versions presented here derive from different editions of what was essentially the same work by the contemporary historian of the Reformation. Note that Foxe drew upon archival sources himself for this vivid account, which names persecutors as well as persecuted and employs direct speech. Also interesting is his appeal to eye-witness evidence in the shape of Mother Hall from Babington.

(a) The wife of Sir Smyth, with six others of Coventry, burned

J. Foxe (1559) *Rerum in ecclesiasia gestarum*, Basel, p. 116.

Coming to mind here, in this series of most excellent women, is the memory of a certain woman of Coventry whose name, however, is unknown, except that her husband, who at one time governed the town, was called Smyth. This wife of Smith thus, around that time or not long after, along with sixc ther comrades of her martyrdom, was led outside the city walls into a hollow ditch, which nowadays . . . is called Heretics' Hollow, and was given up to the fire. It is said, however that for these seven . . . there could not have been any other possible outcome. [. . .] But as rumour had it, she could have escaped that danger, except for a certain document, containing the Lord's prayer in the vernacular idiom, which was perceived by the one who was leading her on . . . and he brought her back, first into the enmity of the bishop and theologians, and then to condemnation. There was, moreover, a considerable number of citizens and craftsmen at that time, converging in groups in the various ditches of the suburbs, to hear the holy word of the Lord: they were treated cruelly by various kinds of punishments. Others also were openly displayed in public ignominy with faggots. Many were hanged in the public market, their ears nailed to the gallows: especially those who despising the pontifical order concerning fasting had not abstained from meat during Lent. Such was either the ignorance of the times, or the cruelty of men.

(b) Mistress Smith, widow of Coventry, with six other men burned

J. Foxe (1563) *Acts and Monuments of these latter and perilous dayes, touching matters of the church*, London: John Daye, p. 420.[1]

Upon Ash Wednesday in this year of our Lord god 1519. In the city of Coventry, John Bond then being mayor, Thomas Dod and Thomas Crampe Shrives. There was taken for heresy (as they call it) . . . six men and one gentlewoman, at which time also one Robert Silkeb fled away and escaped untaken. The names of them that were apprehended were these. Robert Hatchetes, a shoemaker, one Archer, a shoemaker, one Haukins, a shoemaker, Thomas Bound shoemaker, one Wrigsham[2] a glover, one Landsdall a hosier, and one Mistress Smith a widow. The only cause of their apprehension was for that they taught in their houses their children and family, the Lord's prayer, the articles of the Christian faith,[3] and the ten commandments in English, for the which

---

[1] In this volume there is also a lengthy account of the Lollard trials of 1485. See Anthology document 1.28 for some of the depositions from the Lollard trials of 1511–12.

[2] Wrexham.

[3] The Creed.

they were put in prison. Some in places under the ground and some in chambers and other places thereabouts until the next Friday [. . .]. Upon which day, they were sent . . . to a monastery called Maxstock Abbey.[4]

[. . .]

[T]hey being at the said Abbey, there children were sent for to the Grey Friars in Coventry, before one Friar Stafford with others . . . [who] straightly examining their babes of their belief, and what heresy their fathers had taught them, charged them upon pain of such death as their fathers should suffer, that they in no way should meddle with the Lord's prayer [. . . etc] which is abominable heresy. [. . .] Now after that done the children departed thence home again. And on Palm Sunday . . . the fathers of these children were brought back again . . . to the City of Coventry. In which place they had borne (a four years before or more) faggots in their churches and market [. . .] the week before Easter, the Bishop and doctors called before them the fore-named persons, and the said gentlewoman, saying unto them that they should wear fagots portrayed in their clothes,[5] to signify to the people that they were heretics. Then Robert Hatchetes hearing that, said unto the bishop these words, 'Why my Lord (saith he) we desire no more but the Lord's prayer, the articles of the Christian faith, and the commandments in English, which I think surely every Christian man ought to have, and will you punish us for that?' Unto this one doctor answered and said, 'Lo my Lord you may see, what fellows would these be if they might reign?' At which words the bishop cried, 'Away with them', & so gave judgement on them all to be burned, escept the said Mistress Smith widow, which at that time was pardoned & admitted to liberty, & because it was in the evening, she should go home, her sight being somewhat dim to see her way.

[. . .]

Simon Mourton the summoner[6] offered himself to go home with her. Now as he was leading her . . . he heard rattling of a scroll which was in [her] . . . sleeve. [. . .] he said, 'Yea, what have we here?' and so . . . looking therein he espied that it was the Lord's prayer, the articles of the faith, & ten commandments in English. [. . .S]o he said 'Ah sirra come, it is as good now as another time' and so brought her back again to the bishop, where she was immediately condemned, and so

---

[4] Six miles from Coventry.

[5] Badges showing a faggot were commonly worn as a form of penance by those accused of heresy.

[6] An official employed to serve summonses for an ecclesiastical court.

burned with the 6 men ... the 4th April next following, in a place ... called the little park.

[...]

Now when the simple people perceiving this, & considering what the parties were that thus were executed, they grudged there at very sore, & said it was great pity they were put to death. For that they were men of good life, true dealing, & honest conversation. But such is the fruit of these unmerciful tyrants and bloody Papists, that all things may be suffered to be done & practised, saving that which maketh to the glory of God, & the keeping of a good conscience. Yet these cruel hangmen were ashamed of their doing, & therefore to cloak their shameful murder & cruel mischief withal, they sent abroad their scullians, their slaves, their retainers, ... to brute[7] abroad that they were not burned for having the Lord's prayer [etc] ... but because they did eat flesh on Fridays, and other fasting days.

(c) The continuity between Lollardy and the reformed faith[8]

J. Foxe ([1563] 1570), *Acts and Monuments of these latter and perilous dayes, touching matters of the church,* London: John Daye, pp. 922, 1107.

Thus much I thought here good to insert, touching these foresaid men of Coventry, especially for this purpose, because our cavilling adversaries be wont to object against us the newness of Christ's old and ancient religion. To the intent therefore they may see this doctrine not to be so new as they report, I wish they would consider both the time and articles here objected against these for said persons [...]. The principal cause of the apprehension of these persons, was for teaching their children, & family, the Lord's prayer, & X [10] commandments in English.

[...]

And for so much as the people began to grudge somewhat ... at the unjust death of these innocent martyrs, the bishop, with his officers & priests, caused it to be noised abroad, by their tenants, servants and farmers, that they were not burned for having the Lord's prayer [... etc]. The witness of this history be yet alive, which both saw them and

---

[7] Noise.

[8] This edition also includes material on the taking, trial and burning of Robert Silkby in 1521–2.

knew them. Of whom one is by name mother Halle, dwelling now in Babington ii [2] miles from Coventry. By whom also this is testified of them, that they above all other in Coventry pretended most show of worship and devotion, at the holding up of the Sacrament, whether to colour the matter, or no, it is not known. This is certain, that in godliness of life they differed from all the rest of the City.

1.30

Churchwardens' accounts and inventories of church goods from Edward IV to Edward VI

Historians make use of churchwardens' account books and other materials (customarily kept in the proverbial parish chest) to cast light on the parish (and community) life of the period. We have to be extremely careful when using these materials because their purpose was to itemise and record income and expenditure and not to communicate to future generations information about parish activities and organisation. Such sources, however, do contain much useful information. For example, we can gain some impression of the contribution parishioners made to the upkeep of the church over and above tithes (tax of one-tenth, which went to the parson) and offerings. Where there is a long chronological run for a particular parish, they can be exploited to demonstrate historical continuity or change. Where there are a number of such records for different places and different parts of the country they offer opportunities for spatial comparison. These examples have been selected to show the types of goods owned by the medieval ecclesiastical parish and the involvement of lay parishioners in church life (exemplified by All Hallows, London Wall and All Saints Bristol), and the inventories of church goods made by Edward VI's commissioners in Surrey. Major church refurbishment was undertaken at All Hallows and was financed by special collections and a levy on householders according to a sliding scale. Parishioners and clergy at All Saints made significant gifts of money, property and church goods. Parishioners were responsible for the upkeep of the church building itself (with the exception of the chancel, which was the parson's responsibility) and this involved major outlay. From the list of donations we can obtain a good idea of the interior furnishings of this church and their splendour, of the attachment to the saints and Our Lady, of the importance of masses for the dead, of the use of images to tell holy stories to parishioners and so on. Extracts from parish records in the reign of Edward VI [reigned 1547–53] provide data regarding the iconoclasm, and further records from Elizabeth I's reign provide interesting information about the slow reintroduction of Protestant worship after the reign of Mary [reigned 1553–8].

(a) Church of All Hallows, London Wall, 1468

C. Welch, (ed. and trans.) (1912) *The Churchwardens'*
Accounts of the Parish of Allhallows, London Wall, in the
City of London, 33 Henry VI to 27 Henry VIII (A.D.
1455–A.D. 1536), London: privately printed, pp. 8–9, 22–4.

These be the payments paid by the hands of the church wardens Nicholas Cale and John Parrys they being in her office the vii [7] year of the reign of King Edward the fourth.

In primis[1] receved of Thomas Wylkocks[2] & Will Cace they being churchwardens	8s	0d
Item received for the beam light for 4 quarters of a year	8s	5d
Item received of Symond Pratt for the rent of the church house for 3 quarters	30s	0d
Item received of Nicholas Cale for his wife's burying in the church 6s 8d	6s	8d
Item received of John Audley for his maid's burying	1s	0d
SUM:	44s	1d

These be the payments paid by the said wardens in the year abovesaid.

In primis for paving of the cawsey at Pratt's door	6s	0d
Item for washing of the church clothes for a year	1s	6d
Item paid for lamp oil for a year	1s	4d
Item paid for tallow candles for a winter to the church		8d

---

[1] First.

[2] The names in this document are transcribed as in the original with no modernisation of spelling.

Item paid for a key making to the great geste[3] in the vestry		6d
Item paid for flags and garlands		5d
Item paid for birch at midsummer	1s	0d
Item paid for holme[4] and ivy at Christmas		2d
Item paid for paving of a grave in the church		6d
Item paid for ringing of the great bell		4d
Item paid for water to the font		2d
Item paid for wax for Nicholas Boyle for a year	15s	2d
Item paid for palm box & yew		3d
Item paid for mending of 2 surplice at the collar		1d
Item paid for ringing of the great bell		4d
Item paid for a bell rope		6d
Item paid for colys at Easter		½d
Item paid to the parson		3s
SUM TOTAL	28s	2½d
These be the parcels of receipts received by the hands of the church wardens Thomas Wilkocks and William Condy they being in their office the 9th year of the reign of King Edward the fourth first received in ready money in the box	32s	3d
Item received for beamlight at midsummer quarter		9½d
Item received for beamlight at Michaelmas	1s	9½d
Item received for beamlight at Easter	2s	10d
Item received for comm.[uni]on tapers at Easter	2s	7d
Item received for the pascal at Easter	5s	9d
Item received of Sir Thomas Bolton for the pit and knell	10s	0d
Item received of the parson toward the making of the sepulchre[5]	4s	0d
Item received of the anker to the church work	3s	4d
Item received of the beamlight at Michaelmas	2s	2d
Item received of the beamlight at Easter	3s	4d
Item received for the comm[uni]on tapers at Easter	1s	8d
Item received for the pascal at Easter	5s	2d

[3] Chest.

[4] Holly?

[5] This is the Easter sepulchre, a common feature of medieval chancels, at which the resurrection of Christ was celebrated at Easter. The parson was responsible for the chancel and hence made a sizeable contribution to this cost.

Item received for the old sepulchre		3s	4d
Item received of William Wynne for the waste of two torches			8d
Item received for the rent of the church house for two years		80s	0d
Item received of the parishioners toward the making of the Sepulchre that is to say of William Boteler		3s	4d
"	of John Hardyng	3s	4d
"	of Symond Pratte	2s	0d
"	of John Newman	1s	8d
"	of William Condy	1s	8d
"	of Nicholas Cale	1s	8d
"	of John Sistokke	1s	0d
"	of William Cace	1s	0d
"	of Matchyng his wife	1s	0d
"	Richard Trent		4d
"	Richard Barbour		2d
"	Walter May		4d
"	John Abraham		4d
"	William Godale		4d
"	William Hayward		2d
"	John Gilbert		4d
"	Kateryn Grene		4d
"	of Gey Condy	6s	8d
"	Thomas Cherscey	1s	0d
"	Laurance Webe		4d
"	Nycholas Santlowe		4d
"	John Lambe	1s	0d
"	John Conat	4s	0d
"	Rye Wyfelde		4d
"	Will Pudsay		4d
"	Cateryne Kendale		3d
"	John Cagge		1d
"	John Browne		4d
"	John Bole		4d
"	Thomas Hunt		2d
Item received of Pratt for midsummer rent . . . [for the tenth year]		10s	0d
Item received for beamlight at midsummer		2s	0d
Item received of Godeale's wife		11s	0d
Item received of Sir Richard			4d

Item received of Pratt for Michaelmas rent [for the tenth year]	10s	0d
Item received of my lady Noryse for the great bell	3s	4d

These be the parcels of the payments paid by the said wardens in the year abovesaid that is to say by Thomas Wilkokks & William Condy

First paid to the parson of the rent of the church house for two years	7s	0d
Item paid for the making of the Sepulchre	44s	0d
Item paid for painting of the same sepulchre	9s	0d
Item paid for flags and garlands for two years	1s	0d
Item paid for ringing of the great bell		4d

[Items found in other years' accounts include]

Item paid for the clerk's indenture		5d
Item paid for two hundred tile	1s	4d
Item paid for two feet for the rafter	1s	0d
Item paid for lathe and nails		1d
Item paid for mending of the offering dish		4d
Item paid for a tiler for 2 days [at]	1s	8d
Item paid for his labourer 2 days [at]		10d
Item paid to the wax chandler in your first coming in	3s	11½d
Item paid for lamp oil for the year	1s	9d
Item paid for writing of this account		4d
Item paid for 2 images of alabaster to the high altar	6s	8d

This is the account of Richard Barbour & John Clovier church wardens of the parish church of All Hallows at London Wall from the feast of the Annunciation of our lady in the 20th year of the reign of King Edward IV unto the 23rd day of the month of June in the 22nd year of our said King that is to say by the space of 2 years and three months.

First the said wardens account that they had in their hands at such time as they were chosen church wardens by the gathering[6] of them and their wives and of the wife of Symond Pratt	26s	4d
Item received in gathering of people upon Good Friday	4s	8d

---

[6] A special collection.

Item received in gathering upon Easter day	6s	8d
Item received of Walter Wells for my Lady Stokton toward the reparation of the church	5s	0d
Item received for broken boards and broken timber		6d
Item received of gathering in the church toward the clasping of the books . . . [other items include]	1s	0d
Item received of a woman toward a certain thing to be made in the church[7]	4s	
Item received in gathering of alms of divers people toward the church works by the church wardens and their wives at Whitsuntide last past	21s	4d

(b) Church of All Saints, Bristol, c. 1450–c. 1500

Examples extracted from C. Burgess (ed.) (1995) *The
Pre-reformation Records of All Saints Bristol, Part 1*,
Bristol Record Society Publications, vol. 46, Bristol: Bristol
Record Society, pp. 10–27.

Sir Thomas Furber, brother and fellow of the Kaledars, gave to the gilding of the rood loft – £5, and he also caused a priest to sing in this church 1 year.

Sir John Thomas, vicar of this church, from his own goods caused the roof of the choir to be sealed.

These are the names of all the good doers and benefactors unto the said church . . .

Roger le Gurdeler

In primis he gave . . . unto the worship of the precious and glorious sacrament to be borne in, 1 bowl of silver gilded within and without, with 1 cover and 1 crucifix over the head, with precious stones wor- shipfully endowed, and a little cup and 1 spoon both gilded, weighing 45 ozs. And that this said bowl, cup and spoon be not alienated, sold nor broken, under pain of cursing us as it appears by writing under the dean's seal.

God have mercy on his soul. Amen.[8]

Goldsmiths dwelling in the Goldsmith's Row now called Cook Row

[. . .]

---

[7] Anonymous donor.

[8] Most of these donations were made by will. This line of blessing suggests the predomi- nant motive behind making such gifts – they were good works to ensure the soul's peaceful passage to heaven.

[U]nto the worship of almighty God and all the saints let made at their own costs for the high altar 1 tabernacle with gold, silver and precious stones of the coronation of Our Lady with 1 ruby imperial all over the head, . . . £20.

God have mercy on their souls.

Item Emott Chylcombe gave in the said church 1 chalice of 13½ozs. God have mercy on her soul.

Thomas Halleway,[9] that died 13 day of December Anno Domini 1454, and Joan his wife, that died the first day of March Anno Domini 1455, both lie buried by the Cross altar under the great stone. . . .

Inprimis they founded 1 chantry in the said church in perpetuity . . .

Item they gave forever to find the lamp before the precious sacrament in the choir – 8s

Item they gave forever for 1 chamber that the said priest dwelled in, the which they built in the churchyard at their own cost – 6s 8d.

Item they gave unto the said church 1 worshipful jewel with 2 angels called a monstrance to bear the precious sacrament with divers relics enclosed in the same, of 57½ozs.

Item they gave 1 mass book to the high altar.

Item they ordained 1 bell to be rung daily to mass, and hung him and enclosed the rope in one case of lead . . .

Item they gave to the best suit of vestments – £20

Item they gave to the building of the corss aisle – £20

Item moreover most well willed to all good works of the church to oversee the repairs of the church 4 times a year going in his coat.

Item they made the seats in the church before St Dunstan's altar – £3.

God have mercy on their souls.

William Rayne, Isabell and Joan gave . . . 1 ship of silver. Item they gave to a new suit of vestments – £3.

Thomas Fyler and Agnes gave to the said church 1 tenement that they dwelt in.

Item they found in the church a priest 3 years.

Item they gave the roof to cover the south aisle.

[. . .]

Also the said Alice [Chestre] executrix to the said Harry, has let made in carved work, a tabernacle with a Trinity in the middle over the image of Jesus, and also at her own cost had it gilded full worshipfully, with a cloth hanging before to be drawn at certain times when

---

[9] Mayor.

it shall please the vicar and parishioners. [and] . . . has let gild at her own cost Our Lady altar [ad]joining the said image of Jesus, and let made a stained cloth to hang before with imagery of Our Lady, Saint Katherine and Saint Margaret.[10]

Also . . . another tabernacle to the north side of the said altar with 3 stories of Our Lady, one, of the stories of Our Lady of Pity; the second, of the Salvation of Our Lady; and the third, of the Assumption of Our Lady.

[. . .]

Moreover the said Alice, 2 years before her decease, being in good prosperity and health of body, considering the rood loft of this church was but single and no thing [of] beauty, according to the parish entente,[11] she, taking to her counsel the worshipful of this parish with others having better understanding and insights in carving, to the honour and worship of almighty God and his saints, and of her special devotion to this church, has let to be made a new rood loft in carved work filled with [?] 22 images, at her own proper cost; of the which images, three are principal – a Trinity in the middle, a [Saint] Christopher in the north side, and a [Saint] Michael in the south side; and besides this, each of the 2 pillars bearing up the loft has four houses there set on in carved work, with an image in each house.

[. . .]

Memorandum Agnes Bartlett, of the almshouse in All Hallows' Lane, at her decease gave unto the church a silver spoon weighing [?] 1 oz the which is set about with stones under the figure of Jesus.

[. . .]

Item [since the death of her husband, Clement Wiltshire, merchant] his wife Joan Wiltshire alias Baten has given a pair of vestments of blue satin with flowers embroidered of gold – 28s 4d.

(c) Destruction of images in the reign of King Edward VI

1. [Order of Edward VI] we have appointed you to be our special commissioners and by authority hereof do name, appoint and authorise

---

[10] Henry and Alice Chester were major benefactors of the church. In her own right Alice made major gifts, a few of which are listed here. Their son John died in 1488. It is noted that he was 'a special well wisher' who supported his widowed mother in making these gifts.

[11] Intent.

you four or three of you to take and receive a full and just view of all goods, plate, jewels, bells and ornaments of every church and chapel ... [And] cause a true, just and full, perfect inventory to be made of the same [. . .].[12]

2. Paid for pulling down the rood loft and setting up the Scriptures, that is to say the creation of the world, the coming of our saviour Christ, the beatitudes,[13] the ten commandments, the twelve articles of our belief[14] and the Lord's Prayer, the judgement of the world, the king's majesty's arms £3 12s 6d.[15]

3. This inventory taken by the jury aforesaid the 14 day of December in the year above written ...

2 chalices of silver, 1 parcel gilt

2 vestments

2 altar cloths

2 copes of silk

1 cope of dornicken

A cross of tin

2 candlesticks of latten

A diaper towel

A font cloth

In the steeple 2 bells

That these were churchwardens in the first year of the king's majesty's reign that now is.

John Hamon

William Wooden

That there was sold by John Woden the elder and Richard Woder the younger wardens in the 4th year of the king's reign aforesaid 2 small bells and certain latten for 3s.

That there was stolen out of the said church by night 2 altar cloths, a surplice, 2 vestments, 2 corporous with their cases and an old cope but by whom we know not.[16]

---

[12] J.R. Daniel-Tyssen (ed.) (1869) *Inventories of goods and ornaments in the churches of Surrey in the reign of King Edward VI*, London: Wyman & Sons, p. 3.

[13] Taken from the Sermon on the Mount when Jesus pronounced blessings: for example, Blessed are the pure in the heart ...

[14] The Creed (Anthology Document 1.26).

[15] Extract taken from Vernon Staley (1902) *Hierurgia Anglicana, vol. 1: Library of Lituriology and Ecclesiology for English Readers*, London: De La More Press, vol. 3, p. 13 – being extracted from the churchwardens' accounts for a Surrey parish in 1551, following the order from Edward VI that roods were to be dismantled.

[16] Commonly parishioners secreted away especially precious items and these re-emerged during Mary's reign for use again in church services.

(d) The purchase of new Protestant requirements for Lambeth church[17]

Table constructed by Rosemary O'Day, from the most
notable examples in C. Drew (ed.) (1940), *Lambeth
Churchwardens' accounts 1504–1645, part 1*, Surrey
Record Society, vol. 40, London: Surrey Record Society.

1565	For 10 load of lime for whitewashing the whole church and for mean fillings in the roof of the church	10s 10d
	For 150 quarter board to amend the pews and seats in the church	9s 0d
	For 3 boards of wainscot as well to make the pulpit as a new desk for the same and for amending the pews	2s 6d
	To Matthew Allen for writing when the cross and chalice and other vestments were defaced	1s
1566	For a book of prayers and a quire of paper	6d
1569	For a new Bible of the greatest volume 26s of which Mr John Porye Doctore of Divinity paid 13s 4d and so the parish charge	23s 4d
	For a copy of the articles set forth by the bishop to be read to the parish	4d
	For the boarders of the hearse cloth and for the images taken off the communion cloth sold to John Widden	6d
	Three copes of white damask sold to Robert Rundell	16s
1570	Paid for ringing the 17 day of November being the beginning of the Queen's Majesty's reign	2s
	Paid for the new Book of Common Prayer and administration of the sacraments for the use of the church 17 November	5s 4d
	Paid to Hitchens for 2 days' work in making benches and seats for servants to sit on	2s
	The charges of taking down the rood loft with new painting and ceiling [? sealing] the same and other reparations done immediately upon the sale of the vestments making 4 new pews	60s 4d

[17] Much of this expenditure would have been in response to the bishop's regular visitation to the parish.

1571	For a book of articles and canons and table of the degrees of marriage	7d
1574	Paid 3 April for 33 yards of mat at 2d the yard for people to kneel on at the communion and for one hassock for Mr Bullock to kneel on at the communion table	5s 6d
	Paid 6 April to a joiner for 2 new pews . . . and for 2 seats for the clerk and the scholars to sit and say service in	23s 8d
	Paid 21 October for a book of the exposition of certain chapters of the Old Testament commanded to be had in our church	4s 6d
1575	For a new service book for the church	4s
	For boat hire for fetching the same	2d
	For a table of the Ten Commandments	11d
1577	For a case for the communion cup	4s

Chapter 2

The European Reformation, 1500–1600

Introduction

The source extracts in this chapter are all concerned with the European Reformation in the sixteenth century. The first five extracts are from sources concerned with the early years of what became the Reformation, dealing with the evangelical challenge of the 1520s. These were often chaotic years where the evangelical movement had yet to take definite shape and the confessional situation was fluid and social and economic grievances found ideological justification in the evangelical theology.

Documents 2.6 to 2.12 provide insight into two urban Reformations, the first within the Imperial city of Strasburg, focusing on the decade between 1525 and 1535, and the second within the Swiss city of Geneva, concentrating on events from 1538 to 1555. This was a period when the Reformation began to make a profound institutional and political impact across northwestern Europe, and new Protestant churches were established on a confessional basis.

Then follows extracts from sources illustrating the course and nature of the English Reformation, from the Act of Restraint of Appeals to Rome in 1533 (2.13) to documents relating to the heated debate over Anglican clerical vestments (the Vestiarian Controversy) in the 1560s (2.17). The English Reformation offers an example of a gradual Reformation of a country or state, which proved both slow and tortuous. In England, what began with the Act of Supremacy in the reign of King Henry VIII was not concluded until the Elizabethan settlement of the 1560s.

2.1 Luther gesticulates towards the True Church of Salvation on his right, with a Protestant congregation receiving communion before Christ as the Lamb of God. On his left is Damnation, where the pope and his clerics are taken into hell. Beneath the pulpit are the ducal family of Saxony.

Finally, the chapter concludes with extracts from sources relating to the Dutch Revolt during the important years from 1565 to 1582 (documents 2.20 to 2.25). These years saw the creation of the Dutch Republic and the establishment of the Reformed Church within the United Provinces, as the Dutch Republic initially was known. The Dutch Revolt offers a pertinent example of how closely intertwined the themes of state formation and faith (belief and ideologies) often were in Reformation Europe.

The chapter provides a broad collection of different sources to the history of the European Reformation, offering readers a varied impression of the significance of the Reformation to sixteenth century people and institutions. It includes extracts from important books, tracts and treatises of the period, which were widely publicised and inspired men and women to embrace the Reformation. The potentially explosive nature of these publications and the sermons to which they gave rise is particularly in evidence in the documents relating to the Peasants' War, where the social and economic grievances of the peasants found ideological justification in the new evangelical faith. The religious, cultural, social and political effects of the Reformation are amplified in a number of letters both private and public, written by evangelical reformers and lay people won over to the evangelical cause. Similar effects can be seen from the extracts from wills, ballads and historical accounts of events connected with the Reformation. Finally the extracts from government acts, church orders, political statements, etc. all illustrate the significance of the Reformation for early modern state building.

Ole Peter Grell

2.1
Erasmus, *The Praise of Folly*, 1511

Erasmus of Rotterdam (1971) *Praise of Folly and Letter to Martin Dorp, 1515*, trans. B. Radice, introd. & notes A.H.T. Levi, Harmondsworth: Penguin, pp. 164–73. Paragraph numbers added.

Desiderius Erasmus (1466–1536), or Erasmus of Rotterdam as he was more commonly known, thereby linking him with his birthplace, was the greatest Christian humanist scholar of the early sixteenth century. From the start Erasmus' writings emphasised the need for reform of the Catholic Church. His witty and satirical attacks on a worldly and corrupt Church and what he considered a meaningless monasticism quickly found resonance among the educated elite in Europe.

Erasmus wrote *The Praise of Folly* while in London in 1510 and published it the following year in Paris. The work combined a humanist programme for religious and educational reform and proved hugely popular and quickly went through a number of editions. In the book the figure of Lady Folly is preaching a sermon in praise of herself whereby many religious and scholarly traditions of the Church are ridiculed.

1. The happiness of these people is most nearly approached by those who are popularly called 'Religious' or 'Monks'. Both names are false, since most of them are a long way removed from religion, and wherever you go these so-called solitaries are the people you're likely to meet. I don't believe any life would be more wretched than theirs if I didn't come to their aid in many ways. The whole tribe is so universally

loathed that even a chance meeting is thought to be ill-omened – and yet they are gloriously self-satisfied. In the first place, they believe it's the highest form of piety to be so uneducated that they can't even read. Then when they bray like donkeys in church, repeating by rote the psalms they haven't understood, they imagine they are charming the ears of their heavenly audience with infinite delight. Many of them too make a good living out of their squalor and beggary, bellowing for bread from door to door, and indeed making a nuisance of themselves in every inn, carriage or boat, to the great loss of all the other beggars. This is the way in which these smooth individuals, in all their filth and ignorance, their boorish and shameless behaviour, claim to bring back the apostles into our midst! But nothing could be more amusing than their practice of doing everything to rule, as if they were following mathematical calculations which it would be a sin to ignore. They work out the number of knots for a shoe-string, the colour of a girdle, the variations in colour of a habit, the material and width to a hair's breadth of a girdle, the shape and capacity (in sacksful) of a cowl, the breadth (in fingers) of a tonsure, the number of hours prescribed for sleep. But this equality applied to such a diversity of persons and temperaments will only result in inequality, as anyone can see. Even so, these trivialities not only make them feel superior to other men but also contemptuous of each other, and these professors of apostolic charity will create extraordinary scenes and disturbances on account of a habit with a different girdle or one which is rather too dark in colour. Some you'll see are so strict in their observances that they will wear an outer garment which has to be made of Cilician goat's hair and one of Milesian wool next to the skin, while others have linen on top and wool underneath. There are others again who shrink from the touch of money as if it were deadly poison, but are less restrained when it comes to wine or contact with women.

2. In short, they all take remarkable pains to be different in their rule of life. They aren't interested in being like Christ but in being unlike each other. Consequently, a great deal of their happiness depends on their name. Some, for instance, delight in calling themselves Cordeliers, and they are subdivided into the Coletines, the Minors, the Minims and the Bullists. Then there are the Benedictines and the Bernardines; the Bridgetines, Augustinians, Williamists and Jacobines; as if it weren't enough to be called Christians.[1] Most of them rely so much on their ceremonies and petty man-made traditions

---

[1] 'Cordeliers' was a generic name for all Franciscans or friars minor. Folly deliberately chooses some lesser known orders and lesser known names for well known orders.

that they suppose heaven alone will hardly be enough to reward merit such as theirs. They never think of the time to come when Christ will scorn all this and enforce his own rule, that of charity. One monk will display his wretched belly, swollen with every kind of fish. Another will pour out a hundred sacksful of psalms, while another adds up his myriads of fasts and accounts for his stomach near to bursting by the single midday meal which is all he usually has. Yet another will produce such a pile of church ceremonies that seven ships could scarcely carry them. One will boast that for sixty years he has never touched money without protecting his fingers with two pairs of gloves, while another wears a cowl so thick with dirt that not even a sailor would want it near his person. Then one will relate how for over fifty years he has led the life of a sponge, always stuck in the same place; others will show off a voice made hoarse by incessant chanting, or the inertia brought on by living alone, or a tongue stiff with disuse under the rule of silence. But Christ would interrupt the unending flow of these self-glorifications to ask: 'Where has this new race of Jews sprung from? I recognize only one commandment as truly mine, but it is the only one not mentioned. Long ago in the sight of all, without wrapping up my words in parables, I promised my father's kingdom, not for wearing a cowl or chanting petty prayers or practising abstinence, but for per-forming the duties of charity. I don't acknowledge men who acknowl-edge their own deeds so noisily. Those who also want to appear holier than I am can go off and live in the heavens of the Abraxasians, if they like, or give orders for a new heaven to be built for them by the men whose foolish teaching they have set above my own commands.'[2]

3. When they hear these words and see common sailors and wag-goners preferred to themselves, what sort of looks do you think they'll give each other? But for the moment they're happy in their expecta-tions, not without help from me. And although they are segregated from civil life, no one can afford to belittle them, especially the Men-dicants, who know all about everyone's secrets from the confessional, as they call it. They know it's forbidden to publish these abroad, unless they happen to be drinking and want to be amused with entertaining stories, but then no names are mentioned and the facts left open to conjecture. But if anyone stirs up this hornets' nest they'll take swift revenge in their public sermons, pointing out their enemy by insinua-tions and allusions so artfully veiled that no one who knows anything can fail to know who is meant. And you'll have to throw your sop to

---

[2] The Abraxasians were a heretical sect.

Cerberus before they'll make an end of barking.[3] Is there a comedian or cheapjack you'd rather watch than them when they hold forth in their sermons? It's quite absurd but highly enjoyable to see them observe the traditional rules of rhetoric. Heavens, how they gesticulate and make proper changes of voice, how they drone on and fling themselves about, rapidly putting on different expressions and confounding everything with their outcry! This is a style of oratory which is handed down in person from brother to brother like a secret ritual. I'm not one of the initiated, but I'll make a guess at what it's like.

4. They start with an invocation, something they've borrowed from the poets. Then if they're going to preach about charity their exordium is all about the Nile, a river in Egypt, or if they intend to recount the mystery of the cross they'll happily begin with Bel, the Babylonian dragon.[4] If fasting is to be their subject they make a start with the twelve signs of the Zodiac, and if they would expound the faith they open with a discussion on squaring the circle. I myself have heard one notable fool – I'm sorry, I meant to say scholar – who set out to reveal the mystery of the Trinity to a large congregation. In order to display the exceptional quality of his learning and to satisfy the ears of the theologians he made a novel beginning, starting with the alphabet, syllable and sentence, and going on to the agreement of noun with verb, adjective with noun and substantive. There was general astonishment amongst his listeners, some of whom whispered to each other the quotation from Horace, 'What's the point of all this stink?' Finally he reached the conclusion that a symbol of the Trinity was clearly expressed in the rudiments of grammar, and no mathematician could trace a figure so plain in the sand. And that 'great theologian' had sweated eight whole months over this discourse, so today he is blinder than a mole, all his keenness of sight doubtless gone to reinforce the sharp edge of his intellect. But the man has no regrets for his lost sight; he even thinks it was a small price to pay for his hour of glory.

5. I've heard another one, an octogenarian and still an active theologian, whom you'd take for a reincarnation of Scotus himself, set out to explain the mystery of the name of Jesus. He proved with remarkable subtlety how anything that could be said about this lay hidden in

---

[3] 'Mendicant' was a term which covered all the orders who begged for their living and were therefore not cloistered. Certain canonical privileges, particularly associated with confessional jurisdiction, attached to this status. The sacrament of penance, demanding auricular confession, was attacked by all the reformers; the reference to the 'sop for Cerberus' alludes to the *Aeneid*, 6, 419, by the Roman poet Virgil (70–19BCE).

[4] Bel is the dragon of the biblical story of Daniel (Daniel, 14).

the actual letters of his name. For the fact that it is declinable in three different cases is clearly symbolic of the threefold nature of the divine. Thus, the first case (*Jesus*) ends in s, the second (*Jesum*) in m, the third (*Jesu*) in u, and herein lies an 'inexpressible' mystery; for the three letters indicate that he is the sum, the middle and the ultimate. They also concealed a still more recondite mystery, this time according to mathematical analysis. He divided *Jesus* into two equal halves, leaving the letter s in the middle. Then he showed that this was the letter ש in Hebrew, pronounced *syn*; and *syn* sounds like the word I believe the Scots use for the Latin *peccatum*, that is, sin. Here there is clear proof that it is Jesus who takes away the sins of the world. This novel introduction left his audience open-mouthed in admiration, especially the theologians present, who very nearly suffered the same fate as Niobe. As for me, I nearly split my sides like the figwood Priapus who had the misfortune to witness the nocturnal rites of Canidia and Sagana, and with good reason;[5] for when did Demosthenes in Greek or Cicero in Latin think up an 'exordium' like that? These orators held the view that an introduction which was irrelevant to the main theme was a bad one – even a swineherd with no one but nature for a teacher wouldn't open a speech in such a way. But our masters of learning think that their preamble, as they call it, will show special rhetorical excellence if it's wholly unconnected with the rest of the subject, so that the listener will marvel and say to himself 'Now where's that taking him?'

6. In the third place, by way of an exposition, they offer no more than a hasty interpretation of a passage from the gospel as an aside, so to speak, though this should really be their main object. And fourthly, with a quick change of character they propound some theological question the like of which 'has never been known on earth or in heaven',[6] and they imagine this is a further indication of their expertise. At this point there really is a display of theological arrogance as they bombard the ears of their listeners with such high-sounding titles as Worthy Doctors, Subtle or Most Subtle Doctors, Seraphic Doctors, Holy Doctors and Incontrovertible Doctors. Then they let fly at the ignorant crowd their syllogisms, major and minor, conclusions, corollaries, idiotic hypotheses and further scho-

---

[5] The figwood Priapus which cracked in fright at the rites of Canidia and Sagana comes from Horace (*Satires*, 1, 8). The phrase 'where's that taking him?' comes from Virgil (*Bucolics*, 3, 19).

[6] The phrase for what 'has never been known on earth or in heaven' comes from Lucian's *Alexander* which Erasmus had translated.

lastic rubbish. There remains a fifth act, in which an artist can really surpass himself. This is where they trot out some foolish popular anecdote, from the *Mirror of History*, I expect, or the *Deeds of the Romans*, and proceed to interpret it allegorically, tropologically, and anagogically. In this way they complete their Chimaera, a monstrosity which even Horace never dreamt of when he wrote 'Add to the human head etc.'

7. But they've heard from someone that the opening words of a speech should be restrained and quietly spoken. As a result they start their introduction so softly they can scarcely hear their own voices – as if it really did any good to say what is intelligible to none. They've also heard that emotions should be stirred by frequent use of exclamations, so they speak in a low drone for a while and then suddenly lift their voices in a wild shout, though it's quite unnecessary. You'd swear the man needed a dose of hellebore, as if it didn't matter where you raise your voice. Moreover, as they've heard that a sermon should warm up as it goes along, they deliver the various sections of the beginning anyhow, and then suddenly let out their voices full blast, though the point may be of no importance, and finally end so abruptly that you might think them out of breath.

8. Last of all, they've learned that the writers on rhetoric mention laughter, and so they're at pains to scatter around a few jokes. 'O sweet Aphrodite', what polish and pertinence, a real case of 'the ass with the lyre'! They sometimes try satire too, but it's so feeble that it's laughable, and they never sound so servile as when they're anxious to give an impression of plain speaking. In fact their entire performance might have been learned from the cheapjacks in the market squares, who are a long way their superiors, though the two types are so alike that they must have learned their rhetoric from each other. Even so, thanks to me, they find people who'll listen to them and believe they hear a genuine Demosthenes or Cicero, especially among merchants and silly women, whose ears they are particularly anxious to please. For the merchants have a habit of doling out small shares of their ill-gotten gains if they're suitably flattered, and the church finds favour with women for many reasons, the main one being that a priest can provide a bosom where a woman can pour out her troubles whenever she quarrels with her husband.

Now I think you must see how deeply this section of mankind is in my debt, when their petty ceremonies and silly absurdities and the noise they make in the world enables them to tyrannize over their fellow men.

[. . .]

2.2

Martin Luther, *To the Christian Nobility of the German Nation*, 1520

C.M. Jacobs & J. Atkinson (trans.) 'To the Christian Nobility
Concerning the Reform of the Christian Estate' in
H.T. Lehmann (ed.) (1966), *Luther's Works*, vol. 44: *The
Christian Society*, Philadelphia: Fortress Press, pp. 124–5,
126–7, 130. Section numbers added.

Martin Luther (1483–1546) was an Augustinian monk and university teacher when he started what eventually became the Protestant Reformation by nailing his 95 theses to the door of the university church in Wittenberg in October 1517. Between 1518 and 1520 his disagreement with the Catholic Church and the pope widened. Luther's hugely influential tracts of the 1520s such as 'On the Babylonian Captivity of the Church' and 'To the Christian Nobility of the German Nation', eventually resulted in his excommunication in January 1521.

'To the Christian Nobility of the German Nation' was published in August 1520, but rather than being a response to recent attacks on Luther by Catholic polemicists the treatise would appear to have been a carefully prepared work which Luther's colleagues at the University of Wittenberg and his friends at the Saxon court had encouraged him to write. The treatise gave theological substance to the long held complaints by the German nation against the pope and the Church.

1. To His Most Illustrious, Most Mighty, and Imperial Majesty, and to the Christian Nobility of the German Nation, from Doctor Martin Luther.

Grace and power from God, Most Illustrious Majesty, and most gracious and dear lords.

It is not from sheer impertinence or rashness that I, one poor man, have taken it upon myself to address your worships. All the estates of Christendom, particularly in Germany, are now oppressed by distress and affliction, and this has stirred not only me but everybody else to cry out time and time again and to pray for help. It has even compelled me now at this time to cry aloud that God may inspire someone with his Spirit to lend a helping hand to this distressed and wretched nation. Often the councils have made some pretense at reformation, but their attempts have been cleverly frustrated by the guile of certain men, and things have gone from bad to worse. With God's help I intend to expose the wiles and wickedness of these men, so that they are shown up for what they are and may never again be so obstructive and destructive. God has given us a young man of noble birth as head of state,[1] and in him has awakened great hopes of good in many hearts. Presented with such an opportunity we ought to apply ourselves and use this time of grace profitably.

[. . .]

2. The Romanists have very cleverly built three walls around themselves. Hitherto they have protected themselves by these walls in such a way that no one has been able to reform them. As a result, the whole of Christendom has fallen abominably.

In the first place, when pressed by the temporal power they have made decrees and declared that the temporal power had no jurisdiction over them, but that, on the contrary, the spiritual power is above the temporal. In the second place, when the attempt is made to reprove them with the Scriptures, they raise the objection that only the pope may interpret the Scriptures. In the third place, if threatened with a council, their story is that no one may summon a council but the pope.

In this way they have cunningly stolen our three rods from us, that they may go unpunished. They have ensconced themselves within the safe stronghold of these three walls so that they can practice all the knavery and wickedness which we see today. Even when they have been compelled to hold a council they have weakened its power in advance by putting the princes under oath to let them remain as they were.[2] In addition, they have given the pope full authority over all decisions of a council, so that it is all the same whether there are many councils or no councils. They only deceive us with puppet shows and

---

[1] Charles V (1500–58), who had been elected emperor in 1519 when only twenty years of age, and whom Luther appeared before at the Diet of Worms in 1521.

[2] Luther alludes here to the failure of the conciliar movement to reform the church. The movement failed chiefly because the papacy refused to submit to the authority of the council. Furthermore, the papacy refused to cooperate in the convening of councils unless the secular powers first swore not to deprive the pope of his authority. In brief, the papacy refused to submit to the authority of either church or empire. Luther felt that since the church had failed to take the initiative in the matter of reform, the emperor should do so.

sham fights. They fear terribly for their skin in a really free council! They have so intimidated kings and princes with this technique that they believe it would be an offense against God not to be obedient to the Romanists in all their knavish and ghoulish deceits.[3]

May God help us, and give us just one of those trumpets with which the walls of Jericho were overthrown [Joshua 6:20] to blast down these walls of straw and paper in the same way and set free the Christian rods for the punishment of sin, [and] bring to light the craft and deceit of the devil, to the end that through punishment we may reform ourselves and once more attain God's favour.

Let us begin by attacking the first wall. It is pure invention that pope, bishop, priests, and monks are called the spiritual estate while princes, lords, artisans, and farmers are called the temporal estate. This is indeed a piece of deceit and hypocrisy. Yet no one need be intimidated by it, and for this reason: all Christians are truly of the spiritual estate, and there is no difference among them except that of office. Paul says in I Corinthians 12 [:12–13] that we are all one body, yet every member has its own work by which it serves the others. This is because we all have one baptism, one gospel, one faith, and are all Christians alike; for baptism, gospel, and faith alone make us spiritual and a Christian people.

[. . .]

3. Therefore, just as those who are now called 'spiritual,' that is, priests, bishops, or popes, are neither different from other Christians nor superior to them, except that they are charged with the administration of the word of God and the sacraments, which is their work and office, so it is with the temporal authorities. They bear the sword and rod in their hand to punish the wicked and protect the good. A cobbler, a smith, a peasant – each has the work and office of his trade, and yet they are all alike consecrated priests and bishops. Further, everyone must benefit and serve every other by means of his own work or office so that in this way many kinds of work may be done for the bodily and spiritual welfare of the community, just as all the members of the body serve one another [I Corinthians 12:14–26].

---

[3] *Spugnissen*, literally, 'ghosts'. The sense of the passage is that the Romanists have frightened the world with threats of purgatory and hell.

2.3

The Twelve Articles of the Upper Swabian Peasants, February 1525

C. Lindberg (ed.) (2000) *The European Reformation Sourcebook*, Oxford: Blackwell, pp. 91–3.

The 'Twelve Articles' is a complex document. It articulates the grievances and demands of the rebellious Upper Swabian peasants. It is also known as 'The Twelve Articles of Memmingen' after the Imperial city where peasant leaders agreed on a mutual charter. Its authorship is uncertain, but it was probably written by the leader of the Upper Swabian peasants, Ulrich Smid, with the assistance of the evangelical preachers of Memmingen and it is undoubtedly representative of the religious and political aims of the rebellious peasants. It is a typical example of the demands drawn up by many bands of peasants who had taken up arms in other regions of south-west Germany/Switzerland affected by the Peasants' War. It came to serve as a template for similar manifestoes issued by peasant bands or armies across these regions.

First, . . . we want to have the full power for a whole congregation to select and elect its own pastor, and also the power to remove him, if he acts improperly . . .

Second, since a just tithe[1] has been established in the Old Testament, and fulfilled in the New (as the whole Epistle to the Hebrews says), we will gladly pay the just grain tithe to the full – but in the proper way. It should be given to God and distributed to his people, paid to a pastor who clearly proclaims the word of God. . . . We are willing that henceforth our churchwardens, chosen by the congregation, collect and receive this tithe. From it they shall give the parson, who has been elected by the whole congregation, enough to maintain himself and his family modestly, according to the determination of the whole congregation. And whatever is left over should be distributed to the destitute people. . . .

---

[1] Church tithes were commonly divided into the 'great' tithes (of all the major crops) and the 'small' tithes (of animal produce such as chickens and lambs etc.). The latter had always been notoriously difficult to collect.

We will not pay the 'small tithe' [on animals] at all. Since the lord God created cattle freely for mankind (Genesis 1), we regard it as an improper tithe which has been contrived by people. . . .

Third, until now it has been the custom for us to be regarded as a lord's personal property, which is deplorable since Christ redeemed us all with the shedding of his precious blood. . . . Thus, Scripture establishes that we are and will be free. . . . Without a doubt as true and just Christians, you will also gladly release us from serfdom,[2] or show us from the gospel that we should be serfs.

Fourth, until now it has been the custom that no poor man has been allowed the right to hunt game or fowl or to catch fish in flowing water. We think that this is completely improper and unbrotherly; rather, it is selfish and not compatible with the word of God. . . .

Fifth, we also have grievances concerning the use of woodlands. For our lordships alone have appropriated all the woods, and when the poor man needs wood, he must buy it at double the price. It is our conviction that, regardless of the kind of woods involved . . . it should revert to the whole community. . . .

Sixth, we have a serious grievance concerning labor services,[3] which increase from day to day. We want . . . some understanding, and accordingly not to be so severely burdened. . . .

Seventh, henceforth we no longer want to be burdened by a lordship. . . . Lords should not force or compel their peasants, seeking to get more services or other dues from them without payment. The peasant should be able to use and enjoy his property in peace, without being burdened. . . . But if the lord is truly in need of services, the peasant should be at his disposal willingly and obediently, but at an hour and season that are not to the peasant's detriment, and the peasant should be properly paid for his services.

Eighth, we are aggrieved, especially those that have their own land, because these lands cannot sustain the payments [taxes and fees] on them, and because these peasants must then forfeit the land and are ruined. [We demand] that lords let honorable people inspect these pieces of property and establish a payment that is equitable, so that the peasant does not work for nothing. For every laborer is worth his wage. . . .

Ninth, we are burdened by the great outrage that new laws are constantly being made, so that we are punished not according to the

[2] A legal status prevalent in medieval and early modern Europe whereby peasants were tied to the land on which they lived.

[3] Work obligations demanded of serfs on the estate of their landlord, especially in busy times, of sowing and harvesting.

facts of a case, but sometimes out of envy and sometimes out of favoritism. . . .

Tenth, we are aggrieved that some have appropriated meadowland as well as fields which belong to the community. . . . We will take these properties into our hands again, unless they have in fact been legally bought. . . .

Eleventh, we want the custom termed heriot[4] to be completely abolished. For we will never accept that the property of widows and orphans should be taken from them so shamelessly. . . .

Twelfth, it is our conclusion and final conviction that if one or more of the articles we have composed here is not in accordance with the word of God, we will retract these articles, if they can be shown to be improper according to the word of God. . . .

2.4

Strasburg preachers' reply to the Alsatian peasants, 18 April 1525

T. Scott & B. Scribner (eds. & trans.) (1991) *The German Peasants' War: A History in Documents,* New Jersey: Humanities Press International, pp. 109–11.

This reply given by the three leading Strasburg reformers, Wolfgang Capito (1478–1541), Mattheus Zell (1477–1548) and Martin Bucer (1491–1551) was to a request for mediation from the rebellious Alsatian peasants under the leadership of Erasmus Gerber. The peasants evidently hoped for a sympathetic hearing and mediation from the evangelical preachers. The preachers were clearly concerned for the welfare of the peasants, but simultaneously inherently hostile to their use of force, and advised them accordingly.

Wolfgang Capito, Matthäus Zell, and Martin Bucer to their 'dear brothers, Erasmus Gerber from Molsheim and the rulers of the assembly at Altorf'.

---

[4] A feudal obligation which required a dead peasant's family to make payment to a lord for the death of 'his' serf.

The grace and peace of God the Father and our lord Jesus Christ. The dangerous state of affairs and our desire for your welfare have caused us to write to you on the way, before we have returned home. We beg you to read our letter with like gravity, for we have always faithfully striven to help lighten the burdens upon the common man for which we are well recognized to have placed our lives in great danger. Our considered opinion in the light of all the circumstances is that we cannot see that you have cause either in the name of God or in your own interests to reject the proposal put to you by Sir Martin Herlin and lord Bernhard Ottfriedrich[1] and to remain assembled en masse since:

1. The larger the troop grows, the quicker the provisions will be eaten up, thereby leading to division and discord.
2. A larger troop could not remain united if lying weakened, above all once the common soldiers can no longer find provisions in the convents and have to start paying for their food, as must happen with time, especially since negotiations over the Twelve Articles cannot be completed with despatch, as we have informed some of your number.
3. You would do well to be guided by the example of the Swabian assembly, the size of whose larger bands and length of encampment together, alas, did it no good at all, as may clearly be seen.
4. You would do well, dear brothers, to consider that no one engaged on important matters squanders the favor and good will of others without just cause, as you seem to have done. Our gracious lord, the bailiff, and count Bernhard von Eberstein are strongly disposed towards Christian conduct and have at many times and in many places shown themselves eager to promote the Word of God and the interests of the poor [common people]. For, dear brothers, you cannot expect to remain together without your [true] aims and intentions being revealed.
5. You know that the city of Strasbourg has risked much over this affair and is constantly endeavoring to have matters resolved for the best, so that you should not spurn its friendship and good will.
6. No more competent and trusty persons than Martin Herlin and lord Bernhard Ottfriedrich may readily be found. They have taken

---

[1] Herlin and Ottfriedrich were local noblemen who had been appointed mediators by the Strasburg magistracy.

this matter to heart and will doubtless find an acceptable solution as quickly as anyone in the entire troop.

7. You should not worry lest matters drag on, for you have been given assurances that they shall be dealt with as quickly as possible, and that the opposing party will be summoned, together with the committee, which the said lords would not have promised you unless they were able to deliver.

8. You should have no fear that the other lordships will instruct the city of Strasbourg's emissaries to give any undertakings or assurances unless they intend to keep them. For the city of Strasbourg is well enough known for it not to tolerate such a breach of faith. . . .

9. So far we have only given our immediate opinion, but we will now set forth what the Scriptures instruct us in this matter.

10. We declare that it is not in accordance with the Gospel to resist the proposal, for that is a sign that you place your trust in no one, which is contrary to Scripture, or that you desire the temporal more than the eternal, which is also contrary to the Gospel. For to be Christians we must disavow our [worldly] selves. How can we then at the same time seek our ends by rebellion?

11. It is perilous to act without chapter and verse from the Scriptures. We have never read anywhere in the Scriptures that the honor of God and the common weal are advanced by the commons killing an unjust overlord, I Kings 8:6.

12. Whoever chooses to aspire to godliness cannot fail, but he who acts against God's will shall be damned, I Kings 6:[12]. If you seek your own ends under the pretext of the Gospel, or if you should ever seek to advance your cause against [the will of] God, God will punish it and not allow it to triumph, Joshua 7.

13. Lastly, dear brothers, we know that there are many who put not their trust in God but in many, but God wishes all honor to himself alone and commands the faithful not to put our trust in temporal power, Jeremiah 2: [28ff]. As God indeed has manifested, for he commanded the children of Israel to rise up against [the tribe of] Benjamin, who deserved punishment; and the children of Israel numbered eleven tribes and were great in number. But because they relied upon their numbers and strength [alone], God ordained that the unjust Benjamites, who numbered twenty-six thousand, should slay around forty thousand of the children of Israel [Judges 20: 15ff, 21ff], so great is God's wrath if one puts oneself in his place and relies on temporal aid.

Therefore, dear brothers, we beg that you consider our injunction. We are Christians, we should seek peace, we should desire God's honor and not our own, for in this matter it is God alone who counts. What harm would follow, were you to ignore this simple truth! Please receive our loyal, amicable letter in the same spirit, for we much desire your welfare and interests, as far as may be conformable to God. May the grace of God be with you, and may it enlighten you, so that you may go forward in peace and by Christian means. Amen. In haste, at Entzheim.[2]

2.5

Argula von Grumbach, 'A Christian Noblewoman's Missive', 1523

C. Lindberg (ed.) (2000) *The European Reformation Sourcebook*, Oxford: Blackwell, pp. 277–8. Paragraph numbers added.

This is the first of no less than eight pamphlets written by the noblewoman Argula von Grumbach (*neé* Argula von Stauffen c. 1492–1554). She was clearly well educated, even though she did not have Latin, and took a considerable interest in theology and religion from an early age. Later she corresponded with several of the evangelical reformers, including Luther and Andreas Osiander (1498–1552) in Nuremberg. She is representative of a number of noblewomen who took an active part in the first decade of the Reformation. This pamphlet was occasioned by the dismissal of a young student and instructor from the University of Ingolstadt who had been charged with being a Lutheran heretic and forced to recant his evangelical views.

1. I am called a follower of Luther, but I am not. I was baptised in the name of Christ; it is him I confess and not Luther. But I confess that Martin, too, as a faithful Christian, confesses him. God help us never to deny this, whether faced by disgrace, abuse, imprisonment, breaking on the wheel and even death – God helping and enabling all Christians in this. Amen.

---

[2] A village between Strasburg and Altdorf.

2. How in God's name can you and your university [Ingolstadt] expect to prevail, when you deploy such foolish violence against the word of God; when you force someone to hold the holy Gospel in their hands for the very purpose of denying it, as you did in the case of Arsacius Seehofer?[1] When you confront him . . . and use imprisonment and even the threat of the stake to force him to deny Christ and his word?

3. Yes, when I reflect on this my heart and all my limbs tremble. What do Luther and Melanchthon[2] teach you but the word of God? You condemn them without having refuted them. Did Christ teach you so, or his apostles, prophets, or evangelists? . . .

For my part, I have to confess, in the name of God and by my soul's salvation, that if I were to deny Luther and Melanchthon's writing I would be denying God and his word, which may God forfend for ever. Amen. . . .

4. Are you not ashamed that [Seehofer] had to deny all the writings of Martin, who put the New Testament into German, simply following the text? That means that the holy Gospel and the Epistles and the story of the Apostles and so on are all dismissed by you as heresy. It seems there is no hope of a proper discussion with you. . . .

5. I beseech you for the sake of God, and exhort you by God's judgment and righteousness, to tell me in writing which of the articles written by Martin or Melanchthon you consider heretical. In German not a single one seems heretical to me. And the fact is that a great deal has been published in German, and I've read it all. Spalatin[4] sent me a list of all the titles. I have always wanted to find out the truth. . . .

6. Your Princely Grace[3] cannot afford such cashiers as these Franciscans who take nothing and yet rake in everything. It is not I who judge, but Christ in Matthew 23: 'Woe to you, Pharisees, you brood of vipers, you who eat up and devour the houses of widows, all under the semblance of a lengthy prayer. The eternal fire is prepared for you.' As far as I can see the endowment of so many canons and priests and that whole swarm of others does nothing but provide for lovers and their concubines. That is painfully obvious. The pope has followed the advice of the devil; he has forbidden women, and for the sake of money permitted concubines. . . .

---

[1] Expelled student and instructor at the University of Ingolstadt. A former student of Philip Melanchthon in Wittenberg.

[2] Philip Melanchthon (1497–1560), Luther's collaborator and co-teacher at the University of Wittenberg.

[3] William IV, duke of Bavaria (1508–50).

[4] Georg Spalatin [Burkhardus de Spalt] (1484–1545), secretary and adviser to Frederick III, Elector of Saxony.

2.6

Deliberations of the magistracy and guilds in Strasburg on the Peasants' War, May 1525

T. Scott & B. Scribner (eds. & trans.) (1991) *The German Peasants' War: A History in Documents*, New Jersey: Humanities Press International, pp. 190–1.

This document is from the height of the Peasants' War and demonstrates the concern of the Strasburg magistracy and the views of the Strasburg Council of 300 and the city's guilds of how to deal with the potentially dangerous situation for Strasburg in case the rebellious Alsatian peasants decided to march on the city. That the magistracy had chosen to seek the advice of the Council of 300 (the 'Jurors' referred to in the document) and the guilds is indicative of its exceptional concern about the political situation. This is a complex document offering insight into the deliberations which took place within Strasburg from 11–14 May 1525.

What was laid before the Jurors when the assembly of peasants proposed to march upon the city and demand [the surrender of] the goods and persons of those clerics who had come in [for refuge], concluded on Thursday after Jubilate in the year 1525; likewise what was thereafter laid before all the guilds on the Sunday Cantate, 11–14 May 1525.

   III. [Second address to the Jurors]

   ... We have also considered how the common citizenry is burdened with daily guard- and watch-duties and how the weekly markets and income therefrom have declined. For the benefit and welfare of the common citizenry we have therefore decided to grind two thousand quarters of rye and to sell the flour to all needy citizens at six pence the bushel, provided that they present a certificate from their respective guildmasters to the ... corn officials, stating that they are citizens ... No citizen shall receive less than a bushel or more than an *Achtel* [an eighth] weekly, which shall be doled out on Tuesdays at the granary. In this regard, we kindly request all citizens who have no need [of such flour] not to visit the granary and to give the poor unrestricted access to it. Excluded from these provisions are the recipients of alms from the common chest, for they are already provided with a due ration of bread. We have moreover suspended that portion of the toll

124

charges levied at the exchequer [*Fronhof*] on produce brought by the countryfolk which falls to us; we have also managed to persuade the cathedral chapter not to collect its portion until it has consulted our gracious lord the bishop, for we are confident that . . . [he] will give a favorable reply.

IV. Discussion of certain matters raised, to which the Jurors should also be alerted.

[2] Concerning the burdens from which the citizenry desires to be absolved: it was considered that, since . . . we would like to be sure in what respects we may rely on the citizenry, we should deal only with the points raised and exclude all others. At the same time, we should instruct every . . . councillor to consider any comment by the citizens that we are not responding to their articles [of grievance], and that therefore the excise and duties on the retailing of liquor [*Zapfen- und Helblingzoll*] and other taxes should be abolished, by kindly pointing out that without such revenues the city could not maintain its extensive canals and watercourses, its public buildings, and its considerable daily expenditure on running costs. For although the clergy have accepted burgher's rights and civic protection and bear their [share of civic] burdens, these burdens only fall due at the end of the year, which is not yet past. Therefore they [the citizens] should remain calm during the present disturbances and help defend this city and their fatherland. When the unrest has been quelled and the secular and regular clergy's taxes have been levied, the council will abolish whatever [taxes] are capable of remission.

VII. [Submission of the Guilds]

1. The Anchor Guild [of boatmen].

What our lords have laid before us in writing we accept, and pledge our life and property to the protection and defense of the city of Strasbourg and its common citizenry.

Jacob Lutz pledged likewise, but with the proviso that only a certain number of foreign cavalry be admitted, lest they overwhelm us.

Hans Hesch pledged likewise, but with the proviso that the lords [of the council] should be mindful of the poor apprentices and journeymen [*Gesellen*], to see whether the city could do anything to raise their earnings above those of other foreigners, so that they might the better support their wives and children.

2. The clothmakers.

Diebolt Stol says: he hears the peasants are demanding justice . . . If that be the case, he would not oppose them.

Gottfrid Wolff likewise, and added that he would remain by whatever the Word of God upheld . . .

Theoderis Wild says: we are throwing the people into confusion with all the petitions. Doesn't everyone know what they have sworn, by now for the second time? He wishes to remain by the oath which he has sworn to my lords and by those laws which are not against God and brotherly love . . . The remainder are all well disposed and will act as godly folk, although many say [only] in so far as my lords have right on their side.

3. The gardeners in the Steinstrasse.

. . . have agreed that they will place their lives and all their property at our lords' disposal. But four of them . . . declare that if [the peasants] demand [the surrender of] the parsons and their property, our lords should hand them over and afford them no assistance. And, dear lords, in order that we suffer no injury therefrom, [at the least] these parsons and their goods and chattels should be handed over who have only become citizens during these unruly times.

4. The gardeners in the Krutenau.

. . . have decided to place their lives, honor and property at their lords' disposal . . . It has also been decided by common consent that my lords should get rid of the foreign priests and their property and not accept them as burghers, since the city of Strasbourg may suffer disadvantage thereby. Likewise . . . if someone has a claim against a priest whom my lords have admitted [as a burgher], he and his property shall be expelled, in order that no quarrel or strife befall the city . . . Likewise . . . any foreign priest who henceforth immigrates shall receive no protection of any kind . . .

2.7

Sturm and Pfarrer's letter to the Strasburg magistracy, 2 June 1530

H. Virck (ed.) (1882) *Urkunden und Akten der Stadt Strassburg*, vol. 1: *Politische Correspondenz der Stadt Strassburg im Zeitalter der Reformation*, Strasburg, pp. 446–7. Translated from German by Susanne Meurer.

Jacob Sturm (1489–1553) the most prominent civic leader in the Empire during the Reformation period, had become the driving

2.2 Portrait of Mathis Pfarrer (1489–1568), ammeister of Strasburg. Woodcut by Bernhard Jobin, 1568.

force behind Strasburg's foreign policy in 1525 when he was elected stettmeister. Together with the city's ammeister Mathis Pfarrer,[1] Sturm left Strasburg on 22 May 1530 to attend the Imperial Diet of Augsburg. It was Sturm's intention once more to try to join forces with the Lutherans and unify the Protestant camp within the Empire which had recently split due to the differences over the interpretation of the Eucharist. Sturm and Pfarrer's letter of 2 June 1530 to their magisterial colleagues in Strasburg provides an impression of the religious and political difficulties they encountered in Augsburg.

Following our arrival here, we have again busied ourselves and looked at the instructions and proposals regarding religious issues, which Your Honourable Council had sent to us. Since it was suggested in those [proposals] that we should in all respects make as many efforts as possible to ensure that no final decisions will be made here and thus without testimony from scholars and preachers, but that the matter should instead be passed on to a free Christian general council,[2] to which the scholars should be taken and be sufficiently questioned on every point. And since the convening of such a council has been deemed useful and necessary at all previous imperial diets, we thought that perhaps the matter could take place in the following way: Upon an announcement his Imperial Majesty [Charles V] might hear the scholars – considering that the electors and princes from both parties, who are now here, have brought many preachers and scholars with them, and since Eck, Faber, Cochlaeus[3] and others are either here or will surely arrive soon. In addition, the elector[4] is determined that if his Imperial Majesty so desired or else should approve, to also summon Luther, who is thought to be not far from Nuremberg. If such an examination, or something similar should take place here, it may perhaps be of benefit that a number of honourable preachers should also be present, in order to give account and answer questions regarding their teachings and beliefs. As we do not have express orders from here to

[1] The equivalent translation for both Stettmeister and Ammeister is mayor.

[2] This is a reference to a General Council of the Church – much referred to in the Reformation era, but never called.

[3] Johann Eck (1486–1543) Catholic controversialist and Luther's most gifted opponent; Johannes Faber (1470?–1530) Dominican humanist hostile to Luther from the mid-1520s; Johannes Cochlaeus (1479–1552) Catholic polemicist.

[4] The elector of Saxony referred to is Johann the Constant who ruled electoral Saxony from 1525 to 1532.

request anything, we thus submit our subservient request to Your Honourable Council to notify us via messenger, whether, if things take place in the manner outlined above, we should ask and request on behalf of Your Honourable Council to have a number of our preachers also summoned here and cross-examined for sufficient comparison, or how we should act in that case, and we will comply with it. Some kindly [souls] also think that even if this should not be the case, it would still not be futile to have Martin Bucer or Doctor Capito here with us, and to make use of them in any eventualities which may arise. Nevertheless, we did not want to leave Your Honourable Council uninformed about this, so that you may further deliberate on this matter, and – should You consider it a good idea – also to hear the opinions of said two preacher on this matter.

Doctor Luther has put the articles, which were brought forward by the Elector and Margrave George of Brandenburg[5] during the talks at Schwabach[6], into print, of which we herewith send you a copy. And we have also received reliable reports that the Elector of Saxony has sent those same articles to his Imperial Majesty in Innsbruck via his embassy, together with the announcement that these are his beliefs, to which he intends to stick. And since they were written in German, his Imperial Majesty ordered to have them translated into Latin and carefully considered them.

We have handed over our suggestions regarding the division of the sacrament to our gracious lord, the landgrave,[7] etc., but as far as we have heard from his ducal grace, there is little hope that the elector and the other princes who follow Luther will trouble themselves with us any further than to the extent that they do not think that we should be pressed away from our preachers' opinions through deeds or force without a hearing of the matter.

Furthermore, Eisleben[8] is at this moment preaching on the main issues of the sacrament, indicating, in what respect the pope and the Zwinglians, as they are called, are mistaken. And although our dear lord, the landgrave, etc., has ordered his preachers to be repentant in this matter, he has still not managed to stop it among the Saxons. One

[5] Margrave Georg of Brandenburg, referred to as George, who ruled Brandenburg-Ansbach between 1527 and 1543.

[6] The Schwabach Articles – the Protestant confession drawn up by Luther following the Diet of Speyer, 1529.

[7] Landgrave Philip of Hesse (1504–67). A landgrave was a title used in central Europe, comparable to a count, who had feudal duty direct to the Holy Roman Emperor.

[8] This is a reference to Luther, whose birthplace was Eisleben.

should therefore be concerned that such contradictory preachings will not advance the entire Christian cause much, but will win over many to the opposite.

Dated Augsburg, 2 June 1530
Letter signed by Sturm

2.8
Strasburg Church Order, 1534

R. Stupperich (ed.) (1978) *Martin Bucers Deutsche Schriften* [*Martin Bucer's German Writings*], vol. 5: *Strassburg und Münster im Kampf um den rechten Glauben 1532–1534* [*Strasbourg and Münster's fight for the true faith 1532–1534*], Gütersloh: Gerd Mohn, pp. 29–31. Translated from German by Susanne Meurer.

Strasburg did not receive its first evangelical Church Order until 1534. On the request of the city's four prominent reformers, Bucer, Hedio, Zell and Capito, the magistracy, the Senate and the Council of XXI agreed to call a general synod of the church in Strasburg in order to establish a secure doctrinal and ecclesiastical foundation for the new Protestant Church in the city. The synod which formulated the new Church Order consisted of lay members, from elders to prominent political leaders of the city such as Jacob Sturm, and clerical members, i.e. all the evangelical preachers.

[II] How the duties of a parish priest and helper/assistant should be performed and maintained through proper and edifying actions.

Firstly, following the [principle] that the highest degree of love and friendship should exist between the shepherds of Christian pastures and Christ's flock, also St Paul's wish that a bishop should generally be highly regarded by everybody, it is proper to proceed in the approval and appointment of a servant of the church that one should appoint those servants, who, to the best of their abilities, are agreeable to the Christian community. Thus the will of the parish has for a long time been ascertained everywhere in the selection and appointment of servants of the church.

It is therefore recognised that, when a parish becomes vacant, the said examiners of God's teachings[1] should allow one or more [candidates], after they have been deemed agreeable and suited for such offices or assistance in the parish or found fit during the examination, to initially deliver a number of sermons in the parish, which lacks a priest or helper, so that the congregation of that parish can hear them. And following that, namely where a priest is about to be approved, the congregation of the parish should have a pious servant of the Word deliver a sermon on what constitutes a priest's offices and how much depends upon those being administered appropriately, together with the admonition that God should be most earnestly asked to govern and guide such an election and investiture, if that be the case.

Upon this, the elders/churchwardens, in whose parish a priest is to be chosen, should select twelve god-fearing men, whom the parish considers to lead a Christian life and they should hold the election in all earnestness together with the examiners at an appropriate time and place to be named by the examiners, and they should carefully consider and discuss everything amongst each other, which is necessary in such an election. [This type of] consideration and reporting is not possible within a large parish to a necessary degree. Whoever the prescribed examiners, together with the elders/churchwardens and the twelve [members] of the parish, which lacks a priest, choose, should then be indicated to the Honourable Council. And once the Honourable Council has found the chosen [candidate] suitable and endorsed him, then the aforementioned examiners and elders/churchwardens shall once again arrange for and instruct a pious servant of the Word from the same parish for which a priest has been selected, to deliver a sermon. In this, he shall commend the thus elected to the congregation and remind him of his duties towards the congregation, and equally the congregation's duties towards him, and admonish [both] to faithfully beseech and pray to God that He may bestow His Holy Spirit onto both, the priest and congregation, that they should conduct themselves towards each other as their duties require, and that He may thus grant that the priest may serve fruitfully.

When, however, a helper is to be taken on, then the examiners, the elders/churchwardens and the priest of the parish in which a helper is lacking, should hire him. And those, who are considered suitable for such offices should initially be allowed to deliver a number of sermons, with a request to the congregation, which should be issued by the priest, to notify the parish councillors in case someone thinks

---

[1] Some of the Protestant ministers appointed by the magistracy.

that one of those, who have been heard, may perhaps be inadequate and hence not suited to such offices. Equally, whenever more than one has been heard and someone considers there to be special reasons why one should be selected above all the others, then the elders/churchwardens should also be notified of this.

The priest of the said parish should then commend the chosen helper to the congregation in a sermon, he should speak to him of his duties and have prayers said for him. The aforementioned examiners and the elders/churchwardens of the said parish should also carefully observe the teachings and way of life of the selected priests and helpers, and should either be found wanting, they should mend them if possible. Otherwise [they should] dismiss them, and in the case of priests bring the matter before the Honourable Council.

Reason for this article

The office of tending the flock of Christ is so great and important that one can never pay enough careful attention and deliberate enough on the selection of such servants of Christ and shepherds of his flock. The proper tenure of such offices is also so far beyond all human abilities, that God should be beseeched and called upon with truly the highest solemnity and greatest devotion. This is the reason why so much ceremony and solemnity has been observed in the selection and investiture of bishops, which have since the time of the apostles been nothing other than priests.

Convocation[2]

In order to ensure, however, that such teachings of Christ are followed with proper solemnity and in a unanimous Christian fashion by the priests, helpers and preachers and so that they should also conduct themselves appropriate to such teachings in their lives and deeds, an Honourable Council has found it useful and ordered that as they, the preachers, have so far been in the habit of meeting every few weeks in order to discuss amongst each other how the teachings of Christ should be conducted, what the church should at all times bear in mind, and how everything required by their offices should best be executed, from now on three of the twenty-one elders/churchwardens should be delegated to such convocations of the preachers, in order to confer and compare with the preachers on the needs of the church. However, should matters be brought up which they, the elders/churchwardens, deem too complex, or in which they cannot consult with the preachers, then they shall present them to the other twenty-one elders/church-

[2] A church assembly.

wardens, which they may summon, or in front of an Honourable Council. The preachers shall in the meantime rest such matters or not continue with them, but instead wait for the decision of the other elders/churchwardens or of the Honourable Council. And these said convocations shall take place once a fortnight, always, as a rule, on a Thursday. And after the first convocation one of the elders/churchwardens shall leave, while the other two remain and in place of the departing [elder/churchwarden] another shall be delegated, and so on, so that at every convocations there shall always be two old and one new elders/churchwardens so that the newly-arrived elder/churchwarden may receive reports from the old ones on what has been discussed previously. In case of church matters or urgent business, which may not wait for a regular convocation or fortnightly gathering as outlined above, [the period between] such meetings may and should be shortened as opportune to and deemed necessary and useful by the delegated members of the parish council and priests.

All priests and helpers in town, also those from Ruprechtsau and Schilcken[3] should attend such convocations, and without pertinent reason no-one should be absent. Should necessity dictate it, they may also summon the ordinary lecturers, school masters and teachers without exception as they deem necessary and beneficial. Yet, they should not make any significant decisions or innovations, but present them to the Honourable Council, in front of which they should take them.

2.9
Bucer's response to Hoffman, 1534

R. Stupperich (ed.) (1978) *Martin Bucers Deutsche Schriften*
[*Martin Bucer's German Writings*], vol. 5: *Strassburg und
Münster im Kampf um den rechten Glauben 1532–1534*
[*Strasbourg and Münster's fight for the true faith
1532–1534*], Gütersloh: Gerd Mohn, pp. 52–4. Translated
from German by Susanne Meurer.

Martin Bucer (1491–1551), who had originally welcomed Melchior Hoffman (1495–1543) on his arrival in Strasburg in the summer

---

[3] Villages belonging to Strasburg.

of 1529, had by 1533 come to see Hoffman as a dangerous, religious radical. Together with his evangelical colleagues Bucer was instrumental in convincing the Strasburg magistracy to imprison Hoffman in 1533. Bucer's intervention in 1534 was a response to Hoffman's recent statement issued from prison of his religious views which the mainstream Protestant leaders in the city clearly felt could not be left unanswered, not least because of Hoffman's considerable following in Strasburg.

The case, as heard in the public meeting recently held during the synod in Strasburg by the preachers of said place, concerning Melchior Hoffmann and his four noble pieces on Christian teaching and positions, together with a truthful account of the foundations on which Hoffmann builds his fallacies.

May the Holy Ghost lead us to all truth. Amen

When the Honourable Council,[1] our Gracious Lords, granted Hoffmann, at both our own and Hoffmann's request, to present at our synod and open meeting what he considers lacking in our preaching and teaching, this indeed took place on the 11th day of June [1533]. Above all, he declared the following four terrible fallacies with the great and true conviction of being a servant of the Almighty and a tool of our Lord Jesus Christ as awakened by God in order to proclaim these terrible fallacies, which he presents as the true gospel of Christ, to the world and first of all to us here in Strasburg.

Thus he expounds that just as Rome is the spiritual Babylon, Strasburg is the spiritual Jerusalem. And on this he constantly insists, not only in his spoken teachings, but also in his writings and in particular in his inflammatory prophecies, which he had collected and issued in print twice by a simple and silly man, Leonhard Jost,[2] who a while ago was lying in chains in the local hospital because he was out of his mind, and then again by [Jost's] wife, who shares just as much in the spirit of our Lord. From this Jerusalem, he writes, one hundred and forty-four thousand virginal apostolic heralds shall pour forth to spread the brotherhood and the baptism through immersion in water throughout the world.

And this is supposed to begin now, as he writes that this summer the times of persecution of his brethren in baptism and brotherhood shall have passed and that the baptism with blood of those who per-

---

[1] The Strasburg magistracy.

[2] One of the 'Strasburg prophets' – Anabaptists who claimed to have direct revelations from God.

secuted them shall start. Before that, however, Strasburg shall be besieged and much pressured, although [the city] will ultimately be victorious. And there are many other cruel and inflammatory false prophecies, in which he has partly already been found mendacious, because the time, for which he had predicted this siege of Strasburg (although he now denies it and would like to twist his story) has already passed.

Now, although every Christian should easily see that these bloodthirsty and seditious prophecies have arisen from the spirit that has been a murderer from the beginning and not at all from the calm and gentle spirit of Christ, who seeks that which was lost and helps those who are depraved,[3] we still wanted to briefly report [the matter] here and thus make it clear what we think of this and what everyone should rightly think of such esteemed and splendid witnesses of these spirits so that (while this Hoffmann always refers to Strasburg, where we [are said to] pass over this matter in silence) no-one may think that we do not recognise this spirit, or that we should be in league with it.

2.10
Calvin, *Institutes of the Christian Religion*

J. Calvin (1989) *Institutes of the Christian Religion*, trans. H. Beveridge, Grand Rapids, MI.: Eerdmans, pp. 210–11.

John Calvin (1509–64), like Luther, was a copious writer of treatises and biblical commentaries. But, as opposed to Luther, Calvin published one work which came to overshadow all his other publications, namely the *Institutes of the Christian Religion*. First published in March 1536, it gradually developed into a handbook of the Reformed religion. It went through numerous editions in French and Latin, gradually expanding so that the final edition of 1559 was many times larger than the first edition of 1536. The *Institutes* became a fundamental work for trainee Calvinist ministers and theologians in the sixteenth century and was translated into many languages.

---

[3] The Bible John 8:44 and Luke 19:10.

The whole people of Israel are called the Lord's inheritance, and yet there were many foreigners among them. Still, because the covenant which God had made to be their Father and Redeemer was not altogether null, he has respect to that free favour rather than to the perfidious defection of many; even by them his truth was not abolished, since by preserving some residue to himself, it appeared that his calling was without repentance. When God ever and anon gathered his Church from among the sons of Abraham[1] rather than from profane nations, he had respect to his covenant, which, when violated by the great body, he restricted to a few, that it might not entirely fail. In short, that common adoption of the seed of Abraham was a kind of visible image of a greater benefit which God deigned to bestow on some out of many. This is the reason why Paul so carefully distinguishes between the sons of Abraham according to the flesh and the spiritual sons,[2] who are called after the example of Isaac. Not that simply to be a son of Abraham was a vain or useless privilege (this could not be said without insult to the covenant), but that the immutable counsel of God, by which he predestinated to himself whomsoever he would, was alone effectual for their salvation. But until the proper view is made clear by the production of passages of Scripture, I advise my readers not to prejudge the question. We say, then, that Scripture clearly proves this much, that God by his eternal and immutable counsel determined once for all those whom it was his pleasure one day to admit to salvation, and those whom, on the other hand, it was his pleasure to doom to destruction. We maintain that this counsel, as regards the elect, is founded on his free mercy, without any respect to human worth, while those whom he dooms to destruction are excluded from access to life by a just and blameless, but at the same time incomprehensible judgment. In regard to the elect, we regard calling as the evidence of election, and justification as another symbol of its manifestation, until it is fully accomplished by the attainment of glory. But as the Lord seals his elect by calling and justification, so by excluding the reprobate either from the knowledge of his name or the sanctification of his Spirit, he by these marks in a manner discloses the judgment which awaits them. I will here omit many of the fictions which foolish men have devised to overthrow predestination. There is no need of refuting objections which the moment they are produced abundantly betray their hollowness. I will dwell only on those points which either form the subject of dispute among the learned, or may

[1] The Jewish race.
[2] Christians.

occasion any difficulty to the simple, or may be employed by impiety as specious pretexts for assailing the justice of God.

2.11
Establishment of Calvinism in Switzerland

A. Duke, G. Lewis & A. Pettigree (eds.) (1992) *Calvinism in Europe, 1540–1610: A Collection of Documents*, Manchester: Manchester University Press, pp. 25–8, 29–30, 41–5.
Paragraph numbers added.

(a) Calvin's letter to Oswald Myconius, 14 March 1542

John Calvin (1509–64) was an avid letter-writer who realised the need for good relations with Protestant colleagues in the other Swiss cities. The recipient of this letter, Oswald Myconius (1488–1552), was a prominent reformer in Basel who had started his career in Zurich where he had been instrumental in attracting Ulrich Zwingli (1484–1531) to the city. After Zwingli's death, Myconius moved to Basel where he served both as a minister and a professor at the University. Calvin's letter, written shortly after his return to Geneva in the autumn of 1541, provides insight into the problems he expected to encounter in the city, especially with regard to the Reformed Church Order he wanted to introduce.

1. On my first arrival here I could not, as you had requested, write to you with certainty as to the state of this church, because I had not then myself sufficiently ascertained its condition. Since that time also I have not ventured to say anything for certain, while matters were not very settled, that I might not shortly have occasion to repent having praised it so soon. . . . The present state of our affairs I can give you in few words. For the first month after resuming my ministry, I had so much to attend to and so many annoyances, that I was almost worn out: such a work of labour and difficulty had it been to build up once more the fallen edifice. Although certainly Viret[1] had already begun successfully to restore, yet, nevertheless, because he had deferred the complete form of order and discipline until my arrival, it

---

[1] Pierre Viret (1511–71), influential Lutheran preacher in French-speaking Switzerland.

had, as it were, to be commenced anew. When, having overcome this labour, I believed that a breathing space would be allowed me, new cares presented themselves, and those of a kind not much lighter than before. This however somewhat consoles and refreshes me, that we do not labour altogether in vain, without some fruit appearing; which although it is not so plentiful as we could wish, yet neither is it so scanty that there does not appear some change for the better. There appears a brighter prospect for the future if Viret can be left here with me: on which account I am the more desirous to express to you my most thankful acknowledgement, because you share with me in my anxiety that the Bernese may not call him away; and I earnestly beseech, for the sake of Christ, that you will do your utmost to bring that about. [...]

2. Our other colleagues are rather a hindrance than a help to us: they are rude and self-conceited, have no zeal, and less learning. But what is worst of all, I cannot trust them, even though I very much wish that I could; for by many evidences they show their estrangement from us, and give scarcely any indication of a sincere and trustworthy disposition. I bear with them, however, or rather I humour them, with the utmost lenity: a course from which I shall not be induced to depart, even by their bad conduct. But if, in the long run, the sore need a severer remedy, I shall do my utmost and shall see to it by every method I can think of to avoid disturbing the peace of the Church with our quarrels; for I dread the factions which must necessarily arise from the dissensions of ministers. On my first arrival I might have driven them away had I wished to do so, and that is even now in my power. I shall never, however, repent the degree of moderation which I have observed, since no one can justly complain that I have been too severe. These things I mention to you in a cursory way, that you may perceive more clearly how wretched I shall be if Viret is taken away from me. What you observe, from the example of your church, of the great injury which is inflicted by the noisome plague of discord among the ministry, I can confirm from my own experience to the fullest extent, in the calamity that has befallen this church. No persons could be on closer terms of intimacy than we were here with one another. But when Satan had stirred up the deplorable misunderstanding between these brethren and ourselves, you know yourself what followed thereupon. My determination was therefore made at once, that unless with the evidence of an entire reconciliation, I would never undertake this charge, because I despaired of any benefit from my ministry here, unless they held out a helping hand to me. Meanwhile, many in their assembly are not over friendly, others are openly hostile

to me. But this I carefully provide against, that the spirit of contention may not arise among us. We have an intestine seed of discord in the city, as I have already mentioned; but we take special care, by our patient and mild deportment, that the Church may not suffer any inconvenience from that circumstance, and that nothing of that kind may reach the common people. They all know very well by experience the pleasant and humane disposition of Viret. I am in no way more harsh, at least in this matter. Perhaps you will scarcely believe this; it is not the less true, however. Indeed I value the public peace and cordial agreement among ourselves too highly, that I lay restraint upon myself: those who are opposed to us are themselves compelled to award this praise to me. The feeling prevails to such an extent that from day to day those who were once open enemies have become friends; others I conciliate by courtesy, and I feel that I have been in some measure successful, although not everywhere and on all occasions.

3. On my arrival it was in my power to have disconcerted our enemies most triumphantly, entering with full sail among the whole of that tribe who had done the mischief. I have abstained; if I had liked, I could daily, not merely with impunity, but with the approval of very many, have used sharp reproof. I forbear; even with the most scrupulous care I avoid everything of the kind, lest even by some slight word I should appear to persecute any individual, much less all of them at once. May the Lord confirm me in this disposition of mind. It happens, however, sometimes, that it is necessary to withstand our colleagues; but we never do so unless they either compel us by their unseasonable importunity, or some weightier consideration demands our interference. I will relate an instance to you, which the complaint you make in your letter, owing to the similarity of the case in point, brought very forcibly to my recollection. When we were considering about the introduction of ecclesiastical censure, and the Senate had given us a commission to that effect, these worthy persons appeared in public to assent; doubtless because they were ashamed to offer direct opposition in a matter that was so plain and evident. Afterwards, however, they were to be seen going about secretly, dealing separately with each of the senators, exhorting them not to lay at our feet the power which was in their hands (as they said), not to abdicate the authority which God had entrusted them, and not to give occasion to sedition, with many other arguments of a like nature. We dared not close our eyes to such perfidious conduct. We endeavoured, however, to arrange the matter in such a way as not to stir up strife among us.

4. We at length possess a presbyterial court, such as it is, and a form of discipline, such as these disjointed times permit. Do not, however, allow yourself to suppose that we obtained so much without the most vigorous exertion. And besides, those troops of unclean spirits break forth in all directions, who in order that they may escape from healthy discipline, which they can in no way submit to, seek every sort of pretext for slipping away from the authority of the Church. The world, moreover, holds this laxity to be an established custom, which, for the sake of its lust, must reign paramount, because it cannot endure to resign the dominion of the sensual appetites to Christ. But however impostors of this kind may plead the plausible case of the world and the flesh, the Lord will consume them with the breath of his mouth, provided we go forward to the assault with a united courage and resolution, and fight manfully, with a stout heart and unwearied zeal, for that sacred authority over the members of the Church which ought ever to be held inviolable. For indeed, the truth of God shines more brightly of itself in this evangelical order of discipline, than to allow of it being easily overlaid with such lying devices. They adduce Moses and David as examples, as if these two rulers had exercised no other charge over the people than to rule them in the ordinance of civil government. Let those insane pleaders for the authority of the magistrate give us such men for magistrates as were Moses and David, that is excelling in the singular spirit of prophecy, and sustaining both characters, not at their own mere will and pleasure, but by the calling and commission of God, we shall then willingly concede to such persons that authority which they demand. I have no doubt that Moses himself discharged the functions of priesthood before the consecration of Aaron to the office: afterwards he prescribes, by the command of God, what was to be done. David also did not proceed to take order in settling the administration of the Church, before he was invested with that power by the permission of God. Other pious godly kings defended and protected the established order by their authority, as became them; they let the Church alone, however, in the exercise of her peculiar jurisdiction in spirituals, and left to the priests the charge assigned to them by the Lord. . . .

(b) Calvin's letter to William Farel, April 1546

This letter was written in the spring of 1546 at a time when Calvin's attempt to impose an impartial social and religious discipline on Geneva had met with considerable hostility among some of Geneva's leading families, many of whom had previously been firm supporters of the Reformation in the city. The recipient, William Farel (1489–1565), had originally in 1536 invited Calvin to help him reform Geneva. The two men had worked closely together until their expulsion in 1538, when Farel settled in Neuchâtel where he remained a minister until his death, but they remained in regular contact.

1. After your departure the dances caused us more trouble than I had supposed. All those who were present being summoned to the Consistory, with the two exceptions of Corne and Perrin, shamelessly lied to God and us. I was incensed, as the vileness of the thing demanded, and I strongly inveighed against the contempt of God, in that they thought nothing of making a mockery of the sacred obtestations we had used. They persisted in their contumacy.[2] When I was fully informed of the state of the case, I could do nothing but call God to witness that they would pay the penalty of such perfidy; I, at the same time however, announced my resolution of revealing the truth, even though it should be at the cost of my own life, lest they should imagine that any profit was to come of lying. Francisca also, the wife of Perrin, grossly abused us, because we were so opposed to the Favres. I replied as seemed proper, and as she deserved. I inquired whether their house was inviolably sacred, whether it owed no subjection to the laws? We already detained her father in prison, being convicted of one act of adultery, the proof of a second was close at hand; there was a strong report of a third; her brother had openly contemned and derided the Senate and us. Finally I added that a new city must be built for them, in which they might live apart, unless they were willing to be restrained by us here under the yoke of Christ; that so long as they were in Geneva, they would strive in vain to cast off obedience to the laws; for were there as many diadems in the house of Favre as frenzied heads, that would be no barrier to the Lord being superior. Her husband meanwhile had gone to Lyons, hoping that the matter would be silently buried. I thought that they should be forced to a confession of the truth by an oath. Corne warned them that he would by no means suffer them to perjure themselves. They not only confessed what we wished, but that they on that day danced at the house of the widow of Balthazar. They were all cast into prison. The Syndic was an illustrious example of moderation; for he publicly spoke against himself and the whole herd so severely that it was unnecessary

---

[2] Contumacy is contempt of the authority of a church court.

to say much to him. He was, however, severely admonished in the Consistory, being deposed from his office until he gave proof of repentance. They say that Perrin has returned from Lyons; whatever he may do he will not escape punishment.

2. Henri was stripped of his office with our consent. . . . Much was said, backwards and forwards, but the result was that he departed loaded with the reproach and odium of all.[3] Being deprived of his ministry he was at the same time thrust into prison, whence however he was liberated in three days. There he was a strenuous patron of the dances, that he might embitter as far as was in his power the hatred towards me of those who were already more than sufficiently alienated from me. But whatever Satan may essay by the like of him, he will afford a striking example. For two things are already matter of public talk, that there is no hope of impunity since even the first people of the city are not spared, and that I show no more favour to friends than to those opposed to me. Perrin with his wife rages in prison; the widow is absolutely furious; the others are silent from confusion and shame.

(c) Calvin's letter to Heinrich Bullinger, 15 June 1555

Calvin wrote this letter shortly after he and his supporters had finally been able to defeat their opponents from among some of Geneva's leading families. His letter to Heinrich Bullinger (1504–75), Zwingli's successor in Zurich and, apart from Calvin, the most prominent reformer in Switzerland, is an attempt to put events in Geneva in the best possible light. The letter sought to justify events in Geneva which had resulted in the execution and exile of many prominent Genevans and clearly caused alarm in other Swiss cities which did not feel comfortable with the form and direction of the Genevan Reformation under Calvin.

1. With the request contained in your last letter that I should give you a distinct and detailed account of our recent riot, I comply the more willingly, because it is very much our own interest that the affair should be put in a proper light among you and your neighbours. For it is perfectly well known that unfavourable reports are spread about concerning us, and that too by the the artifices of those who for their

---

[3] Henri de la Mare, whom Calvin regarded as the most unreliable of his ministerial colleagues, and whom he subjected to a remorseless persecution.

own advantage wish to render us everywhere an object of detestation. You will therefore do us a very acceptable service, if you will take the trouble to have read over to your illustrious senate the substance of what I am about to write to you. Besides, if it is not taxing your patience too much, I should wish a part of my letter to be copied and sent to our brethren the ministers of Schaffhausen, that they too may acquit our city of the defamatory charges brought against it. Here is an exact statement of the whole affair. There were in the senate two unprincipled men and audacious to the highest pitch of impudence, both also in the most abject poverty. The one was named Perrin, the other Vandel. The former being Captain of the city, had attached to his person a rabble of profligate fellows, by holding out to them the prospect of impunity for their crimes. For whatever knavish, riotous or dissolute act was committed throughout the city, to screen the offender from the punishment of the laws, he was ever ready to undertake his defence. The other was his trusty abetter in all these enterprises. A part of the senate, whom they gained in their flatteries, was at their disposal. They forced, through their fears, certain mean creatures to obsequiousness – creatures who were unable to maintain their rank, if not countenanced by these men. Their kinsmen bound to them by the tie of relationship chimed in with them. By all these means their power had been so firmly established in the lesser council, that scarcely anyone dared resist their humour. Certainly all judicial proceedings had for several years been directed at their pleasure, and this sale of justice was a secret to nobody. Not only the city saw this, but even among our neighbours and foreigners, through their fault, we were very ill-spoken of. And loud were the complaints of a great many, because they were frequently molested by the most atrocious acts of villainy. . . . And when formerly if the lesser council had committed any fault, the Two Hundred were accustomed to afford some remedy for its errors and defects, now they have obtruded on the latter body many of the dregs of the population, partly noisy and turbulent young men, partly individuals of flagitious and dissolute lives. And lest they should fail in having a majority, without paying any attention to the established numbers, they have thrust into the crowd whosoever they think will be the most fit for their purposes. In a word, their license was so disorderly, that certain broke forcibly into the council who were not even elected by themselves. That was the faction which, seeing the judgement of the Church alone opposed a barrier to them and checked the unlimited impunity granted to all kinds of vice, in order that every vestige of discipline should disappear, stirred up a contest with us about the right of excommunication, nor ceased to turn everything upside down, until after much contention we obtained that they should at least consult the churches of Switzerland. But as your answer defeated the hopes and wishes of those profligate men, we afterwards enjoyed a little more tranquillity; not however, that after that time, ever on the watch for an opportunity, and shaking off all sense of shame, they did not attempt to break through every restraint. Moreover, tired of being kept in continual agitation, at length we plucked up courage to attack them in our turn, and so force them to take some decisive step. And here in a wonderful manner God disappointed their expectations. For in that promiscuous rabble, we gained the majority of votes.

2. Soon after followed the elections for the syndics in which an unexpected revolution showed itself. Here indeed these depraved men began to vent their fury openly, because they saw themselves forcibly reduced to order. They began then insolently to attempt many things in order to undermine the existing order. Our party always held it sufficient to quash, without any disturbance, or at least to impair their attempts. But because it was perfectly evident that they were gaping after innovations, the council resolved to oppose an excellent remedy to their license. Of the French sojourners who have long lived here, and whose probity was well known, some were adopted into the rank of citizens, to the number of fifty perhaps. The worthless felt how much more secure the party of the good would be rendered by this succour. They therefore thought that they should leave no stone unturned in order to defeat this design. The affair was discussed among them everywhere in the cross-ways, about the taverns, and clandestinely in private houses. When they had drawn over certain persons to their project, they began to make head against us, not only with murmurings but open threats. The prefect of the city was suborned who, accompanied by a numerous but vile and disreputable crew, going up to the town house, signified to the council the danger of its persisting in its scheme. . . . The council replied with dignity that they were introducing no new precedents, but such as had been sanctioned by the immemorial practice of the city; that it was shameful indeed that now both an ancient usage of the city should be abrogated, and those expelled from the rank of citizens who had been so long and so honourably settled in the city. . . . The prefect was sharply reprimanded for having lent his aid to insolent men, in so unjust a cause. At the same time, a decree was voted for convoking the Two Hundred, and when the affair was carried before them, the decision of the lesser council was ratified, and permission granted them, that

henceforth at their good pleasure they might select from the French sojourners those on whom they wished to confer the rights of citizenship.

3. But before the Two Hundred had passed this last decree, the fury of those suddenly broke out more violently, who as is generally the case in desperate situations, had determined to hazard the most perilous extremities. For from a nocturnal riot the state was brought almost to the brink of ruin. The day preceding this event, a dinner scot-free had been given to a number of scoundrels. The ringleaders feasted elsewhere, of whom one whom I have named Vandel took on himself the expenses of the dinner, Perrin those of the supper. . . . Now it is the custom, when the sentries for the night have been stationed at the gates, for the captain of the watch to go his rounds and inspect the posts. This duty each of the senators takes in his turn. When the sentries of that night are posted in the middle of the city, they hear a shout at no great distance. For in the quarter situated behind the booths of the market-place, an individual hit by a stone cried out that he was killed. The guards in the discharge of their functions run up to him. Against them rush out two brothers, boon companions of Perrin and Vandel, men indeed of the lowest class, confectioners by trade, but who supped gratis at the same table. . . . One of those brothers with drawn sword rushes against the syndic. The syndic, relying on the badge of his authority, lays hands upon him, that he may be led away to prison. Several of the faction fly to the aid of their confederate. The lights are put out in the scuffle, and they declare that they will not suffer an excellent comrade to be dragged to prison. Immediately Perrin presents himself, and at first, feigning a desire for pacification, wrenches away the syndic's rod, whispering in his ear, 'It is mine, not yours.' The syndic, though a man of diminutive stature, was not however inclined to yield it, and struggled manfully and stoutly against this violence. In the meantime a cry was everywhere raised along the streets and spread about almost in a moment, that the Frenchmen were in arms, and the city betrayed by treachery; the house of the senator who was captain of the watch that night was crowded with armed men. Emissaries shouted out tumultuously for those whom they knew to be favourable to their party. Perrin, when he was fully persuaded that his band was sufficiently strong, began to vociferate, 'we are in possession of the syndic's rod, for it is in my hands'. To this cry no mark of approbation was returned, and nevertheless he was surrounded by conspirators, so that it was very evident that they were held back by some mysterious suggestion from God. Then troubled by shame and at the same time terrified, he gave ground a little. But

falling in with the other syndic, a relation of his, he wrested from him by force and with great violence his rod of office. The latter called out for help – that his person was assaulted, that the rights of the city were violated. But as the profligate party was much superior in force of arms, on the complaint of the syndic, no one moved a foot to come to his aid. But again a kind of religious scruple held back some of the very worst from chiming in with Perrin. Thus compelled by fear, he privately gave back the rod of office.

4. There was now in arms a numerous body of villains. One cry was heard everywhere: the Frenchmen must be massacred, the city has been betrayed by them. But the Lord in a wonderful manner, watching over his wretched exiles, partly threw them into so deep a sleep that, during these horrid outcries, they were tranquilly reposing in their beds; partly strengthened their hearts so that they were not dismayed by the threats nor fear of danger. What is certain none of them stirred out of the house. And by this signal miraculous interference of God, the rage of the ungodly was defeated because no one presented himself to the conflict. For they had resolved, as was afterwards discovered, if any should essay to defend themselves, after having dispatched a few, they should fall on the others, as if the sedition had originated with us. Nor were the sojourners alone threatened, but some cried out that their protectors should be put to death, and punishment inflicted on the senate. . . .

5. Nevertheless, contrary to our expectations, through divine interposition this tempest gradually blew over. Two days after, it was decreed that an enquiry should be set on foot respecting this public outrage. The council having spent three days in summoning witnesses, that no one might say that he was crushed under false pretences, call together the Two Hundred. While the evidence is being taken, among the other judges were seated even those who had conspired. According as any of these appeared chargeable with guilt, or violently suspected of doubtful conduct, they were ordered to leave the court, as it was impossible they could be sufficiently impartial to pronounce a proper sentence. But Perrin, seeing his crime detected made his escape with three others. . . . All disturbances have been appeased since their departure. The mist which they had spread over affairs has been dissipated; the laws have recovered their vigour; tranquillity has been restored to the city.

2.12

Marie Dentière's letter to Queen Marguerite of Navarre, 1539

C. Lindberg (ed.), *The European Reformation Sourcebook*, Oxford: Blackwell, 2000, pp. 276–7. Paragraph numbers added.

Marie Dentière (c. 1495–1561) had been an Augustinian prioress in Tournai when in 1521 she had become an evangelical and left her nunnery for Strasburg where she later married a French evangelical preacher, Antoine Froment (1509–81). Together they travelled to Geneva in 1535. Marie Dentière became a firm supporter of Farel and Calvin and wrote a chronicle of the early Reformation in Geneva. Her letter to Queen Marguerite was written on the request of the queen who wanted to know the reasons for the expulsion of the reformers from Geneva in 1538. Marie Dentière is the only known woman to have written in defence of Calvin and Farel and the Genevan Reformation. This passage articulates her defence of women's right to read and interpret the Scriptures and play an active part in the Reformation.

1. I ask, didn't Jesus die just as much for the poor illiterates and the idiots as for the shaven, tonsured, and mighty lords? Did he only say. 'Go, preach my Gospel to the wise lords and grand doctors?' Did he not say, 'To all?' Do we have two Gospels, one for men and the other for women? . . . For we ought not, any more than men, hide and bury within the earth that which God has . . . revealed to us women? [sic]

2. Although it is not permitted to us [women] to preach in public assemblies and churches, it is nevertheless not forbidden to write and admonish one another, in all love. Not only for you, my Lady [Marguerite], have I wished to write this letter, but also to give courage to other women held in captivity, in order that they may not all fear being exiled from their country, relatives and friends, like myself, for the word of God . . . that they may from now on not be tormented and afflicted in themselves but rather rejoicing, consoled, and excited to follow the truth, which is the gospel of Jesus Christ. Till now this gospel has been hidden so that one did not dare to say a word about it, and it seemed that women should read and understand nothing in the holy writings. This is the principal cause, my Lady, which moved

me to write you, hoping in God that in the future women will not be so much despised as in the past. . . . throughout all the world.

3. If God then has given graces to some good women, revealing to them by his Holy Scriptures something holy and good, will they not dare to write, speak, or declare it one to another? . . . Ah! It would be too audacious to wish to stop them from doing it. As for us, it would be too foolish to hide the talent which God has given us.

2.13

Act in restraint of appeals to Rome, 1533

G.R. Elton (ed.) (1960) *The Tudor Constitution*, Cambridge: Cambridge University Press, pp. 344–9.

The preamble of an Act of Parliament (Statute) lays out the rationale for the new legislation. Here an appeal is made to the authority of precedent: England has always been an independent empire and previous monarchs and Parliaments have passed legislation to curb the role of the papacy as a court of appeal. This new legislation seeks to address 'inconveniences and dangers' caused by loopholes in existing laws.

An act that the appeals in such cases as have been used to be pursued to the see of Rome shall not be from henceforth had nor used but within this realm.

Where by divers sundry old authentic histories and chronicles it is manifestly declared and expressed that this realm of England is an empire, and so hath been accepted in the world, governed by one supreme head and king having the dignity and royal estate of the imperial crown of the same, unto whom a body politic, compact of all sorts and degrees of people divided in terms and by names of spiritualty[1] and temporalty,[2] be bounded and owe to bear next to God a natural and humble obedience; he being also institute and furnished by the goodness and sufferance of Almighty God with plenary, whole and entire power, pre-eminence, authority, prerogative and jurisdiction to render and yield justice and final determination to all manner

---

[1] Spirituality – the religious/ecclesiastical part of the realm.
[2] Temporality – the secular part of the realm.

of folk resiants [residents?] or subjects within this realm, in all causes, matters, debates and contentions happening to occur, insurge or begin within the limits thereof, without restraint or provocation to any foreign princes or potentates of the world: the body spiritual whereof having power when any cause of the law divine happened to come in question or of spiritual learning, then it was declared, interpreted and showed by that part of the said body politic called the spiritualty, now being usually called the English Church, which always hath been reputed and also found of that sort that both for knowledge, integrity and sufficiency of number, it hath been always thought and is also at this hour sufficient and meet of itself, without the intermeddling of any exterior person or persons, to declare and determine all such doubts and to administer all such offices and duties as to their rooms spiritual doth appertain. For the due administration whereof and to keep them from corruption and sinister affection the King's most noble progenitors, and the antecessors[3] of the nobles of this realm, have sufficiently endowed the said Church both with honour and possession. And the laws temporal for trial of property of lands and goods, and for the conservation of the people of this realm in unity and peace . . . was and yet is administered, adjudged and executed by sundry judges and administers of the other part of the said body politic called the temporalty, and both their authorities and jurisdictions do conjoin together in the due administration of justice the one to help the other. And whereas the King his most noble progenitors, and the Nobility and Commons of this said realm, at divers and sundry Parliaments as well in the time of King Edward I,[4] Edward III,[5] Richard II,[6] Henry IV[7], and other noble kings of the realm, made sundry ordinances, laws, statutes and provisions for the entire and sure conservation of the prerogatives, liberties and pre-eminences of the said imperial crown of this realm, and of the jurisdictions spiritual and temporal of the same, to keep it from the annoyance as well of the see of Rome as from the authority of other foreign potentates attempting the diminution or violation thereof [. . .]. And not withstanding the said

---

[3] Predecessors.

[4] The Statute of Carlisle was an act against abuse of papal patronage (35 Edward I, st.l).

[5] First Statute of Provisors, 1351 (25 Edward III, st.4) and the First Statute of Praemunire, 1353 (27 Edward III, st.l).

[6] Second Statute of Provisors, 1390 (13 Richard II, st.2) and the Second Statute of Praemunire, 1393 (16 Richard II, c.5).

[7] The Second Statute of Praemunire was confirmed and extended by 2 Henry IV, c.3 (1401) and 9 Henry IV, c.8 (1408).

good statutes and ordinances made in the time of the King's most noble progenitors in preservation of the authority and prerogative of the said imperial crown . . . yet nevertheless . . . divers and sundry inconveniences and dangers not provided for plainly by the said former acts, statutes and ordinances have risen and sprung by reason of appeals sued out of this realm to the see of Rome, in causes testamentary, causes of matrimony and divorces, rights of tithes, oblations [. . . etc.] to the great inquietation, vexation, trouble, costs and charges of the King's Highness and many of his subjects and resiants in this his realm, but also to the great delay and let to the true and speedy determination of the said causes, for so much as the parties appealing to the said court of Rome most commonly do the same for the delay of justice: and forasmuch as the great distance of way is so far out of this realm. So that the necessary proofs nor the true knowledge of the cause can neither there be so well known nor the witnesses there so well examined as within this realm, so that the parties grieved by means of the said appeals be most times without remedy. In consideration whereof the King's Highness, his Nobles and Commons . . . doth therefore by his royal assent and by the assent of the Lords spiritual and temporal and the Commons in this present Parliament assembled, and by authority of the same, establish and ordain that all causes testamentary, causes of matrimony and divorces, rights of tithes, oblations . . . shall be from henceforth heard, examined, discussed, clearly finally and definitely adjudged and determined, within the King's jurisdiction and authority and not elsewhere, in such courts spiritual and temporal of the same as the natures, conditions and qualities of the causes and matters aforesaid in contention or hereafter happening in contention shall require, without having any respect to any custom use or suffereance in hindrance . . . ; any foreign inhibitions, appeals, sentences, summons, citations, suspensions, interdictions, excommunications, restraints, judgements, or any other process or impediments . . . from the see of Rome or any other foreign courts or potentates of the world

[. . .]

II. And it is further enacted . . . that if any person or persons . . . do attempt, move, purchase or procure, from or to the see of Rome or from or to any other foreign court or courts out of this realm, any manner foreign process, inhibitions, appeals, sentences, summons . . . excommunications, restraints or judgements . . . or execute any of the same . . . that then every person or persons so doing, and their . . . abettors . . . shall incur and run in the same pains, penalties and forfeitures ordained and provided by the statute of provision

2.3 Coronation of Henry VIII and Katherine of Aragon, 1509, depicting the couple's heraldic badges, the Tudor Rose (Henry) and the pomegranate (Katherine).

and praemunire made in the sixteenth year of the reign of . . . King Richard II.

2.14
Acts of Supremacy, 1534 and 1559

G.R. Elton (ed.) (1960) *The Tudor Constitution*, Cambridge: Cambridge University Press, pp. 356, 363–8. Additional editing by Rosemary O'Day.

These two extracts from the 1534 and 1559 Acts of Supremacy seem at first glance to show that both Henry VIII (1491–1547) and his daughter Elizabeth (1533–1603) were made supreme heads of the Church of England. Closer inspection will reveal subtle differences, some of which reflect the passage of time and changed circumstances in Elizabeth's reign. The inclusion in the Elizabethan Act of an oath of supremacy, for example, indicates the anticipated resistance of leading church and lay people to the new regime which was replacing that of the Catholic Mary.

(a) Henrican Act, 1534

An Act concerning the King's Highness to be Supreme Head of the Church of England and to have authority to reform and redress all errors, heresies and abuses in the same.

Albeit the King's Majesty justly and rightfully is and oweth to be the supreme head of the Church of England, and so is recognised by the clergy of this realm in their Convocations; yet nevertheless for corroboration and confirmation thereof, and for increase of virtue in Christ's religion within this realm of England, and to repress and extirp all errors, heresies and other enormities and abuses heretofore used in the same, Be it enacted by authority of this present Parliament that the King our sovereign lord, his heirs and successors kings of this realm, shall be taken, accepted and reputed the only supreme head in earth of the Church of England called Anglicana Ecclesia, and shall have and enjoy annexed and united to the imperial crown of this realm as well the title and style thereof, as all honours, dignities, preeminences, jurisdictions, privileges, authorities . . . to the said dignity of supreme head of the same Church belonging and appertaining. And that our said sovereign lord, his heirs and successors . . . shall have full power and authority from time to time to visit, repress, redress, reform, order, correct, restrain and amend all such errors, heresies, abuses, offences, [. . .] whatsoever they be, which by any manner spiritual authority or jurisdiction ought or may lawfully be reformed, ordered, corrected, restrained or amended, most to the pleasure of Almighty God, the increase of virtue in Christ's religion, and for the conservation of the peace, unity and tranquillity of this realm: any usage, custom, foreign laws, foreign authority, prescription or any other things to the contrary hereof notwithstanding.

(b) Elizabethan Act and Oath of Supremacy, 1559

An Act restoring to the Crown the ancient jurisdiction over the state ecclesiastical and spiritual, and abolishing all foreign power repugnant to the same.

[. . .]

And for the better observation [of this act] . . . all and every arch-bishop, bishop, and all and every other ecclesiastical person [. . .] and all and every temporal judge, justicer, mayor, and other lay or temporal officer or minister, and every other person having your Highness' fee or wages within this realm or any your Highness' dominions, shall make, take and receive a corporal oath upon the evangelist,[1] [. . .] according to the tenor and effect here following, that is to say:

I, A.B., do utterly testify and declare in my conscience that the Queen's Highness is the only supreme governor of this realm and of all other her Highness' dominions and countries, as well in all spiritual or ecclesiastical things or causes as temporal, and that no foreign prince, person, prelate, state or potentate hath or ought to have any jurisdiction, power, superiority, pre-eminence or authority ecclesiasti-cal or spiritual within this realm, and therefore I do utterly renounce and forsake all foreign jurisdictions, powers, superiorities, and author-ities, and do promise that from henceforth I shall bear faith and true allegiance to the Queen's Highness, her heirs and lawful successors, and to my power shall assist and defend all jurisdictions, pre-eminences, privileges and authorities granted or belonging to the Queen's Highness, her heirs and successors, or united and annexed to the imperial crown of this realm: so help me God and by the contents of this Book.

2.15
Preambles to wills as indicators of religious belief

In the preamble (first part) of a will the testator made a declara-tion of what they wished to do with their soul's part (or spiritual estate). For some individuals, this implied a declaration of their faith and, in traditional wills, the care they wished to be given to their souls after death. Not all wills, by any means, contain this amount of detail. It became common for lay people to employ lawyers, scriveners and local clergy to write their wills for them and declarations of faith etc. could reflect the views of these

[1] i.e., sworn on the Gospel of John.

professional will-writers rather than of the testator, although one would expect that a testator would object strongly if they disagreed with the preamble.

(a) Will of Joan Brytten, 1540

W.J. Sheils (1989) *The English Reformation, 1530–1570*, Longman Seminar Studies in History, London: Longman, pp. 90–1. Modernised and annotated by Rosemary O'Day.[1]

I Joan Brytten of the parish of St Michael in Woodstreet,[2] sick in my body, bequeath my soul unto Almighty God and unto our blessed Lady[3] and unto all the holy company in heaven, and my body to be buried within the parish church of Saint Gregory's by Paul's[4] under a stone there prepared all ready for me. I bequeath unto the high altar of Saint Michael's for my tithes[5] negligent forgotten 8d. I will have at the time of my burial half a trental of masses 5s 4d.[6] I will have 6 priests besides the parson, the clerk and the sexton[7] and bequeath them for their labour 4s 10d. I will have a fore noon's knell 20d.[8] The peels 6d.[9] I will have 5 lib[10] tapers the price 15d and 5 children to bear them 10d and 200 pound tapers and the children to bear them before the cross 10d.[11] I will that 4s be delivered in obolos bread at the time of my burial, also

---

[1] Entire will printed in I. Darlington (ed.) (1967) *London Consistory Court Wills, 1492–1547*, London: London Record Society, p. 69.

[2] Single women and widows were allowed to make wills; married women might do so only with the explicit consent of their husbands.

[3] Virgin Mary, the mother of Jesus Christ.

[4] Near St Paul's Cathedral.

[5] Lay people had to pay their parson a tenth of all their produce, known as the tithe. Tithes were also levied on wages etc. After the reformation those lay people who had purchased church property (monasteries and the livings they owned) also purchased the right to collect the great tithes belonging to the property.

[6] A trental was thirty masses, so she bequeaths 15 masses. These masses said at the time of burial would absolve the deceased person of parts of their sin, thus reducing the amount of time each spent in purgatory.

[7] Before the Reformation the acolyte and the parish clerk and the sexton were in minor holy orders, while the priests, deacons and subdeacons were in major holy orders. All were distinguished from the laity by the tonsure (a shaved patch on the top of the head) and by the manner and colour of their dress.

[8] A mournful toll of the church bell.

[9] A peal of the bells. Churches often had more than one bell but change ringing of the kind known today was a later development.

[10] A reference to the weight of the tapers, 5 pounds weight.

[11] During the processional.

I will that a dinner be made for them that be out in trust of my will the day of my burial, the price 3s 4d. Also I will at my death a[n] inventory of my plate and of all the rest of my goods be made and so appraised and sold and then when the charges of my burying and my bequests paid the rest of my goods I will that a priest shall sing for my soul, my master Milard's soul, his wife's soul and all Christian souls within the church of St Gregory's in London for one half year,[12] and in the church of St Michael in Woodstreet for the space of one quarter of a year or more if the goods will extend [to such a payment].

(b) Will of Edward Hoppaye of Halifax, 1548

W.J. Sheils (1989) *The English Reformation, 1530–1570,* Longman Seminar Studies in History, London: Longman, p. 91. Modernised and annotated by Rosemary O'Day.[13]

I believe that my redeemer lives, and that at the last day I shall arise out of the earth and in my flesh shall see my Saviour. This my hope is laid up in my bosom unto the last day, that I and all other faithful shall appear before the majesty seat of God [. . .] and touching the wealth of my soul, the faith that I have taken and rehearsed is sufficient, as I believe, without any other man's work or works.[14] My belief is that there is but one God and one mediator betwixt God and man, which is Jesus Christ, so that I accept none in heaven, neither in earth, to be my mediator betwixt God and me,[15] but he onlie [. . .] and touching the distribution of my goods, my purpose is to bestow them that they may be accepted as the fruits of faith, so that I do not suppose that my merit be by bestowing of them, but my merit is faith in Jesus Christ only, by which faith such works are good according to Christ's words, Matthew 25, 'I was hungry and didst give me meat,' etc. And it follows, 'that ye have done to the least of my brethren, you have done it to me'. A good work makes not a good man, but a good man makes good works. For a righteous man lives by faith. And thus I rest in conscience concerning my faith.

---

[12] These were masses to be sung (probably in a chantry chapel) for the souls of the departed. It was believed that such masses would reduce the time spent by the deceased in purgatory.

[13] Originally published in A.G. Dickens (1959) *Lollards and Protestants in the Diocese of York, 1509–1558,* London: Oxford University Press for the University of Hull, p. 217.

[14] Salvation by faith alone, and not works, including masses for the dead.

[15] Rejection of the mediating role of priests, the Virgin Mary and the Saints.

(c) Will of Richard Wenman of Witney, Oxon, 1533 (abstract)

J. Harvey Bloom (ed.) (1922) *Wayman Wills and Administrations Preserved in the Prerogative Court of Canterbury, 1383–1821*, London: Wallace Gandy, pp. 10–11.

My Soul to almighty God, Jesu my redeemer and saviour, and to our Blessed Lady Saint Mary the Virgin and all the holy company of saints. My body to be buried in the chapel of the most glorious resurrection, set in the parish church of Witney. To the high altar of the same for tithes and offerings forgotten, and that the curate there will have my soul recommended in his devout prayers, 13s 4d. To the Cathedral Church of Lincoln, 12d. Every standing light in the church of Witney, three pounds wax, ready made, there to burn at the time of my . . . funeral service and other festival days as long as they maye thereunto endure. Towards the reparation of the bells in the steeple, 40s. To every of five score poor men and women, 6 yards of cotton of the price of 6d to make a gown. To every of the four orders of priors in Oxford; to pray for my soul, the souls of my father and mother, our benefactors' souls, and all Christian souls, £6 13s 4d.

2.16
Prayer books and the struggle for the church under Edward VI

In the reign of the minor Edward VI (reigned 1537–53), ecclesiastical leaders struggled to establish the identity of the Church, in terms of its ritual and doctrine, and to impose order and discipline upon it by providing instruction or rubric[1] on the practice of clergy and congregation. The two prayer books represent different phases in this process.

---

[1] The headings marked in bold were the rubrics or instructions that were originally printed in red in the Book of Common Prayer.

(a) Extracts from the 1549 edition

The booke of the common praier and administracion of the Sacramentes and other rites and ceremonies of the Churche: after the vse of the Churche of Englande (1549), London: Richard Grafton, unpaginated. Modernised by Rosemary O'Day.

The earlier book grew out of Cranmer's *Order of Communion* of 1548. The 1549 *Book of Common Prayer* belongs to a phase when Cranmer strove to follow a *via media* [middle way]. 'Though wholly in the English language,' wrote A.G. Dickens, 'this . . . remained a masterpiece of compromise.'[2] It did not deny Catholic doctrine on the Eucharist explicitly but its author consciously designed ambiguous phrases so that Protestants could use the services with good conscience. Lutheran doctrine and liturgy were rejected. For the first time all the services of the church were contained within one, English volume, which alone was to be used throughout the kingdom. The communion was modelled on the Catholic Sarum (Salisbury) Use and largely retained the old order of service. Within the book can be detected many remnants of the Catholic services of morning prayer (matins),[3] evensong and holy communion (mass) upon which it was based. The Latin names of the services are retained, the vestments emphasised (paragraph 4), the words of the consecration are marked as sanctified (paragraph 7), and there is a marked reluctance to be too specific about the nature of the sacrament of the mass itself. In the end, references to the 'holy mysteries' and to sacrifice were retained (paragraph 9). However, in the Canon (the long prayer containing the consecration of the bread and wine) the idea of a repeated, placatory sacrifice was replaced by an emphasis on thanksgiving and memorial (paragraphs 7, 8).

The Supper of the Lord and the Holy Communion, commonly called the Mass[4]

[2] A.G. Dickens, *The English Reformation*, London, 1989, p. 243.

[3] Term used in several Protestant denominations to describe morning prayers. Matins in the canonical hours of the medieval Catholic church was the service held in the middle of the night.

[4] This book was authorised as the only service book to be used in churches by the First Edwardian Act of Uniformity of 1549.

1. So many as intend to be partakers of the holy Communion, shall signify their names to the Curate,[5] over night: or else in the morning, after the beginning of Matins, or immediately after.

2. And if any of those be an open and notorious ill liver, so that the congregation by him is offended, or have done any wrong to his neighbours by word or deed: The Curate shall call him, and advertise him,[6] in any wise not to presume to the lord's table, until he have openly declared himself to have truly repented, and amended his former naughty life: that the congregation may therefore be satisfied, which afore were offended: and that he have recompensed the parties, whom he hath done wrong unto, or at least be in full purpose so to do, as soon as he conveniently may.

3. The same order shall the Curate use, with those betwixt whom he perceiveth malice, and hatred to reign, not suffering them to be partakers of the Lord's table, until he knows them to be reconciled.

[. . .]

4. Upon the day and at the time appointed for the ministration of the holy communion, the Priest that shall execute the holy ministry, shall put upon him the vesture appointed for that ministration, that is to say: a white alb plain, with a vestment or cope.[7] And where there be many priests, or deacons, there so many shall be ready to help the priest, in the ministration, as shall be requisite: and shall have upon them likewise the vestures appointed for their ministry, that is to say albs with tunicles.[8] Then shall the clerks sing in English for the office,[9] or *introit* (as they call it), a psalm appointed for that day.

[. . .]

Then the priest, turning him to the altar,[10] shall say or sing, plainly and distinctly, this prayer following:

---

[5] The term curate has various meanings. It was applied generally to any clergymen in charge of a cure of souls – i.e. a parish – whether he be a rector, vicar or perpetual curate. This seems to be the meaning here. It was also, however, applied to an assistant to the parish priest and this is the most common usage in the twenty-first century.

[6] Warn him.

[7] For letters discussing the Elizabethan controversy over clerical robes, the Vestiarian Controversy, see Anthology Document 2.17.

[8] Otherwise known as vestments.

[9] In January 1548 Archbishop Cranmer circulated a questionnaire to the English and Welsh bishops asking their views on vernacular church services. Opinion was very divided with some like Archbishop Holgate of York firmly in favour and others like conservative bishops Tunstall and Bonner arguing for just a few English prayers to instruct and inspire the devotion of the laity.

[10] The word altar, referring to the table on which were set the crucifix, candles and the vessels for communion, had sacrificial overtones.

5. Almighty and everliving God, which by thy holy apostle hast taught us to make prayers and supplications, and to give thanks for all men: We humbly beseech thee most mercifully to receive these our prayers, which we offer unto thy divine majesty, beseeching thee to inspire continually the universal church with the spirit of truth, unity, and concord: And grant that all they that do confess thy holy name, may agree in the truth of thy holy word, and live in unity and Godly love. Specially we beseech thee to save and defend thy servant Edward [VI] our King, that under him we may be godly and quietly governed. And grant unto his whole council, and to all that he put under authority under him, that they may truly and indifferently minister justice, to the punishment of wickedness and vice, and to the maintenance of God's true religion and virtue. Give grace (O heavenly father) to all bishops, pastors, and curates, that they may both by their life[11] and doctrine[12] set forth thy true and lively word, and rightly and duly administer thy holy Sacraments: and to all thy people give thy heavenly grace, that with meek heart and due reverence they may hear and receive thy holy word, truly serving thee in holiness and righteousness all the days of their life: And we ... beseech thee ... to comfort and succour all them which in this transitory life be in trouble, sorrow, need, sickness, or any other adversity. And especially we commend unto thy merciful goodness, this congregation which is here assembled in thy name, to celebrate the commemoration of the most glorious death of thy son ... we do give unto thee most high praise ... for the wonderful grace and virtue, declared in all thy saints [. . .] And chiefly in the glorious and most blessed virgin Mary,[13] mother of thy son Jesu Christ our Lord and God, and in the holy Patriarchs, Prophets, Apostles and Martyrs, whose examples [. . .] grant us to follow.

6. We commend unto thy mercy ... all other thy servants, which are departed hence from us, with the sign of faith, and now do rest in the sleep of peace: Grant unto them, we beseech thee, thy mercy, and everlasting peace,[14] and that, at the day of general resurrection,[15] we and all they which be of the mystical body of thy son, may altogether be set on his right hand, and hear ... his most joyful voice, Come unto me, O ye that be blessed of my father, and possess the kingdom [. . .]. Grant this, O father, for Jesus Christ's sake, our only mediator and advocate.

[11] Example.

[12] Teaching.

[13] Protestants found offensive the retention of this prayer.

[14] The prayer for the dead also offended Protestants.

[15] Rising from the dead on the Last Day.

7. O God [. . .] which of they tender mercy didst give thine only son Jesu Christ to suffer death upon the cross for our redemption, who made there (by his one oblation once offered) a full, perfect and sufficient sacrifice, oblation, and satisfaction, for the sins of the whole world, and did institute, and in his holy Gospel commanded us to celebrate a perpetual memory of that his precious death, until his coming again: Hear us . . . and with thy holy spirit and word, vouchsafe to blX[16]ess and sancXtify these thy gifts, and creatures of bread and wine, that they may be unto us the body and blood of thy most dearly beloved son Jesus Christ. Who in the same night that he was betrayed, took bread, and when he had blessed, and given thanks, he brake it, and gave it to his disciples, saying: 'Take, eat, this is my body which is given for you, do this in remembrance of me.'

Here the priest must take the bread into his hands:

8. Likewise after supper he took the cup, and when he had given thanks, he gave it to them, saying, 'drink ye all of this, for this is my blood of the new Testament, which is shed for you and for many, for remission of sins: do this as oft as you shall drink it, in remembrance of me.

Here the priest shall take the cup into his hands.

These words before rehearsed are to be said, turning still to the altar, without any elevation, or showing the sacrament to the people.[17]

9. Wherefore . . . we thy humble servants do celebrate, and make here before thy divine majesty, with these thy holy gifts, the memorial which thy son hath willed us to make, having in remembrance his blessed passion, mighty resurrection, and glorious ascension . . . entirely desiring thy fatherly goodness, mercifully to accept this our sacrifice of praise and thanksgiving [. . .]. Grant us therefore (gracious lord) so to eat the flesh of thy dear son Jesus Christ, and to drink his blood in these holy mysteries, that we may continually dwell in him, and he in us, that our sinful bodies may be made clean by his body, and our souls washed through his most precious blood.[18] Amen.

10. Then shall the priest first receive the communion in both kinds himself, and next deliver it to other ministers . . . (that they may be ready to help the chief minister), and after to the people.

---

[16] Here is inserted, in the text of the original, a cross.

[17] Thus avoiding any suggestion of adoration or worship of the elements of bread and wine.

[18] Such was the ambiguity of this phraseology that even the Catholic bishop Gardiner declared that he (a firm believer in transubstantiation) was content to use these words.

11. And when he delivereth the sacrament of the body of Christ, he shall say to every one these words:

The body of our Lord Jesus Christ which was given for thee, preserve thy body and soul unto everlasting life.

12. And the minister delivering the sacrament of the blood, and giving every one to drink once and no more, shall say:

The blood of our Lord Jesus Christ which was shed for thee, preserve thy body and soul unto everlasting life.

[. . .]

13. Upon Wednesday and Friday the English Litany shall be said or sung in all places, after such form as is appointed by the King's majesty's Injunctions . . . [there will be no communion unless there be other priests present, but only a collect (set prayer) and blessing.]

[. . .]

14. For avoiding . . . dissension, it is meet that the bread prepared for the communion be made, through all this realm, after one sort and fashion: that is to say, unleavened, and round, as it was afore, but without all manner of print, and something more larger and thicker than it was, so that it may be aptly divided in divers pieces . . . and men must not think less to be received in part than in the whole, but in each of them the whole body of our saviour [. . .].

15. And forasmuch as the pastors and curates . . . shall continually find at their costs and charges . . . sufficient bread and wine for the holy Communion . . . it is therefore ordered, that in recompense of such . . . the parishioners of every parish shall offer every Sunday, . . . the just valour and price of the holy loaf . . . to the use of their pastors and curates [. . .].

16. Also, that the receiving of the Sacrament of the blessed body and blood of Christ, may be most agreeable to the institution thereof, and to the usage of the primitive Church

[. . .]

17. [E]very man and woman to be bound to hear and be at the divine service in the parish church where they be resident, and there with devout prayer, or Godly silence and meditations, to occupy themselves. There to . . . communicate once in the year at the least [. . .]. And whosoever willingly upon no just cause doth absent themselves [or behave badly . . .] upon proof, . . . by the ecclesiastical laws of the realm to be excommunicate, or suffer other punishment [. . .].

18. [A]lthough it be read in ancient writers, that the people . . . received . . . the Sacrament of the body of Christ in their own hands . . . yet forasmuch as they many times conveyed the same secretly away, kept it with them, and diversely abused it to superstition and wickedness: lest any such thing hereafter should be attempted [. . .] it is though convenient the people commonly receive the Sacrament of Christ's body, in their mouths, at the priest's hands.

(b) Extracts from the 1552 edition

The boke of common praier, and [ad]ministracion of the sacramentes, and other rites and ceremonies in the Churche of Englande (1552) London: Richard Grafton, unpaginated. Modernised by Rosemary O'Day.

The Book of Common Prayer of 1552 represents a much more radical and evangelical departure from the traditional services and the mass in particular than did the book of 1549. The word 'mass' itself is never used and matins has been transliterated into morning prayer. An attempt is made to strip the services of practices without scriptural warrant. The medieval vestments are explicitly forbidden; only the surplice is required. The words of the administration of communion have been changed to a form with which Zwingli could hardly have disagreed. Such ceremonial as is retained is included, specifically, to ensure that there is uniformity and order in the church (paragraphs 7–11). The memorial character of the Lord's Supper is emphasised: Christ made one sacrifice on Calvary and this is in no sense repeated in this communion service (paragraph 15). Some rituals and practices are excluded to limit the opportunities for Christians to make magical and superstitious associations (paragraph 22). Where a practice such as kneeling is included (paragraph 16), the text makes it crystal clear (paragraph 23) that this is purely for the sake of order and has no connotations of adoration.

It is interesting that in these two documents historians find evidence not only of the order and doctrine that was now imposed but also of the debates raging within the Edwardian church about what were appropriate ceremonies and teachings. In September 1552, John Knox [c. 1513–72] preached before King Edward against the rubric directing communicants to receive the sacrament kneeling (see paragraph 16). Although copies of the Prayer

Book were already in the press, a hurried amendment was made, known as the Black Rubric (see paragraph 23 below), denying all intention to suggest that the sacrament should be worshipped.

[I] **Preface**[19]

1. There was never any thing by the wit of man so well devised, or so sure established, which [...] hath not been corrupted: as [...] it may plainly appear by the common prayers in the Church commonly called divine service: the first [...] ground whereof... he shall find that the same was not ordained but for a good purpose, and for a great advance of godliness. For they so ordered the matter that all the whole Bible ... should be read over once in the year intending thereby that the clergy ... should ... be stirred up to godliness themselves, and be more able also to exhort other by wholesome doctrine, and to confute them that were adversaries to the truth.... And ... the people ... should continually profit more and more in the knowledge of God.... But these many years past, this godly ... order hath been so altered ... by planting in uncertain stories, legends, responses, verses, vain repetitions, ... that commonly when any book of the Bible was begun, before three or four chapters were read out, all the rest were unread.... And ... whereas Saint Paul would have such language spoken to the people in the Church, as they might understand ... the service in this Church of England ... hath been read in Latin to the people, which they understood not.
[...]
2. [H]ere is set forth such an order, whereby the seem shall be redressed ... here is drawn out a calendar for that purpose which is plain and easy to understand.... here you have an order for prayer (as touching the reading of holy scripture) much agreeable to the mind and purpose of the old fathers.... It is more profitable, because here are left out many things, whereof some be untrue, some uncertain, some vain and superstitious, and is ordained nothing to be read, but the very pure word of God ... and that in such a language and order, as is most easy and plain for the understanding both of the readers and hearers.... Furthermore by this order, the curates shall

---

[19] This prayer book was imposed officially in advance on England and Wales by the Second Edwardian Act of Uniformity of April 1552. The new Prayer Book was to come into use as of November 1552. It was in use for just a few months prior to Edward VI's premature death on 6 July 1553.

need none other books for their public service, but this book, and the Bible: [therefore] . . . the people shall not be at so great charge for books, as in time past.

[. . .]

3. And where heretofore there hath been great diversity in saying and singing in churches within this realm, some following Salisbury use, some of Hereford use, some the use of Bangor, some of York, and some of Lincoln. Now from hence forth, all the whole realm shall have but one use.

[. . .]

4. And for as much as nothing can almost be so plainly set forth, but doubts may rise in the use and practicing of the same [. . .] for the resolution of all doubts concerning the manner how to understand, do and execute the things contained in this book: the parties . . . shall always resort to the bishop of the diocese [. . .]. And if the bishop of the diocese be in any doubt, then may he send . . . unto the Archbishop.

[. . .]

5. And all priests and deacons shall be bound to say daily the morning and evening prayer, either privately or openly, except they be letted[20] by preaching, studying of divinity, or by some other urgent cause.

6. And the curate that ministreth in every parish church or chapel . . . shall say the say in the parish Church or chapel . . . and shall toll a bell thereto, a convenient time before he begin, that such as be disposed may come to hear God's word, and to pray with him.

[II] **Of Ceremonies**
Why some be abolished, and some retained.

7. Of such ceremonies as be used in the church, and have had their beginning by the institution of man: some at the first were of Godly intent and purpose devised, and yet at length turned to vanity and superstition: some entered into the church by indiscreet devotion, and such a zeal as was without knowledge: and for because they were winked at in the beginning they grew daily to more and more abuses: which not only for their unprofitableness, but also because they have much blinded the people, and obscured the glory of God, are worthy to be cut away and clean rejected. Other there be, which although they have been devised by man, yet it is thought good to reserve them still, as well for a decent order in the church . . . as because they pertain

---

[20] Allowed not to.

to edification; And although the keeping or omitting of a ceremony . . . is but a small thing: yet the wilful and contemptuous
transgression and breaking of a common order and discipline,
is no small offence before God.

[. . .]

8. And whereas as in this our time, the minds of men are so
diverse, that some think it a great matter of conscience to
depart from a piece of the least of their ceremonies (they be so
addicted to their old customs) and again on the other side, some
be so new fangled, that they would innovate all things, and so
do despise the old, that nothing can like[21] them, but that is new:
it was thought expedite,[22] not so much to have respect how to
please and satisfy either of these parties, as how to please God
and profit them both. And yet lest any man should be offended . . . here be certain causes rendered why some of the accustomed ceremonies be put away, and some retained.

[. . .]

9. Some are put away, because the great excess and multitude
of them hath so increased . . . that the burden of them was intol-
erable. . . . and many of them so dark, that they did more confound and darken, than declare and set forth Christ's benefits
unto us.

10. And besides Christ's Gospel is not a ceremonial law (as
much of Moses' law was) but it is a religion to serve God [. . .]
in the freedom of spirit being content only with those ceremonies, which do serve to a decent order and godly discipline, and
such as be apt to stir up the dull mind of man, to the remembrance of his duty to God, by some notable and special signification, whereby he might be edified.

[. . .]

11. [B]ut now as concerning those persons, which peradven-
ture will be offended, for that some of the old ceremonies are
retained still: if they consider, that without some ceremonies it
is not possible to keep any order or quiet discipline in the
church, they shall easily perceive just cause to reform their
judgements [. . .]. Furthermore [. . .] For as those be taken away,
which were most abused, and did burthen men's consciences
without any cause: so the other that remain are retained for a
discipline and order, which (upon just cause) may be altered
and changed, and therefore are not to be esteemed equal with

[21] Please.
[22] Expedient.

God's law. And moreover they be neither dark nor dumb ceremonies: but are so set forth, that every man may understand what they do mean, and to what use they do serve.

[. . .]

[XII] **The order for the administration of the Lord's Supper or Holy Communion.**

12. So many as intend to be partakers of the holy Communion, shall signify their names to the Curate over night, or else in the morning, afore the beginning of morning prayer[23]**, or immediately after.**

[The next two paragraphs are a repetition of clauses 2 and 3 in the Preface of the 1549 book].

[. . .]

13. The table[24] **having at the Communion time a fair white cloth upon it, shall stand in the body of the Church, or in the chancel, where morning prayer and evening prayer be appointed to be said. And the priest standing at the north side of the table, shall say the Lord's Prayer, with this collect following:**

14. Almighty God, unto whom all hearts be open, all desires known, and from whom no secrets are hid . . .

15. Then the priest standing up shall say [. . .]:

Almighty God our heavenly father, which of thy tender mercy didst give thine only son Jesus Christ, to suffer death upon the cross for our redemption, who made there (by his one oblation of himself once offered) a full, perfect and sufficient sacrifice, oblation and satisfaction, for the sins of the whole world, and did institute, and in his holy Gospel command us to continue, a perpetual memory of that his precious death, until his coming again: Hear us . . . and grant that we, receiving these thy creatures of bread and wine, according to thy son our saviour Jesus Christ's holy institution, in remembrance of his death and passion, may be partakers of his most blessed body and blood: who, in the same night that he was betrayed, took bread, and when he had given thanks, he brake it, and gave it to his disciples, saying: Take, eat, this is my body which is given for you. Do this in remembrance of me. Likewise after supper he took the cup, and when he had given thanks, he gave it to them, saying: Drink ye all of this, for this is my blood of the new testament, which is shed for you and for many, for remission of sins: do this as oft as ye shall drink it in remembrance of me.

---

[23] Note that this is no longer called Matins as in the 1549 book.

[24] Note that it is no longer called an altar as in the 1549 book.

16. Then shall the minister first receive the Communion in both kinds himself, and next deliver it to other ministers [. . .] and after to the people in their hands kneeling.[25]

17. And when he delivereth the bread, he shall say:

Take and eat this in remembrance that Christ died for thee, and feed on him in thy heart by faith, with thanksgiving.

18. And the minister that delivereth the cup, shall say:

Drink this in remembrance that Christ's blood was shed for thee, and be thankful.

[. . .]

19. Upon the holy days, if there be no Communion, shall be said all that is appointed at the Communion, until the end of the homily[26]

[. . .]

20. And there shall be no celebration of the Lord's Supper, except there be a good number to communicate with the priest, according to his discretion.[27]

[. . .]

21. And to take away the superstition, which any person hath, or might have in the bread and wine, it shall suffice that the bread be such, as is usual to be eaten at the table with other meats, but the best and purest wheat bread, that conveniently may be gotten. And if any of the bread or wine remain, the curate shall have it to his own use.

22. And note, that every parishioner shall communicate, at the least three times in the year: of which Easter to be one: and shall also receive the Sacraments, and other rites, according to the order in this book appointed. And yearly, at Easter, every parishioner shall reckon with his Parson, Vicar or Curate . . . and pay to them . . . all ecclesiastical duties, accustomably due,[28] **then and at that time to be paid.**

23. [. . .] Whereas it is ordained in the book of common prayer, in the administration of the Lord's Supper, that the communicants kneeling should receive the holy communion: which thing being well meant, for a signification of the humble and grateful acknowledging of the benefit of Christ, given unto worthy

---

[25] This insistence that communicants should kneel to receive the sacrament of the body was contentious.

[26] Homilies were authorised printed sermons.

[27] This was a reinforcement of the view that the communion was not a repeat of Christ's sacrifice but rather an act of remembrance in fellowship.

[28] Customarily.

receiver, and to avoid the prophanation and disorder, which . . . might else ensure: Lest yet the same kneeling might be thought or taken otherwise, we do declare that it is not meant thereby, that any adoration is done, or ought to be done unto the sacramental bread or wine there bodily received, or unto any real and essential presence there being of Christ's natural flesh and blood. For as concerning the sacramental bread and wine, they remain still in their very natural substances, and therefore may not be adored, for that were idolatry to be abhorred of all faithful Christians.[29] And as concerning the natural body and blood of our saviour Christ, they are in heaven and not here. For it is against the truth of Christ's true natural body, to be in more places than in one, at one time.

2.17
Zurich letters: correspondence between leaders of the early Elizabethan church and continental churchmen, 1559–65

H. Robinson (ed.) (1842–5) *The Zurich Letters, comprising the correspondence of several English bishops and others, with some of the Helvetian reformers, during the early part of the reign of Queen Elizabeth*, ed. H. Robinson, Cambridge: Cambridge University Press for the Parker Society, vol. 1 (1842) pp. 52–9, 63–5, 72–5, 133–4, 153–5, 168–71; vol. 2 (1845) pp. 38–41.

Many evangelical English clergymen had gone into exile in Europe during Mary's reign, and they were heavily influenced by continental reformers. When the exiles returned to England at Elizabeth's accession, they kept in close contact with European leaders, such as Peter Martyr,[1] Heinrich Bullinger[2] and Martin

---

[29] This is a denial of the doctrine of transubstantiation.

[1] Peter Martyr (Pietro Martire Vermigli 1499–1562), a former Augustinian who lived in England between 1547 and 1553. From 1548 he was Regius Professor of Divinity at Oxford. At the time of this correspondence he was professor of Hebrew at Zurich.

[2] Heinrich (Henry) Bullinger (1504–75) had succeeded Zwingli as leader of the church in Zurich and was highly regarded as a mediator in the great quarrels that broke out within and between the different reformed churches.

Bucer,[3] continually informed them of developments in both England and Scotland, and deferred to them for their opinions on the acceptability of various elements in the Elizabethan settlement. John Jewel[4] was among those who agitated for the return of Peter Martyr to his old post at Oxford.

These letters shed light on the nature of the relationship between the early Elizabethan church of England and the continental reformed churches, and also provide information about the imposition of the Elizabethan settlement and the pace of reform. Several former exiles, including Jewel, served on a royal commission in the summer and autumn of 1559 to root out what they described as 'popery' and 'superstition'. Elizabeth's continued use of the crucifix in the Chapel Royal made radical evangelicals despair of thorough reformation. Some, like Thomas Sampson[5], refused to become bishops in Elizabeth's church.

One of the most serious religious controversies of Elizabeth's reign centred on her insistence that there be uniformity of clerical dress.[6] The most radical English Protestant churchmen had always objected to wearing the surplice and also the cope, on the grounds that they were associated with popery and idolatry and made an unwelcome division between Christians, that is, between clergy and laity. In Lent 1565 Bishop Grindal[7] of London, reluctantly bade his clergy attend a fashion show at which a clerical mannequin modelled the correct ordinary costume of surplice and cap rather than the Genevan gown. Thomas Sampson and Laurence Humphrey[8] asked for the opinions of Martyr and Bullinger regarding the obligation to obey such royal orders. As Grindal's letter makes clear, Bullinger came down on the side of the bishops.

---

[3] Martin Bucer (1491–1551) a former Dominican, Bucer lived in England from 1549 to his death in 1551. He was Regius Professor of Divinity at Cambridge.

[4] John Jewel (1522–71), bishop of Salisbury, 1559–71. Jewel is best known for his important defence of the Anglican Church, *Apologia Ecclesiae Anglicanae*, of 1562, in which he accused the Roman Church of innovation.

[5] Thomas Sampson (1517–89), Dean of Christ Church, Oxford, 1559, was deprived of his living for refusal to wear vestments and follow ceremonial in 1565.

[6] A clause in the Act of Uniformity of 1559 restored clerical vestments, including copes, as they had been at the start of Edward VI's reign.

[7] Edmund Grindal (?1519–83), bishop of London, 1558–76, and archbishop of Canterbury, 1576–83. He refused to obey Elizabeth I's orders to suppress prophesyings and was suspended from office from 1577–82.

[8] Laurence Humphrey (1527–90), President of Magdalen College, Oxford, was likewise deprived in 1565.

(a) John Jewel to Peter Martyr, 5 November 1559

I have at last returned to London with a body worn out by a most fatiguing journey. You probably supposed me dead, because I did not write: meanwhile I was kept away three whole months by this very tedious and troublesome commission [. . .].

But what, you will say, has been done after all by this commission of yours? Receive then in one word, what it took me a long time to investigate. We found every where the people sufficiently well disposed towards religion, and even in those quarters where we expected most difficulty. It is however hardly credible what a harvest, or rather what a wilderness of superstition had sprung up in the darkness of the Marian times. We found in all places votive relics of saints, nails with which the infatuated people dreamed that Christ had been pierced, and I know not what small fragments of the sacred cross. The number of witches and sorceresses had everywhere become enormous. The cathedral churches were nothing else but dens of thieves, or worse [. . .]. If inveterate obstinacy was found any where, it was altogether among the priests, those especially who had once been on our side. [. . .] But let them make what disturbance they please; we have in the mean time disturbed them from their rank and office [. . .].[9]

(b) John Jewel to Peter Martyr, 16 November 1559

Religion among us is in the same state which I have often described to you before. The doctrine is every where most pure; but as to ceremonies and maskings, there is a little too much foolery. That little silver cross, of ill-omened origin, still maintains its place in the queen's chapel. Wretched me! This thing will soon be drawn into a precedent. There was at one time some hope of its being removed; and we all of us diligently exerted ourselves, and still continue to do, that it might be so. But as far as I can perceive, it is now a hopeless case [. . .]. The slow-paced horses retard the chariot. Cecil[10] favours our cause most ardently. The bishops are as yet only marked out [for promotion], and their estates are in the mean time gloriously swelling the exchequer. Both our universities, and that especially which you heretofore culti-

---

[9] In some cases, over half the clergy of cathedral chapters refused to take the Oath of Supremacy and Uniformity.

[10] William Cecil (1520–98), later Lord Burghley. He was at this time Secretary of State, an MP and also Chancellor of Cambridge University.

vated with so much learning and success, are now lying in a most wretched state of disorder, without piety, without religion, without a teacher, without any hope of revival.

(c) Thomas Sampson to Peter Martyr, 6 January 1560

I implore you therefore . . . to pray God most earnestly on our behalf. Contend for this, for this I say, that the truth of the gospel may be neither obscured nor overturned in England.

[. . .]

The consecration of some bishops has already taken place [. . .]. Dr Parker,[11] of Canterbury, Cox,[12] of Ely, Grindal, of London, Sandys,[13] of Worcester . . . Bentham of Coventry,[14] and your friend Jewel of Salisbury, will follow shortly [. . .]. Let others be bishops; as to myself, I will either undertake the office of a preacher, or none at all.

[. . .]

Oh! My father, what can I hope for, when the ministry of the word is banished from court? While the crucifix is allowed, with lights burning before it? The altars indeed are removed, and images also throughout the kingdom; the crucifix and candles are retained at court alone [. . .]. What can I hope, when three of our lately appointed bishops are to officiate at the table of the lord, one as priest, another as deacon, and a third as subdeacon, before the image of the crucifix . . . with candles, and habited in the golden vestments of the papacy; and are thus to celebrate the Lord's supper without any sermon? What hope is there of any good, when our party are disposed to look for religion in these dumb remnants of idolatry, and not from the preaching of the lively word of God?

[. . .]

I will propose this single question for your resolution . . . whether the image of the crucifix, placed on the table of the lord with lighted candles, is to be regarded as a thing indifferent; and if it is not so considered, but as an unlawful and wicked practice, then, I ask, suppose the queen should enjoin all the bishops and clergy, either to admit this image together with the candles into their churches, or to

---

[11] Matthew Parker (1504–75), archbishop of Canterbury. Parker was one of the few early Elizabethan bishops not to have been in exile during Mary's reign, although he had lived in hiding.

[12] Richard Cox (1500–81), bishop of Ely. He had once been Edward VI's tutor. He had gone into exile during Mary's reign, chiefly in Frankfurt.

[13] Edwin Sandys (d. 1571), bishop of Worcester, 1559–71.

[14] See headnote to Document 2.18.

retire from the ministry of the word, what should be our conduct in this case? Should we not rather quit the ministry of the word and sacraments, than that these relics . . . should be admitted? Certain of our friends . . . appear . . . inclined to regard these things as matters of indifference [. . .]. I am altogether of opinion, that should this be enjoined, we ought rather to suffer deprivation . . . what is the opinion of you all, I mean yourself, Bullinger and Bernadine. His authority, I know, has very great weight with the Queen . . . she is indeed a child of God. But she has yet great need of such advisers as himself.

(d) Peter Martyr to Thomas Sampson, 1 February 1560, from Zurich

I come to the subjects upon which you require information. In the first place, I exhort you, by reason of the great want of ministers in your country, not to withdraw yourself from the function offered you: for if you, who are as it were pillars, shall decline taking upon yourselves the performance of ecclesiastical offices, not only will the churches be destitute of pastors, but you will give place to wolves and antichrists . . . if you sit at the helm of the church, there is a hope that many things might be corrected.

[. . .]

As to the square cap and external Episcopal habit, I do not think there is need of much dispute, seeing it is unattended by superstition, and in that kingdom especially there may be a political reason for its use. Touching the garments which they call holy . . . I wonder they are so pertinaciously retained. I should wish every thing to be done with the greatest possible simplicity. I think however that if peace could obtain between the churches of Saxony and our own with respect to doctrine, this sort of garments would never make a separation [. . .]. You may therefore use these habits either in preaching, or in the administration of the Lord's supper, provided however you persist in speaking and teaching against the use of them. But I can never recommend any one . . . to have the image of the crucifix upon the table.

(e) Edwin Sandys to Peter Martyr, 1 April 1560

The doctrine of the Eucharist, as yet by God's blessing unimpugned, remains to us . . . pure and inviolate [. . .]. We had not long since a controversy respecting images. The queen's majesty considered it . . . rather for the advantage of the church, that the image of Christ crucified, together with Mary and John, should be placed, as heretofore, in some conspicuous part of the church, where they might more readily be seen by all the people. Some of us thought far otherwise, and more especially as all images of every kind were at our last visitation not only taken down, but also burnt, and that too by public authority; and because the ignorant and superstitious multitude are in the habit of paying adoration to this idol above all others. As to myself, because I was rather vehement in this matter . . . I was very near being deposed from my office [. . .]. But God, in whose hands are the hearts of kings, gave us tranquility instead of a tempest, and delivered the church of England from stumbling blocks of his kind; only the popish vestments remain in our church, I mean the copes;[15] which, however, we hope will not last very long.

(f) Laurence Humphrey to Henry Bullinger, Oxford, 16 August 1563

Health in Christ, and everlasting peace! [. . .].

Respecting the subject of the habits,[16] I wish you would again write me your opinion, either at length, or briefly, or in one word: first, whether that appears to you as indifferent which has been so long established with so much superstition, and both fascinated the minds of the simple with its splendour, and imbued them with an opinion of its religion and sanctity: secondly, whether at the command of the sovereign (the jurisdiction of the pope having been abolished) and for the sake of order, and not of ornament, habits of this kind may be worn in church by pious men, lawfully and with a safe conscience. I am speaking of that round cap and popish surplice,[17] which are now enjoined us, not by the unlawful tyranny of the pope, but by the just and legitimate authority of the queen. To the pure, then, can all these things be pure, and matters of indifference? I ask your reverence to let me know very exactly what is your opinion.

(g) Thomas Sampson to Henry Bullinger, 16 February 1566

Reverend father in Christ, I wrote you a letter six months since, and should have satisfied the wishes of many of my brethren, if . . . I had

---

[15] An ornate embroidered cloak worn by the priest during high mass and other ceremonial occasions.

[16] Clerical costume or uniform.

[17] Possibly the cope is meant. Reformers seemed to be confused concerning the various vestments and when and where they were to be worn.

received an answer from your worthiness. But . . . I am under the necessity of repeating what I before stated.

Our church remains in the same condition as was long since reported to you. For, after the expiration of seven years in the profession of the gospel, there has now been revived the context about habits, in which Cranmer, Ridley, and Hooper, most holy martyrs of Christ, were formerly wont to skirmish.[18] The state of the question, however, is not in all respects the same, but the determination of those in power is more inflexible.

[. . .]

But that you may more readily understand the matter in controversy, I have thought it best to reduce it into certain questions, which are these:

I. Whether a peculiar habit, distinct from that of the laity, were ever assigned to the ministers of the gospel in better times, and whether it ought now to be assigned to them in the reformed church?

II. Whether the prescribing habits of this kind be consistent with ecclesiastical and Christian liberty?

III. Whether the nature of things indifferent admits of coercion; and whether any violence should be offered to the consciences of the many who are not yet persuaded?

IV. Whether any new ceremonies may be instituted, or superadded to what is expressly commanded in the word?

V. Whether it be lawful to revive the Jewish ceremonies respecting the habit of the priesthood, and which were abolished by Christ?

VI. Whether it be expedient to borrow rites from idolaters or heretics, and to transfer such as are especially dedicated to *their* sect and religion to the use of the reformed church?

[. . .]

XII. Whether good pastors, of unblemished life and doctrine, may rightfully be removed from the ministry on account of their non-compliance with such ceremonies?

Here you have, most esteemed Sir, our difficulties. Here many pious men are hesitating; for the sake of whom I again ask . . . you, that . . . you will plainly state your opinion.

---

[18] In 1550, John Hooper (1495/1500–55) had initially refused to be consecrated bishop of Gloucester wearing vestments, and had quarrelled with Archbishop Cranmer (1489–1556) and Bishop Nicholas Ridley (c. 1502–55) over the issue.

(h) Edmund Grindal to Henry Bullinger,
27 August 1566

Health in Christ, most illustrious master Bullinger. Master John Abel gave me the letter from you, addressed to the bishops of Winchester and Norwich in common with myself, together with what you have written on the controversy about the habits [...]. I return you my best thanks, both for manifesting so much interest for our churches, and for acquainting me, a man personally unknown to you, with what has been written to our brethren concerning the matters in dispute.

It is scarcely credible how much this controversy about things of no importance has disturbed our churches, and still, in great measure, continues to do so. Many of the more learned clergy seemed to be on the point of forsaking their ministry. Many of the people also had it in contemplation to withdraw from us, and set up private meetings; but however most of them, through the mercy of the Lord, have now returned to a better mind. Your letter, replete with piety and wisdom, has greatly contributed to this result; for I have taken care that it should be printed, both in Latin and English. Some of the clergy, influenced by your judgment and authority, have relinquished their former intention of deserting their ministry. And many of the laity also have begun to entertain milder sentiments, now that they have understood that our ceremonies were by no means considered by you as unlawful, though you do not yourself adopt them; but of this, before the publication of your letter, no one could have persuaded them. There are nevertheless some, among whom are masters Humphrey and Sampson, and others who still continue in their former opinion. Nothing would be easier than to reconcile them with the queen, if they would be brought to change their mind; but until they do this, we are unable to effect anything with her majesty, irritated as she is by this controversy. We, who are now bishops, on our first return, and before we entered our ministry, contended long and earnestly for the removal of those things that have occasioned the present dispute; but as we were unable to prevail, wither with the queen or the parliament, we judged it best, after a consultation on the subject, not to desert our churches for the sake of a few ceremonies, and those not unlawful in themselves, especially since the pure doctrine of the gospel remained in its integrity and freedom; in which, even to this day ... we most fully agree with your churches, and with the confession you have lately set forth.[19] And we do not regret our resolution; for . . . our churches are enlarged and established, which under other circumstances would have become a prey to the Ecebolians,[20] Lutherans and semi-papists. But these unseasonable contentions about things which . . . are matters of indifference, are so far from edifying, that they disunite the churches, and sow discord among the brethren.

2.18

Copy letter book of Thomas Bentham, bishop of Coventry and Lichfield, 1560s

Aberystwyth, National Library of Wales MS 4919D; extracts published in R. O'Day & J. Berrlatsky (eds.) (1979) *Camden Miscellany XXVII*, London: Royal Historical Society, pp. 113–238. Additional editing and modernisation of spelling by Rosemary O'Day.

Correspondence provides one of the most valuable (but uncommon) sources for the history of the English Reformation in the dioceses and parishes. Thomas Bentham (1513–79) became bishop of the sprawling midland diocese of Coventry and Lichfield in March 1560. He had been in exile in Zurich and Basel for part of Mary I's reign but had returned to England and ministered, at great personal risk, to the secret Protestant congregation in London. His letter book, one of only two surviving Elizabethan episcopal letter books of comparable quality,[1] demonstrates the financial and religious predicament of the bishop and also the image of himself that the bishop wished to portray.[2]

---

[19] Bullinger published his 'Second Helvetic Confession' in 1566.

[20] Ecebolus taught rhetoric to the emperor Julian (known as Julian the apostate) in the fourth century and followed his heresy.

---

[1] Letter books or copy letter books contained either full copies or short abstracts of letters sent. For the other, see Ralph Houlbrooke (ed.) (1975) *The Letter-book of John Parkhurst, Bishop of Norwich, Compiled During the Years 1571–5*, Norwich: Norfolk Record Society, Volume xliii.

[2] For a discussion of Bentham's plight and of other documentation that throws light upon it, see Rosemary O'Day (1972) 'Thomas Bentham: a case study in the problems of the early Elizabethan episcopate', in *Journal of Ecclesiastical History*, XXIII, pp. 135–59.

Item 17: Letter from Bishop Thomas Bentham of Coventry and Lichfield diocese[3] to Mrs Kate Ashley,[4] Woman of the Bed-chamber to Queen Elizabeth 1, 10 Sept 1560

As I have been always bold with you present right worshipful Mistress Ashley, so I have great need of your help being absent. It is so that necessity hath compelled me to write unto the Queen's Highness a rude supplication which I beseech you help to deliver if need shall require or else when it is delivered to speak a good word to prosper it for surely if I had known this much being at London I should hardly have come in to this country, but now, seeing I am in the briars, I must get forth when I may and as I may. In the mean time having need of all good men's help, I pray you speak for me when you see best occasion and most apt time. And although I be not able to deserve it, yet will I heartily pray God to recompense it, to whose blessed protection I commit your worship. Written this xth [tenth] of September 1560 at my poor castle of Eccleshall.

Your good worship's to command.

Item 22: A bill testifying to the good reputation of Elizabeth Thickyns, 28 October 1560[5]

Moved as well by the knowledge and intelligence that we have as also by the honest testimony that Mistress Mary Hales and Mrs Lucy hath given of one Elizabeth Thickyns, with whom she hath been conversant a many of years;[6] being also requested to give our judgement of the said Elizabeth, do judge of her that she is an honest and sober woman and such a one that for her conditions is worthy to be coupled with some honest and discreet mate. In witness whereof we the bishop and justices of peace have set our hands to this bill.

Item 30: Thomas Bentham to Thomas Lever,[7] Archdeacon of Coventry, 4 August 1560

---

[3] This diocese contained four archdeaconries, Coventry (part of Warwickshire), Derby (part of Derbyshire), Salop (Shropshire) and Stafford (Staffordshire).

[4] Katherine Ashley (d. 1565) was the wife of John Ashley, one of the Marian exiles. She was a noted Protestant who had had close association with Elizabeth from her childhood onwards.

[5] The twenty-ninth Royal Injunction of 1559 recognised clerical marriage, but the consent of the diocesan bishop and two JPs, as well as the good will of the woman's parents, kin, or master, was required.

[6] Possibly Elizabeth Thickyns had been in the service of Mrs Lucy of Charlecote, Warwickshire.

[7] Thomas Lever (1521–77) was archdeacon of Coventry from 1560 to his death. He was a noted radical reformer, held in high regard by the returned Marian exiles.

Item to convent [charge] the parson or curate of Solihull for disorder about the communion; last to ride to Salop to preach if he can.

Item 33: Thomas Bentham to Ralph Egerton in London, 5 August 1560
A letter written to my brother Ralph Egerton to, for the forbearing of his money which I do owe him.[8]

Item 43: Thomas Bentham to Ralph Egerton August 1560
Item a letter to my brother Egerton to forbear his money unto I can receive my rents.

Item 49: Thomas Bentham to Thomas Lever at Coventry, 26 August 1560
Item a letter written to Mr Lever to Coventry, concerning his visitation which I would have had deferred one week longer by reason of harvest. As touching the injunctions,[9] I like them well, save the first and 2nd of the last to be more meet for Coventry and such towns than the villages far distant in the country. Moving him to add likewise interrogatories accordingly as the archdeacon of London hath done.[10] But concerning his setting them forth in the name of the archdeacon of Coventry having not yet his mandate and, indeed, I doubt whether it will be prejudice.[11] Last of all I am about my chapel with slow work men but I will make what haste I can.

Item 52: Thomas Bentham to Dr Robert Weston, Chancellor of the diocese,[12] 27 August 1560
Item a letter to Dr Weston in the behalf of William Mansfield for the parsonage of Boyleston[13] void by lapse.[14]

---

[8] Sir Ralph Egerton of Wrinehill, Betley, Staffs (d. 1596) was perhaps Bentham's brother-in-law. He became commissioner-general of the diocese on 18 April 1561 and Bentham recommended him as a JP in 1564.

[9] These were injunctions or orders for his archidiaconal visitation (inspection).

[10] John Mullins, archdeacon of London (d. 1591).

[11] Lever was preacher of St John's, Bablake and his appointment as archdeacon had not yet come through.

[12] Son of John Weston of Lichfield.

[13] A Derbyshire parish which had just thirty-one households in 1563.

[14] To pass to another through neglect or omission. If the landowner or other person entitled to nominate a clergyman to a vacant parsonage (living) failed to do so within a given amount of time, his right to do so became void and the bishop of the diocese then could appoint a parson.

Item 56: Thomas Bentham to James Weston, Registrar of the Diocese,[15] September 1560

Item a letter to James Weston to publish[16] the administration of orders which shall be ministered upon Saint Matthew's day, viz 21 September.[17]

Item 58: Thomas Bentham to Thomas Lever at Coventry, 9 September 1560

After my hearty commendations in the Lord unto you and yours etc. These are to signify unto you that I have appointed the 21st day of this month to give orders upon at Eccleshall,[18] at what time I would have you repair thither with such as you know meet to enter into the ministry. If you could come ii [2] days before I would be glad and then let Pemberton cause the vicar of Coleshill to come also,[19] who as I hear sheweth much stubbornness, wherefore I purpose to talk with him. I intend the same 21st day to ride at after noon towards Shrewsbury and therefore I purpose to despatch betimes. If you can well and conveniently ride with me, I would have your company. Thus leaving other things to your coming, I commit you to God & me to your prayers this 9th of September at Eccleshall 1560.

Your friend to command.

Item 74: Thomas Bentham to Dr Robert Weston, Chancellor, 25 September 1560

Item a letter to Doctor Weston to make process for one John Marchald of London who hath gotten Maud Ashelake with child and is run away because he will not get god fathers to christen it.

Item 78: Thomas Bentham to Ralph Egerton at London, 2 October 1560

[. . .] so shortly as I can gather up my rents, I will send you some money, by the grace of God. In the mean time, I pray you put none of the Bibles nor psalm books away for I would have them all, and rather more than fewer, and I would have them bound as handsomely as may in paste, with some golden letters. Further I thank you for paying of Philip Nicholls for my horse's grass, which you shall have

---

[15] James Weston (d. 1589) was brother of the Chancellor Robert Weston.

[16] Advertising a forthcoming ordination in local churches.

[17] Ordination of priests and deacons by the bishop took place on given days during the church's year.

[18] The episcopal palace.

[19] John Fenton, vicar of Coleshill (d. 1566).

again with thanks. At the talk of money I have not above £5 in my house, and that is not now increased. I hear say that I am much slandered of negligence, coldness and weakness, with many other grievous faults, whereunto I say nothing, but wish them that slander me if they would do more and better in my place. What they be I know not but I believe they never felt such a burden as I am compelled to bear daily. Being so many ways vexed as I am and having so little help and comfort as I find, no marvel if I satisfy not all men's expectation, for indeed I do not content myself . . . Written this second of October at my poor and cold castle of Eccleshall . . . your friend most assuredly to command.

Item 89: Thomas Bentham to Henry Techoo,[20] vicar of Montford, Shropshire, 4 October 1560

Item a letter to Sir Henry Techoo vicar of Manford to come and answer why he serveth not his cure as he ought to do and why he hath hid 4 of their images with their cases or tabernacles which I have charged him to bring with him to be some part of his satisfaction.

Item 101: Thomas Bentham to George Torperley, Shropshire, 12 October 1560

For as much as I do plainly understand by experience of my self in many places made that the most part of churches within this part of my diocese hath not only yet their altars standing but also their images reserved and conveyed away contrary to the Queen's Majesty's injunctions,[21] hoping and looking for a new day as may be thereby conjectured. Which thing ought neither to enter into any true Christian or faithful subject's heart. These are to will you to take such pains as to go, together with my summoner, to those churches which be nigh unto you and call for their images and such books as the Queen's injunctions doth appoint. And in case any man shall either contentiously trouble you or wilfully resist you in this doing, take his name that he may be presented unto me with convenient speed and I shall take order therein.

[. . .]

Item 102: Thomas Bentham to George Lee of Shrewsbury,[22] 12 October 1560

---

[20] Techoo had been deprived, for marrying, during Mary I's reign (London, British Library, Harley MS.421 fo.59).

[21] Royal Injunctions, 1559.

[22] Possibly bailiff of Shrewsbury.

Item a letter to Mr George Lee of Shrewsbury signifying that upon hope I am contented to defer the correction of Sir Henry Techoo, how be it I can not suffer those that bear 2 faces in one hood, to marry and love images etc.[23]

Item 109: Thomas Bentham to the Dean and Chapter of Lichfield, 23 October 1560

Item a letter to the dean and chapter concerning the reformation of Eccleshall's church,[24] both to examine the churchwardens of their oath taken at Lichfield and also of the register which they should keep according to law, of marriages, christenings and burials.

Item 137: Thomas Bentham to James Weston, Registrar, 15 November 1560

Item a letter to James Weston . . . to help him to some process for his tenths, so much as law will bear, for because I use so much softness, it maketh the proud and peevish papists stout and bold, but I must begin to traverse with them and purpose, God willing, to do with the proudest of them.

[. . .]

Item 177: Thomas Bentham, from London, to Thomas Lever, Archdeacon of Coventry, 17 February 1561

After my hearty commendations in our Lord Jesus etc. these may be to signify that as I do perceive the godly zeal and affection of your flock daily to increase, so I pray unto almighty God that in such godliness they may not only be fervent but also constant to the end. As you have moved me to make haste and dispatch my business: truly my affection and conscience towards my charge moveth me no less, but my state is so troublesome and my charges so great every way that I know not how or where with I shall live when I come. Although I have nothing here to live upon, yet through my acquaintance in London I can now and then borrow something to help me, which in the country I can not do.

[. . .]

Item 198: Thomas Bentham to Matthew Parker, archbishop of Canterbury, 11 April 1561

[23] Marriage being a characteristic of Protestant ministers and loving images an attribute of Catholic clergy.

[24] Eccleshall was in the jurisdiction of the Dean and Chapter and not of the bishop. The bishop nonetheless had his palace at Eccleshall.

... these may be to desire the same most earnestly to be so favourable unto me in my great need, as to license Dr Weston towards the end of the term, to make such speed homeward, as he doth well know to be very necessary for the reformation of divers and sundry things far out of order, almost in my whole diocese, whereof he is able to give your grace understanding by private talk ... further, whereas one Mr Aston,[25] a godly preacher within these parts of my diocese, is preferred to a benefice in the diocese of Lincoln, whereupon he should by order of law be resident, my request ... is, that it would please [you] ... to show so much favour ... unto the said Mr Aston, for that he hath now begun a good work to the furtherance of a school in Shrewsbury which if he should presently depart were like not to proceed or else much to be hindered. In consideration whereof ... you shall not only do a great pleasure to the town of Salop but also to me in these parts of my diocese, which have here no other preacher but him.

[. . .]

Item 229: Thomas Bentham to Peter Morewyn,[26] chaplain, at London 7 May 1561

Commending me to you and your wife etc. These are to will you learn what my lord of London doth in his visitation, besides his articles which you sent me. I would also have those articles or injunctions and homilies, which I hear say are set forth by my lord of Canterbury. And if you can get me the table of the degrees of marriage I would have it. What other things you see to be needful for me to know, let me understand by your letters from time to time, so long as you shall tarry there. Speak to Mr Sears to get me the Statutes of King Edward, and also the statutes of Queen Mary well bound severally: and at Michaelmas he shall have money for them and such things as I shall send for hereafter. Commend me to my brother Ralph Egerton and to his wife. And to all other my friends in Christ, who prosper all their doings, this 7 of May at Eccleshall.

Item 235: Thomas Bentham to Edwin Sandys, Bishop of Worcester, 18 May 1561

---

[25] Thomas Aston or Ashton (d. 1578), first headmaster and virtual founder of Shrewsbury School.

[26] B.A. of Bentham's old college, Magdalen, Oxford. He was ordained deacon and priest in spring 1560 and was appointed Bentham's personal chaplain. He was appointed by the bishop to the rectory of Longford, Derbyshire, in July 1560, after the removal of John Ramridge, lately archdeacon of Derbyshire under Queen Mary, and then presented to the rectory of Norbury, Staffs in 1561 after the deprivation of Henry Cumberford.

Item, a letter to my Lord of Worcester thanking him for his pains taking in those parts of my diocese, and signifying unto him how weary I am of my seat and know not where to complain for the amendment of the same.

2.19

Come over the born, Bessy: A song between the Queen's Majesty and England

V. de Sola Pinto & A.E. Rodway (eds.) (1965) *The Common Muse: An Anthology of Popular British Ballad Poetry, 15th–20th Century*, Harmondsworth: Penguin, pp. 60–2. Adapted by Rosemary O'Day. Numbers added to verses.

Contemporary ballads can sometimes provide historians with insights regarding popular attitudes to historical persons and events, although such evidence should not be taken at face value. The ballad from which the verses below are extracted celebrated the accession of Elizabeth 1 on 17 November 1558 in the form of a conversation between E. (England) and B. (Bessy = Elizabeth). Caution seems all the more appropriate when one notes that 'A New Ballad of the Marigold' heralded the accession of Elizabeth's Catholic sister Mary in 1553.

1.
E. Come over the born Bessy / come over the born Bessy
Sweet Bessy come over to me
And I shall thee take / and my dear lady make
Before all other that ever I see.

2.
B. Me think I hear a voice / at whom I do rejoice
And answer thee now I shall.
Tell me I say / what art thou that bids me come away
And so earnestly dost me call?

3.
E. I am thy lover fair / hath chose thee to my heir
And my name is merry England.
Therefore come away / and make no more delay
Sweet Bessy give me thy hand.

4.

B. Here is my hand / my dear lover England.
I am thine with mind and heart
For ever to endure / thou mayest be sure
Until death do us two depart.

5.

E. Lady this long space / have I loved thy grace
More than I darest well say
Hoping at the last / when all storms were past
For to see this joyful day.

6.

B. Yet my lover England / you shall understand
How fortune on me did lower.
I was tumbled and lost / from pillar to post
And prisoner in the Tower.

7.

E. Dear Lady we do know / how that tyrants not a few
Went about to seek thy blood
And contrary to right / they did what they might
That now bear two faces in one hood.

[. . .]

11.

E. Why dear lady I trow / those mad men did not know
That you were daughter unto King Harry
And a princess of birth / one of the noblest on earth
And sister unto Queen Mary.

12.

B. Yes, yet I must forgive / all such as do live
If they will hereafter amend
And for those that have gone / God forgive them everyone
And his mercy on them extend.

13.

E. Yet my lover dear / tell me now here
For what cause had you this punishment?
For the commons did not know / nor no man would them show
The chief cause of your imprisonment.

14.

B. No nor they themselves / that would have decayed my wealth
But only by power and abusion

They could not detect me / but that they did suspect me
That I was not of their religion.

[. . .]

16.
B. Yet my lover dear / mark me well here
Though they were men of the devil
The Scripture plainly saith / all they that be of faith
Must needs do good against evil.

17.
E. O sweet virgin pure / long may you endure
To reign over us in this land
For your works do accord / you are the handmaid of the lord
For he hath blessed you with his hand.

18.
B. My sweet realm be obedient / to God's holy commandment
And my proceedings embrace
And for that that is abused / shall be better used
And that within short space.

19.
E. Dear Lady and Queen / I trust it shall be seen
You shall reign quietly without strife
And if any traitors there be / of any kind or degree
I pray God send them short life.

20.
B. I trust all faithful hearts / will play true subjects' parts
Knowing me their Queen and true heir by right
And that much the rather / for the love of my father
That worthy prince King Henry the eighth.

21.
E. Therefore let us pray / to God both night and day
Continually and never to cease
That he will preserve your grace / to reign over us long space.

22.
Both
All honour laud and praise / be to the lord God always
Who hath all princes' hearts in his hands
That by his power and might / he may give them a right
For the wealth of all Christian lands.

God save the Queen.
William Birch

2.20

Letter of Philip II to the duchess of Parma, 17 October 1565

E.H. Kossman & A.F. Mellink (eds.) (1974)
Texts concerning the Revolt of the Netherlands,
Cambridge: Cambridge University Press, pp. 53–6.
Paragraph numbers added.

Philip II (1527–98), king of Spain and lord of the Netherlands, ruled the Netherlands through a succession of governors/ governesses-general. In 1565, the governess-general was his half-sister, Margaret, duchess of Parma (1522–86) who eventually resigned two years later in December 1567. The letter concerns the recent changes in state and church in the Netherlands introduced by Philip II and provides guidelines for Margaret's government to follow.

1. Madame my dear sister, I answer your letter of 22 July in which you told me, as you did in your preceding letters, how you have started to comply with the instructions transmitted by my cousin the prince of Gavre, and have been trying to remedy the religious problems. I understand that, as I had ordained, you have convoked at Brussels the bishops of Ypres, Namur and St Omer and the presidents of Flanders and Utrecht with the councillor, Muelerus, and also the theologians and Doctors Tiletanus and Jansenius, nominated as bishop of Ghent, and with them Doctor Wulmarus, canonist, whose statements in Latin, signed in their own handwriting, you have sent me together with the minutes. I am very pleased to learn that the assembly was constituted by men of such quality and such zeal for our religion and I value their advice on various points, and also on matters in which it does not seem suitable to make innovations, as you will see from the enclosed answers to their statements. I have added some other points which I think are important in the matter of religion and I instruct you to have these executed without fail in the best manner possible. I rely upon you in this.

2. You say that I did not make it clear in the afore-mentioned instruction that it was not my intention to ask you or the seigniors of the state council in the Netherlands for more advice in this matter but in fact you were made to understand my definitive intention. As to whether I

would wish to ask the advice of the private and great councils and of the governors and provincial councils, this would be a considerable waste of time since my mind is made up. I have not asked others at all but followed the advice of the above-mentioned assembly as much as possible and as seemed fitting, and I have been very pleased to hear that you have already begun to apply the other canonical remedies, such as having good preachers and pastors, founding good schools and reforming the ecclesiastics in accordance with my instruction, and, moreover, publishing the decrees of the council and all that is connected with it . . .

3. As to the proceedings of the inquisitors of Louvain,[1] you must endeavour to support them as well as the others in all that concerns the exercise and administration of their charges. For this makes for the strength and maintenance of religion.

I cannot but be very much affected by the lampoons which are continually spread abroad and posted up in the Netherlands without the offenders being punished. This, of course, happens because the authors of earlier ones were not punished. You should consider what remains of my authority and yours, and of the service of God, when it is possible to do such things with impunity in your very presence. Therefore I pray you, take the necessary measures so that this does not remain unpunished. These things are not so secret but that several men hear of them and if some are not seen to be punished, the daring increases daily and in the end so much liberty is taken that we must fear most dangerous consequences . . .

4. As to the resentment you have noticed at some of the things which the prince of Gavre[2] says I told him and which don't seem to correspond with my letters from Valladolid [13 May 1565] and with the negotiations in progress over the matter of religion, I don't see or understand that I wrote anything different in these letters from what was entrusted to the prince of Gavre. For as to the inquisition, my intention is that it should be carried out by the inquisitors, as they have done up till now and as it appertains to them by virtue of divine and human rights. This is nothing new, because this was always done in the days of the late emperor my seignior and father, whom God has in His glory, and by me. If one fears disturbances there is no reason to think that they are more imminent and will be greater when one does allow the inquisitors to perform their proper duties and when one

---

[1] The theological faculty of the university of Louvain had played an important part in the fight against heresy.

[2] Lamorel (1522–68), count of Egmont, prince of Gavre, a Spanish governor in the Netherlands.

does assist them. You know the importance of this and I command you urgently to do in this matter all that is so necessary and not to agree to any different policy. You know how much I have these things at heart and what pleasure and satisfaction this will give me.

I have heard how insubstantial are the objections raised by the inhabitants of Bruges against Titelman;[3] you would do well not to permit anything to be done to undermine his authority. I am sure that being well-informed of what happens (as I believe you are) you won't fail to take the necessary steps.

5. As to the Anabaptists, what I wrote to you about them was in answer to what you asked me about the punishment of some prisoners.[4] This did not differ from what the prince of Gavre reported. For though you have to deliberate about proposals for altering punishments, this does not mean that they should cease until a resolution is taken. These prisoners must be punished as I told you in my letter from Valladolid. This also answers your representations to me in your letter of 22 July about state-affairs. I cannot refrain from telling you that considering the condition of religious affairs in the Netherlands as I understand it, this is no time to make any alteration. On the contrary, His Majesty's edicts should be executed; I think that the cause of the past evil and its subsequent growth and advance has been the negligence, leniency and duplicity of the judges, about which I will give you more particulars later. I told the prince of Gavre that since the men condemned to die advance to execution not in silence, but as martyrs dying for a cause you should consider whether they ought not to be executed in secret in some way or other (though it is true that a public execution also serves to set an example) . . .

6. For the rest I can only thank you for all you propose to me, but assure you that my orders are designed for the welfare of religion and of my provinces and are worth nothing if they are not obeyed. In this way you can keep my provinces in justice, peace and tranquillity. Now that you know the importance of this, I pray you again to take steps to bring this state of affairs into being. Thus I shall be most satisfied with you and with the seigniors who are with you. You must pass on my wishes to them. I trust that they won't fail to do what I want as they know what satisfaction this will give me. Thus they will do their duty according to their rank and to the obligation they have to serve

---

[3] Peter Titelman, a notorious inquisitor in Flanders.

[4] This concerned a lawsuit against repenting Anabaptists, for whom the Assembly of Nine had advocated milder penalties.

God and me, and to further the common welfare of the provinces in the Netherlands on which they are themselves dependent.

So far, etc.

From the Segovia woods, 17 October 1565

2.21

Petition of Compromise, 5 April 1566

E.H. Kossman & A.F. Mellink (eds.) (1974) *Texts Concerning the Revolt of the Netherlands*, Cambridge: Cambridge University Press, pp. 62–4.

Around 400 nobles, mainly lesser nobles, signed the Petition of Compromise which requested Philip II to halt the religious persecution in the Netherlands conducted through royal edicts and the Inquisition. William of Orange (1533–84), Floris, count of Culemburg (1537–98) and Henry, baron of Brederode (1531–68) were its main architects and became the leaders of the confederates as they became known. Escorted by more than 200 armed supporters, they personally handed the petition to the governess-general, Margaret, duchess of Parma.

Madame! [Duchess Margaret]

It is common knowledge that throughout Christendom the people of these Netherlands have always been praised for their great fidelity to their seigniors and natural princes, and this is still the case, and that the nobles have always been prominent in this respect, since they have spared neither life nor property to conserve and increase the greatness of their rulers. And we, very humble vassals of His Majesty [Philip II], wish to do the same and to do even more, so that night and day we are ready to render him most humble service with life and property. And considering the condition of affairs at present, we prefer rather to incur some people's anger than to hide from your Highness something which might afterwards be to the prejudice of His Majesty and undermine the peace and quiet of his provinces. We hope that time will show that of all the services which we have ever rendered or shall in future render to His Majesty, this may be reckoned among the most

189

notable and useful, and we are firmly convinced that Your Highness will highly value our action.

We are not in doubt, Madame, that whatever His Majesty formerly ordained and now again ordains regarding the inquisition and the strict observance of the edicts concerning religion, has some foundation and just title and is intended to continue all that the late emperor, Charles[V] – blessed be his memory – decreed with the best of intentions. Considering however that different times call for different policies, and that for several years past those edicts, even though not very rigorously executed, have caused most serious difficulties, His Majesty's recent refusal[1] to mitigate the edicts in any way, and his strict orders to maintain the inquisition, and to execute the edicts in all their rigour, makes us fear that the present difficulties will undoubtedly increase. But in fact the situation is even worse. There are clear indications everywhere that the people are so exasperated that the final result, we fear, will be an open revolt and a universal rebellion bringing ruin to all the provinces and plunging them into utter misery. The extent of the danger that menaces us being, in our view, so manifest, we have hoped up till now that eventually either the Seigniors[2] or the States of the provinces would draft a remonstrance to Your Highness, with the purpose of remedying that evil by striking at its cause. But since for reasons unknown to us they have not come forward, and the evil is meanwhile daily augmenting, so that open revolt and universal rebellion are imminent, we consider it our bounden duty, incumbent upon us because of our oath of fidelity and homage as well as our zeal to serve His Majesty and our fatherland, to wait no longer but to be the first to come forward and do what we are obliged to do.

We speak the more frankly because we have sufficient reason to hope that His Majesty will not blame us at all for warning him. The matter concerns us more deeply than anyone else, for we are most exposed to the disasters and calamities, which usually spring from such rebellions. Our houses and lands are situated for the greater part in the open fields, and cannot be defended. Moreover, as a result of His Majesty's order to execute the edicts in all their severity, not one of us, or even of all inhabitants of the whole country, whatever his condition, will not be found guilty and sentenced to forfeit his life and property, as all of us will be subject to the defamatory testimony of

---

[1] The king's letters from Segovia of 17 October 1565 (see document 2.20).

[2] When they met at Hoogstraten in March, the great nobles could not agree upon combined action, mainly because Egmont refused to take part.

whoever might like to accuse us on the pretext of the edicts in order to obtain part of our confiscated goods. Only thanks to the duplicity of the responsible officer shall we be able to escape this fate and our lives and property will be entirely at his mercy.

Because of this we have every reason very humbly to implore Your Highness, as we do in this petition, to put these matters right and to dispatch a suitable courier to His Majesty as soon as possible to inform him and entreat him most humbly on our behalf,[3] that he be pleased to take measures to prevent this happening now and in the future. This will never be possible, if the edicts are left in force, for they are the source and origin of all difficulties; thus His Majesty should be asked kindly to repeal them. This is not only very necessary to avert the total ruin and loss of all his provinces, but is also in keeping with reason and justice. And so that he may have no reason to think that we, who only seek to obey him in all humility, would try to restrain him or to impose our will on him (as we don't doubt that our adversaries will say to our disadvantage), we implore His Majesty very humbly that it may please him to seek the advice and consent of the assembled States General for new ordinances and other more suitable and appropriate ways to put matters right without causing such apparent dangers.

We also most humbly entreat Your Highness that while His Majesty is listening to our just petition and making his decisions at his good and just pleasure, Your Highness may meanwhile obviate the dangers which we have described by suspending the inquisition as well as the execution of the edicts until His Majesty has made his decision. And finally we declare with all possible emphasis before God and men that in giving this present warning we have done all we can do according to our duty, and state that if there should occur disasters, disorder, sedition, revolt or bloodshed later on, because no appropriate measures were taken in time, we cannot be criticised for having concealed such an apparent abuse. For which purpose we call God, the king, Your Highness and the members of your council together with our conscience to witness that we have proceeded as becomes the king's good and loyal servants and faithful vassals, keeping within the bounds of our duty. Therefore we are entitled to implore Your Highness to assent to this, before further evils ensue and to do what is right.

---

[3] John Glimes, marquis of Bergen, and Florence Montmorency, baron of Montigny were very shortly entrusted with this mission.

2.22

Two accounts of hedge-preaching in the Netherlands, 1566

A. Duke, G. Lewis & A. Pettigree (eds.) (1992) *Calvinism in Europe, 1540–1610: A Collection of Documents*, Manchester: Manchester University Press, pp. 143–7. Paragraph numbers added.

The first account (a) of illegal Calvinist preaching activity in the countryside (hedge-preaching) was enclosed in a report written by the local governor of Lille, Douai and Ochies to the governess-general and refers to preaching in the evening of 29 June 1566 two miles outside Lille on the road to Tournai. The second account (b) was written by a certain Marcus van Vaernewijk, who evidently was not a Protestant, and refers to two hedge-preaching incidents near Ghent on two consecutive Sundays (30 June and 7 July).

(a) Maximilien Vilain de Gand, baron de Rassenghien, governor of Lille, Douai and Orchies, to Margaret of Parma. Lille, 30 June 1566.

1. ... I am bound, furthermore, to inform Your Highness that two more preachings took place last night, the chief of which, attended by some 4,000 people, was held about two leagues from this town on the road to Tournai by a preacher whose name, I understand, is Cornille de La Zenne, the son of a blacksmith from Roubaix, who has long been a fugitive from this country on account of the religion. According to the report, which some reliable persons have submitted to me, whom I know to have been at the said preaching, the said preacher exhorted his auditors, among other things, not to start any trouble or [commit] any seditious act, because in such a case no one would assist them, but if anyone arrested them or examined them for no other reason than their faith, or for having gone to the preachings, they might all be assured that they would be helped before any ill befell them, and in conclusion he spoke more or less as follows: we pray to God that He may grant the destruction of this papist idolatry; be of good heart for we are quite strong, but our time has not yet come. And we pray God that He may keep the people of Tournai and Armentières in their convictions and likewise confirm the good start we see among the inhabitants of Lille. And when the said sermon was over, the preacher

disappeared so quickly through the crowd with the help of twenty hackbutters, who escorted him, that it was impossible to know whither he had retired.

2. And in another preaching which took place a few days ago near the border with Tournaisis, three leagues from here, some rabble among the auditors told the preacher at the conclusion that they had decided on returning home to invade a certain house, I do not know which, in the vicinity of Tournai. He strongly warned them against this, saying that the time was not yet ripe and that he would tell them when the hour had come and that he hoped that it would be quite soon. Your Highness may judge sufficiently from these remarks that when the time and opportunity are favourable, they will be very ready somewhere to play a trick on some unsuspecting monastery in the countryside or some undefended town. We are afraid that once the corn has been harvested and gathered into the barns, which will be in two or three weeks' time at the outside here, they will try to seize control of the countryside somewhere, before the towns have the means to obtain supplies, in order in this manner to starve the towns and to recruit by poverty a larger following, for which reason it would be expedient to give orders in good time and to find a way in advance of averting their assemblies. People have told me that many French gentlemen secretly hold themselves in readiness in order when sedition first occurs to offer their services, boasting that instead of the 4,000 Spanish soldiers whom the Catholic King sent to France, they could send 4,000 gentlemen to Flanders and that the Constable [Anne, duc de Montmorency] must have replied a few days ago to some Catholics in Paris, grumbling about the Huguenots, that it was time to importune the King there and that they waited first to see what measures the Catholic King would take in Flanders. I hope, however, that we may place our trust in the nobility of the Low Countries and that the members of the Request [Compromise] have no understanding with the assemblies of these rabble sectaries, and that we can yet find a means to undo the schemes of the people without violence, by some declaration from the said nobility. If Your Highness would find it expedient to enter into discussions with the leading members of the Request in order to ascertain their intentions in the matter of the assemblies (which are harmful to both the consideration and the publication of any provisional edict Your Highness might think good to make), for some of the leaders of their deputation are present in each quarter [of the country], I do not doubt but that this would be most beneficial, for it would both remove the mistaken impression held by the infected people and also greatly reassure the judges and officers of the good intentions of the said

nobility. Nevertheless I leave everything to the noble discretion of Your Highness, for whom I would always do everything in my power to obey.

Madame, I pray that Our Lord may give Your Highness the fulfilment of her highest and most virtuous desires, after having most humbly kissed your hands. From Lille on the last day of June 1566.

(b) 1. [Sunday 30 June 1566] . . . then someone preached, dressed like the other [preacher] in lay attire, with an ermine-trimmed gown and a fine felt hat. [He was] short of stature and aged about thirty, and seemed, to judge from his speech, to hail from Kortrijk. Close to the chapel outside St Lievenspoort [he preached], bare-headed and with great modesty, on a small hill surrounded by copses and plantations. He sat on some hoods and cloaks, lent him by those who had come to listen, and he had in front of him a book, from which he read from time to time, before closing it again and continuing with his sermon. Before he preached, he knelt folding his hands together very devoutly. To avoid being arrested or surprised, he was led into the enclosure in a group of six people in such a way that no one knew who out of the six was the preacher until he made ready to speak. He expounded the Gospel of the day, reproved sins and prayed for the magistrates, the King and the Pope that God might enlighten their minds so that the Word of God (as they called their doctrine) might go forward peacefully. He had promised to preach at three o'clock in the afternoon, but he began at two o'clock.

2. Those present sat in three separate, closely-packed small companies made up of men, women and young girls; each of these had about as many members as the preacher had years. Each company had its teacher and the members had small books in their hands and from time to time sang the psalms; you could buy books there in which the psalms were printed in metrical form for a stiver. Many onlookers stood around; they had come to see what was going on there because it was for everyone a strange, unheard-of event, especially for those who lived in Flanders. I was told this by my washerwoman with whom I strongly remonstrated. I said to her that we were threatened by a great evil and danger, if it were not quickly stopped, but, like many simple folk, she thought it was quite innocent and even edifying. . . .

3. On Sunday 7 July [1566] they preached again, in defiance of the authorities, at Stallendriesche at high noon. Thousands of people attended from the town and from the surrounding countryside, including many of the common people, who were not very well-versed in the

Holy Scriptures and the Church Fathers. They [the Calvinists] gave these the impression that now for the first time the truth had been revealed and the Gospel preached aright because the preachers especially cited the Scriptures most valiantly and stoutly. They let the people check each passage in their testaments to see whether or not they preached faithfully, [when they said that] the New Testament contained the Word which the Lord had commanded all men to proclaim; not the human inventions and institutions, with which the papists (as they call them) had busied themselves; having raised these above God's Word or allowed these to obscure God's Word, it could not advance as it should and must [instead] be bent and give ground in order to accommodate human invention and contrivance; that it was much more proper that human laws should yield and make way for the sacred and blessed Word of God, for this, not rosaries, pilgrimages, voyages, and many suchlike superstitions, will prevail at the Last Judgement; that we are also under a far greater obligation (as the Apostles tell us) to obey the Word of God than men or magistrates, even though we are forbidden to hear this on pain of death, for the Lord says that we should not be afraid of those who would take the body captive, but only those who would cast the body and the soul into the everlasting fires of Hell; and that He shall be ashamed to confess before His heavenly Father and the angels of God those who are ashamed to confess Him in this world; that also Christ (who cannot lie) has prophesied that those who preach and hear His Word in its naked purity shall be oppressed and persecuted for as long as the world exists.

4. With these and other similar arguments they struck such a marvellous chord in the hearts of good and uneducated people that many of them declared that they were ready to forfeit both their property and their lives for the Word of God and Christ's name. This sprang, alas, more from a naïve fervour than from any judicious circumspection, for if they had heeded and properly understood the counter-arguments, they would have come to the opposite conclusion. Not everything that claims to be the Word of God is in fact the Word of God. You must search out what has been the judgement of the Holy Spirit of God, which lies hidden under the letter of God's Word. It was not without good cause that St Paul said that the letter kills but the Spirit brings life.

2.23
The Council of Troubles in Brill, 1566–7

A. Duke, G. Lewis & A. Pettigree (eds.) (1992) *Calvinism in Europe, 1540–1610: A Collection of Documents*, Manchester: Manchester University Press, pp. 155–8.

This document relates how 83 men from Brill (Den Briel) and the surrounding area were investigated for their activities during the revolt of 1566–7. They were subsequently convicted by the Spanish tribunal, the Council of Troubles on 20 October 1568, initiated by the new governor of the Spanish Netherlands, Fernand Alvarez de Toldeo, 3rd duke of Alba [Alva] (1508–82). The men were banished and their estates were confiscated.

Willem van Treslong, having been a gentleman in the household of the Heer van Brederode, a member of the Compromise of the Nobility, having been a signatory to their pernicious and seditious league and for this reason present at the presentation of the Request,[1] as is notorious, and also at the meeting at St Truiden, having seduced his eldest brother Jan van Treslong also to appear and to sign the said Compromise and in January 1567 to have presented the last Request of the Heer van Brederode to Her Highness, according to which they demanded complete freedom to exercise the new religion in return for laying down their arms . . . ; Nicolaas van Sandijck,[2] having also been a member of the said Compromise, and having been a signatory to their seditious league and having maintained two horses in the service of the Heer van Brederode, and who gave refuge and advice to the imagebreakers of the town of Den Brielle. Hugo Quirynsz was present in the chamber of the Rhetoricians in the town hall on Ash Wednesday 1567 and there with other brother rhetoricians to have mocked the mass by drinking from the chalice belonging to the altar of the same fraternity. On this occasion the missal, the canon of the mass and the statue of St Rochus were put on trial, and, after psalms had been sung by way of a refrain, they sentenced the said missal, canon of the mass and the statue of St Rochus to be burnt; this was carried out and the whole lot thrown on the fire. Corvinck Thonisse and Jan Thysse, deans

---

[1] 3 April 1566.
[2] Former bailiff of Den Briel.

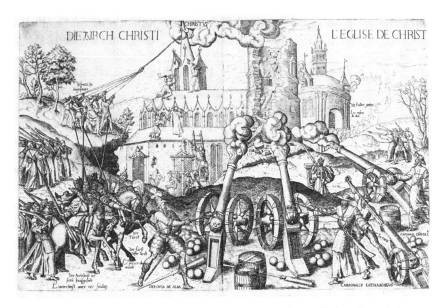

2.4 'The Church of Christ', anonymous engraving, 1568, allegorising an attack on the Protestant Church by the duke of Alba and the cardinal of Lorraine with cannons, and the Spanish Inquisition with ropes and axes. The pope ('Antichrist') brings reinforcements of Catholic princes, clergy and demons.

of the rhetoricians, were present during the said blasphemies and abominations, when four statues from the altar of St Rochus (which had been removed from the parish church and taken to the said chamber to keep them from being broken) were likewise condemned to be burnt, and indeed thrown into the fire, together with the ornaments and furnishings belonging to the said altar. Dierick de Nayer also drank from the said chalice. Aert Daniels, Pieter Michielsz., Jan Commersz., and Jan Lenartsz. were very thoroughly involved in the new preachings, and had carried messages for the members of the consistory, and had shown great favour to the image-breakers and had been commissioned by the sectaries to go the Prince of Orange and the Heer van Brederode; and the said Pieter Michielsz. had been present during the image-breaking in the convent of the Poor Clares, instructing the iconoclasts what they ought to smash, [and] when a Catholic asked him 'if the Gospel commanded the breaking [of images]' he replied that 'it was necessary and that the Whore of Babylon must be overthrown'. The said Hugo Pietersz., Jacob Cornelisz., Mr. Pieter van der Heyde and Andries de Wever had been deacons; and the said Jan Commersz., Mr Pieter and Andries de Wever had broken in the parish church of Maerlant; and the said Hugo Pietersz. held the consistory in his house; and the said Mr. Pieter, besides having one of his children baptised in the Calvinist way, had been the ringleader and one of the chiefest of the said breakers. Jacob Jacobsz. Coster, having been detained on account of the past troubles, had broken prison and escaped; [he] was charged with having led his pupils to the burial of someone of the new religion and there made them sing psalms. Eeuwout Cornelisz., until recently the *schout* [bailiff] of the said town, and Willem Willemsz. *Apotheker* [pharmacist] had been foremost in promoting and encouraging the iconoclasm there and had themselves broken [images]. The said Eeuwout Cornelisz. had been commissioned by the sectaries and put in charge of the ordnance drawn up on the town fortifications and in front of the gates of the same to defend them and to have worn the badge of the Beggars. Boudewyn Jansse [was] also a member of the Compromise and had been a signatory to their seditious league under the Heer van Brederode and to have worn their badge and dress. Mathys Andriesse and Jacob his son had also broken in the convent of the Poor Clares as have also broken . . . [54 names follow], all of whom have been convicted of having broken images. The said Simon Jansse Sleeper has been a member of the said Compromise of the nobility, having been a signatory to their seditious league and had one of his children baptised in the new way and having broken statues. Jan van Delft also broke [images] and attended the aforementioned abominable insolence perpetrated against the service of the mass. Adriane de Kleermaeker had been a messenger for the consistory and broken images in the convent of the Poor Clares. Cornelis Heyndricxz., a burgomaster in 1566, had lodged a minister of the sectaries. Mr Cornelis Rutgersz. had shown great favour towards the image-breakers and was alleged to have hired some of them to break the said statues and to have expressed several blasphemous remarks against the Catholic religion and the venerable Sacrament [of the altar]. Pieter Jansz. Coninck [was charged with being] thoroughly involved in the new religion and their preachings, [with] having made several journeys on behalf of the consistory, received the sums collected on behalf of the Heer van Brederode and [with having] held the consistory at his house. Lenaert Benoyt alias de Wael [was charged with being] deeply involved in the said new religion and preachings, having been a member of the said Compromise and a signatory to their league; also [with having] received money for the said Heer van

Brederode. Mr Dirck Cock, rector and schoolmaster, is one of the foremost authors of the alteration of the old religion and of the introduction of the sects and new preachings, having infected all his pupils with his false and erroneous doctrines and having instructed them in Calvin's catechism and taught them to sing the psalms, no longer leading them to mass on feast-days and Sundays or to any other church service, yet taking them to the graveside of those buried in the new way to sing the psalms there, in these ways alienating them completely from the ancient Catholic and Roman religion so that most of the youth of the town are infected by the said false doctrines; and when he was summoned before the magistrates and asked whether he would not instruct his said pupils in the old way, he roundly replied that he would not, but that he wanted to teach what he had recently learned; having also ripped up the missal and other books in the convent of St Catherine; and the said Jan Smeet de Borst having gone into hiding because he had married a nun who had fled from the convent of St Catherine.

Having also seen the evidence shown by the said *procureur-generaal* in support of the facts set out above . . . His Excellence [the Duke of Alba] banishes all those who have been cited.

Done in Antwerp 20 October 1568.

2.24

The prince of Orange's warning to the inhabitants of the Netherlands, 1 September 1568

E.H. Kossman & A.F. Mellink (eds.) (1974) *Texts Concerning the Revolt of the Netherlands*, Cambridge: Cambridge University Press, pp. 84–6. Paragraph numbers added.

William of Orange had initially refrained from joining the armed revolt against Spain in 1566–7 and instead sought refuge in his German possessions at Dillenburg. However, with the death of his friend Brederode in the first half of 1568 and his own condemnation by the Council of Troubles, and subsequent confiscation of all his possessions in the Netherlands, he had no alternative but to take up the leadership of the armed revolt against Spain. His proclamation (warning) to the inhabitants of the Netherlands provided a justification for the invasion he was in the process of launching with troops recruited in Germany.

1. Firstly, we would remind you of something that is clear to every one, that the Netherlands have always been ruled and reigned over by their princes and overlords with all gentleness, right and reason and wholly in accordance with their freedoms, rights, customs, traditions and privileges, which have always been observed there and were obtained in former times from emperors, kings, dukes, counts and seigniors by the inhabitants of the country, great friends and supporters of their liberty and enemies to all violence and oppression. The princes as well as the subjects of the country have always had to commit themselves by a formal contract and to swear a solemn oath that they would maintain these rights and realise them. The inhabitants therefore owe obedience to the rulers only on condition that the freedoms are maintained – and it should be added that respect for the privileges brought our dear fatherland all that power, richness and prosperity which one found there in the past.

2. Neither can it be denied, since it is so plain and definite, that for over fifty years since the time when the countries of Spain came by marriage together with the Netherlands under one sovereign[1] some grandees of Spain have been intent on somehow obtaining power to govern and tyrannise over so prosperous a country as they do elsewhere. And though the freedoms and privileges of the Netherlands always meant that their attempts failed, nevertheless they did not cease to be on the watch for opportunities to mislead the benevolent prince so completely that ultimately they would achieve their aim. It is also only too obvious that Cardinal Granvelle[2] and his adherents took an unfair advantage of the faith of the trustful and good prince and, seeking only to rule and dominate the Low Countries completely in order to satisfy their ambition, avarice and other passions, proposed all those leagues, practices and strange innovations that were to serve as means utterly to enslave the conscience, persons and possessions

---

[1] The marriage of Philip the Fair with Joanna of Aragon in 1496. She became heiress to the Spanish throne through the deaths of her brother and elder sisters.

[2] Cardinal Antoine Perrenot Granvelle (1517–86), councillor to Philip II. Served as Philip's special representative in the Netherlands and was responsible for many of the changes introduced.

of the whole population, nay to rob them of all their freedoms, rights and privileges. Of course all this was given the appearance of holy zeal and said to be done in the name of religion as well as of the majesty and service of the king, but in reality it was greatly to the disservice of God, the king and the country. It was to this end that so many strange innovations, cruel persecutions, bloody edicts, an unbearable inquisition, the supersession of the bishops, the capture of the abbeys,[3] the proclamation of the regulations of the council,[4] cruel executions of the Christians and more unheard of inventions against the freedom of the country and the will of the people were proposed and executed.

3. We and other seigniors and brethren who sought and are seeking only to serve God, the king and the country well and continually and to further the freedom and prosperity of subjects and inhabitants, protested several times and showed how wrong all this was. We have always said that it is better to act with gentleness than with severity and we think that it is better and more reasonable to keep promises than to break them and to violate oaths. For these reasons the cardinal and his adherents and those who collaborated with him in Spain not only conceived a great hatred and unjustified envy for us, but also contrived to obscure and to distort the truth with false and deceitful practices and denunciations so that the gracious king, ill-informed about all these matters, thought that our loyal advice, actions and services originated from ambition and that his good loyal subjects were rebellious, disobedient and refractory (though this was quite untrue). Thus they succeeded in being allowed to proceed at discretion, which was what they had desired for so long.

It is clear that the inquisitions, executions, mandates, persecutions, innovations and proposals of the cardinal and his men (usurping on the powers not only of the governess but also of the king) damaged and harmed the country very much and alarmed, drove away, robbed and killed a very large number of the inhabitants. At the same time they impaired and hindered the old customary freedom. Nevertheless we see nowadays with great heart-ache, and it is to be feared that if God does not help us – what we trust He will do and what we are preparing ourselves for to the utmost of our ability – we may see on an even larger scale, how greatly and grievously all the afore-mentioned innovations, proposals, oppressions, inquisitions, persecutions,

---

[3] Abbeys were incorporated into the new bishoprics in order to ensure the latter sufficient revenues.

[4] The decrees of the Council of Trent.

murders, seizures, executions and tyrannies have increased and multiplied, and how totally inhuman they have become since the duke (in name of the king and shielding himself with the king's authority) arrived here with his Spanish soldiers.[5] And we also see how these countries have fallen from the greatest prosperity into the utmost misery, how the worthy inhabitants who enjoyed freedom in former times have been brought into unbearable slavery and how piteously the privileges and rights of the country together with the religion of God are lying there oppressed and destroyed.

2.25

Letters to the Dutch Church in London

A. Duke, G. Lewis & A. Pettigree (eds.) (1992) *Calvinism in
Europe, 1540–1610: A Collection of Documents,*
Manchester: Manchester University Press, pp. 161–3, 189–90.
Paragraph numbers added.

These two letters were written by Reformed ministers who were closely associated with the influential Dutch Reformed Church in London. The Dutch Church in London had quickly realised the importance of supplying the emerging Reformed churches in the Netherlands with ministers.

(a) Letter of Bartholdus Wilhelmi, 29 August 1572

Among the first to leave the London Dutch Church was Bartholdus Wilhelmi who, after having served the London Dutch Community was appointed minister to the Reformed Church in Dort (Dordrecht) in August 1572. His letter was written on his arrival.

1. . . . Most dear brethren and fellow ministers in the Lord. You will be pleased to know that I arrived at Dordrecht on 27 August in good health and without meeting any danger from the enemy of God, for which I cordially beseech you to praise the Lord for this Grace. . . .

---

[5] The duke of Alba arrived at Brussels on 22 August 1567.

Further that you will, as you promised, inform the congregation why I travelled here without taking my leave, namely for no other reason than to prevent the danger that was consequently to be expected and not out of any contempt or negligence, and therefore ask the congregation not to take it amiss. . . .

2. Further, because those of Dordrecht ask for still more ministers, since the harvest grows but the workers are very few, I beseech you (on behalf of the notables of this town, who have also desired the same from me), that you will show in this matter the love which you owe to both God and his Holy Congregation and send at least four or five of our ministers of the Word as quickly as possible. There are not only still some deficiencies in Dordrecht, but in addition there are some ten or twelve places in the neighbourhood, both towns and villages, with neither ministers nor services. The inhabitants of these same places daily complain and cry out, 'alas, we are like sheep without shepherds, we live without religion and hear nothing of God'. In one place you will find eight unbaptised children, in others six or four, and it is impossible to improve matters and to assist them in their great need unless we have more ministers, for much depends on Dordrecht and therefore this place in particular must be provided. All the ministers whom you send across shall be well received and looked after. The town governor himself[1] was so delighted by my arrival that he did not know how he could sufficiently thank the congregation and consistory of London for the love they had shown by sending one of their ministers. Should this not move us, my dear brethren, more and more to help advance the preaching of the Gospel which has begun? Should we not consider how many sheep who have strayed may in this way be brought, by God's grace, to the sheepfold? Likewise, how precious they stand in the sight of Christ, for did He not also shed His blood for the same on the wooden cross? Oh, what fruits there shall be if they can be won for Christ. Ought we not to ponder on this and still other matters, too long to enter into here?

3. And since almost no one in Dordrecht and thereabouts has ever heard anything about the reformation of worship or has been in Reformed congregations, you will readily appreciate that we need ministers with some knowledge of the government of the Church, who can set matters in good order. And who is more apt in this respect than our brother [Godfried] van Winghen, who has long experience with the congregation, or Silvanus [Joris Wybo], if he be fit, or [Pieter] Carpentier, or [Jan] Lamoot, [Johannes] Cubus, etc. Therefore do your

[1] Johan de Hornes, baron of Boxtel.

best in this matter so that the Lord's dilapidated house may again by the Lord's grace be built up. I do not doubt that as you have begun well you shall likewise continue. . . . I would have written more, but as the shipmaster wants to sail I have not been able to complete everything as I would have wished. Therefore you shall take it in good part on this occasion. Farewell. From Dordrecht, 29 August 1572.

Greet my wife and continue to comfort her in my absence . . . and take good care, dear brethren, of the flock that God has acquired by his blood, for there will be a time of reckoning so that you may always have a good conscience before God. . . .

Your fellow brother and servant, so far as I am able, Bartholdus Wilhelmi.

Any letters you want to send me should be addressed: to Cornelis Franssen Wittesz. on the Nieuwe Haven.

(b) Letter of Daniel de Dieu, 9 August 1582

Daniel de Dieu had been among the first alumni of the Dutch Church in London, which sponsored the education of a number of Reformed ministers destined for the Reformed communities in the Netherlands. De Dieu had studied both in Geneva and Heidelberg before returning briefly to London to serve as a trainee minister before he was allowed to accept a position as minister to the Reformed Church in Brussels. De Dieu's letter was written after he had served the Brussels community for more than a year.

1. Honourable brethren, since an opportunity has arisen to write to England, I have not wanted to delay greeting all the brethren any longer. . . . As for the state of our oppressed fatherland, we may well compare it, as the prophet Isaiah [1: 5–6] does his Jewish people, to a wretched man, whose whole head is sick and his whole heart has grown weary and in whom nothing wholesome can be found; from the soles of his feet to his head there are only wounds, stiffness and ulcers, which can neither be closed, bound up nor soothed with oil. For the Lord does lay aside His wrath, but His hand remains stretched forth and the land is still filled with idolatry, injustice, treachery and every kind of infamy. God's Holy Word is received by few and read by still fewer. Everywhere you find multitudes of atheists and libertines, some of whom openly scoff at religion and call it a fable and invention, saying that it is nothing more than a matter of policy, devised by crafty

and cunning rulers to keep simple folk in fear and obedience. These therefore regard those who do, and suffer, so much for the sake of religion as mad. Others who wish to conceal their contempt for God say that such a variety of contending beliefs has arisen in our fatherland that they neither know which is true nor what they should believe. Some set their cap to the wind and outwardly conform with all sorts of religion. Others extol the peace and prosperity of everything under popery and make out that God's Word is the cause of all this misfortune and strife. It is therefore not surprising that the wrath of God is still kindled against the country. We on the other side too, who should have been all the more godly as the world grows more godless, have by our sins also increased the fire. Instead of bringing water, we together carry oil to it so that it burns more fiercely than ever. For this reason we see that the Lord gives advancement to the enemy and sets us back. He makes his horses sturdy and his soldiers strong and bold and by contrast He makes ours fearful and timid.

2. Thus God has also allowed our fellow brethren at Lier to be treacherously surprised and wretchedly treated.[1] Some of these escaped naked and many others, having no money to buy their ransom, were miserably murdered, among whom one of the ministers, a virtuous god-fearing man (by name Jan Schijve: he had earlier served at Mechelen) was according to reports most cruelly put to death. The chief men and leaders of the country are not exempt from all sorts of assaults on their person, as was quite recently planned and about which you will have certainly heard.[2] What then should anyone think? Shall we allow ourselves to become discouraged and bereft of all comfort? Our answer is no, certainly not. For we know that, although we shall have tribulation in the world (John 16), we nevertheless have peace in Christ. Recently we had here a great mutiny of our garrison; they seized the court, grievously threatened the burghers and forcibly removed some officers, both from the magistracy and from the council of war, from their houses. Whereupon some burghers, both Papists and others, were given arms to protect the market, the town hall and magistrates from any insolence, though not to fight the soldiers, for that would have been the height of folly. Nevertheless the situation was as a result far worse because the servants of the mass and malcontented spirits strove thereby to incite the soldiers against us by

---

[1] A Scottish captain in the service of the States betrayed Lier to Alessandro Farnese (1545–92), duke of Parma on 2 August 1582. The Walloon troops sacked the town.

[2] On 18 March 1582 Jean Jaureguy made an attempt on William of Orange's life in Antwerp.

spreading many slanders and threats so that it seemed as though the soldiers and our people would have fallen on one another with their swords. But the affair has been settled and entirely made up so that our pro-Spanish party has not yet achieved their boast. Soon afterwards we were warned from all sides that the enemy was coming to besiege us and great preparations were laid, but this cloud also seems to have passed over. Our mass-enticers have now been pressing the Duke [of Anjou][3] for several months on end to be allowed to take possession of the church on the Koudenberg close by the Court (which is used by the Walloon congregation) and openly to celebrate mass. But so far they have failed and only time will tell what they shall obtain hereafter once the Duke comes. God will meanwhile keep away all idolatrous services from us. Brussels, 9 August 1582.

[3] Hercule François, duke of Anjou (1555–84), a younger brother of the French king who became involved in the Dutch revolt on the side of the rebels.

Chapter 3

The wars of the three kingdoms, 1640–90

Introduction

The extracts reproduced in this chapter all relate to the civil wars in the British Isles and their aftermath, and cover the period from the 1620s to 1689. They deal with the origins of the breakdown between the king and his subjects, aspects of the wars in different parts of the British Isles, the post-war reconstruction of the countries and the events and developments of the Glorious Revolution of 1688.

The material ranges from extracts from diaries and letters (not always the private documents that they became in later periods), to such public documents as parliamentary proceedings and court reports. Their primary function is to show what kinds of source historians of the period have to work on: this was a great era of cheap print and the absence of censorship in 1640–60 led to the appearance of many novel and revolutionary ideas. Documents have particularly been selected for providing a sense of the voices of the people of the time and to demystifying the words of the past. Fifty years after the event, Mrs King wrote vividly of her schooldays during the 1650s and the assault on her by a child who disliked her (royalist) father's politics: we can see 'the scars I have yet to be seen' (document 3.3). Charles I's words at his trial, 'England was never an elective kingdom, but an hereditary kingdom for near these thousand years; therefore let me know by what authority I am called hither' conjure up the character of a proud but defeated monarch (document 3.17 (a)). The words of the governor of Londonderry's account of the final days

of the siege in 1689 hover between farce and tragedy: 'We were under so great necessity that we had nothing less unless we could prey upon one another: A certain fat gentleman conceived himself in the greatest danger and, fancying several of the garrison looked on him with a greedy eye, thought fit to hide himself for three days' (document 3.21).

The documents have also been chosen for what they can say about state formation, especially the constitutional developments of the period; there are documents relating to the constitutional challenges to Charles I, the governments of the 1650s, and the Restoration settlement. Documents touching the subject of beliefs and ideologies show the importance of religious belief and the significance of the ecclesiastical records of the time. We see, through the material on provisioning the armies in the civil wars, how producers and consumers were affected by the civil wars. The documents also show how devastating for a society a civil war is and how long-lasting and terrible its after-effects can be.

Anne Laurence

3.1
Writing the history of the English civil war: John Rushworth

J. Rushworth (1659–1701), *Historical Collections of Private Passages of State, Weighty Matters of Law, Remarkable Proceedings in Five Parliaments*, 7 vols., London, vol. 1 (1659), Preface, unpaginated.

John Rushworth (1612?–90) lawyer, clerk to parliament, and secretary to the Council of War and to the commander-in-chief, Sir Thomas Fairfax (1612–71), began to make a record of events in the 1630s. In 1659 he started to publish his *Historical Collections*, a collection of original documents from the civil war period with a commentary. The first volume was dedicated to Richard Cromwell (1626–1712).

3.1 [facing] Charles I on trial in Westminster Hall, January 1649. The king sits in the dock, with his back to the viewer, facing his accusers.

I began early to take in characters, speeches and passages at confer-
ences in parliament, and from the king's own mouth, when he spake
to both the Houses; and have been upon the stage continually, and as
an eye- and ear-witness of the greatest transactions; employed as an
agent in, and entrusted with affairs of weighty concernment; privy also
both to the debates in parliament, and to the most secret results of
councils of war, in times of action. Which I mention without ostenta-
tion; only to qualify me to report to posterity. [. . .] Such practices, and
the experience I had thereof, and the impossibility for any man in after-
ages to ground a true history, by relying on the printed pamphlets in
our days, which passed the press whilst it was without control,[1] obliged
me to all the pains and charge I have been at for many years together,
to make a great Collection; and whilst things were fresh in memory to
separate truth from falsehood, things real from things fictitious or
imaginary. Whereof I shall not at all repent, if I may but prove an ordinary instrument to undeceive those that come after us.

If you demand why my Collections commence so early, and start at
such a distance of time so remote, I must answer, That it was at first
my purpose to begin with the parliament which met Nov. 3 1640.[2] But
after I had perused, ordered and compared my printed and manuscript
relations of the first year of that parliament, I found they pointed at,
and were bottomed [grounded] upon some actions of the late king
[Charles I (b. 1600; reigned 1625–49)], in dissolving four preceding
parliaments: and thereupon, the zeal I had to clear the truth of the
differences between king and parliament, forced me to a longer adventure; especially seeing the essay had been very imperfect, and but a
mere fragment, if I had only writ the death and not the life of a prince,
who, in the first speech that ever he made in his first parliament, did
reflect upon some passages in a former parliament, that advised his
father to break off the two treaties with Spain touching a marriage,[3]
and the restitution of the Palatinate[4] and so engaged the father in a
war, which the son was, by him, left to prosecute.[5] And this consideration put me upon a further enquiry concerning the aforesaid treaties,
the causes and grounds of the war in the Palatinate, and how far the
same concerned England and the oppressed Protestants in Germany:

[1] Censorship of the press lapsed in 1640 and was not fully reinstated until 1660.

[2] The opening of the Long Parliament.

[3] James I (b. 1566; king of Scotland, 1567–1625; king of England, 1603–25) was proposing
to marry his son Charles to the daughter of the king of Spain.

[4] James had committed a force to help his son-in-law, Frederick V (1596–1632), the Elector
Palatine, recover his lands after they had been over-run by imperial forces in 1623.

[5] Charles I continued the policy of supporting the Elector after his succession as king
in March 1625.

and finding those proceedings to have their rise in the year 1618 (in which year the blazing star appeared) I resolved that the very instant should be the *Ne plus ultra* [highest point] of my retrospect . . .

I have heartily studied to declare myself unbiased, and to give an instance, that it is possible for an ingenuous [sic] man to be of a party, and yet not partial.

I pretend only in this work to a bare narrative of matter of fact, digested in order of time; not interpolating my own opinion, or interpretation of actions. . . . If I speak of any transactions which I myself did not see or hear, I do so with all the caution imaginable, having first consulted records, conferred with persons of unquestionable esteem, interested in the very actions, or perused their known hand-writings of those times; and where I make mention of any letters or passages scattered in print, I first weighed the same, and out of whose closets they came, and found many of them concredited [accredited] before I inserted them.

3.2
Rewriting the history of the civil war: John Nalson

J. Nalson (1682–3), An Impartial Collection of the Great Affairs of State from the beginning of the Scotch Rebellion in the Year 1639 to the Murther of King Charles, London, 2 vols., vol. 1, pp. i–vi.

John Nalson (1638?–86) historian and Anglican clergyman, wrote a number of anti-Whig works in the 1670s and 1680s. His collection of original documents was published as a corrective to Rushworth under the patronage of Charles II (b. 1630; crowned king of Scotland, 1651–85, king of England, 1660–85). Only the first two volumes appeared, taking the account to 1642.

Nothing is more certain, than, that to pursue the heels of time in the historical account of the affairs of a man's own country, at too near a distance, is an attempt not without discouragement, and sometimes danger.

[. . .]

I must confess, in the following discourse I have not tied myself strictly to the rules of a bare collector, but indulged myself in the liberty of an historian, to tie up the loose and scattered papers with the circumstances, causes and consequences of them. [. . .] I have always myself esteemed those histories which do not only tell us the bare tale of great transactions and revolutions of states and kingdoms. [. . .] I have therefore not only told the reader a long story that such great and uncommon events have happened, but I have also endeavoured to acquaint him with the real grounds, causes and occasions of those memorable transactions.

[. . .]

. . . I had these prospects, as the basis and foundation of the following discourses.

First, To prevent those false impressions which have been endeavoured to be made upon the minds of the subjects of this ancient and most admirably constituted hereditary monarchy, by prepossessing them with partial and false accounts of the late tragical revolutions. And in order to that,

Secondly, To manifest the innocence of government, and vindicate it from those notorious detractions and calumnies, which some factious and turbulent spirits, who have had all along a design to subvert the establishment both of church and state, have always endeavoured to fix upon it; persuading the nation of strange designs to introduce arbitrary government, and re-establish popery . . .

And lastly, in perfect charity to succeeding ages to set up buoys, beacons and light-houses upon the dangerous coast of disloyalty, and to give a true chart of the quicksands of popularity, and the dangerous rocks, which lie undiscovered under the smooth surface of pretences, to maintain liberty, property, Protestant religion, and privileges of parliament, betrayed us into the most deplorable shipwrack [sic] that England ever saw . . . and . . . prevent and avoid a second shipwrack.

[. . .]

I do not lie under the least temptation to quarrel with Mr Rushworth, being not so much as personally known to him, or having ever exchanged an hour's conversation with him. [. . .] [O]ne must conclude him, besides the strong bent of having been an actor upon the stage, almost within the danger of being an ingrate, if he did not endeavour as much as they will bear it, to palliate, at least, if not justify, the proceedings and actions of those men and times . . . and though it was Mr Rushworth's misfortune, as it was of many more, to mistake the short-lived meteor Richard Cromwell,[1] for the rising sun, yet the early adoration of dedicating his labours to the son of the usurper [Oliver Cromwell], may have been one great reason why they were calculated for that meridian; it being very improper to expect preferments and rewards, by telling the son his father was a rebel and a murderer, and was advanced to that height of usurpation by all the methods and artifices of villainy and wickedness.

3.3
Mrs Frances King's account of the war and its aftermath

Oxford, Bodleian Library, MS J. Walker c. 1, fo. 26. Line numbers added.

In the early eighteenth century a dispute broke out about who had suffered the more in the civil wars and at the Restoration: the Puritan clergy ejected from their livings in 1660–2 or the royalist clergy ejected from their livings in the 1640s and 1650s. John Walker (1674–1747), a Devon vicar, contacted many hundreds of people to collect information about the fate of royalist clergymen all over the country and published *An Attempt towards recovering an Account of the Numbers and Sufferings of the Clergy*, London, 1714. This letter was written to Walker in 1704 by the daughter of the royalist rector of Cottenham Cambridgeshire.

Haddenham March 25th, 1704

[. . .] I thought I was in duty obliged to endeavour to preserve the memory of my dear father who was a deep sufferer, in those calamitous times, and one of the earliest began withal, and hope his name may be inserted, amongst the rest, which was John
5   Manby, Doctor of Divinity, rector of Cottenham in the County of Cambridge, and within four miles of that town, a living of

---

[1] The first volume of Rushworth's *Historical Collections* was dedicated to Richard Cromwell, although he would later support the Restoration of the monarchy.

about £500 a year,[1] which was taken from my father, and given
for a portion[2] to Oliver Cromwell's sister Robina, married to one
Peter French.[3] [. . .] Committee men[4] being set up, and seques-
10 trators[5] made, the country went to wrack presently. Arms being
taken up on both sides, (viz) king's and parliament, declar[at]ions
was sent abroad, as victories were gotten, with order to be read
in churches, my father refused to read the parliament's, but read
the king's. For this and other his loyalty and religion, he was
15 first imprisoned in St John's College in Cambridge (the students
being turned out to make room for the king's good subjects) and
a soldier to keep him, and follow him where ever he went, being
commanded, to suffer none to speak a word to him but what he
should hear, no not my mother, when she came to see him, but
20 the soldier would stand by her. He was there a year and [a] half,
and often booted and spurred, to be taken away, he knew not
whither. Then some hasty news would come of the king's prevailing, and so he escaped them dangers. One time the king and
Prince Charles, passing through Cambridge by the college, my
25 father stood upon the leads [roof], over the gate, with his back
against a chimney, so soon as he was turned from the place, a
pistol was shot, charged, with a bullet, and hit the place where
he stood, but through God's providence missed him. While he
was kept there, he was plundered of all he had, by 2 sequestra-
30 tors, his parishioners, who lived in his parish. The one named
John Wright, a collar-maker by trade (who often worked in my
father's hall mending horse gears [harness and equipment] and
glad of a pot of strong beer) the other John Tailer, a husband-
man. These seized all within doors, all without doors, corn in
35 the barns, corn in the chambers, and corn growing on the land,
drove his cattle to the market, and sold them, sequestered all
his estate and one Major Jordan, captain at Cambridge and his
soldiers came, and French with them, who stood in the yard,

---

[1] This was a very valuable living. The poorest ones were worth perhaps £10 a year.

[2] Marriage portion or dowry.

[3] Canon of Christ Church, Oxford.

[4] In 1643 parliament appointed committees to administer all the counties that were
under parliamentary control; their primary purpose was to levy and collect the assessment
(tax).

[5] The Sequestration Ordinance set up local committees to confiscate and administer
estates of delinquents (royalists and Catholics). Sequestrators were officials of the committees and were responsible for assessing and collecting property sequestrated from
individuals for such offences as using the Book of Common Prayer, refusing to acknowledge the new church settlement or expressing opposition to Parliament.

40   until they entered the house, with their pistols cocked, and their swords drawn in their hands, their matches[6] [a]light and took my mother by the arm, and me in her arms, sucking on her breasts, and 4 small children more, and turned out of doors, and all her family, and put French in. Meat was at the fire, roasting for dinner, they seized that, and gobbled it up, and left none for

45   the owner. But put us into the street, the heavens to be our covering, and ground our lodging, for they took no care, to provide an habitation for us, and every one was afraid to give us shelter. . . . Having lost all here, [John Manby] was patron of a living in Yorkshire, near Beverly, called Middleton on the

50   Wolds, and the incumbent being dead, he went to serve it himself, hoping he might be suffered to keep that but after he had stayed there a year, the sequestrators there seized it, turned him out, put in an intruder, and would not give him one farthing for his labour. [. . .] One time Wright charged my mother with receiving

55   letters from my father, and see them he would, and searched her pockets to find them, which so frighted my mother, that it caused a miscarriage of a child, and much endangered her life. Another time my father was riding through the street, and Wright met him, who took his horse by the bridle, led him to the

60   common pound, put the horse in, father on his back, and locked the pound gate again. . . . Many were the indignities, affronts, and spiteful pranks this sequestrator used to my poor father, at last the Drs [lawyers] procured him to be bound over in the Kings Bench,[7] to his good behaviour, and then my father had a

65   little more quiet who lost his estate 18 years. My sister being owner of a little commonable house, in the town, and my father not being suffered to keep anything, stocked her with some cows, to keep a dairy. These sequestrators took her cows, drove them to market, sold them, and put the money into their own

70   pocket [. . .] They sent a bell man about the town to forbid every one that owed him money to pay him. The parliament allowed my mother the fifth part out of the living to maintain her[8] and her children, but Nye[9] would not pay one farthing. Then went off the king's head, and my father being treated thus in the

---

[6] Glowing match for igniting matchlock guns.

[7] King's Bench, principal criminal court for England.

[8] The families of ejected royalist clergymen were entitled to petition for the award of one-fifth of the value of the living vacated to allow them to survive since the husband and father was disabled from earning a living.

[9] John Nye who became rector after Peter French, who displaced Manby.

75 country removed his family to London, to try better fortune,
thinking to follow something of his employ, as teaching school,
or what he could mete withal. But they silenced him, and would
not suffer him to follow any thing. Then came he down again to
a town near Cottenham, called Histon, and there he settled,
80 having a little estate, was my eldest sister's, for the nourishment
of his family till King Charles the second's restoration to the
crown and my father to his living again which God after all
these endeavours to starve him and his brought to pass. . . . I
myself saw Wright riding bareheaded before Oliver Cromwell
85 who came to Cottenham in great pomp, to see his sister, with
his troop of soldiers, and Wright rid his horse to death in per-
forming that service. When the Presbyterian government was
set up it was highly commended in Cottenham church by Nye,
in his sermon, and he bid those that liked it to hold up their
90 hand, which the man did immediately, and a certain gentlewoman held up her foot. These with a great many more which
I cannot give account of were the sufferings of my poor father,
which ruined his family for though he lived to be restored to his
living, he was old and could not recruit his losses . . . but what
95 I have writ is true what I have heard from my father, and mother's own mouths, and servants that then lived with him, my
aunt, uncle and neighbours, after we came amongst them again
and what I know myself, in all my growing up, who groaned
with my parents, under these hardships.

[. . .]

100 Their [the parliamentarians'] very children were so full of
hatred taking it from their parents, that if I and my sister, had
straggled out on a holiday, to see them play, they would leave
off, and not company with us, and myself being very young, at
school with a master in Cottenham, where boys and girls were
105 taught together, at playtime in the yard; some boys pretended
to espy a wonder upon a house that joined with the yard, and I
running amongst the rest to see, a boy, son to an adversary, took
up a fork, and struck the tines into my head, a little above my
forehead, the scars I have yet to be seen, my father durst no
110 more let me go amongst them. [. . .] So leaving this to the author
of the book to put into right order, hoping my father's name may
be placed amongst those pious sufferers, and begging pardon
for all mistakes or errors in this writing I being a woman, and
doing it myself. I desire to know the price of the book when
115 finished.

3.4

Resistance to ship money, 1639

K. Lindley (ed.) (1998), *The English Civil War and Revolution: A Sourcebook*, London: Routledge, pp. 36–7.

Ship money was originally an emergency tax levied on maritime counties in exceptional circumstances. From 1635, the king levied the tax on inland counties, meeting considerable resistance. All householders were required to pay and county officials were empowered to seize (distress or distrain) possessions from non-payers.

4 August 1639

Middlesex. Robert Markes, clerk to the under sheriff of Middlesex, and William Caninge, a bailiff, being authorised to warrant from the high sheriff of the county of Middlesex for the levying of many arrears for his majesty's service within the parish of Harrow upon the Hill and other parishes within the hundred[1] of Gore were much abused in the execution of their office by several persons in many particulars calling them thieves, rogues, assaulting them, throwing scalding water upon them, rescuing distresses[2] taken, threatening suits against them in case they brought not the distresses to them back again and saying they came progging[3] and prowling up and down the country to cheat them by whose examples many men are encouraged to oppose the said service; many affirming they are to be borne out by some particular persons though they oppose.

The names of such [as] were most obstinate about the service being distrained [including]:

Distress taken. Mrs Miller of Pinner being distrained and a piece of cloth now in custody; more was brought to them by one Mr Hatch. She would question them for felony.

Distress. Rescue. John Edlyn of Pinner March being distrained and a horse in custody: the said William Caninge the bailiff, was much beaten by the servant of the said Edlyn and the horse rescued away: Edlyn having had notice to pay the money the night before yet refused and bade them take their course.

[. . .]

---

[1] An administrative unit below that of county.
[2] Legal seizure of goods as means of enforcing payment.
[3] Poking about, foraging.

217

There hath been about forty distresses taken in Harrow and near thereabouts; most of them refusing to pay without distresses saying they can but pay at last and there is no for it.

3.5
Episcopal visitation articles and returns of the 1630s

Conformity to the ecclesiastical canons, the laws regulating the conduct of the Church of England, was enforced by archbishops, bishops and their subordinates by means of visitations when the churchwardens of each parish were asked to respond to a set of questions. Bishop Matthew Wren,[1] supported the ecclesiastical changes proposed by Archbishop Laud.[2]

(a) Headings and extracts from *Articles to be enquired of within the Diocese of Hereford in the first visitation of the reverend Father in God, Matthew Lord Bishop of Hereford,* 1635

K. Fincham (ed.) (1998), *Visitation Articles and Injunctions of the Early Stuart Church,* vol. II, Church of England Record Society vol. 5, pp. 129–44.

1. Concerning religion and doctrine
1. Whether be there any abiding in your parish, or resorting to it, who have wilfully maintained any heresies, errors or false opinions, contrary to the faith of Christ and holy scripture? Or are that do impugn any of the 39 articles of religion agreed upon in *anno* 1562, and established in the Church of England? And is the declaration which the king's majesty prefixed before those 39 Articles concerning the settling of questions in difference, duly observed by all within your parish, according to his majesty's commandment?

---

[1] Matthew Wren (1585–1667) was bishop of Hereford 1635, of Norwich 1635–8 and of Ely 1638–67. He was strongly associated with the Laudian reforms.
[2] William Laud (1573–1645), archbishop of Canterbury from 1633.

The Souldiers in their passage to York turn unto reformers pull down Popish pictures, break down rayles, turn altars into Tables,

3.2 Parliamentarian soldiers reacting against Laud's ecclesiastical canons and destroying altar rails and altars, 1646. This was a favoured image of Royalist propaganda, depicting their opponents all as fervent puritans, out to destroy the Church of England and impose their own form of piety on the populace.

2. Concerning public prayer and administration of the holy sacraments

1. [. . .] do any preach, speak or declare, that the book of common prayer containeth any thing, that is repugnant to the holy scripture, or not meet to be used?

[. . .]

3. Concerning the church, the furniture, and possessions thereof

2. Whether have you in your church or chapel, a font of stone, set in the ancient usual place, whole and clean, and fit to hold water, a convenient and decent communion table, with a carpet of silk, or some other decent stuff, continually laid upon the table at the time of divine service; and a fair linen cloth laid thereon at the time of administering the communion? And whether is the same table placed conveniently, so as the minister may best be heard in his administration, and the greatest number may reverently communicate [take holy communion]? Ordinarily doth it stand up at the east end of the chancel, where the altar in former times[3] stood, the ends

---

[3] i.e., before the Reformation.

thereof being placed north and south? Is it at any time used unreverently, by leaning or sitting on it, throwing hats or anything else upon it, or writing on it, or is it abused to any profane or common use? And whether are the ten commandments set up on the east end of your church, or chapel, where the people may see and read them, and other chosen sentences also written upon the walls of your said church or chapel, in places convenient for the said purpose.

[. . .]

6. Is there any in your parish that hath or doth refuse to contribute towards the reparation of your church . . . ?

[. . .]

4. Concerning the ministers of God's holy word, and preachers and lecturers

9. Whether your minister, preacher, and lecturer every year four times, of purpose and expressly, at large teach and declare the lawful authority which the king hath over the state, both ecclesiastical and civil, and the just abolishing of all foreign power or jurisdiction over the same.

[. . .]

5. Concerning matrimony

3. Whether do any persons being lawfully married, live asunder unlawfully; and in whom is the default?

[. . .]

6. Concerning the churchwardens and sidesmen[4]

4. Do the churchwardens and sidesmen, or assistants, diligently see that all the parishioners do duly resort to the church, upon all Sundays and holidays . . . ?

[. . .]

7. Concerning the parishioners

12. Whether have you any in your parish that are commonly known, or reputed to be blasphemers of God's holy name, common and usual swearers, drunkards, usurers, filthy-speakers, adulterers, fornicators, incestuous persons, bawds, concealers or harbourers of fornicators or adulterers? Have any in your parish been detected of such notorious crimes, and what penance have they done for the same?

[. . .]

---

[4] An assistant to a churchwarden, responsible for greeting the congregation, seating arrangements, and for taking the collection.

15. Whether have any in your parish, received or harboured any women gotten with child out of wedlock, and suffered her to depart without punishment first inflicted on her by the ordinary [bishop or bishop's deputy]? You shall truly present as well the party harbouring, as harboured, and who is suspected to be the father of the child?

[. . .]

8. *Concerning schoolmasters, physicians, surgeons, midwives and parish clerks*

2. What physician or surgeon have you in your parish? Who not being a doctor of physic in either of the universities, doth notwithstanding practise physic? What other persons have you among you, male or female, who take upon themselves to profess physic or surgery? And who be midwives within your parish?

(b) Extract from *Bishop Matthew Wren's Orders for Norwich Diocese*, 1636

K. Fincham (ed.) (1998), *Visitation Articles and Injunctions of the Early Stuart Church*, vol. II, Church of England Record Society vol. 5, p. 157.

3. That the communion table in every church do always stand close under the wall of the chancel, the ends thereof north and south, unless the ordinary give particular direction otherwise. And that the rail be made before it (according to the archbishop's late injunctions) reaching across from the north wall to the south wall, near one yard in height, and so thick with pillars, that dogs may not get in.

(c) Extract from *Articles to be Inquired of within the Diocese of Ely in the First Visitation of the Right Reverend Father in God Matthew Lord Bishop of Ely*, 1638

Articles to be Inquired of within the Diocese of Ely in the First Visitation of the Right Reverend Father in God Matthew Lord Bishop of Ely, London, 1638, unpaginated.

3.2 Have you in your church or chapel a font of stone set and fastened in the ancient usual place, whole and clean and fit to hold water? A convenient and decent communion table, with a carpet of silk, or some other decent stuff, continually laid upon the table at the time of divine service; and a fair linen cloth thereon laid, at the time of administering the communion? What did either of them cost? What be they now worth in value? And is the same table placed conveniently, so as the minister may be heard in his administration, and the greatest number may reverently communicate? To that end doth it ordinarily stand up at the east end of the chancel where the altar in former times stood, the ends thereof being placed north and south? Is it at any time used irreverently, by leaning or sitting on it, throwing hats or anything else upon it, or writing on it; or is it abused to any other profane or common use? Are there any ascent or steps in your chancel up to the communion table? Have you also a decent rail of wood (or some other comely enclosure covered with cloth or silk) placed handsomely above those steps, before the holy table, near one yard high and reaching cross from the north wall to the south (except by the order of the diocesan it be made with the ends returning unto the east wall) with two convenient doors to open before the table: and if it be a rail, are the pillars or balusters thereof so close, that dogs may not anywhere get in? Also are the Ten Commandments set up in your church or chapel where the people may see and read them; and other chosen sentences written upon the walls of your said church or chapel, in places convenient to the same purpose.

(d) Extract from the answers of the parish of Shepreth, Cambs to the questions in Bishop Wren's 1638 Visitation

W.M. Palmer & H.W. Saunders (eds.) (1926), *Documents Relating to Cambridgeshire Villages* no. III, Cambridge: Cambridge University Press, pp. 53–6.

Ch. 1, Concerning religion &c.
We answer we have nothing to present
Ch. 2, Concerning public prayers
We answer
1. We have none that have procured any minister either to read public prayer or to administer any sacrament otherwise than is mentioned in the Book of Common Prayer nor have we any interrupters or disturbers of the minister officiating.
2 & 3. Baptism hath been duly performed, hath not been deferred, always after the 2nd lesson . . .

8 & 9. The sacrament of the lord's supper hath been duly & reverently administered thrice every year whereof once at Easter, likewise devoutly received, all humbly kneeling

Ch. 3 Concerning the church

1, 2, 3 We have a parish [church] and chancel now standing & useful, a bible in folio & of use the last translation, the Book of Common Prayer, Jewel's Works,[5] canons ecclesiastical, the book of homilies, the form and services for the 5 November and 27 March,[6] a font of stone for use, a clean & decent table with a carpet but defective & a fair linen cloth. What they cost we know not but are worth 20 shillings. Our communion table is placed at the east end of the chancel and stands ended north and south but not conveniently that the minister may be heard in his administration. We have an ascent unto the table, a rail of wood close made from the north wall to the south with two doors, the ten commandments & other sentences of scripture upon the walls. . . .

8. There is one Philip Hale, gent. that refuseth to pay part of a rate[7] made for the repair of our church, which comes to about 15 shillings or thereabouts.

Ch. 4 Concerning the ministers, preachers and lecturers

1–5. Our minister is a graduate master of Arts, his name is Stephen Wilson, a licensed preacher by a late revered bishop of Ely of this diocese and preacheth usually in his own cure in such ornaments as is prescribed and observeth that form of exhortation to prayer prescribed in the canon. . . .

11, 12, 13 Our minister declareth the king's sovereign authority for all causes and over all persons ecclesiastical and civil, abolishing popery and all civil power. Neither hath he published any new doctrine dissenting from the truth of God's word nor from the articles of faith agreed on *anno domini* 1562 and so observeth the administration of baptism after the second lesson, using therein the sign of the cross and all other things and ceremonies as is prescribed in the rubric of the Book of Common Prayer.

Ch. 5 Concerning matrimony

. . . None lawfully married live asunder. No recusants,[8] none that have been divorced, nor any that companies together, but such as are known to be lawfully married.

---

[5] John Jewel, bishop of Salisbury (1522–71) See Document 2.17, footnote 4.

[6] The anniversaries of the Gunpowder Plot and the accession of King Charles I.

[7] A local tax levied in each parish.

[8] The word recusants is commonly used to mean Roman Catholics but actually means everyone who refused to go to church.

Ch. 7 Concerning parishioners

12. We present John Frevill of our town for abusing our minister being in holy orders with contumelious words and uncivil gestures, behaving himself rudely and unreverently towards him, tending to the scorn and dishonour of his person, calling him devil, and comparing him to Judas[9] &c.

3.6

The National Covenant, 1638

From G. Donaldson (ed.) ([1970] 1974), *Scottish Historical Documents*, Glasgow: Neil Wilson, pp. 199–200.

The National Covenant, drafted in February 1638 by Alexander Henderson (c. 1583–1646) and Archibald Johnston of Wariston (c. 1611–63), was sent round Scotland for subscription by anyone who decried the Laudian innovations in the Church of Scotland.

We noblemen, barons, gentlemen, burgesses, ministers and commons under subscribing, considering divers times before and especially at this time, the danger of the true reformed religion, of the king's honour, and of the public peace of the kingdom: By the manifold innovations and evils generally contained, and particularly mentioned in our late supplications, complaints and protestations, do hereby profess, and before God, his angels, and the world solemnly declare, that, with our whole hearts we argue and resolve, all the days of our life, constantly to adhere unto, and to defend the foresaid true religion, and (forbearing the practice of all [in]novations, already introduced in the matters of the worship of God . . .) to labour by all means lawful to recover the purity and liberty of the gospel, as it was [e]stablished and professed before the foresaid novations. [. . .] We promise and swear by the great name of the lord our God, to continue in the profession and obedience of the foresaid religion: that we will defend the same, and resist all these contrary errors and corruptions, according to our vocation, and to the uttermost of that power that God hath put in our hands, all the days of our life: and in like manner with the same heart, we declare before God and men, that we have no intention nor desire to attempt

---

[9] The disciple who betrayed Christ.

anything that may turn to the dishonour of God, or to the diminution of the king's greatness and authority.

Acts of the General Assembly at Glasgow, 1638

3.7

G. Donaldson (ed.) ([1970] 1974), *Scottish Historical Documents*, Glasgow: Neil Wilson, pp. 203–5.

The General Assembly of the Kirk (the representative governing body of the Church of Scotland) met in 1638 for the first time since 1618, after riots against the proposed ecclesiastical innovations. The Assembly condemned them and abolished those it most hated, asserting the power of the Assembly alone to govern the church.

Condemnation of the Prayer Book, Canons and High Commission
The Assembly having diligently considered the Book of Common Prayer, lately obtruded upon the reformed kirk within this realm ... findeth that it hath been devised and brought in by the pretended prelates, without direction from the kirk, and pressed upon ministers without warrant from the kirk. [...] The Assembly, therefore, all in one voice, hath rejected and condemned and by these presents doth reject and condemn the said book, not only as illegally introduced, but also as repugnant to the doctrine, discipline and order of this reformed kirk ... and doth prohibit the use and practice thereof.
[...]
The Assembly also, taking into their consideration the Book of Canons, and the manner how it hath been introduced, findeth that it hath been devised by the pretended prelates, without warrant or direction from the General Assembly. ... Therefore the Assembly all in one voice hath rejected and condemned ... the said book, as contrary to the Confession of our Faith, and repugnant to the established government, the Book of Discipline, and the acts and constitutions of our kirk.
[...]

Condemnation of episcopacy

The whole Assembly most unanimously, without contradiction of anyone (and with hesitation of one Allarnly) professing full persuasion of mind, did voice that all episcopacy different from that of a pastor over a particular flock, was abjured in this Kirk, and to be removed out of it.

3.8
The Nature of the Irish, 1610

B. Rich (1610), *A New Description of Ireland: Wherein is Described the Disposition of the Irish Whereunto they are Inclined*, London, pp. 15–16.

[handwritten: potential bias]

Barnaby Rich (?1540–1617), an Englishman, served as a soldier in France and the Low Countries before taking service in Ireland in the 1570s. He then moved to London and took to writing romances, reminiscences and pamphlets exposing contemporary vices. In the 1580s he returned to military service in Ireland and published a number of accounts of the country and its people, capitalising on the popularity in England of travel literature.

To speak now of the Irish more at large. [. . .] And though that in the remote places, the uncivil sort so disfigure themselves with their glibs,[1] their trows [trews],[2] and their misshapen attire, yet they appear to every man's eye to be men of good proportion, of comely stature, and of able body. Now to speak of their dispositions, whereunto they are addicted and inclined. I say, besides they are rude, uncleanly, and uncivil, so they are very cruel, bloody minded, apt and ready to commit any kind of mischief. I do not impute this so much to their natural inclination, as I do to their education, that are trained up in treason, in rebellion, in theft, in robbery, in superstition, in idolatry, and nuzeled [nurtured] from their cradles in the very puddle of popery. [. . .] From hence it proceedeth, that the Irish have ever been, and still are, desirous to shake off English government. [. . .] From hence it is, that the Irish had rather still retain themselves in their sluttishness, in their

---

[1] A hanging lock of hair.

[2] Close fitting trousers worn with stockings by Irish men and Scots Highlanders.

uncleanliness, in their rudeness, and in their inhumane loathsomeness, than they would take any example from the English, either of civility, humanity, or any manner of decency.

Protestant depositions in Ireland, 1641

Following the Catholic rising in Ireland in October 1641 and the murder and spoliation of Protestant settlers there, a number of Protestant clergymen and special commissioners took sworn statements from Protestant refugees about their losses and the extent of the damage they had suffered over the period 1641–7. Many of the statements recalled events that had taken place four or five years previously. Thirty-two manuscript volumes of the statements survive.

(a) Deposition of Honora Beamond, 7 June 1643

M. Hickson (1884), *Ireland in the Seventeenth Century or the Irish Massacres of 1641–2, their Causes and Results*, London: Longmans, Green and Co., 2 vols., vol. 1, p. 191.

Honora Beamond, relict [widow] of William Beamond, innkeeper, late of Clouness [Clones], in the county of Monaghan, sworn and examined, deposeth and saith, that on or about the 23rd of October 1641, she and her husband were deprived, robbed and otherwise despoiled of their goods, chattels, profits of a garden, and the benefit of a lease worth £30 per annum, by Redmond MacRory MacMahon, of the Dartry, a captain of rebels, Rory MacPatrick MacMahon, another captain of the rebels, their soldiers and followers, whose names she knows not. And at that time the rebels aforesaid hanged eighteen Scottish Protestants on the church gate of Clouness, and murdered one James Whitehead, an English Protestant, who had been a good housekeeper, after they had robbed him of all his goods when he was going on a message for one Mr Willoughby. And they also murdered about the same time James Dunshiel, another Protestant, and robbed and stripped of their clothes this deponent, her husband and children, and all the Protestants in the country thereabouts. And the rebels burned this deponent's house and the town and church of Clouness, and this deponent herself saw the corpses of sixteen Protestants, nearly all women and children, near the common mill, after the rebels had there drowned them in a bog or pit, all which corpses were buried in one hole in the highway, near the ditch or bog where they were drowned, in the presence of this deponent. And after she and her husband were robbed as aforesaid, the rebels imprisoned and restrained them, so as they would not suffer them to depart out of the country until about Midsummer 1642, during which time they endured extreme want and misery. But at length the great God in His mercy sent thither the Lord Moore,[1] with an army, who enlarged them from the rebels and brought them to Dublin, where her said husband nine days after died, leaving her this deponent and her children in great want, distress and misery.

Honora Beamond + her mark

Jurat [sworn] 7th June 1643
W[illia]m Aldrich
Hen[ry] Brereton

(b) Deposition of Margaret Farmenie and Margaret Leathley, 3 January 1642

M. Hickson (1884), Ireland in the Seventeenth Century or the Irish Massacres of 1641–2, their Causes and Results, London: Longmans, Green and Co., 2 vols., vol. 1, pp. 168–9.

Margaret Farmenie and Margaret Leathley, widows, both of Acrashannig, in the parish of Clowniss [Clones], county of Fermanagh, sworn and examined, deposeth that on October 24th, 1641, in the morning, Laughlin Duffe; Patrick MacMahon; Laughlin MacCarroll; Philip Roe Shane MacCullen, and certain others of the rebels in the said county, to the number of one hundred or thereabouts, robbed those deponents of their goods, and further saith that the rebels bound those deponents' hands behind them, urging to confess they had money. And they bound the husband of the said Margaret Farmenie, and then they dragged him up and down in a rope, and cut his throat in her own sight, with a skene [dagger], having first knocked him down and stripped him. And having also there murdered fourteen persons more, all English Protestants, they, the said rebels, alleging that they had the king's broad seal to strip and stone all the English and that they were the king's soldiers. And as these deponents came up to

---

[1] Charles Moore, Viscount Moore of Drogheda (1603–43). Protestant commander.

Dublin, being aged women of seventy-five years old or thereabouts, the said rebels bidding them go on and look for their God, and let him give them clothes.

Margaret + Farmenie

Margaret + Leathley

Jurat. [sworn] January 3rd 1641 [/2]

Coram [in the presence of] John Sterne

  W[illia]m Hitchcock

(c) The humble petition of Elizabeth Birche to the Right Honourable Lords Justices and Council, c. 1643

Dublin, Trinity College, MS 840, no 124.

Shewing that your petitioner's husband being one of the Earl of Strafford's troop,[2] on Saturday last was grazing his horse at Baggotrath, and there was taken by the rebels, and carried away into the county of Wicklow and now remains prisoner with them. Now so it is that your petitioner is informed that there is one Ellen Aspoole now prisoner at the Naas who hath remained there since Christmas last who they willingly accept if your honours be pleased to give order that the said Ellen may be released and delivered on exchange for your petitioner's husband.

3.10

Extracts from the Grand Remonstrance, 1641

J.P. Kenyon (1986), *The Stuart Constitution 1603–1688: Documents and Commentary*, 2nd edn, Cambridge: Cambridge University Press, pp. 207–17.

The Grand Remonstrance was presented as a petition from the House of Commons to the king on 1 December 1641. It was

---

[2] Thomas Wentworth, 1st earl of Strafford (1593–1641), English statesman and Lord Lieutenant of Ireland (1632–40). He was a strong supporter of the king and systematically enforced increasing 'anglicisation' of finance, administration and the Church in Ireland. He was recalled to England to become Charles I's chief adviser in 1639. Strafford bore the brunt of Parliament's attempts to curtail the king's powers in 1640: he was convicted of treason under a Bill of Attainder (legal process without a trial) and executed on 12 May 1641.

prompted by the outbreak of rebellion in Ireland in October and fears about what the king would do if equipped with a substantial army. It set out the reasons for the recent divisions and in addition to the terms below demanded that the church settlement be referred to a synod of divines from England and other European Protestant communities. It passed by eleven votes.

Preamble

The duty which we owe to your Majesty and our country cannot but make us very sensible and apprehensive that the multiplicity, sharpness and malignity of those evils under which we have now many years suffered are fomented and cherished by a corrupt and ill-affected party.

[. . .]

For preventing whereof, and the better information of your Majesty . . . we have been necessitated to make a Declaration of the state of the kingdom . . . which we do humbly present to your Majesty, without the least intention to lay any blemish upon your royal person. . . . We your most humble and obedient subjects do with all faithfulness and humility beseech your Majesty:

1. That you will be most graciously pleased to concur with the humble desires of your people in a parliamentary way, for the preserving the peace and safety of the kingdom from the malicious designs of the Popish party:

For depriving the bishops of their votes in parliament, and abridging their immoderate power usurped over the clergy, and other your good subjects, which they have perniciously abused to the hazard of religion and great prejudice and oppression to the laws of the kingdom and just liberty of your people;

For the taking away such oppression in religion, church government and discipline as have been brought in and fomented by them;

For uniting all such your loyal subjects together as join in the same fundamental truths against the papists, by removing some oppressive and unnecessary ceremonies by which divers weak consciences have been scrupled, and seem to be divided from the rest, and for the due execution of those good laws which have been made for securing the liberty of your subjects.

2. That your Majesty will likewise be pleased to remove from your council all such as persist to favour and promote any of those pressures and corruptions wherewith your people have been grieved, and that for the future your Majesty will vouchsafe to employ such persons

in your great and public affairs, and to take such to be near you in places of trust, as your parliament may have cause to confide [have confidence] in;

[...]

Which humble desires of our being graciously fulfilled by your Majesty, we will, by the blessings and favour of God, most cheerfully undergo the hazard and expense of this war [in Ireland].

3.11

Newsbook accounts of an engagement at Warrington, 8 April 1643

Numerous newsbooks were published during the civil war. Some appeared in no more than two or three issues, others survived for much longer and were semi-official mouthpieces for parliament or the king.

(a) *Mercurius Aulicus* (Royalist newsbook)

Mercurius Aulicus, 14th week, 2–9 April 1643, p. 179.

The principal royalist newsbooks were published in Oxford, the king's headquarters, but were often sold and sometimes reprinted in London. *Mercurius Aulicus* was published weekly as the official royalist mouthpiece, edited by Dr Peter Heylin (1599–1662) from offices in Oriel College, Oxford.

Saturday April 8

The first news of this day was of a double defeat given by the Earl of Derby[1] to Sir William Brereton,[2] at Warrington in Lancashire, a town very near the borders of Cheshire, Brereton coming thither upon an hope of hindering the Earl's proceedings: who was going with part of his forces towards Manchester. But Brereton being well beaten at the

---

[1] James Stanley, 7th earl of Derby (1607–51) was commander of the king's forces in Lancashire and Cheshire.

[2] Sir William Brereton (1604–61) was commander of the parliamentary forces there.

first onset, with the loss of many of his men and some of his colours, had no mind to go away until he had perfected the Earl's victory, and his own overthrow, and therefore drew into the field again, with the accession of some new forces from Manchester, to play double or quits. Which being perceived by the Earl of Derby, he purposely held off from accepting the battle, till the dusk of the evening, and then sent some of his own men under Brereton' s colours to make towards them; who being taken (and indeed mistaken) for their own party, were suffered to join with them, or come very near them on the one side; and then the Earl charging very hotly upon the other, they made a great impression on both sides, and having thus caught them in a trap, defeated them with greater slaughter, and little labour.

(b) *The Kingdomes Weekly Intelligencer* (Parliamentarian newsbook)

The Kingdomes Weekly Intelligencer sent abroad to prevent misinformation, 4–11 April 1643, pp. 118–19.

The *Weekly Intelligencer*, published on Tuesdays, was started in January 1643 and ran until 1649. It broadly supported parliament. Its editor, Richard Collings, was more outspoken than other editors and more insistent on the evils of the royalist cause. He reduced the coverage of parliament's proceedings and reported military engagements in detail.

The next lord, whose name begins with D, is that grand patron of papists also, the Earl of Derby, whose forces being about fourteen hundred at least at Wigan in Lancashire, the only place of receipt for the papists' treasure and goods, were there soundly beaten by the honest-headed Clubmen,[3] who if the nobility and gentry of the kingdom still go on to make the Commons of England gentle slaves in their religion and liberty, they themselves (that is) so many of them as run these courses, may happen to be taken before they die, at least in esteem inferior to Commons. And in that fight about eight hundred were taken prisoners, and five hundred more quite routed, and above one thousand arms, besides ordnance taken, and treasure and goods of papists to the value of twenty thousand pounds.

---

[3] Clubmen movements emerged in several counties opposing the forces of both sides and the demands they made on householders for money, livestock, quarter, food etc.

The stout Manchesterians with their honest German engineer[4] rested not here, they marched on to Warrington, a place of strength and great resort, have taken the town, and beaten the popish forces into the church and steeple; and some write, that the Earl of Derby is there with those forces; more of this next week. If every week, the parliament's forces (who are the only men in this kingdom that truly fight for God and religion) prevail against the other lords according to the alphabet,[5] they will quickly put a period [end] to the popish and malignant [royalist] peers.

(c) *A Continuation of certaine Speciall and Remarkable Passages from both Houses of Parliament*

A Continuation of certaine Speciall and Remarkable Passages from both Houses of Parliament, no. 40, 6–13 April 1643, unpaginated.

This publication ran from October 1642 to June 1643 and appeared on Wednesdays. It may have been published by Samuel Pecke.

More letters from Lancashire confirms (sic) the taking of Wigan from the Earl of Derby by Sir John Seaton[6] and the Manchester forces, and that they took there 800 prisoners, 21000 arms, besides other ammunition, money and goods of the papists, to the value of 20000 pound.

And that after the taking of Wigan they went to Warrington, where the Earl of Derby with his most considerable forces then lay, and after a very fierce assault and hot skirmish on both sides they forced their entrance into the town and drove the enemy into the church, against which they have made some battery, but wanted [lacked] ordnance [cannon] for the present to force it, but make no doubt to be master of it suddenly, and put an end to the Lancashire distractions, if the Earl of Derby be there (as is supposed), however the malevolents in London do strongly affirm that the Earl of Derby hath again taken

---

[4] John Rosworme (fl. 1630–60), a German engineer, contracted with the citizens of Manchester to defend the town against the earl of Derby. He later became engineer-general of all the garrisons and forts in England.

[5] The author had noted that many of the people in the news were lords whose names began with the letter D.

[6] Local parliamentarian commander.

Wigan from the parliament's forces, which is not only improbable but a mere falsity.

<hr>

3.12

The religious provisions of the Solemn League and Covenant, September 1643

S.R. Gardiner (ed.) (1906), *The Constitutional Documents of the Puritan Revolution 1625–60*, Oxford: Clarendon Press, 3rd edn revised, pp. 268–9.

The Solemn League and Covenant embodied the terms of the alliance between parliament and the Scots under which, in return for military assistance, parliament agreed to pay for the Scots forces, reform the Church of England, and to ensure that all English military personnel and office holders subscribed to the document.

[We] do swear,

1. That we shall sincerely, really and constantly, through the grace of God, endeavour in our several places and callings, the preservation of the reformed religion in the Church of Scotland, in doctrine, worship, discipline and government, against our common enemies; the reformation of religion in the kingdoms of England and Ireland, in doctrine, worship, discipline and government, according to the Word of God, and the example of the best reformed churches; and we shall endeavour to bring the Churches of God in the three kingdoms to the nearest conjunction and uniformity in religion, confession of faith, form of church government, directory for worship and catechising, that we, and our posterity after us, may, as brethren, live in faith and love, and the Lord may delight and dwell in the midst of us.

2. That we shall in like manner, without respect of persons, endeavour the extirpation of Popery, prelacy (that is, Church government by Archbishops, Bishops, their Chancellors and Commissaries, Dean, Deans and Chapters, Archdeacons, and all other ecclesiastical officers depending on that hierarchy), superstition, heresy, schism, profaneness, and whatsoever shall be found to be contrary to sound doctrine and the power of godliness, lest we partake in other men's sins, and

thereby be in danger to receive of their plagues; and that the Lord may be one and His name one in the three kingdoms.

YES | *PERHAPS*

Agitators and Levellers, 1647

G.E. Aylmer (ed.) (1975), *The Levellers in the English Revolution*, London: Thames and Hudson, pp. 89–91; 109–12.

(a) An Agreement of the People

The first *Agreement of the People* was written in October 1647, probably by civilian Levellers[1] (despite the statement in the text that it was written by the agents of five new Model Army cavalry regiments). It was, in effect, a draft proposal for a constitution to be submitted to the people of England. It distilled the demands of civilian and army Levellers.

An Agreement of the People for a form and present peace, upon grounds of common-right and freedom as was proposed by the Agents of the five regiments of horse; and since by the general appro-bation of the army, offered to the joint concurrence of all the free Commons of England. . . . 1647

Having by our late labours and hazards made it appear to the world at how high a rate we value our just freedom, and God having so far owned our cause, as to deliver the enemies thereof into our hands: we do now hold ourselves bound in mutual duty to each other, to take the best care we can for the future, to avoid both the danger of returning into a slavish condition, and the chargeable remedy of another war: for as it cannot be imagined that so many of our countrymen would have opposed us in this quarrel, if they understood their own good, so may we safely promise to our selves, that when our common rights and liberties shall be cleared, their endeavours will be disappointed, that seek to make themselves our masters: since therefore our former

---

[1] The Leveller movement grew up in London and in the New Model Army during the mid-1640s. Their demands included religious toleration for Protestants, frequent parliaments and an enlarged franchise for men. *which upset Cromwell & Ireton*

oppressions, and scarce yet ended troubles have been occasioned, either by want of frequent national meetings in council, or by rendering those meetings ineffectual. . . . We declare

I. That the people of England being at this day very unequally distributed by counties, cities and boroughs, for the election of their deputies in parliament, ought to be more indifferently proportioned, according to the number of the inhabitants.

[. . .]

IV. That the power of this, and all future representatives of this nation, is inferior only to those who choose them, and doth extend, without the consent or concurrence of any other person or persons; to the enacting, altering, and repealing of laws; to the erectings and abolishing of officers and courts; to the appointing, removing, and calling to account magistrates, and officers of all degrees; to the making war and peace, to the treating with foreign states: and generally, to whatsoever is not expressly, or impliedly reserved to the representatives themselves

Which are as followeth

1. That matters of religion, and the ways of God's worship, are not at all entrusted by us to any human power, because therein we cannot remit or exceed a tittle of what our consciences dictate to be the mind of God, without wilful sin: nevertheless, the public way of instructing the nation (so it be not compulsive [compulsory]) is referred to their discretion.

2. That the matter of impressing and constraining any of us to serve in the wars, is against our freedom. . . .

3. That after the dissolution of the present parliament, no person be at any time questioned for anything said or done, in reference to the late public differences. . . .

4. That in all laws made, every person may be bound alike. . . .

5. That as the laws ought to be equal, so they must be good, and not evidently destructive to the safety and well-being of the people.

[. . .]

(b) Extracts from the debates at Putney, 29 October 1647

Between 28 October and 1 November 1647, the General Council of the Army, 'agitators' (representatives of regiments in the New Model Army) and civilian Levellers met in Putney church to debate the terms of *An Agreement of the People*. The debates were taken down in shorthand by William Clarke (1623/4–66), secretary to the army council, and the first three days of discussion subsequently transcribed by him into longhand.

John Wildman:[2] Our case is to be considered thus: that we have been under slavery, that's acknowledged by all. Our very laws were made by our conquerors. [. . .] We are now engaged for our freedom; that's the end [purpose] of parliaments. [. . .] Every person in England hath as clear a right to elect his representative as the greatest person in England. I conceive that's the undeniable maxim of government: that all government is in the free consent of the people.

[. . .]

Henry Ireton:[3] A man ought to be subject to a law that did not give his consent, but with this reservation, that if this man do think himself unsatisfied to be subject to this law, he may go into another kingdom; and so the same reason doth extend in my understanding, that a man that hath no permanent interest in the kingdom, if he hath money, his money is as good in another place as here; he hath nothing that doth locally fix him to this kingdom . . . in every kingdom, within every land the original of power, of making laws of determining what shall be law in the land, doth lie in the people who have a permanent interest in the land.

[. . .]

Colonel Rainsborough:[4] There are many thousands of us soldiers who have ventured our lives; we have had little propriety [property] in the kingdom as to our estates, yet we have had a birthright; but it seems now, except a man hath a fixed estate in this kingdom, he hath no right in this kingdom. I wonder we were so much deceived. If we had not a right to the kingdom, we were mere mercenary soldiers. There are many in my condition, that have as good a condition; it may be little estate they have at present, and yet they have as much right as those too who are their lawgivers, as any in this place. I shall tell you in a word my resolution. I am resolved to give my birthright to none, whatsoever may come in the way. [. . .] I do think the poor and

---

[2] Wildman (1622/3–93) had served in the New Model Army but by 1647 was a civilian. He was one of those who probably drafted *An Agreement of the People*.

[3] Ireton (1611–51) was commissary-general of the New Model army, an MP and Cromwell's son-in-law.

[4] Thomas Rainsborough MP (d. 1648), had served in the navy and at this time was a New Model colonel of foot.

meaner of this kingdom . . . have been the means of the preservation of this kingdom.

3.14

Charles I's Engagement with the Scots, 1647

G. Donaldson (ed.) ([1970] 1974), *Scottish Historical Documents*, Glasgow: Neil Wilson, pp. 214–15.

After the fall of Oxford in 1646 and the collapse of negotiations between king and parliament, the king escaped from the custody of the parliamentary army and joined the Scots where he concluded this agreement with them in December 1647.

His Majesty, so soon as he can with freedom, honour and safety be present in a free parliament, is content to confirm the said [Solemn] League and Covenant by Act of Parliament in both kingdoms . . . provided that none who is unwilling shall be constrained to take it. His Majesty will likewise confirm by Act of Parliament in England, presbyterial government, the directory for worship and assembly of divines at Westminster,[1] for three years, so that his Majesty and his household be not hindered from using that form of Divine Service he hath formerly practised; and that a free debate and consultation be had with the Divines at Westminster, twenty of His Majesty's nomination being added unto them, and with such as be sent from the Church of Scotland, whereby it may be determined by His Majesty and the two Houses [of parliament] how the church government, after the said three years, shall be fully established as is most agreeable to the Word of God: that an effectual course shall be taken by Act of Parliament, and all other was needful or expedient, for suppressing the opinions and practices of Anti-Trinitarians, Anabaptists, Antinomians, Arminians, Familists, Brownists, Separatists, Independents, Libertines, and Seekers,[2] and generally for suppressing all blasphemy, heresy, schism, and all such scandalous doctrines and practices . . .

---

[1] The Westminster Assembly of Divines was set up in June 1643 by parliament to plan and implement the reform of the Church of England.

[2] All radical religious sects outside the mainstream churches.

3.15 YES

Supplying a provincial garrison

J.H.P. Pafford (ed.) ([1940] 1966), *Accounts of the
Parliamentary Garrisons of Great Chalfield and
Malmesbury 1645–46*, Wiltshire Record Society vol. 2,
pp. 59–60, 69–70.

Great Chalfield, Wiltshire, was a parliamentary garrison from October 1644, of about 200 men and 100 horse. The medieval manor house was not fortified, but was moated and partially walled. Wiltshire was occupied by both royalists and parliamentarians, each of whom levied taxes to maintain garrisons in the areas they controlled. The garrison collected the weekly assessment levied on 24 parishes and paid to them in money, in labour or in kind. It also bought supplies for the soldiers.

(a) Receipts for the assessment for the parish of Winsley and Stoke, 1644

		£:s:d
	Charged	96:15:0
Imprimis brought in to the garrison from thence		
183 lb of cheese, 6 bushels of oats and 5 bushels and a half of wheat; valued at		3:11:2
Item	204 lb of cheese	2:9:0
"	6 bushels of wheat and 2 cheeses	1:4:0
"	8 bushels of oats 9s 4d, 2 bushels of wheat 7s 4d	0:16:8
"	220 lb of cheese	2:10
"	5 labourers 29 days	0:19:4
"	3 bushels of good wheat	0:11:0
"	6 bushels of oats and 8 bushels of wheat	1:16:0
"	24 bushels of oats	1:12:0
"	58 lb of cheese and 6 bushels of wheat	1:16:4
"	4 bushels of malt 10s, 8 bushels of oats 10s	1:0:0
"	Received in money thence by Captain Dymock before I [1]came to the garrison	2:0:0
	Sum total	20:5:6
	Received in money	21:16:0
		42:1:6
	Remains [in] arrears	54:13:6

[1] William Tarrant was receiver of taxes at the garrison.

3.3 Great Chalfield Manor, Wiltshire, built c. 1480. Most of the fortifications and the moat which made it suitable as a civil war garrison post no longer survive.

(b) Disbursements for the garrison of Great Chalfield

16 March [1645]		£:s:d
Paid	To the porter for his week's pay	0:5:0
"	For poultry	0:5:0
"	Jo[hn] Collett for a quarter of malt at 2 s 8 d the bushel	1:1:4
"	Samuel Bussell of Attworth towards his wages for work at the bulwarks	0:3:0
"	W[illia]m Charles of Attworth for his work likewise	0:2:8
"	For washing table linen	0:5:0
"	For Hector Mallard one of the Major's company when he was sick, by the Governor's direction	0:2:0
"	For a barrel of beer for the table	0:3:0
"	The gunsmith further towards his wages	0:5:0
"	Lieut. Cliffe for guides he took up to guide him the footway from Malmesbury hither by night	0:3:0
"	The Lieut. Col.[2] For the use of the garrison	0:5:0
"	The saddler's wife of Trowbridge for 4 bridles for the troopers	0:3:0

[2] Lieutenant-colonel Pudsey, governor of the garrison.

16 March [1645]		£:s:d
Paid	For 5 lb of butter	0:1:10
"	For eggs	0:1:0
"	For earthen wares for the house	0:1:6
"	For another barrel of beer from Holt	0:3:0
"	Which the Lieut. Col. gave the soldiers that fott [fetched] the widow Somner's oxen	0:10:0
"	The Lieut. Col. at Trowbridge	0:8:0
"	For washing the Lieut. Col.'s linen	0:2:0
"	For poultry	0:4:0
"	For butter	0:4:0
"	To a spy by the Lieut. Col.'s appointment	0:5:0
"	For a couple of capons	0:3:0
"	To Christofer Longe in part payment of £4 for 20 bushels of bay [sea] salt received of him	1:0:0
"	For a messenger 3 times to Melksham	0:1:6
"	For making the cannon and musket baskets	1:4:2
"	To Hugh Batten the gunsmith towards his wages	0:8:0
22 March		
Paid	The Lieut. Col. for a fortnight's pay for the foot[3]	30:0:0

3.16 *yes*

Passages from Isabella and Roger Twysden's Diaries, 1645

How well-informed?

Isabella (1605–57) was daughter and sole heir of Sir Nicholas Saunder of Nonsuch, Surrey, who had been ruined in an imprudent investment. In 1635 she married Sir Roger Twysden, of Royden Hall, East Peckham, Kent, with whom she had six children. After her husband's imprisonment in 1643 she continued to live at their home at Royden Hall. Sir Roger (1597–1672) was an MP in the 1620s and in the Short Parliament. He spent most of his time improving his estates and in scholarly pursuits. He opposed the king's financial expedients, but the attacks on bishops and ministers caused him to join the king's party. In spring 1642 he collaborated in producing the Kentish petition

---

[3] Soldiers in the garrison received half pay (4d for foot soldiers) and 'diet'.

Domestic events w/ what happens in war.

supporting the Church of England and was eventually, after having been arrested and released on bail, confined to London. In 1643 for failing to pay his contribution towards the monthly assessment and after trying to escape abroad he was imprisoned and his estates in Kent sequestrated. He compounded for his estates (by paying a fine) and returned to Kent in 1650. After the Restoration he served as JP and deputy-lieutenant in Kent.

The spelling and punctuation have not been modernised to show how different the writing of two individuals from the same background might be.

(a) Isabella Twysden

F.W. Bennitt (ed.) (1940 for 1939), 'The diary of Isabella, wife of Sir Roger Twysden, baronet, of Royden Hall, East Peckham, 1645–1651', *Archaeologia Cantiana*, 51, pp. 116–19.

The first of Janua [1645] M[r] Jo: hothum[1] was beheaded on tower hill.

The 2 of Janu S[r] Jo: hothum (father to Mr hothum) was beheaded on tower hill.

The 10 of Janu: my lo: of canterbury[2] was beheaded on tower hill and was buried at barking church.[3]

the meeting over uxbridg[4] about professions[5] was the 30 of Janu:

m[r] white[6] the churc man about ministeres, died the 27 of Ja: and was buried the 30. in the tempell church.

the 8 febri, I came to peckham great with child, and rid all the waye a hors back,[7] and I thank god had no hurt.

---

[1] John Hotham (1610–45), son of Sir John (1589–1645), was beheaded for deserting his post as general of the parliamentary forces in Lincolnshire and for negotiating with the royalists to change sides. Sir Roger Twysden's nephew was married to Sir John Hotham's daughter.

[2] Archbishop William Laud.

[3] His remains were removed to St John's College, Oxford in 1663.

[4] Negotiations between king and parliament.

[5] The king was asked to agree to changes which would make the Church of England more like the Church of Scotland.

[6] John White, MP for Southwark and chairman of parliamentary committee to enquire into the immorality of the clergy.

[7] She rode pillion with a manservant.

the 6 of march 1644 [1645] between one and 2 in the morning I was brought to bed of a boye,[8] the 7 he was chrissened and named charles, the gossops [godparents] were my bro: Tho: and Fra: Twysden[9] and my la: astlye,[10] Jamme stood for hir. He was born at peckham being Thursday.

the 11 of march there was the terriblest wind, that had been knowne sence ever the like, it did a great dele of hirt. . . .

the 13 aprill there begane a rising[11] in Kent about mersam[12] and thereabouts, but it was presently laid being but a few. . . .

the 21 S[r] mills Lissys [Sir Miles Livesey's?] tropes came into Kent to Senack[13] for there paye the trane bands [militia] was rased agane to goe against them, they were sent back with promises of there paye.

the first of aprill nurs Jane had 12[d] for a month nursing of charles the month was not up till 2 dayes after.

the 14 of June S[r] Tho: fairfax had a great victory at nasby where he took 12 peces of ornance 4000 foote sholders, and the Sc. [secret?] letters.[14] . . .

the 28 June there was brought in to Lambeth hous from the atillirer yard 680 pore prisoners, part of those which were taken at nasby.

my part in Stockenbury wood for my 5th part,[15] July 2 1645 was 74 cord and 6 feet and 2 load of turners timber and 2200 bavines[16]. . . .

My nan[17] went with my Serv[t] whitfield into the contry to blechinly July 17. . . .

the 24 July 1645 I had a letter from my sis war[18] telling me my bro. napers[19] death about 6 week before and harry naper like to dye. . . .

nan went the 14 to M[r] harrys in surrey, august. . . .

---

[8] Her sixth and last child.

[9] Brothers-in-law.

[10] Agnes Impel, the Dutch wife of the royalist military commander Sir Jacob Astley (1579–1652).

[11] A popular rising against the war against the Covenant, illegal taxes, the abolition of the Prayer Book and impressment for the army.

[12] Mersham, near Ashford.

[13] Possibly Senlac, ancient name for the site of the battle of Hastings.

[14] At Naseby, a cabinet of the king's letters to his wife was seized, revealing his plans to bring in troops from Ireland and help from the duke of Lorraine (Charles IV (1604–75; duke 1624–34)). The letters were published in July.

[15] The families of royalists whose property had been sequestered were entitled to petition parliament for one fifth of the income.

[16] Brushwood or firewood.

[17] Daughter Anne (1636–?)

[18] Frances, Isabella's sister, wife of Edward Warham.

[19] Napper or Napier, husband of Isabella's sister Elizabeth.

the 21 august major palet about 8 o'clock at night departed this life a right honest good man he was, and was buried the 22 in the church at Lambeth.

the 9 Sep Mr Strod,[20] on[e] of the five members, a parlement man died.

the 11 of Sep 1645 princ rupert[21] delivered up bristoll on treaty to Sr Tho: farfax for the parlement.

the 18 Sep: my bro: and sister yelverton came from peckham agane to London.

the 12 Sep: sary Stiles went away.

the 26 nell duck came up to Lambeth to be my maid,

the 12 octo, was the first day I had the third day ague [fever]. . . .

the 24 nov: my sister warham went from London to goe home to dorset there she came to London on milmas [michaelmas] day before. . . .

the 10 desem: my lord and lady of Kirry went away from Lambeth.

The 14 desem my nan came home from M^r harry.

(b) Roger Twysden

L.B. Larking, (ed.) (1858), 'Sir Roger Twysden's journal'. *Archaeologia Cantiana*, 4, pp. 145–7.

This year [1645], my dear Wife looking after my businesse, I had the liberty of following my studies; and finding humane nature can never bee absolutely idle, put out ye Lawes of Henry ye I compared wth the red booke in the Exchequer, never beefore printed . . . and so past them to ye presse wth a preface of my owne: wch is ye first I ever appeered in print.[22]

In January, 1644/5, my wife informed the Committee of Lords and Commons she could get no expedition from ye Committee of

---

[20] William Strode (1594–1645), MP for Bere Alston, Devon, one of the five MPs whom Charles I had attempted to arrest in January 1642.

[21] Rupert, Count Palatine of the Rhine, duke of Bavaria (1619–82) was a younger son of Frederick V, the Elector Palatine, and Elizabeth Stuart (1596–1662), and hence a nephew of Charles I, who created him duke of Cumberland. Rupert was Commander-in-Chief of the royalist cavalry.

[22] Αρχάινομίά, *sive de priscis Anglorum legibus libri, sermone Anglico vetustate antiquissimo aliquot ab hinc seculis conscripti, atq; nunc demum . . . e tenebris in lucem vocati, G. Lambardo interprete. Anglo-Sax. & Lat.*, London, 1644.

Kent, according to their order,[23] for her mansion howse or lands about it. But from theise she could get no reliefe. . . . And heere I may not forget that she taulking one day with one of them, he told her, they must defend their Committees against me; for they were for them, when they knwe me against them. And when she asked, what had I done to shew it? he replyed, they knwe my thoughts. Thus they conclude when they are guilty of those injuries to others themselves cannot pardon.

My deere Wife, great wth child, and now ready to lye in, the 8th of february went downe in to Kent. And though she rid all the way on horseback beehynd George Stone, yet God so enabled her, a weak body, she had no hurt: To hym, therefore, bee the prayse, for that and all his other goodnesse to me and her, for ever and ever, Amen. But whither her many journies on my errands, an unhappy Midwife, or what elce, I know not, she had a very ille tyme after her beeing delivered; and indeede never recovered her former strength during all her life. In so much as she returned not to me again tyll the 23 May following.

The 11 March 1644/5, there was brought to Lambeth a Warrant, subscribed by John Leech, Clark to y[e] Committee for the advance of the Scottish Lones, directed to the keeper of the Prison in Lambeth. The effect of it was, That, Whereas the hon[ble] howse of Commons had set a fine upon me, and by their Order y[e] 4th of that instant March, referred to them the care of levying it, to desire hym to cause me and S[r] Wingfield Bodenham,[24] if he were in hys custody, to bee brought to Gouldsmiths' Hall,[25] on Tuesday y[e] same day, at three of the Clock in the after noone, there to give in my answer.

According to this Warrant, I attended them; there beeing then present M[r] Ash, S[r] Anthony Irby, S[r] Davyd Watkins,[26] and other whom I knwe not, six or eight, more or lesse. They used me very civily, by all means would have me sit downe, when they told me the howse of Commons had imposed on me a fine of 3000 1. [£3,000], that it was referd to them to see it levyed, who for y[t] end had sent to confer wth me.

---

[23] To pay her a fifth of the annual value of Sir Roger's estate.
[24] A royalist gentleman, fl. 1642–8, antiquary.
[25] The Committee for Compounding sat at Goldsmiths' Hall.
[26] Members of the Committee for Compounding. Some were MPs.

The immensenesse of this Summe imposed on me, with out ever beeing heard or sent unto; not acquainted by me how my estate stoode; not knowing what I could say for myself; made me see the Starchamber[27] was remoeved to ye other end of Westminster Hall. I pleaded for myself as well as I could; desired to know my fault. Some sayd y^t was not referd to them; One read out of a paper, y^t it was for abetting a petition came out of Kent. I sayd, I nether framed, nor deliverd it, nor sub-scribed, oherwise then I gave out a trwe Copy, w^ch, on the howse of Commons' command I immediately called in.

Upon this Mr John Ash that was in the Chayr spake these formall words, 'Wee sit here to oppresse no man. For my part I think this gen-tleman to have had a very hard measure: but wee can doe hym no good, other then giving hym tyme for payment.' And so they seemed to think all. I asked them then, 'if they could not how might I bee redrest'. They sayd, 'by petitioning the howse.' I beesought them, y^t one of themselves would bee pleased to deliver me a petition; but they replyed, it was not proper for them. And so they dismist me. Beefore I had quite done, in came Captayne Augustine Skinner,[28] who, as I heard after from hymself, spake in my favor of the hardnesse of my censure.

And heere, having mentione Mr Ashe, I can not but say this in short of that gentleman; that, whilst I attended the Committee, I found hym, however observant of the Orders of ye howse of Commons, yet willing to hear reason in poynt of debts; or otherwise to dispatch men out of their misery; and to moderate, not their paiments, (for y^t was impos-sible, at least not in hys Power) but other things as much as he could. And let no man think I speak this out of any favor I received from hym; for I protest I payd 400l. [£400] for my fifth and twentyeth part, meerely for hys eyther wilfully or ignorantly mistaking the order of ye howse. . . .

Now alone, my wife gon from me, I beegan to consider of the power and Privileges of the two howses, as they stoode apart, and did not joyn wth the King; especyally of the howse of Commons; – and how far they might legally requyre obedience from ye subject.

---

[27] Star Chamber, one of the prerogative courts most complained of by the king's oppo-nents, had been abolished in 1641.
[28] One of the two MPs for the county of Kent.

3.17 *PERHAPS*

The trial of Charles I, 1649

(a) Extracts from the trial proceedings

T.B. Howell (ed.) (1816), *A Complete Collection of State Trials . . . in 21 Volumes*, London, vol. 4, pp. 995–6, 999–1000, 1017–18.

This account of the king's trial 'published by authority, to prevent false and impertinent relations' by Gilbert Mabbot (c. 1622–70) was one of a number. Mabbot seems to have had access to the full verbatim record of the trial taken down by shorthand writers. The trial was conducted 20–27 January 1649 in a specially constituted High Court of Justice, meeting in Westminster Hall. One hundred and fifty men were named 'commissioners', to be judges and jury. Sixty never sat at all (some were absent army officers); fifty-nine signed the death warrant.

Saturday 20 January 1649

Lord President:[1] Charles Stuart, king of England, the Commons of England assembled in Parliament, being deeply sensible of the calamities that have been brought upon this nation, which is fixed upon you as the principal author of it, have resolved to make inquisition for blood; and according to that debt and duty they owe to justice, to God, the kingdom, and themselves, and according to the fundamental power that rests in themselves, they have resolved to bring you to trial and judgment; and for that purpose have constituted this High Court of Justice, before which you are brought.

This said, Mr Cook,[2] Solicitor for the Commonwealth, standing within a bar on the right hand of the prisoner, offered to speak: but the king having a staff in his hand, held it up, and laid it upon the said Mr Cook's shoulder two or three times, bidding him hold. Nevertheless, the Lord President ordering him to go on, he said:

Mr Cook: My lord, I am commanded to charge Charles Stuart, King of England, in the name of the Commons of England, with treason and high misdemeanours; I desire the said charge may be read.

[1] John Bradshaw (1602–59), lawyer and provincial judge.
[2] John Cook (1608–60), barrister.

... the Lord President ordered it should be read; but the king bid him hold. Nevertheless, being commanded by the Lord President to read it, the Clerk begun, and the prisoner sat down again in his chair, looking sometimes on the High Court, sometimes up to the galleries; and having risen again, and turned about to behold the guards and spectators, sat down, looking very sternly, and with a countenance not at all moved, till these words, viz. 'Charles Stuart to be a tyrant and traitor', &c were read; at which he laughed, as he sat, in the face of the Court.

The charge being read, the Lord President replied:

Lord President: Sir, you have now heard your charge, containing such matter as appears in it; you find, that in the close of it, it is prayed to the Court, in the behalf of the commons of England, that you answer to your charge. The Court expects your answer.

King: I would know by what power I am called hither; I was not long ago in the Isle of Wight;[3] ... there I entered into Treaty with both Houses of Parliament, with as much public faith as it is possible to be had of any people in the world. I treated there with a number of honourable lords and gentlemen, and treated honestly and uprightly; I cannot say but they did very nobly with me, we were upon the conclusion of the treaty. Now I would know by what authority, I mean lawful; there are many unlawful authorities in the world, thieves and robbers by the highways; but I would know by what authority I was brought from thence, and carried from place to place, and I know not what: and when I know what lawful authority, I shall answer. Remember I am your king, your lawful king ... I have a trust committed to me by God, by old and lawful descent; I will not betray it. ...

Lord President: If you had been pleased to have observed what was hinted to you by the Court, at your first coming hither, you would have known by what authority; which authority requires you, in the name of the people of England, of which you are elected king, to answer them. ...

King: England was never an elective kingdom, but an hereditary kingdom for near these thousand years; therefore let me know by what authority I am called hither: I do stand more for the liberty of my people, than any here that come to be my pretended judges.

[. . .]

Monday 22 January 1649

King: Sir, by your favour, I do not know the forms of law; I do know law and reason, though I am no lawyer professed; but I know as

[3] The king was held prisoner in Carisbrooke Castle on the Isle of Wight from November 1647.

much law as any gentleman in England; and therefore (under favour), I do plead for the liberties of the people of England more than you do. . . .

Lord President: Sir, I must interrupt you. . . . Sir, the vote of the Commons of England assembled in Parliament, it is the reason of the kingdom. . . . Sir, you are not to dispute our authority, you are told it again by the court. Sir, it will be taken notice of, that you stand in contempt of the court, and your contempt will be recorded accordingly.

King: I do not know how a king can be a delinquent . . . [I] demand to be heard with my reasons; if you deny that you deny reason. . . . I say, sir, by your favour, that the Commons of England was never a court of judicature; I would know how they came to be so.

Lord President: Sir you are not to be permitted to go on in that speech and these discourses.

Then the clerk of the court read as followeth:

'Charles Stuart, king of England, you have been accused on behalf of the people of England of High Treason, and other high crimes; the court have determined that you ought to answer the same'.

King: I will answer the same so soon as I know by what authority you do this. . . . I do require that I may give in my reasons why I do not answer, and give me time for that.

Lord President: Sir, it is not for prisoners to require.

King: Prisoners! I am not an ordinary prisoner.

[. . .]

Wednesday 24 January 1649

The clerk read the sentence, which was drawn up in parchment:

'Whereas the Commons of England in Parliament had appointed them an High Court of Justice, for the trying of Charles Stuart, king of England, before whom he had been three times convened; and at the first time a charge of High Treason, and other crimes and misdemeanours, was read in the behalf of the kingdom of England etc. [here the clerk read the charge]. . . . For all which treasons and crimes, this Court doth adjudge that the said Charles Stuart, as a tyrant, traitor, murdered and a public enemy, shall be put to death, by the severing his head from his body'.

After the sentence read, the Lord President said, This sentence now read and published, it is the act, sentence, judgment, and resolution of the whole court.

Here the Court stood up, as assenting to what the President said.

King: Will you hear me a word, Sir?

Lord President: Sir, you are not to be heard after the sentence. . . .

King: I am not suffered to speak: expect what justice other people will not have.

[Serjeant at Arms]: O yez: all manner of persons that have anything else to do, are to depart at this time, and to give their attendance in the Painted Chamber;[4] to which place this court doth forthwith adjourn itself.

Then the court rose, and the king went with his guard to Sir Robert Cotton's,[5] and from thence to Whitehall.

(b) Depositions taken against the king

T.B. Howell (ed.) (1816), *A Complete Collection of State Trials ... in 21 Volumes*, vol. 4. pp. 1104, 1107.

A number of depositions were taken from men who had witnessed the king in various military engagements. Thirty-three witnesses were examined on the morning of 25 January 1649 to establish the king's personal involvement in the war.

(i) William Brayne of Wixall in the county of Salop, gent, being sworn and examined, deposeth, That about August 1642, this deponent saw the king at Nottingham, while the standard was set up, and the flag flying; and that he (this deponent) much about the same time marched with the king's army from Nottingham to Derby, the king himself being then in the army: and about September the said year, he (this deponent) was put upon his trial at Shrewsbury as a spy, before Sir Robert Heath, and other commissioners of Oyer and Terminer [judges], the king being then in person in Shrewsbury.

(ii) Diogenes Edwards of Carston, in the county of Salop, butcher, aged 21 or thereabouts, sworn and examined, saith, That in June 1645, he (this deponent) saw the king in the head of his army an hour and a half before the fight in Naseby field, marching up to the battle, being then a mile and a half from the said field: and this deponent saith, that he did afterwards the same day see many slain at the said battle.

---

[4] The Painted Chamber had been the king's bedchamber and audience chamber in the Palace of Westminster in the Middle Ages, before Whitehall became the court's base in London. In the sixteenth and seventeenth centuries, the Painted Chamber was the location of important state ceremonies, including the State Opening of Parliament.

[5] Situated between the river and Westminster Hall where the trial was held.

(c) Parliament and king, 27–30 January 1649

Journals of the House of Commons from September the 2nd 1648 . . . to August the 14th 1651, London, 1803, p. 126.

Following the king's trial and sentencing, the Rump Parliament had hastily to deal with the legal and constitutional consequences before the king was executed. The first and second readings of the bill took place on 27 January. The Commons Journals were the official record of debates and decisions taken in parliament.

30 January 1649 post meridiem [p.m.]

An Act prohibiting the proclaiming any person to be king of England or Ireland, or the dominions thereof was this day read the third time; and upon the question passed: [and ordered it] be forthwith proclaimed by Serjeant Dendy, Serjeant at Arms, with sound of trumpet, in Cheapside, the Old Exchange, and Westminster.

[. . .]

That Mr Lisle[6] and Mr Love[7] do withdraw and prepare a letter to be sent to the several sheriffs within the kingdom of England and dominion of Wales, to publish and proclaim the Act entitled, An Act prohibiting the proclaiming of any person to be king, &c. in all market towns, and other public places, within their several counties, and to give this House a speedy account thereof.

The said committee did withdraw; and did prepare the said letter accordingly.

Ordered, that the three votes of the fourth of January instant:

Viz. Resolved &c. that the Commons of England, in Parliament assembled, do declare, that the people are, under God, the original of all just power;

And do also declare, That the Commons of England, in Parliament assembled, being chosen by and representing the people, have the supreme power in this nation.

And do also declare, That whatsoever is enacted or declared for law by the Commons, in parliament assembled, hath the force of a law; and all the people of this nation are concluded thereby, though the consent and concurrence of the king, or House of Peers, be not had thereunto.

Ordered, that these three votes be forthwith printed.

[6] John Lisle (1610–64), MP for Winchester.
[7] Nicholas Love (1608–82), MP for Winchester.

3.18

Scotland under the Commonwealth

(a) The diary of John Nicoll, December 1651

J. Nicoll (1836), *A Diary of Public Transactions and other Occurrences Chiefly in Scotland From January 1650 to June 1667,* Edinburgh: Bannantyne Club, pp. 68–70.

John Nicoll (c. 1590–1668) was a Scots lawyer. Little else is known of him apart from his observations on current events.

December 1651

General Lambert[1] having urged the town of Edinburgh's Common Council to appropriate to him the East Kirk of Edinburgh, being the special kirk and best in the town, for his exercise at sermon, the same was rendered to him for that use; wherein there was divers and sundry sermons preached, as well by captains and lieutenants and troopers of his army, as by ordiner [official] pastors and English ministers; which captains, commanders and troopers, when they entered the pulpits, did not observe our Scottish forms [of worship], but when they ascended, they entered the pulpits with their swords hung at their sides, and some carrying pistols up with them; and after their entry, laid aside within the pulpits their swords till they ended their sermons. It was thought these men were well gifted, yet were not orderly called, according to the discipline oft observed within this kingdom of Scotland.

It was observed, that in the English army there was oft times good discipline against drunkenness, fornication, and uncleanness; whipping fornicators . . . and by shooting to death sundry others who had committed mutiny. . . .

From the incoming of the English army to Scotland [July 1650] to this very day, the last of December 1651, there was no supreme judicature in Scotland, such as Secret [Privy] Council and [Court of] Session to minister justice, so that the people of the land, for lack of the Scottish laws, did suffer much.

---

[1] John Lambert (1619–84) was second in command to Cromwell when the English invaded Scotland in 1650. In 1651 he was one of the parliamentary commissioners sent to Scotland to settle the government there.

(b) The diary of John Lamont, 1652

J. Lamont (1830) *The Diary of Mr John Lamont of Newton, 1649–1671*, Edinburgh: Maitland Club, pp. 37–8.

John Lamont (fl.1636–71) is known primarily as a diarist, commenting on current events as well as on family affairs. He was the son of a minister and may have been a factor [agent] on an estate in Fife.

20 January 1652

The commissioners appointed by the parliament of England, for settling affairs in Scotland, came to this kingdom, viz. 8 in all. . . . They had their instructions in write from the parliament. They sat in Dalkeith in Lothian; they discharged the printing of diurnals at Leith, or elsewhere; they discharged also all judicatories in this kingdom, viz. Lords of Session and Council, shire courts and commissary courts etc. They caused proclaim the parliament of England's declaration (at the several market crosses of the kingdom), for faulting all these that were at Duke [of] Hamilton's Engagement[2] in the year 1648, and all that were at Worcester in England, with K. Charles the 2, Anno Domini 1651, September 3. For church government by presb[yteries] they left it arbitrary for men to do as they list, etc. They caused commissioners in every shire and burgh come in and agree with them for their several shires and burghs. The conditions they propound to the Scots commissioners were mainly two: 1. that this kingdom should be one united commonwealth with England, without king or House of Lords; 2. that they should live peaceably at their own dwellings. . . . In April they caused publish and proclaim at Leith and elsewhere, a proclamation of union, uniting England and Scotland together in one commonwealth . . . They returned to England about the end of April 1652.

[. . .]

---

[2] James Hamilton, 1st duke of Hamilton (1606–49) was Charles I's chief adviser on Scottish affairs and served as a commander of royalist armies on several occasions. In July 1648, he led a large Scottish army into England in support of the newly captured king but was defeated by Cromwell at the Battle of Preston, fought over 17–19 August.

3.19

The rule of the Major-Generals, 1655–7

T. Birch (ed.) (1742) *A Collection of the State Papers of John Thurloe, esq*, 7 vols., London, vol. 4, pp. 224–5; 486.

Following Penruddock's[1] abortive royalist rising in March 1655, Cromwell and the Council of State created a militia in England and Wales, funded by a new tax (the decimation) and administered by army officers. Thomas Kelsey[2] was appointed major-general in charge of Kent and Surrey in October 1655. John Thurloe (1616–68), 'Cromwell's master spy', was in charge of the intelligence services. His immense correspondence was edited and published in the eighteenth century.

(a) Major-General Kelsey to Secretary Thurloe, Maidstone, 20 November 1655

Sir, This day we had a meeting at Maidstone, in order to the putting of his highness and council's orders in execution, where met near 20 commissioners, who all unanimously seem to be very hearty and cordial to the work, and rejoice to see, that such a check and discouragement is put upon their old enemies, and encouragement to their friends, who have issued out orders for delinquents to appear before us at our next meeting. I am not able to make a judgement of what we shall be able to raise, but if we had power to assess [raise assessment tax from] all persons of £50 per annum we should raise almost as much more in this county as now we shall do.... I am able at present to do little as to disarming malignants [royalists], till I have put the other business in some forwardness. Tomorrow I intend to go into Surrey, to meet the gentlemen at Kingston upon Thursday. I must confess the Lord hath given my unbelieving heart the lie, by vouchsafing unto me more of his presence and comfort in this uncoth [unfamiliar] employment, than I could expect. The Lord give me a heart to

---

[1] Sir John Penruddock (1619–55), leader of the uprising and member of the Sealed Knot, a secret royalist association. Penruddock and his forces took Salisbury on 11 March but were heavily defeated three days later in Devon, and the revolt collapsed. Penruddock was among the survivors who were executed.

[2] Kelsey (d. c. 1676). London draper, rose to the rank of colonel in the New Model Army. A radical Independent in religion.

answer his goodness towards me, and make me able to answer the expectations of his highness and council, which is all from, your most humble servant, Thomas Kelsey.

(b) Major-General Kelsey to the Protector, early 1656

May it please your highness, Being at Maidstone with the rest of the commissioners, where we received a complaint from several honest men against one Coppin[3] of Rochester for preaching and maintaining several blasphemous tenants [tenets], saying Christ's human nature was defiled with sin, and that he offered sacrifice for his own sins, as well as for the people's, and that all men should be saved; denying hell or heaven to be any other than what was within him; and many such damnable tenants, and drew many followers after him, and the soldiers there many of them did begin to adhere unto him, and some officers too much favoured him; upon which we sent to apprehend him, but he was not to be found. [. . .] We examined witnesses concerning the said Coppin; and finding the things charged against him was testified by several witnesses, did commit him to the gaol; but knowing that many scandalous professors [believers], that have fallen off from the worship and services of God, and ready to follow after anything that is evil, are ready to cry out for liberty of conscience, and are not backward to say it's persecution worse than in the bishops' time, and the like; and knowing not how things may be presented to your highness, I make bold to give your highness this account. I could wish, and do humbly offer it as my opinion, that he may be sent out of the land, as you have done Bedell;[4] and I further offer it to your highness as my humble opinion, that it would be convenient to remove the soldiers that are at Rochester to some other place, and to send some other in their rooms; for that I am afraid, they have drunk in so much of these tenants, that I fear they may do hurt by lying there, because many townsmen being tainted will be ready to strengthen them in their opinions. All which I leave to your Highness's consideration, and remain Your Highness's most humble servant Thomas Kelsey.

---

[3] In the late 1640s Richard Coppin (fl. c. 1645–59) preached a gospel directly received from God, his *Divine Teachings* (1649) influenced the Ranters in the 1650s. In 1652 he was charged for maintaining that all men would be saved and that God was as much in everyone as in Christ.

[4] Probably John Biddle (1616–62) who denied the divinity of Christ and argued for a literal reading of the scriptures. In 1655 he was exiled to the Isles of Scilly, but released in 1658, reimprisoned in 1660 and died in gaol.

3.20

Extract from the Declaration of Breda, 4 April 1660

J.P. Kenyon (1986), *The Stuart Constitution: Documents and Commentary*, 2nd edn, Cambridge: Cambridge University Press, pp. 331–2.

The Declaration, probably drafted by Edward Hyde,[1] was issued by Charles II from his exiled court at Breda in the Low Countries before the Convention Parliament met. Its pacific tone formed the basis for negotiations which resulted in parliament's decision to recall the king and for a vote on 5 May that the government of the country was vested in king, lords and commons.

Charles, by the grace of God, king of England, Scotland, France and Ireland, Defender of the Faith &c., to all our loving subjects, of what degree or quality soever, greeting. If the general distraction and confusion which is spread over the whole kingdom doth not awaken all men to a desire and longing that those wounds which have so many years together been kept bleeding may be bound up, all we can say will be to no purpose.

[...]

And to the end that the fear of punishment may not engage any, conscious to themselves of what is passed, to a perseverance in guilt for the future, by opposing the quiet and happiness of their country in the restoration both of king, peers and people to their just, ancient and fundamental rights, we do by these presents declare, that we do grant a free and general pardon, which we are ready upon demand to pass under our Great Seal of England, to all our subjects, of what degree or quality soever, who within forty days of the publishing hereof shall lay hold upon this our grace and favour, and shall by any

---

[1] Edward Hyde (1609–74), lawyer, historian, royalist MP and member of Charles I's Privy Council. He responded to a summons to join Prince Charles and the court-in-exile in 1648. After the Restoration, he would become chief minister to Charles II and was created earl of Clarendon.

public act declare their doing so, and that they return to the loyalty and obedience of good subjects (excepting only such persons as shall hereafter be excepted by parliament). . . . We desiring and ordaining that henceforward all notes of discord, separation and difference of parties be utterly abolished among all our subjects, whom we invite and conjure to a perfect union among themselves, under our protection, for the resettlement of our just rights and theirs in a free parliament, by which, upon the word of a king, we will be advised.

And because the passion and uncharitableness of the times have produced several opinions in religion, by which men are engaged in parties and animosities against each other, which, when they shall hereafter unite in a freedom of conversation, will be composed and better understood, we do declare a liberty to tender consciences . . . and that we shall be ready to consent to such an act of parliament as, upon mature deliberation, shall be offered to us for the full granting that indulgence.

And because, in the continued distraction of so many years and so many and great revolutions, many grants and purchases of estates have been made to and by many officers, soldiers and others, who are now possessed of the same, and who may be liable to actions at law upon several titles, we are likewise willing that all such differences, and all things relating to such grants, shall be determined in parliament, which can best provide for the just satisfaction of all men who are concerned.

And we do further declare, that we will be ready to consent to any act or acts of parliament to the purposes aforesaid, and for the full satisfaction of all arrears due to the officers and soldiers of the army under the command of General Monk,[2] and that they shall be received into our service upon as good pay and conditions as they now enjoy.

Given under our Sign Manual [signature] and Privy Signet [signet ring seal], at our court at Breda, this 4/14 day[3] of April 1660, in the twelfth[4] year of our reign.

---

[2] George Monk or Monck (1608–70), parliamentary commander and general-at-sea, created duke of Albemarle in 1660.

[3] The continental calendar was 10 days ahead of the calendar used in Britain.

[4] The start of Charles II's reign was dated from the death of his father in 1649.

3.21

Extract from George Walker's account of the siege of Derry, 1689

A True Account of the Siege of Londonderry. By the Reverend Mr George Walker, Rector of Donoghmoore in the County of Tirone, and Late Governour of Derry in Ireland, London, 1689, pp. 39–41.

George Walker (1646–90) was governor of Derry during its siege from April 1689 until its relief by a naval expedition on 30 July. A Church of Ireland clergyman, he took over command of the garrison when the governor, Ralph Lundy, left. He published his account of the 105-day siege in 1689 in the form of a diary.

July 22 The garrison is reduced to 4973 men
July 25 The garrison is reduced to 4892 men. . . .
July 27. The garrison is reduced to 4456 men, and under the greatest extremity for the want of provision, which does appear by this account taken by a gentleman in the garrison, of the price of our food.

	£	s	d	
Horseflesh sold for		1	8	Per pound
A quarter of a dog		5	6	Fattened by eating the bodies of the slain Irish
A dog's head		2	6	
A cat		4	6	
A rat		1	0	
A mouse			6	
A small flook [fish] taken in the river not to be bought for money, or purchased under the rate of a quantity of meal				
A pound of greaves [tallow refuse]		1	0	
A pound of tallow		4	0	
A pound of salted hides		1	0	
A quart of horse blood		1	0	
A horse pudding			6	
An handful of sea wrack			2	
An handful of chickweed			1	
A quart of meal when found		1		

hard fat melted down to form candles

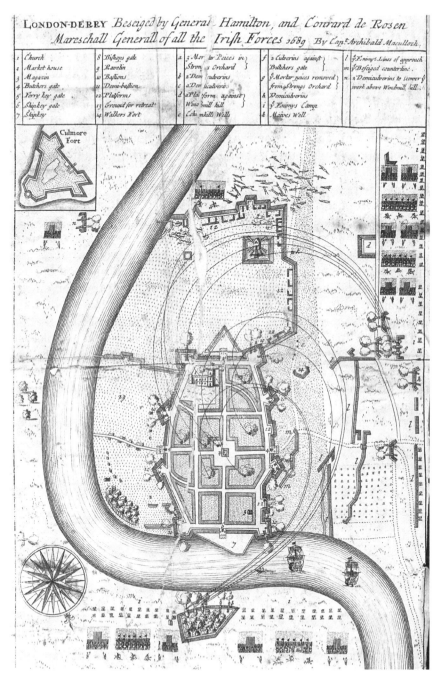

3.4 Plan of Londonderry, 1689, showing the position of the besieging troops.

We were under so great necessity that we had nothing less unless we could prey upon one another: A certain fat gentleman conceived himself in the greatest danger and fancying several of the garrison looked on him with a greedy eye, thought fit to hide himself for three days. Our drink was nothing but water, which we paid very dear for, and could not get without great danger: we mixed in it ginger and aniseeds, of which we had great plenty; our necessity of eating the composition of tallow and starch, did not only nourish and support us, but was an infallible cure of the looseness [diarrhoea]; and recovered a great many that were strangely reduced by that distemper, and preserved others from it. . . .

30 July. About an hour after sermon being in the midst of out extremity, we saw some ships in the lough make towards us. . . .

At length the ships got to us, to the unexpressible joy and transport of our distressed garrison, for we only reckoned upon two days life, and had only nine lean horses left, and among us all one pint of meal to each man; hunger and the fatigue of war had so prevailed among us, that of 7500 men regimented, we had now alive but about 4300, whereof at least one fourth part were rendered unserviceable.

This brave undertaking added to the great success God had blessed us with in all our attempts, so discouraged the enemy, that on the last of July, they ran away in the night time, robbed and burnt all before them for several miles, leaving nothing with the country people, but what they hid the night before, in which their care was so great, that provision grew very plentiful after it.

3.22

A Jacobite account of the battle of the Boyne, 1690

R.H. Murray (ed.) (1912), *The Journal of John Stevens: Containing a Brief Account of the War in Ireland 1689–1691*, Oxford: Clarendon Press, pp. 123, 126.

John Stevens (c. 1662–1726) was a Catholic Englishman who, after various employments abroad, joined the army of King James II (1633–1701; reigned 1685–8) in Ireland where he served as a lieutenant. He kept a journal of the campaign which was probably written up from contemporaneous notes taken day by day.

I thought the calamity had not been so general till viewing the hills about us I perceived them covered with soldiers of several regiments, all scattered like sheep flying before the wolf, but so thick they seemed to cover the sides and tops of the hills. The shame of our regiment's dishonour only afflicted me before; but now all the horror of a routed army, just before so vigorous and desirous of battle and broke without scarce a stroke from the enemy, so perplexed my soul that I envied the few dead, and only grieved I lived to be a spectator of so dismal and lamentable a tragedy. Scarce a regiment was left but what was reduced to a very inconsiderable number by this, if possible, more than panic fear. Only the French can be said to have rallied, for only they made head against the enemy, and a most honourable retreat, bringing off their cannon, and marching in very good order after sustaining the shock of the enemy who thereupon made a halt, not only to the honour of the French but the preservation of the rest of the scattered army . . . if it be lawful for me to give my sentiments on the matter in my opinion much may be laid upon mismanagement, but much more upon cowardice, and am apt to believe all the clamour of treason was raised by some who had given the most eminent signs of fear to cover their and the general disgrace.

Chapter 4

Slavery and freedom

Introduction

The extracts in this chapter all relate to 'New World' slavery and the struggles to abolish the Atlantic slave trade and emancipate the slaves. They are drawn from the years between c. 1760 and c. 1840, a period when the slave trade and the institution of slavery came under sustained moral and political assault. They represent a tiny and eclectic sample of the massive documentation available to historians of 'New World' slavery and were selected for specific teaching purposes.

The material ranges from encyclopaedia entries to anti-slavery pamphlets and the confessions of slaves who had participated in the Jamaican slave rebellion of late 1831, early 1832. Documents 4.2 and 4.3 offer conflicting first-hand testimony on what is one of the most contentious issues in the history of Atlantic slavery: the impact of the external demand for slaves on African societies. Was the provision of slaves for the Atlantic trade an incidental by-product of African institutions and the conflicts between African kingdoms and religions? Or was the external demand for slaves itself the prime cause of social violence? Documents 4.1, 4.4 and 4.5 illustrate the beliefs and ideologies held by 'enlightened' Europeans with regard to Africans and slavery in the later eighteenth century. We should note that the racist Edward Long was a champion of freedom – for British subjects – and a disciple of John Locke, the philosopher of political liberalism. Long represented that paradoxical conjunction of slavery and freedom

262

4.1 'Am I not a man and a brother?', plaque design produced by Josiah Wedge-wood, 1787. The design is taken from the seal of the Society for the Abolition of the Slave Trade.

which was such a striking feature of the eighteenth-century Anglophone Atlantic world.

Document 4.7 shows us the French commander in Saint Domingue, General Leclerc, vainly struggling to reverse the only successful slave rebellion of modern times: Leclerc died shortly after these despairing missives and the black republic of Haiti was inaugurated on 1 January 1804. Documents 4.8 and 4.9 were penned by two of the leading anti-slavery activists in Britain, Thomas Clarkson and Elizabeth Heyrick. The presence of the latter is a tacit reminder that women's activism in the emancipation movement led eventually to the movement for women's emancipation.

Every student of slavery will want to attend to the voices of the slaves themselves: whether the confessions and witness testimonies reproduced in document 4.11 are wholly authentic is a moot point, since they were taken down by an Anglican rector with little or no sympathy for the slaves' aspirations for personal freedom or their religious non-conformity. We must judge the authenticity of these statements from the internal evidence. Document 4.12, from Alexis de Tocqueville's classic analysis of American democracy, would seem to illustrate how society 'goes on behind the backs' of even its most perceptive observers: Tocqueville concluded, in the early 1830s, that slavery was in decay in the US South. In fact, in the 1840s and 50s, it flourished as never before.

Bernard Waites

4.1
Africans as a sub-species of humanity: an eighteenth-century view

E. Long (1774) *History of Jamaica*, London, 3 vols., vol. III, pp. 353–6.

Edward Long (1734–1813) served as a judge in Jamaica in the 1750s and 1760s and was a member of the House of Assembly. His *History* gained notoriety for arguing that Africans were inferior beings, of separate descent from whites, whose depraved and brutish natures fitted them for slavery. The argument contradicted the Biblical account of a common human ancestry and anticipated nineteenth-century 'scientific' racism.

I shall next consider their [the Negroes'] disparity, in regard to the faculties of the mind. Under this head we are to observe that they remain at this time in the same rude situation in which they were found two thousand years ago.

In general, they are void of genius, and seem almost incapable of making any progress in civility or science. They have no plan or system of morality among them. Their barbarity to their children debases their nature even below that of brutes. They have no moral sensations; no taste but for women; gormondizing, and drinking to excess; no wish but to be idle. Their children, from their tenderest years, are suffered to deliver themselves up to all that nature suggests to them. Their houses are miserable cabbins [sic]. They conceive no pleasure from the most beautiful parts of their country, preferring the more sterile. Their roads, as they call them, are mere sheep-paths, twice as long as they need be, and almost impassable. Their country in most parts is one continued wilderness, beset with briars and thorns. They use neither carriages, nor beasts of burden. They are represented by all authors as the vilest of the human kind, to which they have little more pretension of resemblance than what arises from their exterior form.

In so vast a continent as that of Africa and in so great a variety of climates and provinces, we might expect to find a proportionable diversity among the inhabitants, in regard to their qualifications of body and mind: strength, agility, industry, and dexterity, on the one hand; ingenuity, learning, arts, and science on the other. But on the contrary, a general uniformity runs through all these various regions of people; so that, if any difference be found, it is only in degrees of the same qualities and, what is more strange, those of the worst kind; it being a common known proverb, that all people on the globe have some good as well as ill qualities, except the Africans. Whatever great personages this country might anciently have produced, and concerning whom we have no information, they everywhere degenerated into a brutish, ignorant, idle, crafty, treacherous, bloody, thievish, mistrustful and superstitious people ... This brutality somewhat diminishes, when they are imported young, after they become habituated to cloathing [sic] and a regular discipline of life but many are never reclaimed, and continue savages in every sense of the word, to their latest period.

[...]

When we reflect on the nature of these men, and their dissimilarity to the rest of mankind, must we not conclude, that they are a different species of the same *genus*? Of other animals, it is well known, there are many kinds, each kind having its proper species subordinate thereto; and why shall we insist, that man alone, of all other animals,

265

is undiversified in the same manner, when we find so many irresistible proofs which denote his conformity to the general system of the world? In this system we perceive a regular order and gradation, from inanimate to animated matter; and certain links, which connect the several *genera* one with another; and, under these *genera*, we find another gradation of species, comprehending a vast variety, and, in some classes, widely differing from each other in certain qualities.

<hr>

4.2
Letters of John Matthews, 1787–8

E. Donnan (ed.) (1931) *From Documents Illustrative of the History of the Slave Trade to America*, Washington D.C.: Carnegie Institute, pp. 567–71. Paragraph numbers added.

John Matthews was a lieutenant in the Royal Navy, serving in Sierra Leone between 1785 and 1787. While there, he wrote seven letters home, which were published as *A Voyage to the River Sierra Leone, on the Coast of Africa, containing an Account of the Trade and Production of the Country* . . . (1791). Matthews gave evidence to the committee of the Privy Council which investigated the slave trade, and claimed that the trade did not exacerbate violence in Africa. The Liverpool slave merchants formally thanked him for his testimony.

SIERRA-LEONE, February 15, 1787.
1. . . . When the adventurer arrives upon the coast with a suitable cargo – which for this place consists of European and Indian cotton and linen goods, silk handkerchiefs, taffities, coarse blue and red woollen cloths, scarlet cloth in grain, coarse and fine hats, worsted caps, guns, powder, shot, sabres, lead bars, iron bars, pewter basons, copper kettles and pans, iron pots, hardware of various kinds, earthen and glass ware, hair and gilt leather trunks, beads of various kinds, silver and gold rings and ornaments, paper, coarse and fine check, and linen ruffled shirts and caps, British and foreign spirits and tobacco – he dispatches his boats properly equipped to the different rivers. On their arrival at the place of trade they immediately apply to the head man of the town, inform him of their business, and request his protection; desiring he will either be himself their landlord, or appoint a

respectable person, who becomes security for the person and goods of the stranger, and also for the recovery of all money lent, provided it is done with his knowledge and approbation. This business finished, and proper presents made, (for nothing is done without) they proceed to trade either by lending their goods to the natives, who carry them up into the country, or by waiting till trade is brought to them. The former is the most expeditious way, when they fall into good hands; but the latter is always the safest.

2. When the country people come down themselves to trade with the whites, they are obliged to apply to the inhabitants of the villages where the factories are kept, to serve as brokers and interpreters.

When a slave is brought to be sold he is first carefully examined, to see that there is no blemish or defect in him; if approved, you then agree upon the price at so many bars, and give the dealer so many flints or stones to count with; the goods are then delivered to him piece by piece, for which he returns so many stones for each, agreeably to their denominated value; and they always take care to begin with those articles which they judge most essentially necessary.

Exclusive of this method of dealing directly with the natives, transient ships, or those who only come for a small number, generally barter with the white traders resident on the coast, or with the factories established there, who take their whole cargo at once, and deliver them slaves, camwood, ivory, etc. according to their agreement, in a certain time.

From the great number of slaves which are annually exported, and which, from this place and the parts adjacent, including Sherbro' and the Riomoonas,[1] amounts to about three thousand annually, one would be led to imagine the country would, in time, be depopulated; instead of which no diminution of their numbers is perceived; and, from every account we have been able to acquire from the natives themselves, who travel into the interior country, it is extraordinarily populous: but how such a number of slaves are procured, is a circumstance which I believe no European was ever fully acquainted with.

3. The best information I have been able to collect is, that great numbers are prisoners taken in war, and brought down, fifty or a hundred together, by the black slave merchants; that many are sold for witchcraft, and other real, or imputed, crimes; and are purchased in the country with European goods and salt; which is an article so highly valued, and so eagerly sought after, by the natives, that they will part with their wives and children, and every thing dear to them,

[1] Rio Nuñez.

to obtain it, when they have not slaves to dispose of; and it always makes a part of the merchandize for the purchase of slaves in the interior country; yet, notwithstanding salt is in such great demand, the natives of the sea-coast will not permit the import of it in European vessels, because it would interfere with the only article of their own manufacture, which they have for inland trade. . . . Death or slavery were, and still are, the punishments for almost every offence. And every prisoner taken in battle was either put to death or kept as a slave. The fate of prisoners was also in a great measure determined by the season of the year, and the occasion they had for their services. If they were taken after the harvest was over, they were seldom spared; but those who were captured before the commencement of the rice season, experienced a different fate, as they were reserved to cultivate ·the rice-ground; and sold, after the harvest, to those tribes bordering on the sea, who had no other means of acquiring slaves than by purchase; or were kept as labouring slaves, and for ever fixed to the spot. This was the ancient custom of the country, and the modern practice is nearly similar, as they seldom dispose of their new slaves till the rice is in the ground, or until it is cut. Hence, though the Europeans by the eagerness with which they push this trade may be censurable so far, as they may some times, by their competition with each other, excite the avarice of individuals to procure slaves, by means as repugnant to their own laws as any act of dishonesty is to ours; yet I believe we may safely conclude, that slavery can never be abolished in a country like Africa, consisting of a prodigious number of small independent states, perpetually at variance, and under no restraining form of government, where the people are of a vindictive and revengeful spirit, and where the laws make every man a slave who is convicted of the most trifling offence. During the late war in which England was engaged with France,[2] when the ships did not visit the coast as usual, and there were no goods to purchase the slaves which were brought down, the black merchants suffered many of them to perish for want of food, and said they should not come down again till the ships arrived. When questioned what the inland people would do with their slaves? They replied 'cut their throats, as they used to do before white men came to their country'.

[. . .]

[2] France allied with the United States in their War of Independence against the British in February 1778; the war was formally ended by the Treaty of Paris in September 1783.

LIVERPOOL, Feb. 20, 1788.

4. ... A description of the method of procuring slaves in the part of Africa where I resided, I have, in some measure, anticipated in my former letters from Sierra-Leone, which were written at a time when I had no idea of a design to abolish that trade being formed, or I should have applied myself with greater industry to have acquired a more particular knowledge of the manners and customs of the natives of the interior counties; I shall however endeavour to combat such assertions as are made use of by the advocates for the abolition of this commerce, as my own knowledge and information may suggest. That slaves are often captives taken in war, is a position I readily accede to; but that those wars are undertaken merely for the purpose of procuring slaves is by no means the case; for it is necessary to observe, the king, or chief of a tribe, has not power to make war upon any other tribe without the consent and approbation of the principal people of his nation; and it can scarcely be conceived that such consent could be obtained to a measure that would draw down upon them the resentment of the neighbouring states. Neither is it (as is alledged) in any instance which has occurred to my observation or inquiries, by the instigation of the European traders; for, whenever the people on the sea-coast are at war, it puts an entire stop to trade; and I always found it to my interest, as well as my inclination, to reconcile their differences, and to preserve peace. ...

In answer to the charge of kidnapping slaves, I can only say that I never heard of such a practice, nor do I know a word in their language expressive of such a custom ever having had existence. ...

5. The nations which inhabit the interior parts of Africa, east of Sierra-Leone, profess the Mahometan religion;[3] and, following the means prescribed by their prophet, are perpetually at war with the surrounding nations who refuse to embrace their religious doctrines (and I have before shewn the zeal with which the Mandingoes[4] inculcate their faith).

The prisoners made in these religious wars furnish a great part of the slaves which are sold to the Europeans; and would, I have reason to believe, from the concurring testimony of many of the most intelligent natives, be put to death if they had not the means of disposing of them.

---

[3] Islam.

[4] People from the region of French West Africa, modern-day Senegal and the Gambia.

That death would be the fate of their prisoners, the example of the inhabitants of Madagascar, is sufficient proof; for since the Portuguese have declined dealing with them they put all their prisoners to death. . . .

It is also given as a reason for the abolishing this traffic; that the distinctions of crimes are multiplied, and every transgression punished with slavery, in consequence of their intercourse with Europeans.

Upon this head I shall observe, that the crimes of murder, poison, witchcraft, adultery, and theft, are always considered as capital, and have been punished with either death or slavery from time immemorial.

That the punishment of death, for the commission of these crimes, is remitted by their becoming slaves, I believe, in many instances, to be the case; yet, surely no one would adduce this circumstance as a proof of its inhumanity. . . .

4.3

Thomas Clarkson, *An Essay on the Comparative Efficiency of Regulation or Abolition . . . , 1789*

E. Donnan (ed.) (1931) *From Documents Illustrative of the History of the Slave Trade to America,* Washington D.C.: Carnegie Institute, pp. 571–3. Paragraph numbers added.

Thomas Clarkson (1760–1846) was a founder member of the Committee for the Abolition of the Slave Trade (set up in May 1787) and its principal investigator and publicist. He published these accounts from the journals of men who had served on the African coast to draw attention to the violence played in acquiring slaves and the horrors of the Middle Passage. He divided the work into three sections: the first dealt with the seizure of Africans in Africa, the second dealt with the Middle Passage, and the third dealt with African slaves in the colonies. This extract includes material from the first two sections.

[Section 1]

1. GOREE, *Oct. 17, 1787.* On making inquiries to day, relative to the history of a certain negro woman, I found that she came from the country about Cape Rouge, and that in the absence of her husband she had been stolen and forcibly dragged away. Her case was attended with this additional circumstance of cruelty, that she was torn from her children, who, being too young to undergo the fatigue of the journey, were left behind.

Oct, 19th 1787. Inquiring to day of a negroe lad, how he came into the situation of a slave, he informed me, that he had been stolen from his parents, in the interior country above Cape Rouge; that the inhabitants of the shore usually came up in bodies for this purpose, and that they unfortunately met with him, and brought him to Goree, in company with others, whom they had taken in the same manner.

2. JOAL, *Nov. 5th 1787.* Since our arrival here, the king of Barbasin has twice sent out his military to attack his own villages in the night. They have been very unsuccessful, having taken but three children. They had no better fortune last night, having brought in but one girl.

I had two opportunities of seeing how slaves were procured in the River of Old Calabar. I resided with the king of New Town for four months, and he allowed me to go up the river with him to trade for slaves. I went with him twice within that time. In the first expedition, there was a fleet consisting of from ten to twelve canoes, which were properly manned and armed. With this fleet we set out to trade. In the day time we called at the villages as we passed, and purchased our slaves fairly, but in the night we made several excursions on the banks of the river. The canoes were usually left with an armed force: the rest, when landed, broke into the villages, and, rushing into the huts of the inhabitants, seized men, women, and children promiscuously. We obtained about fifty negroes in this manner, in our first expedition.

In our second, the same practices were in force: for we traded fairly by day, and became robbers in the night. We were more successful, in points of the number procured in the second, than in the first expedition. . . .

3. I was resident for seven months at a factory in Mossula Bay, in the kingdom of Angola. I know of no other way of making slaves there, than by robbery. Our factory was supplied by four traders, one of whom, with his party, was always out. These parties consisted usually of forty or fifty in number. They were always armed when they went out. They took no goods with them, but yet returned with slaves. Their time of staying out was sometimes a month, and sometimes less. It depended on circumstances, for if in a previous expedition they had

brought off a few from the skirts of a town, they were obliged to go much farther for the remainder the next. For the negroes, when so attacked, immediately leave their habitations, and go farther inland. They are continually in a wandering, uncertain state, on account of these frequent depredations.

In the year 1787, I was lying at Cape Palmas. I was told by the natives there, that they intended to attack a village on the third night. I asked them if the inhabitants had done them any injury. They replied, no; but that there was a considerable number of fine stout young men belong- ing to it, who were good for trade. This was their only reason. On the same day, on the evening of which their attack was to commence, I had occasion to go to another village, which was within about two miles from that which was marked for pillage, and lay in the same track. I slept at a trader's house that night. At about two in the morning he awakened me to see the fire. I jumped up instantly from a chest on which I lay, and saw the village in flames. The next day more than fifty young men were brought down, all of whom had been taken during the conflagration.

[. . .]

[Section 2]

4. The misery, which the slaves endure in consequence of too close a stowage, is not easily to be described. I have heard them frequently complaining of heat, and have seen them fainting, and almost dying for want of water. Their situation is worst in rainy weather. We do every thing for them in our power. In all the vessels in which I have sailed in the slave-trade, we never covered the gratings with a tarpawling, but made a tarpawling awning over the booms. Notwithstanding which, I have seen the slaves after a rain, panting for breath, and in such a situation, that the seamen have been obliged to get them immediately upon deck, fearing lest they would otherwise have fainted away, and died. In one of my voyages, which was particularly unhealthy, we have found eight or ten dead in a morning. In the ____ we purchased 350 slaves, and buried 6; in a second voyage, in the same ship, we purchased 350, and buried 200; and in the ____ we purchased about 370, and buried about 100. . . .

5. The slaves frequently complain of heat on a calm night, but much more so when it rains, as we are then obliged to spread a tarpawling over them; and notwithstanding that it is kept at a considerable height from the gratings by means of a ridge rope, and stretched out by means of nettles to give them every advantage in point of air, they are still in a miserable state. I have been in their rooms to see them on these occasions and have found them in a violent perspiration. I have wiped

them with cloths myself, and have seen that others have wiped them also. I have no doubt but that in full slave-vessels their sufferings must be inconceivably great. In the ____ we purchased about 700 slaves, and lost 250. In the ship ____ we purchased about 300, out of which we buried about 17. In the sloop ____ 25 were bought, and 2 buried. In the ____ we bought 180, and lost about 25. In the ____ 350 were purchased, and 25 were lost as before. In the ____ about 500 were purchased, and 150 buried; and out of 250 bought in the ____ 5 died.[1] . . .

4.4
Enlightenment definitions of slavery

D. Diderot & J. d'Alembert ([1751–65] 1772) *Encyclopédie, ou Dictionnaire raisonné des sciences, des arts et des métiers*, Geneva: Édition Panckoucke-Cramer, 17 vols., vol. V (1760), pp. 1234–5; & vol. XVI (1760), pp. 859–60. Translated from French by Fabienne Evans & Rachel C. Gibbons.

These extracts are encyclopaedia articles contributed by Louis, Chevalier de Jaucourt to the great *Encyclopédie*, which offer a magisterial summation of the French Enlightenment's optimistic rationality. Slavery and the slave trade came under intellectual assault during the Enlightenment because they were seen as a violation of human rights derived from natural law, as these extracts from the summa of 'enlightened' thinking testify.

(a) Slavery

SLAVERY (Nat[ural] law, Religion, Ethics)
Slavery is the establishment of a right based on force, which makes a man belong to another man in such a way that he is the absolute master of his life, his belongings and his freedom.

This definition applies almost equally to civil *slavery* and political *slavery*: to draw its origin, its nature and its foundations, I will borrow

---

[1] One of Clarkson's accounts comes from a witness who had served on two French and two English slave-ships. In the first, from Bordeaux, 500 slaves were purchased, 200 were buried; in the second, from Brest, 20 were lost out of 400; in the third, from London, 50 out of 370; and in service on 'an old man of war' he saw 1115 purchased and 845 buried.

freely from the author of *The Spirit of the Laws*, without digressing to praise the solidity of his principles because I cannot add any more to his glory.

All men are born free; in the beginning, they had only a name, a condition: Nature made them all equal; but we did not keep this natural equality for long, we gradually moved away from it, servitude settled in by stages and it is likely that it was established on free conventions, although necessity had been the source and origin.

As a consequence of the increase in the number of human beings, we became bored with the simplicity of the first centuries, we looked for new ways of increasing the comforts of life and acquiring non-essentials; it seems very much that rich people hired poor people to work for them for a wage. This arrangement being very convenient for everyone, some resolved to secure their conditions and to maintain forever their position into someone's family as long as food and all other necessities of life were provided; thus servitude was first formed by a willing consent and by a contract 'to work in order to be kept': *do ut facias*. This society was based on conditions, at least for certain things, according to the laws of each country and the conventions of the parties concerned; in a word, such slaves were only servants or mercenaries, quite similar to our domestics.

But we did not stop there; we found so many advantages to make others do what we would have had to do ourselves that, as we wanted to expand through war, we established the custom of granting life and corporal freedom to prisoners of war on the condition that they would still serve as slaves for the people who had conquered them.

As we still had some resentment for the poor souls whom we had reduced to *slavery* by warfare, we usually treated them very harshly; cruelty seemed excusable against people from whom we could have had suffered the same fate; therefore we thought that such slaves could be killed, with impunity, through a fit of anger or for any trivial faults.

Once sanctioned, this licence was widened, under an even less credible pretext, to those who were born from such slaves and even to those whom we bought or acquired in any way. Thus servitude became natural, so to speak, by the force of war: those who had been favoured by fortune and left in the state that nature had created them were called *free*; those on the other hand whose weakness and misfortune had subjugated them to the victors were called *slaves*. And philosophers, judges of the merits of men's actions, considered the conqueror's behaviour as charity, turning the defeated man into a slave instead of taking his life.

The law of the strongest, the right of war injurious to nature, ambition, thirst for conquests, love of domination, and apathy introduced *slavery*, which, to the shame of humanity, has been accepted by nearly all the peoples of the world. Indeed, we could not look at Biblical history without discovering the horrors of servitude: classical history, of the Greeks, the Romans and of all other people who are believed to have been the most civilised, are testimony to this ancient injustice committed with more or less violence all over the earth, according to times, places and nations.

There are two sorts of *slavery* or servitude, the real and the personal: real servitude is the one which consigns the slave to the very lowest level of existence, personal servitude concerns household management and is more related to the personality of the master. The extreme abuse is when it is both personal and real. This is how foreigners' servitude was at the hand of the Jews; they were treated in the harshest way: in vain, Moses was telling the Jews 'you shall not have any rigorous domination over your slaves, you shall not oppress them'.[1] He never managed, by exhortations, to soften the harshness of his fierce nation: he therefore tried with law to bring a few remedies.

[. . .]

The freedom of man is a principle recognised long before the birth of Christ, by all nations that have professed generosity. The *natural* freedom of man is to not suffer any sovereign power on earth and not to be subjected to the legal authority of what has to be done, but to only follow the laws of Nature: freedom *in society* is to submit to a legal power established by the consent of the community, and not to be subjected to whims, to the flimsy, uncertain and arbitrary will of one single man in particular.

This freedom, by which one is not subjected to an absolute power, is so closely linked to the preservation of man, that it can only be detached by what destroys at the same time that very preservation and life. Whoever tries to impose an absolute power upon someone else by doing so puts himself in a state of war with him, so that the other can only see his action as a manifest attempt against his life. Indeed, from the moment a man wants to subject me to his authority against my will, I have good reason to presume that, if I fall in his hands, he will treat me according to his whims and will have no scruples to kill me, when he feels like it. Freedom is, so to speak, the bulwark of self-preservation and the foundation of all things that

---

[1] The Bible, Leviticus 25:43.

belong to me. Therefore, if anyone in the natural state wants to reduce me to slavery, I am justified by the principle of natural liberty in resisting him by any means to secure my person and belongings.

All men having by nature an equal freedom, one cannot strip them of this freedom, without resorting to some criminal actions. Certainly, if a man, in the natural state, has forfeited his life to someone he has sinned against, and who in this case has become the master of his life, the latter can, when he has the culprit in his hands, deal with him, and take him into his service, that way he does not do him any wrong; because fundamentally, when the criminal finds his *slavery* more burdensome and tiresome than the loss of his life, he has the means to bring on the death he deserves by resisting and disobeying his master.

What makes the death of a criminal, in civil society, a lawful matter, is that the law which punishes him has been made in his favour. A murderer, for instance, has benefited from the law which condemns him; it has preserved his life at all times; he therefore cannot claim against this law. It would not be the same for the *slavery* law; the law which would establish *slavery* would be in all cases against the slave, without ever being for him; which is contrary to the founding principle of all societies.

The rights of ownership of men and of belongings are two very different things. Whatever a sovereign says about the one subjected to his dominion, *this person belongs to me*; the ownership he has over such a man is not the same as the one he can claim when saying *these goods are mine*. The ownership of goods gives a full right of usage, to consume them, and to destroy them, either for some benefit or for a simple whim; so that whichever way we use the goods, we do not do them any wrong; but the same expression used for a person, only means that the master, and no other, has the right to control him and stipulate his laws, while at the same time, he is himself subjected to various obligations towards this person and, in any case, his power on this person is very limited.

Whatever damages inflicted on us by another man, humanity does not allow us, once we have reconciled ourselves with him, to reduce him to a condition where there is no trace of the natural equality of all men, and therefore to treat him like an animal, whom we can dispose of as we please. People who have treated slaves like goods that they could dispose of at will are little more than barbarians.

Not only can we have no right of ownership over people; but moreover, it is also distasteful to think, that a man who has no power over his own life, could give to another man, without his consent or by any conventions, the right he has not got himself. Therefore it is not true that a free man could sell himself. The sale supposes a price; the slave selling himself, all his belongings become his master's ownership. Thus, the master would give nothing and the slave would receive nothing either. He would receive a small earning, one might say, but this small amount is incidental to the person. The freedom of each citizen is part of the public freedom: this status, in a people's state, is even part of sovereignty. If freedom has a price for the one who buys it, it has no price for the one who sells it.

Civil law, which gave men the division of property, did not include people amongst the goods to be shared by men. When contracts cause a loss, civil law ensures that there is restitution, therefore it cannot help but go against an agreement which contains the largest flaw of all. *Slavery* therefore conflicts no less with civil rights than natural rights. Which civil law could prevent a slave saving himself from servitude, he is not part of society and therefore no civil law concerns him? He can only be retained by family law, by his master's law, which is the law of the strongest.

If *slavery* shakes natural and civil law, it also offends the best forms of government: it goes against monarchical government, in which it is supremely important not to weaken and degrade human nature. In democracy, where everyone is equal, and in oligarchy, where the laws must ensure that everyone is as equal as the nature of their government will allow it, slaves are against the constitutional spirit; they would only give citizens the power and luxury that they should not have.

Besides, in all governments and countries, however hard is the work demanded by society, everything can be achieved with free men, by encouraging them with rewards and privileges, by adjusting their tasks to their strengths, or by replacing them with machines invented by skill, and applies according to places and needs. You can see this in M. de Montesquieu.[2]

Finally we can add more with this illustrious author, that *slavery* is useful neither to the master nor to the slave: to the slave because he cannot do anything by virtue of it; to the master, because he acquires when acquiring his slaves all sorts of vices and bad habits, against the laws of society; he imperceptibly gets accustomed to flout

[2] Charles-Louis de Secondat, baron de la Brède et de Montesquieu (1689–1755), was a French political and legal theorist. He is famous particularly for his championing of the separation of powers between the executive, the legislative and the judiciary, taken for granted in modern discussions of government and implemented in many constitutions all over the world.

all moral virtues; he becomes arrogant, moody, quick-tempered, hard-hearted, voluptuous, cruel.

(b) The slave trade

SLAVE TRADE (African commerce)

The purchase of negroes that Europeans make on the African coasts, to employ these poor souls in their colonies as slaves. This purchase of negroes, to reduce them to slaves, is a trade that violates religion, ethics, the laws of nature and all rights of human nature.

A modern Englishman full of enlightenment and humanity says that negroes have not become slaves by the right of war; neither do they willingly give themselves to servitude, and therefore their children are not born as slaves. Everybody is aware that we buy them from their princes, who claim to have the right of disposing of their freedom, and that traders have them transported in the same way as any other goods, either to their colonies or to America where they are put on sale.

claim

If a trade of this kind can be justified by a moral code, there is no crime, however atrocious it is, that we cannot legitimize. Kings, princes and magistrates are not the owners of their subjects, therefore are not entitled to control their freedom, and to sell them as slaves.

On the other hand, no man has the right to buy them or to become their masters; men and their freedom are not goods to be traded; they can neither be sold, bought nor paid for at any price. From this we must conclude that a man whose slave escapes should blame himself, as he had acquired for money illicit goods, and that this purchase was forbidden by all laws of humanity and equity.

Thus, not one of these poor souls that we only consider as slaves should be denied the right to freedom, as he has never lost his freedom; that he could not lose it; and that his prince, his father or anyone else in the world did not have the right to dispose of it; therefore, the sale which took place is invalid in itself: this negro cannot ever be stripped of and/or even deprive himself his natural right; he bears it everywhere with him and can demand that we let him enjoy it anywhere. Thus it is an evident inhumanity on the part of judges in the free countries to where he is transported not to enfranchise him straightaway by declaring him to be free, because he is one of them, having a soul like them.

There are some authors who set themselves as political legal experts, boldly telling us that questions relating to the welfare of the people should be decided by the laws of the countries to which they belong and therefore that a man who is declared a slave in America and transported from there to Europe, should be regarded as a slave here as well; but this is deciding of human rights by the civil laws of the gutter, as Cicero said.[3] Do magistrates of a nation, by consideration for another nation, not have any attention for their own species? Does their deference to a law which does not bind them to anything require them to trample on the law of nature, which obligate all men in all times and places? Is there any law as binding as the eternal laws of equity? Can we question if a judge is more bound to observe them [the latter] rather than respecting the arbitrary and inhuman practices of the colonies?

Some may say that if the slave trade was abolished it would cause the ruin of the colonies. But, if it was the case, should it be concluded from this that the rights of mankind should be horribly infringed so that we can get richer or provided with luxury? It is true that the purses of highway robbers would be empty if theft disappeared completely: but do men have the right to get richer by cruel and criminal means? What right has a brigand to rob passers-by? Who is entitled to become wealthy by making his fellow man miserable? Maybe it is legitimate to deprive mankind of its most sacred rights, solely to satisfy one's own miserliness, vanity or personal passions? No – May the European colonies be destroyed rather than create so many poor souls!

But I think it is untrue that the abolition of slavery would bring about their ruin. Trade would suffer for a while: I want it – that is how it works for all new arrangements, because in this case we could not find instantly the means to follow another system; but a lot of advantages would come out of this abolition.

It is this *slave trade*, this use of servitude, which has prevented America becoming populated as rapidly as it should have without this practice. Let us set the slaves free and, within a few generations, this vast and fertile country will have numerous inhabitants. Skills and talents will flourish; and instead of being populated with savages and ferocious beasts, it would soon be occupied only by industrious people. It is freedom and industry which are the real sources of abundance. As long as people preserve this industry and freedom, they have nothing to fear. Industry, as well as poverty, is resourceful and inventive; it finds a thousand different means to create wealth; and, if one

---

[3] Marcus Tullius Cicero (BCE 106–43), prominent Republican politician and enemy of Caesar, and much-published orator and rhetorician.

of the channels to wealth is blocked, hundreds of others open instantly.

Sensible and generous souls will no doubt applaud these reasons in favour of humanity; but miserliness and greed which dominate the earth, will never want to hear them.

Adam Smith, *An Inquiry into the Nature and Causes of the Wealth of Nations*

A. Smith ([1776] 1991) *The Wealth of Nations*, ed. & introd.
D.D. Raphael, Everyman's Library Classics, London:
Everyman, pp. 344–6.

As part of his inquiry into the *Wealth of Nations*, Adam Smith (1723–90) offered a critique of slavery as economically irrational, as the least productive form of human labour. Though false in premise, his argument was significant in his day and remained hugely influential up to the 1960s.

If little improvement was to be expected from such great proprietors, still less was to be hoped for from those who occupied the land under them. In the ancient state of Europe, the occupiers of land were all tenants at will. They were all or almost all slaves; but their slavery was of a milder kind than that known among the ancient Greeks and Romans, or even in our West Indian colonies. They were supposed to belong more directly to the land than to their master. They could, therefore, be sold with it, but not separately. They could marry, provided it was with the consent of their master; and he could not afterwards dissolve the marriage by selling the man and wife to different persons. If he maimed or murdered any of them, he was liable to some penalty, though generally but to a small one. They were not, however, capable of acquiring property. Whatever they acquired was acquired to their master, and he could take it from them at pleasure. Whatever cultivation and improvement could be carried on by means of such slaves was properly carried on by their master. It was at his expense. The seed, the cattle, and the instruments of husbandry were all his. It was for his benefit. Such slaves could acquire nothing but their daily maintenance. It was properly the proprietor himself, therefore, that, in this case, occupied his own lands, and cultivated them by his own bondmen. This species of slavery still subsists in Russia, Poland, Hungary, Bohemia, Moravia, and other parts of Germany. It is only in the western and south-western provinces of Europe that it has gradually been abolished altogether.

But if great improvements are seldom to be expected from great proprietors, they are least of all to be expected when they employ slaves for their workmen. The experience of all ages and nations, I believe, demonstrates that the work done by slaves, though it appears to cost only their maintenance, is in the end the dearest of any. A person who can acquire no property, can have no other interest but to eat as much, and to labour as little as possible. Whatever work he does beyond what is sufficient to purchase his own maintenance can be squeezed out of him by violence only, and not by any interest of his own. In ancient Italy, how much the cultivation of corn degenerated, how unprofitable it became to the master when it fell under the management of slaves, is remarked by both Pliny[1] and Columella.[2] In the time of Aristotle[3] it had not been much better in ancient Greece. Speaking of the ideal republic described in the laws of Plato, to maintain five thousand idle men (the number of warriors supposed necessary for its defence) together with their women and servants, would require, he says, a territory of boundless extent and fertility, like the plains of Babylon.

The pride of man makes him love to domineer, and nothing mortifies him so much as to be obliged to condescend to persuade his inferiors. Wherever the law allows it, and the nature of the work can afford it, therefore, he will generally prefer the service of slaves to that of freemen. The planting of sugar and tobacco can afford the expense of slave-cultivation. The raising of corn, it seems, in the present times, cannot. In the English colonies, of which the principal produce is corn, the far greater part of the work is done by freemen. The late resolution of the Quakers in Pennsylvania to set at liberty all their negro slaves

---

[1] Gaius Plinius Secundus (Pliny the Elder) (23–79 CE), Roman military officer and scholar. His encyclopaedic *Historia Naturalis* (Natural History, published in 77 CE) contains much information on agriculture, horticulture and estate management, as well as astronomy, chemistry, geography, medicine and geology.

[2] Lucius Junius Moderatus Columella (4–70 CE), whose twelve-volume *De Re Rustica* (On Country Ways) is the most important surviving source on Roman agriculture.

[3] Aristotle (384–322 BCE), Greek logician, scientist and philosopher. In his *Politics*, exploring theories of government, Artistotle criticises the 'ideal republic' proposed in *The Republic* (published 390 BCE) by Plato, founder of the Academy of Athens where Aristotle studied philosophy.

may satisfy us that their number cannot be very great. Had they made any considerable part of their property, such a resolution could never have been agreed to. In our sugar colonies, on the contrary, the whole work is done by slaves, and in our tobacco colonies a very great part of it. The profits of a sugar-plantation in any of our West Indian colonies are generally much greater than those of any other cultivation that is known either in Europe or America; and the profits of a tobacco plantation, though inferior to those of sugar, are superior to those of corn, as has already been observed. Both can afford the expense of slave-cultivation, but sugar can afford it still better than tobacco. The number of negroes accordingly is much greater, in proportion to that of whites, in our sugar than in our tobacco colonies.

4.6
The Saint Domingue Revolution, 1790s

D.P. Geggus (2002) *Haitian Revolutionary Studies,*
Bloomington: Indiana University Press, pp. 135–6.

These letters were written at the height of the conflict between Republican French forces and Spanish and British invaders of San Domingue (modern-day Haiti), who had allied with supporters of the *ancien régime* amongst the French planters. François-Dominique Toussaint L'Ouverture (c. 1743–1803) was born a slave on the Bréda plantation. At the time of the slave uprising in August 1791, he was a freeman who joined the rebellion some time after its outbreak and became its most able commander. In 1794, Toussaint was in command of black Republican forces who had invested the port of Gonaïves.

(a) Letter of Toussaint L'Ouverture to the Reverend Father, Vicar of Gonaïves

Gonaïves, May 5, 1794

Most Reverend Father,

I am most sincerely affected by the harsh necessity that compelled you to leave the House of our adorable creator. Having been unable to

4.2 Toussaint Breda or L'Ouverture (c. 1743–1803), one of the leaders of the Haitian revolution.

foresee such a disastrous event fills my soul with despair. You, Minister of Almighty God, instrument of his wishes, come back, I beseech you, come back and reconcile us with Him. Have no doubts as to my sincerity. I dare believe you will give it sufficient credence to return without delay.

I have the honor to be with great respect, most reverend father, your most humble and obedient servant.

Signed Toussaint Louverture,
True Copy, Signed Salazard

(b) Letter of Toussaint L'Ouverture to Messieurs the refugee inhabitants of Gonaïves

Gonaïves, May 5, 1794

Gentlemen,

It is without doubt painful for me to have been unable to foresee the unhappy events that have just transpired and have obliged you to leave your properties. Such regret can be felt by me alone. Be assured, Sirs, that I did not at all participate and that everything was done without my knowledge and consequently against my wishes. God who knows our most secret thoughts and who sees all, is witness to the purity of my principles. They are not founded on this barbarous ferocity that takes pleasure in shedding human blood. Come back, Sirs, come back to your homes. I swear before our divine Creator that I will do everything to keep you safe. I have already given my orders on this matter. Nothing will be neglected to ensure they are precisely carried out.

I dare hope that you will have confidence in my sincerity, and believe that I have the honor to be, Sirs, your most humble and obedient servant.

Signed Toussaint Louverture.

P.S. On second thoughts, I request that you do not return until after I have come back from Marmelade, for I am going up there today.

True copy, signed
Salazazy [sic].

4.7

Letters of General Leclerc to Napoleon Bonaparte, August 1802

C.L.R. James ([1938] 1989) *The Black Jacobins: Toussaint L'Ouverture and the San Domingo Revolution*, London: Allison and Busby, pp. 343–5, 349–50. Paragraph numbers added to (a).

General Leclerc (1772–1802), brother-in-law of Napoleon (1769–1821), had been sent by the First Consul to restore French authority over Saint Domingue in February 1802. In August, Leclerc learned that Napoleon had reinstated slavery in the French empire on 11 May and wrote a series of anguished letters protesting how this decision had undermined his pacification strategy.

(a) Letter of 6 August 1802

1. Death has wrought such frightful havoc among my troops that when I tried to disarm the North a general insurrection broke out.
... I fear nothing from Christophe, but I am not so sure of Dessalines.[1] The first attacks have driven the rebels from the positions they occupied; but they fell back to other cantons and in the insurrection there is a veritable fanaticism. These men get themselves killed, but they refuse to surrender. ...

I entreated you, Citizen Consul, to do nothing which might make them anxious about their liberty until I was ready, and that moment was rapidly approaching. Suddenly the law arrived here which authorises the slave-trade in the colonies, with business letters from Nantes and Havre asking if blacks can be sold here. More than all that, General Richepanse[2] has just taken a decision to re-establish slavery in Guadeloupe. In this state of affairs, Citizen Consul, the moral force I had obtained here is destroyed. I can do nothing by persuasion. I can depend only on force and I have no troops.

2. ... Now, Citizen Consul, that your plans for the colonies are perfectly known, if you wish to preserve San Domingo, send a new army,

---

[1] Two generals of the rebel black army, Henry Christophe (1761–1820) and Jean-Jacques Dessalines (1758–1806).

[2] Antoine Richepanse (1770–1803), captain-general of French possessions in South America.

send above all money, and I assure you that if you abandon us to ourselves, as you have hitherto done, this colony is lost, and once lost, you will never regain it.

My letter will surprise you, Citizen Consul, after those I have written to you. But what general could calculate on a mortality of four-fifths of his army and the uselessness of the remainder, who has been left without funds as I have, in a country where purchases are made only for their weight in gold and where with money I might have got rid of much discontent? Could I have expected, in these circumstances, the law relating to the slave-trade and above all the decrees of General Richepanse re-establishing slavery and forbidding the men of colour from signing themselves as citizens?

I have shown you my real position with the frankness of a soldier. I am grieved to see all that I have done here on the point of being destroyed. If you had been a witness of the difficulties of all sorts which I have overcome, and the results I had obtained, you would grieve with me on seeing my position; but however disagreeable it may be, I still have hopes of succeeding. I make terrible examples, and since terror is the sole resource left me, I employ it. At Tortuga, of 450 rebels I had 60 hanged. To-day everything is in perfect order.

All the proprietors or merchants who come from France speak of slaves. It seems that there is a general conspiracy to prevent the restoration of San Domingo to the Republic.

3. . . . Send me immediately reinforcements, send me money, for I am in a really wretched position.

I have painted a pessimistic picture of my situation. Do not think that I am in any way cast down by what is happening. I shall be always equal to circumstances whatever they may be, and I shall serve you with the same zeal as long as my health permits me. It is now worse, and I am no longer able to ride. Bear in mind that you must send me a successor. I have no one here who can replace me in the critical situation in which the colony will be for some time. . . . Jérémie is in revolt. I have no other news from that quarter.

Christophe and Dessalines have begged me not to leave them here after my departure. That allows you to judge of the confidence they have in me. I hope in the first days of Brumaire to be able to send to France or elsewhere all disruptive persons. . . . When I leave, the colony will be ready to receive the régime which you wish to give it, but it will be for my successor to take the final step. If you agree, I shall do nothing contrary to what I have proclaimed here.

General Richepanse conducts himself in a manner which is very impolitic and very clumsy in so far as San Domingo is concerned; if I had not cut off many heads here, I should have been chased from the island long ago, and would not have been able to fulfil your plans.

[. . .]

(b) Letter of 26 September 1802

My position becomes worse from day to day. I am in such a miserable plight that I have no idea when and how I will get out of it . . . I had believed up to the present that the ravages of the malady would stop in Vendémiaire. I was wrong; the malady has again taken new strength and the month of Fructidor[3] cost me more than 4,000 dead. I had believed from what the inhabitants told me that the malady would stop in Vendémiaire.[4] They tell me to-day that it may possibly last to the end of Brumaire.[5] If that happens and it continues with the same intensity the colony will be lost. Every day the party of the rebels grows larger and mine diminishes by the loss of whites and the desertion of blacks. . . . Dessalines, who up to now had never thought of insurrection, thinks of it to-day. But I have his secret; he will not escape me. This is how I discovered his thoughts. Not being strong enough to finish up with Dessalines, Maurepas[6] and the others, I use one against the other. All three are ready to be party leaders, no one declares himself so long as he will have the others to fear. In consequence he has begun to make reports against Christophe and Maurepas, insinuating to me that their presence was harmful to the colony.

I reiterate what I have told you. San Domingo is lost to France if I have not received on the 16 Nivôse[7] 10,000 men who must all come at the same time.

I have told you my opinion on the measures taken by General Richepanse at Guadeloupe. . . .

I have painted my position in dark colours; this is what it really is and that is the entire truth. Unfortunately the condition of the colonies is not known in France. We have there a false idea of the Negro, and that is why I send you an officer who knows the country and has fought in it. The colonists and the men of business think that a decree of the French Government would be sufficient to restore slavery. I cannot say what measures I shall take, I do not know what I shall do. . . .

---

[3] Fructidor, the twelfth month of the French Republican calendar, beginning on August 18/19. The calendar was in use from 1793 until abolished by Napoleon at the end of 1805.

[4] The first month, Vendémiaire, began at the Autumn equinox on September 22/23.

[5] The second month, Brumaire, began between October 22 and October 24.

[6] Jacques Maurepas, another black general of the rebel army.

[7] 6 January 1803.

4.8

Thomas Clarkson and the Abolition Movement

T. Clarkson ([1808] 1968) *The History of the Rise, Progress, and Accomplishment of Abolition of the African Slave Trade by the British Parliament,* London: Frank Cass & Co., 2 vols., vol. 1, pp. 255–6, 277–9, 282–91, 415–16, 469–71. Paragraph numbers added.

In investigating the evils of the Atlantic slave trade, Thomas Clarkson was a fearless and tireless campaigner. In the course of his enquiries, irate slavers attempted to drown him in Liverpool docks. When he went to Paris in 1789–90 to try to persuade the Revolutionary leaders to outlaw the trade, he took with him the plan of the slave ship 'The Brookes', showing how slaves were packed together for the Middle Passage. It became one of the Abolition movement's most widely circulated images. These extracts are from the 'classic' insider's account of the abolition movement, written immediately after the 1807 Act outlawing the slave trade for British nationals.

1. At the time appointed, I met my friends. I read over the substance of the conversation which had taken place at Mr. Langton's.[1] No difficulty occurred. All were unanimous for the formation of a committee. On the next day we met by agreement for this purpose. It was then resolved unanimously, among other things, That the Slave-trade was both impolitic and unjust. It was resolved also, That the following persons be a committee for procuring such information and evidence, and publishing the same, as may tend to the abolition of the Slave-trade, and for directing the application of such moneys as have been already, and may hereafter be collected for the above purpose.

Granville Sharp.

William Dillwyn.
Samuel Hoare.
George Harrison.
John Lloyd.
Joseph Woods.

[1] Bennet Langton (1737–1801), a key Establishment figure who became a valuable supporter of the Abolitionist movement.

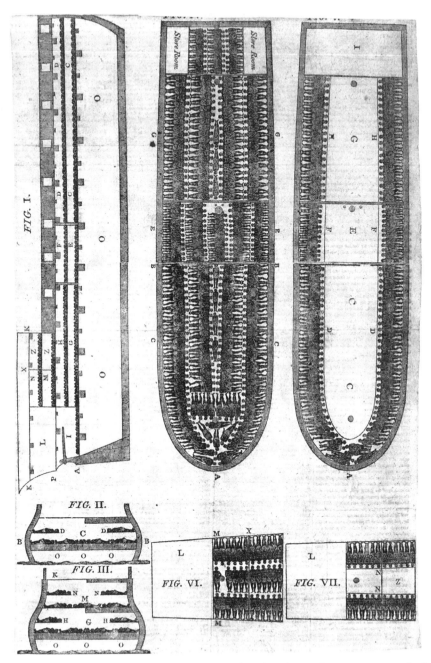

4.3 Plan of 'The Brookes' slaver ship, showing how slaves were packed tightly together on the Middle Passage from West Africa to the Americas. Thomas Clarkson, c. 1789.

Thomas Clarkson.
Richard Phillips.

John Barton.
Joseph Hooper.
James Phillips.
Philip Sansom.

All these were present.
[. . .]
2. At this meeting it was resolved also, that no less than three members should form a quorum; that Samuel Hoare should be the treasurer; that the treasurer should pay no money but by order of the committee; and that copies of these resolutions should be printed and circulated, in which it should be inserted that the subscriptions of all such, as were willing to forward the plans of the committee, should be received by the treasurer or any member of it.

On the twenty-fourth of May the committee met again to promote the object of its institution.

The treasurer reported at this meeting, that the subscriptions already received, amounted to one hundred and thirty-six pounds.

As I had foreseen, long before this time, that my Essay on the Slavery and Commerce of the Human Species [1786] was too large for general circulation, and yet that a general circulation of knowledge on this subject was absolutely necessary, I determined, directly after the formation of the committee, to write a short pamphlet consisting only of eight or ten pages for this purpose. I called it A Summary View of the Slave-trade, and of the probable Consequences of its Abolition. It began by exhibiting to the reader the various unjustifiable ways in which persons living on the coast of Africa became slaves. It then explained the treatment which these experienced on their passage, the number dying in the course of it, and the treatment of the survivors in the colonies of those nations to which they were carried. It then announced the speedy publication of a work on the Impolicy of the Trade, the contents of which, as far as I could then see, I gave generally under the following heads: – Part the first, it was said, would show, that Africa was capable of offering to us a trade in its own natural productions as well as in the persons of men; that the trade in the persons of men was profitable but to a few; that its value was diminished from many commercial considerations; that it was also highly destructive to our seamen; and that the branch of it, by which we supplied the island of St. Domingo [St Domingue] with slaves, was peculiarly impolitic on that account. Part the second, it was said, would show, that, if the slaves were kindly treated in our colonies, they would increase; that the abolition of the trade would necessarily secure such a treatment to them, and that it would produce many other advantages which would be then detailed.

This little piece I presented to the committee at this their second meeting. It was then duly read and examined; and the result was, that, after some little correction, it was approved, and that two thousand copies of it were ordered to be printed, with lists of the subscribers and of the committee, and to be sent to various parts of the kingdom.

[. . .]

3. At this sitting, at which ten members were present out of the twelve, a discussion unexpectedly arose on a most important subject. The committee, finding that their meetings began to be approved by many, and that the cause under their care was likely to spread, and foreseeing also the necessity there would soon be of making themselves known as a public body throughout the kingdom, thought it right that they should assume some title, which should be a permanent one, and which should be expressive of their future views. This gave occasion to them to reconsider the object, for which they had associated, and to fix and define it in such a manner, that there should be no misunderstanding about it in the public mind. In looking into the subject, it appeared to them that there were two evils, quite distinct from each other, which it might become their duty to endeavour to remove. The first was the evil of the Slave-trade, in consequence of which many thousand persons were every year fraudulently and forcibly taken from their country, their relations, and friends, and from all that they esteemed valuable in life. The second was the evil of slavery itself, in consequence of which the same persons were forced into a situation, where they were deprived of the rights of men, where they were obliged to linger out their days subject to excessive labour and cruel punishments, and where their children were to inherit the same hard lot. Now the question was, which of the two evils the committee should select as that, to which they should direct their attention with a view of the removal of it: or whether, with the same view, it should direct its attention to both of them.

It appeared soon to be the sense of the committee, that to aim at the removal of both would be to aim at too much, and that by doing this we might lose all.

4. The question then was, which of the two they were to take as their object. Now in considering this question it appeared that it did

not matter where they began, or which of them they took, as far as the end to be produced was the thing desired. For, first, if the Slave-trade should be really abolished, the bad usage of the slaves in the colonies, that is, the hard part of their slavery, if not the slavery itself, would fall. For, the planters and others being unable to procure more slaves from the coast of Africa, it would follow directly, whenever this great event should take place, that they must treat those better, whom they might then have. They must render marriage honourable among them. They must establish the union of one man with one wife. They must give the pregnant women more indulgencies. They must pay more attention to the rearing of their offspring. They must work and punish the adults with less rigour. Now it was to be apprehended that they could not do these things, without seeing the political advantages which would arise to themselves from so doing; and that, reasoning upon this, they might be induced to go on to give them greater indulgencies, rights, and privileges in time. But how would every such successive improvement of their condition operate, but to bring them nearer to the state of freemen? In the same manner it was contended, that the better treatment of the slaves in the colonies, or that the emancipation of them there, when fit for it, would of itself lay the foundation for the abolition of the Slave-trade. For, if the slaves were kindly treated, that is, if marriage were encouraged among them; if the infants who should be born were brought up with care; if the sick were properly attended to; if the young and the adult were well fed and properly clothed, and not overworked, and not worn down by the weight of severe punishments, they would necessarily increase, and this on an extensive scale. But if the planters were thus to get their labourers from the births on their own estates, then the Slave-trade would in time be no longer necessary to them, and it would die away as an useless and a noxious plant. Thus it was of no consequence, which of the two evils the committee were to select as the object for their labours; for, as far as the end in view only was concerned, that the same end would be produced in either case.

5. But in looking further into this question, it seemed to make a material difference which of the two they selected, as far as they had in view the due execution of any laws, which might be made respecting them, and their own prospect of success in the undertaking. For, by aiming at the abolition of the Slave-trade, they were laying the axe at the very root. By doing this, and this only, they would not incur the objection, that they were meddling with the property of the planters, and letting loose an irritated race of beings, who, in consequence of all the vices and infirmities, which a state of slavery entails upon those

who undergo it, were unfit for their freedom. By asking the government of the country to do this, and this only, they were asking for that,
which it had an indisputable right to do; namely, to regulate or abolish
any of its branches of commerce; whereas it was doubtful, whether it
could interfere with the management of the internal affairs of the colonies, or whether this was not wholly the province of the legislatures
established there. By asking the government, again, to do this and this
only, they were asking what it could really enforce. It could station its
ships of war, and command its custom-houses, so as to carry any act
of this kind into effect. But it could not ensure that an act to be
observed in the heart of the islands should be enforced. To this it was
added, that if the committee were to fix upon the annihilation of
slavery as the object for their labours, the Slave-trade would not fall
so speedily as it would by a positive law for the abolition; because,
though the increase from the births might soon supply all the estates
now in cultivation with labourers, yet new plantations might be opened
from time to time in different islands, so that no period could be fixed
upon, when it could be said that it would cease.

6. Impressed by these arguments, the committee were clearly of
opinion, that they should define their object to be the abolition of the
Slave-trade, and not of the slavery which sprung from it. Hence from
this time, and in allusion to the month when this discussion took
place, they styled themselves in their different advertisements, and
reports, though they were first associated in the month of May, The
Committee instituted in June 1787, for effecting the Abolition of the
Slave-trade. Thus, at the very outset, they took a ground which was
for ever tenable. Thus they were enabled also to answer the objection,
which was afterwards so constantly and so industriously circulated
against them, that they were going to emancipate the slaves. And I
have no doubt that this wise decision contributed greatly to their
success; for I am persuaded that, if they had adopted the other object;
they could not for years to come, if ever, have succeeded in their
attempt.

Before the committee broke up, I represented to them the necessity
there was of obtaining further knowledge on all those individual
points, which might be said to belong to the great subject of the abolition of the Slave-trade. In the first place, this knowledge was necessary for me, if I were to complete my work on the Impolicy of this
Trade, which work the Summary View, just printed, had announced to
the world. It would be necessary also, in case the Slave-trade should
become a subject of parliamentary inquiry; for this inquiry could not
proceed without evidence. And if any time was peculiarly fit for the

procuring of such information or evidence, it was the present. At this time the passions of men had not been heated by any public agitation of the question, nor had interest felt itself biassed to conceal the truth. But as soon as ever it should be publicly understood, that a parliamentary inquiry was certain, (which we ourselves believed would be the case, but which interested men did not then know,) we should find many of the avenues to information closed against us. I proposed therefore that some one of the committee should undertake a journey to Bristol, Liverpool, and Lancaster, where he should reside for a time to collect further light upon this subject; and that if others should feel their occupations or engagements to be such as would make such a journey unsuitable, I would undertake it myself. I begged therefore the favour of the different members of the committee, to turn the matter over in their minds by the next meeting, that we might then talk over and decide upon the propriety of the measure.

The committee held its fourth meeting on the twelfth of June. Among the subjects, which were then brought forward, was that of the journey before mentioned. The propriety and indeed even the necessity of it was so apparent, that I was requested by all present to undertake it, and a minute for that purpose was entered upon our records.

[. . .]

7. I now took my departure from Liverpool, and proceeded to Manchester, where I arrived on the Friday evening. On the Saturday morning Mr. Thomas Walker, attended by Mr. Cooper and Mr. Bayley of Hope, called upon me.[2] They were then strangers to me. They came, they said, having heard of my arrival, to congratulate me on the spirit which was then beginning to show itself, among the people of Manchester and of other places, on the subject of the Slave-trade, and which would unquestionably manifest itself further by breaking out into petitions to parliament for its abolition. I was much surprised at this information, I had devoted myself so entirely to my object, that I had never had time to read a newspaper since I left London. I never knew therefore, till now, that the attention of the public had been drawn to the subject in such a manner. And as to petitions, though I myself had suggested the idea at Bridgewater, Bristol, Gloucester, and two or three other places, I had only done it provisionally, and this without either the knowledge or the consent of the committee. The

---

[2] Thomas Walker, George Barton, Thomas Cooper and Thomas Butterworth Bayley had all been signatories to a letter to Clarkson and his fellow Committee members in 1787 from prominent citizens of Manchester, supporting the formation of the Society for the Abolition of the Slave Trade.

news, however, as it astonished, so it almost overpowered me with joy. I rejoiced in it because it was a proof of the general good disposition of my countrymen; because it showed me that the cause was such as needed only to be known, to be patronised; and because the manifestation of this spirit seemed to me to be an earnest, that success would ultimately follow.

[. . .]

8. By this time the nature of the Slave-trade had, in consequence of the labours of the committee and of their several correspondents, become generally known throughout the kingdom. It had excited a general attention, and there was among people a general feeling in behalf of the wrongs of Africa. This feeling had also, as may be collected from what has been already mentioned, broken out into language: for not only had the traffic become the general subject of conversation, but public meetings had taken place, in which it had been discussed, and of which the result was, that an application to parliament had been resolved upon in many places concerning it. By the middle of February not fewer than thirty-five petitions had been delivered to the commons, and it was known that others were on their way to the same house.

This ferment in the public mind, which had shown itself in the public prints even before the petitions had been resolved upon, had excited the attention of government. To coincide with the wishes of the people on this subject, appeared to those in authority to be a desirable thing. To abolish the trade, replete as it was with misery, was desirable also: but it was so connected with the interest of individuals, and so interwoven with the commerce and revenue of the country, that an hasty abolition of it without a previous inquiry appeared to them to be likely to be productive of as much misery as good. The king, therefore, by an order of council, dated February the eleventh, 1788, directed that a committee of privy council should sit as a board of trade, 'to take into their consideration the present state of the African trade, particularly as far as related to the practice and manner of purchasing or obtaining slaves on the coast of Africa, and the importation and sale thereof, either in the British colonies and settlements, or in the foreign colonies and settlements in America or the West-Indies; and also as far as related to the effects and consequences of the trade both in Africa and in the said colonies and settlements, and to the general commerce of this kingdom; and that they should report to him in council the result of their inquiries, with such observations as they might have to offer thereupon.'

[. . .]

4.9
Elizabeth Heyrick's call for a total end to slavery

E. Heyrick (1824) *Immediate Not Gradual Emancipation, or an Inquiry into the shortest, safest and most effectual means of getting rid of West Indian slavery*, London: J. Hatchard & Son.

Elizabeth Heyrick (1769–1831) was a Quaker convert who became actively involved in the antislavery campaign. Her important pamphlet went into three editions. The punctuation in this text has been retained.

The enemies of slavery have hitherto ruined their cause with the senseless cry of *gradual* emancipation. It is marvellous that the wise and the good should have suffered themselves to have been imposed upon by this wily artifice of the slave holder, - for with him must the project of gradual emancipation have first originated. The slave holder knew very well that his prey would be secure, so long as the abolitionists could be cajoled into a demand for *gradual* instead of *immediate* abolition. He knew very well, that the contemplation of a gradual emancipation would beget a *gradual indifference to emancipation itself*. He knew very well, that even the wise and the Good, may, by habit and familiarity, be brought to endure and tolerate almost any thing. [. . .] He caught the idea, and knew how to turn it to advantage. --- He knew very well, that the faithful delineation of the horrors of West Indian slavery, would produce such a general insurrection of sympathetic and indignant feeling; such abhorrence of the oppressor, such compassion for the oppressed, as must soon have been fatal to the whole system. He knew very well, that a strong moral fermentation had begun, which, had it gone forward, must soon have purified the nation from this foulest of its corruptions, -- that the cries of the people for emancipation, would have been too unanimous, and too importunate for the Government to resist and that slavery would, long ago, have been exterminated throughout the British dominions. Our example might have spread from kingdom to kingdom, from continent to continent, - and the slave trade, and slavery, might, be this time have been abolished - all the world over: -- 'A sacrifice of a sweet savour,' might have ascended to the Great Parent of the Universe; -- 'His kingdom might have come and his will (thus far) have been done on earth, as it is in Heaven.'

But this GRADUAL ABOLITION has been the grand marplot of human virtue and happiness; the very master piece of satanic policy. By converting the cry for immediate, into gradual emancipation, the prince of slave- holders 'transformed himself, with astonishing dexterity, into an angel of light,' - and thereby 'deceived the very elect.' -- He saw very clearly, that if public justice and humanity, especially if *Christian* justice and humanity could be brought to demand only a *gradual* extermination of the enormities of the slave system; if they could be brought to *acquiesce*, but for one year, or for one month, in the slavery of our African brother, -- in robbing him of all the rights of humanity, -- and degrading him to a level with the brutes; that then, they could imperceptibly be brought to acquiesce in all this for an unlimited duration. He saw, very clearly, that the time for the extermination of slavery was precisely, that, when its horrid impiety and enormity were *first distinctly known and strongly felt.* He knew, that every moment's unnecessary delay, between the discovery of an imperious duty, and the setting earnestly about its accomplishment, was dangerous, if not fatal to success. He knew, that strong excitement, was necessary to strong effort, - that intense feeling was necessary to stimulate intense exertion; -- that as strong excitement and intense feeling are generally transient, in proportion to their strength and intensity, -- the most effectual way of crushing a great and virtuous enterprise, -- was to gain time, -- to defer it to 'a more convenient season', when the zeal and ardour of the first convictions of duty had subsided -- when our sympathies had become languid; -- when considerations of the difficulties and hazards of the enterprise, the solicitations of ease and indulgence should have chilled the warm glow of humanity, - quenched the fervid heroism of virtue; -- when familiarity with relations of violence and outrage, crimes and miseries, should have abated the horror of their first impression, and, at length, induced indifference.

The father of lies, the grand artificer of fraud and imposture, transformed himself therefore, on this occasion, pre-eminently, 'into an angel of light,' -- and deceived, not the unwary only, the unsuspecting multitude, -- but the wise and the good, by the plausibility, the apparent force, the justice, and above all, by the *humanity* of the arguments propounded for gradual emancipation. He is the subtlest of all reasoners, the most ingenious of all declaimers. He, above all other advocates, 'can make the worse appear the better argument;' can, most effectually, pervert the judgment and blind the understanding, -- whilst they seem to be most enlightened and rectified. Thus, by a train of most exquisite reasoning, has he brought the abolitionists to the conclusion, - that the interest of the poor, degraded, and oppressed *slave* as well as that of his master, will be best secured by his *remaining in slavery* ...

4.10
Report on the Sam Sharpe rebellion

Correspondence and Papers relating to Slavery and the Abolition of the Slave Trade, 1831–34 (1969) Irish University Press Series of British Parliamentary Papers, Slave Trade 80, Shannon: Irish University Press, pp. 191–2.

This official report from a Committee of the Jamaican House of Assembly was submitted to the Westminster government in the aftermath of Sam Sharpe's rebellion of late December 1831 to early January 1832. The rebellion began as a sit-down strike after the slaves were persuaded that the Crown had introduced an emancipation measure which the planters and colonial assembly were refusing to implement. Crops and property were destroyed in the brief uprising, which was put down by the Jamaican militia within two weeks.

The primary and most powerful cause arose from an evil excitement created in the minds of our Slaves generally, by the unceasing and unconstitutional interference of His Majesty's Ministers with our Local Legislature, in regard to the passing of laws for their government, with the intemperate expression of the sentiments of the present Ministers, as well as other individuals in the Commons House of Parliament in Great Britain, on the subject of Slavery; such discussions, coupled with the false and wicked reports of the Anti-Slavery Society, having been industriously circulated, by the aid of the press, throughout this Island as well as the British Empire.

Secondly, from a delusive expectation produced among the whole of the Slave Population of the machinations of crafty and evil-disposed persons, who, taking advantage of the prevailing excitement, imposed upon their disturbed imaginations a belief that they were to be free after Christmas; and in the event of freedom being withheld from them, they 'must be prepared to fight for it.'

Thirdly, from a mischievous abuse existing in the system adopted by different religious sects in this Island, termed Baptists, Wesleyan Methodists and Moravians, by their recognizing gradations of rank among such of our Slaves as had become converts to their doctrines, whereby the less ambitious and more peaceable among them were made the dupes of the artful and intelligent who had been selected by the preachers of those particular sects to fill the higher offices in their chapels under the denomination of rulers, elders, leaders and helpers.

And lastly, the public discussions of the free inhabitants here, consequent upon the continued suggestions made by the King's Ministers regarding further measures of amelioration to be introduced into the Slave Code of this Island, and the preaching and teaching of the religious sects called Baptists, Wesleyan Methodists and Moravians, (but more particularly the sect termed Baptists), which had the effect of producing in the minds of the Slaves a belief that they could not serve both a Spiritual and a Temporal Master; thereby occasioning them to resist the lawful authority of their Temporal, under the delusion of rendering themselves more acceptable to a Spiritual Master.

4.11

Sam Sharpe rebellion – witness testimonies and confessions from convicted prisoners, 1832

Correspondence and Papers relating to Slave Trade,
1831–3 (1969), Irish University Press Series of British
Parliamentary Papers, Slave Trade 80, Shannon:
Irish University Press, pp. 217–18, 223–6.

These confessions and testimonies from slaves who had participated in Sam Sharpe's rebellion were appended to the Committee's Report (Document 4.10).

(a) Voluntary confession of Linton, a prisoner in Savannah la Mar Gaol, under sentence of death, March 1832

I have been led into this business; I thought it was a good business from what I was told, and I put my hand and heart to it; besides, if I had not joined in the business with a willing mind, the others would have been 'more than me,' and forced me, for what can a man do against 'a multitude.' You, sir, M'Kinley, and I, are shut up in this room; if we two choose it, could we not this moment take your life, and if we were to do it we could not suffer more for it than we are now going to do. No, sir, bad advice! bad advice! This business has been providing for for more than two or three years, even as far back as the Argyle war. Every year back at Christmas or October we were to begin, but were afraid to jump off until this year; we were very near beginning it either in last March or last October. There are a great many people concerned in this business, but I will not speak of the chief heads, excepting Gardner and Sharp. If I chose I could tell a great deal about this business, but as I am going to die let it all go with me; I do not like to speak of 'Gardner's friends, trumps;' if he and they escape judgment here, they cannot escape it in the day of judgment. If I had been sentenced to transportation or flogging, perhaps I might have told more than people think for, but if I do so now, people will say that I did so because I was afraid to die, and because I knew that I could not be present (alive) to prove it. I will tell this only, we were all sworn upon the Bible to do our best to drive white and free people out of this country. The head people among all of us negroes were then to divide the estates among us, and to work them with the common negroes, who were not to get their freedom, but work as they do now. I might as well tell the truth, though they would have had bad treatment from us; we could not treat them as white people now treat them; we would have been obliged to rule them hard to keep them down; but this is nothing; we all believed this freedom business, from what we were told and from what we heard in the newspapers, that the people in England were speaking up very bold for us; we all thought the King was upon our side. Gardner constantly kept telling us that he and the other head people had been told that the King had given orders for his soldiers here not to fight against us, and that he was sending out powder and arms, and the governor was to go away and leave the country to us. In about three or four years the negroes will break out again, for they cannot help believing that the King has given them freedom, especially as they hear so much about it from newspapers.

Those who cannot read always give a 5d. to those who can to read the papers to them when they hear they contain good news for them. Besides this one religion says we cannot serve two masters, but must only serve Jesus Christ. I tell you again, if the gentlemen do not keep a good look out, the negroes will begin this business in three or four years, for they think the Lord and the King have given them the gift, and because those who were joined in this business were all sworn. I will not tell any more, if you wish to know go and ask Gardner and his friends that advise him; you cannot do anything for us, sir, therefore please to order our feet back in irons, I have been very happy, and now look at what I am to come to.

(signed)   Thomas Stewart,
Rector of Westmorland.

(b) Confession of Robert Gardner, alias Colonel Gardner, taken in Savannah la Mar Gaol, 11 February 1832

The whole business of the rebellion was settled upon in Montego Bay; I had often heard the thing spoken of in a casual manner before Christmas, but I never gave much heeding to it; the first time I heard that the time was fixed and the thing determined upon was in Christmas, at Montego Bay. It was determined upon after we had been to morning prayers at our chapel (Baptist): there General Samuel Sharp belonging to Mr. Gray, Taylor to Mr. Boyd the saddler, Johnstone to Retrieve (who was afterwards killed in the battle of Montpelier), Guthrie to Colonel Grignon, Dove to Belvidere, Tharp to Hazelymph, myself, and some others of the head people were present; General Sharp spoke first, he said, 'The thing is now determined upon, no time is to be lost; the King of England and the Parliament have given Jamaica freedom, and it is held back by the whites; we must at once take it. The King sent the law since March last, and it has been withheld by the whites; rise at once and take it.' Sharpe kept on talking in this way, which roused us and made us nearly mad; at last he stopped, and I said, 'Sharpe, I do not like this business at all; let us done away with it.' Sharp then became very furious, and said, 'What is to become of all the men I have sworn, then, they might as well obey me as to die from not doing so.' George Duncan also said, he did not like the business. Guthrie then said, the thing must be done, and was very violent. Guthrie then wanted us to take 'pot luck' with him at three o'clock, in his room at Montego Bay. We went; Guthrie then commenced talking of the thing again; he asked us what we would drink, we said wine; he filled our glasses, and then took up his, and said, 'In a few days may we get our rights, and may Little-breeches (that being the name Colonel Grignon was called by amongst us), and the other gentlemen who oppose us lay at our feet.' I would not drink the toast, and declared, that I would have nothing to say to it, which Duncan, an old carpenter belonging to Hazelymph, can prove; they then laughed at me and drank the toast. Taylor also said, 'Let us not spill a drop of blood; if we do, it will bring a prosecution upon our church (the Baptist).' Guthrie then said, 'I will be up on Tuesday to Barneyside, and I will be on your side on Wednesday (meaning Greenwich, &c.) I will put the first ball into the man (meaning Colonel Grignon).' The matter was then talked over again, Sharp was the head planner, and mentioned how everthing was to be done, and that he had sworn all the people under him; we then separated, and I went home to Greenwich. A few days previous to Christmas I had been sent with a cart from Greenwich by my overseer to a neighbouring estate to bring over a puncheon of rum for the negroes for Christmas, when I came home, Dehaney told me, that General Sharp had sent a person to me who was very anxious to see me; I heard no more of Sharp till we all met on the Christmas-day at chapel, at Montego Bay; after we all separated on Christmas-day at George Guthrie's, I returned, as I before said, to my own home at Greenwich. On Tuesday night after Christmas-day, Sharp sent a great number of men for me to command, and to urge the others in the neighbourhood to join. I heard the multitude coming, and, although at supper, I got up and slipped out at my back-door, because I knew what they were coming for, and wished to have nothing to do with it. I waited concealed a long time, but being hungry and finding that the men would not go away without seeing me, I returned into my house; they then all surrounded me and said that Sharp had sent them to me to command that I was to take them, and all the people in the district, as 'a force' to go against Westmorland and Hanover. They said that Sharp desired them to tell me that he had a multitude of people under his command; that they consisted of all the people in St. James's and part of Trelawny, extending up to Chesterfield, Ginger Hill, &c.; that he would command in person; that the thing was determined upon, and that it must begin at once. I was overruled, and went to Hazelymph immediately, that being the rendezvous. While I was at supper with Fred. Zuicke, at Hazelymph, I heard General Sharp's army coming. They were wild, furious, blowing shells, and making a great shouting. That night the business was all talked over there. It was then determined to commence at once by setting fire to Hazelymph. The trash-house was accordingly set on fire, but being very wet the trash would not burn; it was tried three times but would not catch. A man named Blake, belonging to the property, made a great resistance to the place being set fire to, but he was soon compelled to be quiet. When it was found that they could not set the trash-house on fire, a regiment of Sharp's, under the command of Captain Johnstone 'rushed' immediately to Belvidere, and I presently saw it in flames. Different regiments were then detached to different places, and the work began everywhere. I declare, however, that I entreated them to burn no place. I told them that the best way to do would be this: on Wednesday, the day the negroes were expected to turn out to their work, they should every one go peaceably into the high road near Montpelier (Gravel Hill), and wait there till they should see some respectable gentleman passing by; they should then ask him if it was really true that they were freed from Christmas? if the gentleman should say, no, they were to return to their work; if he said, yes, they were of course to do no work. This was my advice; for we heard so much from newspapers, and people talking, that we did not know what to believe or do. The negroes, however, would not take my advice, but said, if they went into the road as I told them, the white people would come and destroy them. Oh, Sir, if I had had any good friend to tell me the real truth, as I now find it to be, I never would have been brought to this! I feel that I deserve all that I now suffer; and I feel it more from the kind manner in which all the white gentlemen have treated me since I gave myself up. I particularly ordered the negroes to take no man's life. I was at Cow Park, on the hill, when the militia surprised us. I was very tired and hungry, and had fallen asleep, when I was awakened towards morning by the firing of the militia. I fled. We left some of our arms behind us. I did not go into the cave. From that time we never rallied. The men were scattered, and are now wandering about in small parties. I saw from a hill, to which I retreated after the Cow Park business, that the negroes were returning to their duty, and at work on the estates. I saw, therefore, that it was quite useless to remain out any longer. I would then have come in, but I was afraid to do so. I would have come in 10 days before I did if I had not been afraid to do so. A few days before I gave myself up I fell in with Dove, who had been separated from me. We both thought it better to come in, as it was quite useless to stay in the woods and starve. Dehaney fell in by accident with us in the woods, and told us that the militia officer, M'Neel, commanding at Greenwich, appeared to be treating those who came in very mildly. I told him we wished to deliver ourselves up. He said, we had better do so. We then agreed at once to join, and asked if he would take us to M'Neel. He said he would; accordingly we went at once with him; when we got as near to M'Neel's camp as a little more than the length of this jail-yard (but which we could not see on account of a turning between us and the camp), Dehaney said, 'I will leave you here and go and call M'Neel;' shortly after M'Neel came to where we were left by Dehaney, and we gave ourselves up to him. As soon as M'Neel came up to us he offered us his hand, and by his own offer we walked arm and arm with him. I never sent to make any agreement with M'Neel, as to what was to be done with Dove and myself. I never sent to tell him to come unarmed to us, we gave ourselves up of our own accord, because we could not stay out any longer in the woods.

The above confession of Robert Gardner, *alias* Colonel Gardner, was this day taken in Savanna la Mar gaol, this 11th day of February 1832, by me.

(signed)   Thomas Stewart.

(c) Questions put to Robert, alias Colonel Gardner, by Thomas Stewart, and the answers given by him, 11 February 1832, in Savannah la Mar Gaol

Were you sworn to secrecy in this business, and if so, by whom? – Samuel Sharp swore every man all round, from the parish of St. James, part of Trelawny, part of St. Elizabeth, Hanover, and the upper part of Westmorland. I was not sworn, neither was Dove.

The oath was, that every man should fight and do his utmost to drive the white and free people out of Jamaica; if they succeeded, a governor was to be appointed to each parish.

Was Samuel Sharp the only ruler; if so, how did he get that appointment? – At first, Samuel Sharp was the only ruler. He was in the habit of going two or three times a week to Montego Bay, and must have got his appointment there. He can read, and used to read the newspapers, and hear the people talk at the Bay; he would then bring up all the news, and spread it among the negroes; sometimes he would bring the newspapers from the Bay, and read them to the negroes. There is a man named Tharp, belonging to Hazelymph, who is a great ruler; he is a very dangerous man to this country if the white gentlemen want to keep peace. George Guthrie is also another; they should both be taken at once. There is another named Ramsay.

Were there no white's [sic] or free people concerned in the rebellion? – Excepting Alfred Smith, I know of no other; there may be and perhaps there are, but I cannot speak from my own knowledge. I heard Tharp, of Hazelymph, say, that a white man at Lethe taught the negroes how to cut the road, and to make cartridges.

Are the leaders of the several Baptist classes the head engaged among the slaves in the rebellion? – The most of the captains are leaders of classes in our church; the duty of leaders is, to go round to the estates belonging to our church, and to see how the negroes are getting on, and to report the same to the minister.

If you were not directed by some white or other person besides Samuel Sharp, what encouraged you to listen to his advice? – I declare upon my dying words that I firmly believed that the negroes were free by order of the King and the Parliament (these are the words used by Gardner himself); I heard that the order came out in March last. I believed that we were freed, because I have read in the newspapers, and heard other people read, that the people in England wished it, and were on our side. Samuel Sharp read a newspaper to me and to several others, in which it said that the people in England met together to make us free, and that they said we must fight for it, and they would stand by and help us on. After this Samuel Sharp brought another newspaper, in which we read that the gentlemen in the Parliament were speaking on our side, and saying that we ought to be set free at once. This gave us great encouragement, especially when we saw that neither the King nor any one in the Parliament said no it was not to be given to us. We went down to Montego Bay and heard the same thing there. Our chief place for meeting and consulting was always Montego Bay. We did not think that the King's soldiers or sailors would fight against us. I even heard that the King had taken away the governor some weeks ago, and that the country was left to ourselves; and that Colonel Williams, who is master of plenty of slaves, was joining in keeping back our freedom, and to get himself made the governor down this side. I also thought that other gentlemen who were in other parts, and had plenty of slaves, were doing as Colonel Williams was trying to do. Samuel Sharp often told us that God never intended us to be slaves; that we had but one master, Jesus Christ, to obey, and that we could not serve Christ and our master at the same time.

I have always been treated by the different overseers and attorneys of Greenwich, to which I belong, with great confidence. Until this business I never had a charge laid against me. If Dove and I were to be stripped, our skins would be found as smooth as any white man's, for we have never been flogged. I was quite happy.

The above questions were put to Robert, *alias* Colonel Gardner, by me, and the above answers given by him to them this 11th February 1832, in the Savanna la Mar Gaol.

(signed)   Thomas Stewart.

Upon questioning Gardner again respecting Smith, the impression on my mind was that Tharp had forcibly detained him, and compelled him to make cartridges, &c. Gardner's words were, 'Tharp told me he had taken up a white man at Lethe.' I said, 'Tharp, if you have, you have done a very bad thing.'

4.12

Alexis de Tocqueville, *Democracy in America*, 1835–40

C. Alexis H.M. de Tocqueville ([1835] 1899) *Democracy in America*, trans. H. Reeves, revised edn., 2 vols., New York: Colonial, vol. 1, pp. 364–70.

Alexis de Tocqueville (1805–59) was amongst the penetrative political analysts of his day and the 'founding father' of political sociology. He visited the United States in 1831 and published his celebrated study of American democracy in two parts in 1835 and 1840. In this passage he compares industry, agriculture and social mores in the free state of Ohio and the slave state of Kentucky.

I see that in a certain portion of the territory of the United States at the present day, the legal barrier which separated the two races is tending to fall away, but not that which exists in the manners of the country; slavery recedes, but the prejudice to which it has given birth remains stationary. Whosoever has inhabited the United States must have perceived that in those parts of the Union in which the negroes are no longer slaves, they have in no wise drawn nearer to the whites, On the contrary, the prejudice of the race appears to be stronger in the States which have abolished slavery, than in those where it still exists; and nowhere is it so intolerant as in those States where servitude has never been known.

It is true, that in the North of the Union, marriages may be legally contracted between negroes and whites; but public opinion would stigmatize a man who should connect himself with a negress as infamous, and it would be difficult to meet with a single instance of such a union. The electoral franchise has been conferred upon the negroes in almost all the States in which slavery has been abolished; but if they come forward to vote, their lives are in danger. If oppressed, they may bring an action at law, but they will find none but whites amongst their judges; and although they may legally serve as jurors, prejudice repulses them from that office. The same schools do not receive the child of the black and of the European. In the theatres, gold cannot procure a seat for the servile race beside their former masters; in the hospitals they lie apart; and although they are allowed to invoke the same Divinity as the whites, it must be at a different altar, and in their own churches, with their own clergy. The gates of Heaven are not closed against these unhappy beings; but their inferiority is continued to the very confines of the other world; when the negro is defunct, his bones are cast aside, and the distinction of condition prevails even in the equality of death. The negro is free, but he can share neither the rights, nor the pleasures, nor the labor, nor the afflictions, nor the tomb of him whose equal he has been declared to be; and he cannot meet him upon fair terms in life or in death.

In the South, where slavery still exists, the negroes are less carefully kept apart; they sometimes share the labor and the recreations of the whites; the whites consent to intermix with them to a certain extent, and although the legislation treats them more harshly, the habits of the people are more tolerant and compassionate. In the South the master is not afraid to raise his slave to his own standing, because he knows that he can in a moment reduce him to the dust at pleasure. In the North the white no longer distinctly perceives the barrier which separates him from the degraded race, and he shuns the negro with the more pertinacity, since he fears lest they should some day be confounded together.

Amongst the Americans of the South, nature sometimes reasserts her rights, and restores a transient equality between the blacks and the whites; but in the North pride restrains the most imperious of human passions. The American of the Northern States would perhaps allow the negress to share his licentious pleasures, if the laws of his country did not declare that she may aspire to be the legitimate partner of his bed; but he recoils with horror from her who might become his wife.

Thus it is, in the United States, that the prejudice which repels the negroes seems to increase in proportion as they are emancipated, and inequality is sanctioned by the manners whilst it is effaced from the laws of the country. But if the relative position of the two races which inhabit the United States is such as I have described, it may be asked why the Americans have abolished slavery in the North of the Union, why they maintain it in the South, and why they aggravate its hardships there? The answer is easily given. It is not for the good of the negroes, but for that of the whites, that measures are taken to abolish slavery in the United States.

[. . .]

A century had scarcely elapsed since the foundation of the colonies, when the attention of the planters was struck by the extraordinary fact, that the provinces which were comparatively destitute of slaves, increased in population, in wealth, and in prosperity more rapidly than those which contained the greatest number of negroes. In the former, however, the inhabitants were obliged to cultivate the soil themselves, or by hired laborers; in the latter they were furnished with hands for which they paid no wages; yet although labor and expenses were on the one side, and ease with economy on the other, the former were in possession of the most advantageous system. This consequence seemed to be the more difficult to explain, since the settlers, who all belonged to the same European race, had the same habits, the same civilization, the same laws, and their shades of difference were extremely slight.

Time, however, continued to advance, and the Anglo-Americans, spreading beyond the coasts of the Atlantic Ocean, penetrated farther and farther into the solitudes of the West; they met with a new soil and an unwonted climate; the obstacles which opposed them were of the most various character; their races intermingled, the inhabitants of the South went up towards the North, those of the North descended to the South; but in the midst of all these causes, the same result occurred at every step, and in general, the colonies in which there were no slaves became more populous and more rich than those in which slavery flourished. The more progress was made, the more was it shown that slavery, which is so cruel to the slave, is prejudicial to the master.

But this truth was most satisfactorily demonstrated when civilization reached the banks of the Ohio. The stream which the Indians had distinguished by the name of Ohio, or Beautiful River, waters one of the most magnificent valleys that has ever been made the abode of man. Undulating lands extend upon both shores of the Ohio, whose soil affords inexhaustible treasures to the laborer; on either bank the air is wholesome and the climate mild, and each of them forms the extreme frontier of a vast State: That which follows the numerous windings of the Ohio upon the left is called Kentucky, that upon the right bears the name of the river. These two States only differ in a single respect; Kentucky has admitted slavery, but the State of Ohio has prohibited the existence of slaves within its borders.

Thus the traveller who floats down the current of the Ohio to the spot where that river falls into the Mississippi, may be said to sail between liberty and servitude; and a transient inspection of the surrounding objects will convince him as to which of the two is most favorable to mankind. Upon the left bank of the stream the population is rare; from time to time one descries a troop of slaves loitering in the half-desert fields; the primæval forest recurs at every turn; society seems to be asleep, man to be idle, and nature alone offers a scene of activity and of life. From the right bank, on the contrary, a confused hum is heard which proclaims the presence of industry; the fields are covered with abundant harvests, the elegance of the dwellings announces the taste and activity of the laborer, and man appears to be in the enjoyment of that wealth and contentment which is the reward of labor.

The State of Kentucky was founded in 1775, the State of Ohio only twelve years later; but twelve years are more in America than half a century in Europe, and, at the present day, the population of Ohio exceeds that of Kentucky by two hundred and fifty thousand souls. These opposite consequences of slavery and freedom may readily be understood, and they suffice to explain many of the differences which we remark between the civilization of antiquity and that of our own time.

Upon the left bank of the Ohio labor is confounded with the idea of slavery, upon the right bank it is identified with that of prosperity and improvement; on the one side it is degraded, on the other it is honored; on the former territory no white laborers can he found, for they would be afraid of assimilating themselves to the negroes; on the latter no one is idle, for the white population extends its activity and its intelligence to every kind of employment. Thus the men whose task it is to cultivate the rich soil of Kentucky are ignorant and lukewarm; whilst those who are active and enlightened either do nothing or pass over into the State of Ohio, where they may work without dishonor.

It is true that in Kentucky the planters are not obliged to pay wages to the slaves whom they employ; but they derive small profits from their labor, whilst the wages paid to free workmen would be returned with interest in the value of their services. The free workman is paid, but he does his work quicker than the slave, and rapidity of execution is one of the great elements of economy. The white sells his services, but they are only purchased at the times at which they may be useful; the black can claim no remuneration for his toil, but the expense of his maintenance is perpetual; he must be supported in his old age as well as in the prime of manhood, in his profitless infancy as well as in the productive years of youth. Payment must equally be made in order to obtain the services of either class of men: the free workman receives his wages in money, the slave in education, in food, in care, and in clothing. The money which a master spends in the maintenance of his slaves goes gradually and in detail, so that it is scarcely perceived; the salary of the free workman is paid in a round sum, which appears only to enrich the individual who receives it, but in the end the slave has cost more than the free servant, and his labor is less productive.

The influence of slavery extends still further; it affects the character of the master, and imparts a peculiar tendency to his ideas and his tastes. Upon both banks of the Ohio, the character of the inhabitants is enterprising and energetic; but this vigor is very differently exercised in the two States. The white inhabitant of Ohio, who is obliged to subsist by his own exertions, regards temporal prosperity as the principal aim of his existence; and as the country which he occupies presents inexhaustible resources to his industry and ever-varying lures to his activity, his acquisitive ardor surpasses the ordinary limits of human cupidity: he is tormented by the desire of wealth, and he boldly enters upon every path which fortune opens to him; he becomes a sailor, a pioneer, an artisan, or a laborer with the same indifference, and he supports, with equal constancy, the fatigues and the dangers incidental to these various professions; the resources of his intelligence are astonishing, and his avidity in the pursuit of gain amounts to a species of heroism.

But the Kentuckian scorns not only labor, but all the undertakings which labor promotes; as he lives in an idle independence, his tastes are those of an idle man; money loses a portion of its value in his eyes; he covets wealth much less than pleasure and excitement; and the energy which his neighbor devotes to gain, turns with him to a passionate love of field sports and military exercises; he delights in violent bodily exertion, he is familiar with the use of arms, and is accustomed from a very early age to expose his life in single combat. Thus slavery not only prevents the whites from becoming opulent, but even from desiring to become so.

As the same causes have been continually producing opposite effects for the last two centuries in the British colonies of North America, they have established a very striking difference between the commercial capacity of the inhabitants of the South and those of the North. At the present day it is only the Northern States which are in possession of shipping, manufactures, railroads, and canals. This difference is perceptible not only in comparing the North with the South, but in comparing the several Southern States. Almost all the individuals who carry on commercial operations, or who endeavor to turn slave labor to account in the most Southern districts of the Union, have emigrated from the North. The natives of the Northern States are constantly spreading over that portion of the American territory where they have less to fear from competition; they discover resources there which escaped the notice of the inhabitants; and, as they comply with a system which they do not approve, they succeed in turning it to better advantage than those who first founded and who still maintain it.

Were I inclined to continue this parallel, I could easily prove that almost all the differences which may be remarked between the characters of the Americans in the Southern and in the Northern States have originated in slavery; but this would divert me from my subject, and my present intention is not to point out all the consequences of servitude, but those effects which it has produced upon the prosperity of the countries which have admitted it.

The influence of slavery upon the production of wealth must have been very imperfectly known in antiquity, as slavery then obtained throughout the civilized world; and the nations which were unacquainted with it were barbarous. And indeed Christianity only abolished slavery by advocating the claims of the slave; at the present time it may be attacked in the name of the master, and, upon this point, interest is reconciled with morality.

[. . .]

Chapter 5

Creating nations, 1789–1871

Introduction

The extracts in this chapter are examples of the kinds of documents used by historians interested in the major changes that occurred in Europe during the nineteenth century. The century began with the wars of the French Revolution and Napoleon during which, arguably for the first time, battles were fought between armies and navies that claimed to be fighting for a nation state rather than serving as mercenaries in dynastic quarrels between monarchs or as warriors in religious conflicts. In Britain at least, these wars coincided with a crucial stage in the formation of an industrialised economy.

French revolutionaries prided themselves on the abolition of feudalism; the Industrial Revolution is commonly seen as creating a class society. Some of the documents that follow here reflect the old world, notably the extract from Agricol Perdiguer's *tour de France* as a young artisan (document 5.12) and the descriptions of riots over high prices (5.13). Many of the others are illustrative of the changing world. Thus the extracts from the Code Napoleon (document 5.3) emphasise the equality of all citizens, though it is important to note here that, while the differences of order have been abolished, those of gender are formally proclaimed. Similarly, several of the extracts, ranging from Karl Marx's call for revolution in 1848 to the protests of worker-activists in the same period, pick up on what they perceive as the 'class' divisions created by the new society. And if men were called upon to fight for their nation state, why should they not

5.1 'Vox Populi [voice of the people], or A Bully that must be put down', 7 December 1867. Cartoon from *The Tomahawk*, weekly satirical magazine.

have a say in the way in which their nation state was organised and governed?

The *Communist Manifesto* (document 5.16) is an historical document, but it is also an analysis of the way in which society was developing that relies upon an interpretation of history. Many of the documents in the second part of this section and which focus on 'nation' are rather similar in as much as they are presenting an analysis of national and state development. The nation states of nineteenth-century Europe (as well as some of the 'nations' that had no state) used history to boost their legitimacy; and the same period also witnessed the development of 'history' as a specialist academic profession within universities. The documents here have been selected to demonstrate this development as well as to show how history could be presented to both the popular reader and the student at school.

Clive Emsley

5.1

Decree of the National Convention
(*levée en masse*), 23 August, 1793

Archives parlementaires de 1787 à 1860 (Première Série, 1787 à 1799) (1969), Nendeln (Lichtenstein): Kraus Reprint, vol. 72, pp. 688–9. Translation from French by Clive Emsley.

The decree of the *levée en masse* was adopted by the National Convention on 23 August 1793. A measure of this sort had been urged on the revolutionary government by petitions from the revolutionary clubs in Paris during mid-August. The idea was to enlist the entire resources of France for the war effort. By the late summer of 1794 the French had an army of just over a million men. Only about three-quarters of these were fully trained and equipped but even these constituted the largest army of its sort ever seen in Europe.

1. From this time forth, until the enemies of France have been expelled from the territory of the Republic, all Frenchmen are in a state of permanent requisition for the army. The young men will go to battle;

married men will make arms and transport food and supplies; women will make tents and uniforms and work in hospitals; children will seek out old rags for bandages; old men will go out into the public places to stir up the courage of the warriors, the hatred of kings and the unity of the Republic.

2. Public buildings are to be converted into hospitals; public squares into workshops for armaments; the soil of cellars is to be washed down for the extraction of saltpetre.

3. Muskets are to be held only by those who march to fight the enemy; in the interior military service will be carried out using sporting guns and side-arms.

4. Riding horses are to be requisitioned for the cavalry; draught horses, excepting those used in agriculture, are to be used to pull artillery and supplies.

5. Without delay the Committee of Public Safety is to take all measures to establish an extraordinary factory for all kinds of weaponry to cater for the determination and energy of the French people; [the committee] is therefore authorised to set up as many establishments, factories, workshops and mills as are necessary to carry out the work, as well as to require, for this purpose, throughout the Republic, artisans and workers who can contribute to its success.

[. . .]

5.2
Le chant du départ (The Song of Departure), c. 1794

G. & G. Marty (1988) *Dictionnaire des Chansons de La Révolution*, Paris: Tallandier, pp. 185–8. Translated from French by Clive Emsley.

The words were written by Marie-Joseph de Chénier. The precise origin of the song is unclear. It has been said that he wrote it specifically to celebrate the storming of the Bastille and that it was sent by the Committee of Public safety to the National Institute of Music to be sung during a concert on 14 July 1794. It has also been said that the song was played on the battlefield of Fleurus (26 June 1794), the scene of a French victory over the Austrians.

1794

A deputy of the people:
Singing, victory opens the barrier for us,
Liberty guides our steps.
From the north to the south
The warlike trumpet
Has sounded the hour of battle.
Tremble enemies of France,
Kings drunk on blood and pride,
The sovereign people advances,
Tyrants sink into your coffins

Refrain:
The Republic calls us
So we know how to conquer or to perish.
A Frenchman should live for her,
For her a Frenchman should die.

The mother of a family:
Don't fear the tears from our maternal eyes.
Away from us grief-making cowards!
When you take up arms we must triumph;
It is for kings to shed tears.
We gave you life;
Warriors, that life is no longer yours;
All your days belong to the Motherland,
She is your mother before us.

Refrain:

Two old men:
Let paternal iron arm the hand of the brave;
Think of us when you are on the field of Mars.
Consecrate the iron blessed by your old men
In the blood of kings and slaves.
And, bringing home to your hearths
Wounds and virtues,
Come close our eyelids
When tyrants are no more.

Refrain:

Three warriors:
On iron, before God, we swear to our fathers,
To our wives, our sisters,

ROUSE, HIBERNIANS

(1798)

TEXT: Song reproduced in Musgrave's *Memoirs of the Different Rebellions in Ireland*, Vol. II, p. 321. «This was found on the mother of Dogherty, a United Irishman who was killed by Woollaghan at Delgany, in the county of Wicklow in autumn 1798. She was seen to throw it out of her pocket, yet she swore she never saw it.»

Rouse, Hibernians, from your slumbers!
See the moment just arrived
Imperious tyrants for to humble,
Our French brethren are at hand.

Chorus

Vive la, United heroes,
Triumphant always may they be,
Vive la, our gallant brethren
That have come to set us free.

Erin's sons, be not faint-hearted,
Welcome, sing then «Ca ira»,
From Killala they are marching
To the tune of «Vive la».

To arms quickly, and be ready,
Join the ranks and never flee,
Determined stand by one another
And from tyrants you'll be free.

Cruel tyrants who oppressed you,
Now with terrors see their fall!
Then bless the heroes who caress you,
The Orange now goes to the wall.

Apostate Orange, why so dull now?
Self-willed slaves, why do you frown?
Sure you might know how Irish freemen
Soon would put your Orange down.

NOTE: 1100 French troops under General Humbert landed at Killala Bay, County Mayo, on 22nd August, 1798.

Our representatives, our sons, our mothers,
That we will annihilate oppressors.
Everywhere, while plunging feudalism
Into the darkest night,
The French will give the world
Peace and Liberty.

Refrain:

5.3

The Napoleonic Code, 21 March 1804

*The Code Napoleon or, The Civil Code, literally translated
from the original and official edition published at Paris,
in 1804, By a Barrister of the Inner Temple (1824),
London, Books I and III.*

The Civil Code *(la Code Civile des Français)* was first promulgated on 21 March 1804. It became known officially as the Code Napoleon in September 1807. Napoleon, as First Consul, played a major role in the discussions of the code in the Council of State. He interfered personally and notably when the rights of women were under discussion; it has been suggested that his own experience of being married to an unfaithful wife who was no longer able to bear children had some influence here.

Book I: Of Persons
Title 1: Of the Enjoyment and Privation of Civil Rights
Chapter I: Of the Enjoyment of Civil Rights
7. The exercise of civil rights is independent of the quality of citizen, which is only acquired and preserved conformably to the constitutional law.
8. Every Frenchman shall enjoy civil rights.
9. Every individual born in France of a foreigner, may, during the year which shall succeed the period of his majority, claim the quality of Frenchman . . .
[. . .]
Title V: Of Marriage
Chapter I Of the Qualities and Conditions required in order to be able to contract Marriage

144. A man before the age of 18, and a woman before 15 complete, are incapable of contracting marriage.

145. The government shall be at liberty nevertheless, upon weighty reasons, to grant dispensation of age.

[. . .]

148. The son who has not attained the full age of 25 years, the daughter who has not attained the full age of 21 years, cannot contract marriage without the consent of their father and mother; in case of disagreement, the consent of the father is sufficient.

149. If one of the two be dead, or under the incapacity of manifesting his or her will, the consent of the other is sufficient.

[. . .]

Chapter VI: Of the respective Rights and Duties of Married Persons

212. Married persons owe to each other fidelity, succour, assistance.

213. The husband owes protection to his wife, the wife obedience to her husband.

214. The wife is obliged to live with her husband, and to follow him to every place where he may judge it convenient to reside: the husband is obliged to receive her, and to furnish her with every thing necessary for the wants of life, according to his means and station.

215. The wife cannot plead in her own name, without the authority of her husband, even though she be a public trader, or non-communicant, or separate in property.

[. . .]

217. A wife, although non-communicant or separate in property, cannot give, alienate, pledge, or acquire by free or chargeable title, without the concurrence of her husband in the act, or his consent in writing.

[. . .]

Title VI: Of Divorce

Chapter I: Of the Causes of Divorce

229. The husband may demand a divorce on the ground of his wife's adultery.

230. The wife may demand divorce on the ground of adultery in her husband when he shall have brought his concubine into their common residence.

231. The married parties may reciprocally demand divorce for outrageous conduct, ill-usage, or grievous injuries, exercised by one of them towards the other.

[. . .]

Title IX: Of Paternal Power

371. A child, at every age, owes honour and respect to his father and mother.

372. He remains subject to their control until his majority or emancipation.

373. The father alone exercises this control during marriage.

374. A child cannot quit the paternal mansion without permission of his father unless for voluntary enlistment after the full age of eighteen years.

375. A father who shall have cause of grievous dissatisfaction at the conduct of a child, shall have the following means of correction.

376. If the child have not commenced his sixteenth year, the father may cause him to be confined for a period which shall not exceed one month ...

377. From the age of sixteen years commenced to the majority or emancipation, the father is only empowered to require the confinement of his child during six months at the most ...

378. There shall not be in either case, any writing or judicial formality, except the order itself for arrest, in which the reasons thereof shall not be set forth.

The father shall only be required to subscribe an undertaking to defray all expenses and to supply suitable support.

379. The father is always at liberty to abridge the duration of the confinement ...

[...]

Title XI: Of Majority, Interdiction and the Judicial Advisor

Chapter I: Of Majority

488. Majority is fixed at twenty-one years completed; at this age a person is capable of all acts regarding civil life, saving the restrictions contained under the title '*of Marriage*'.

Book II: Of Property, and the Different Modifications of Property

Title I: Of the Distinction of Property

[...]

Chapter III: Of Property with Reference to those who are in Possession of it

537. Private persons have the free disposition of the property belonging to them, subject to the modifications established by the laws.

[...]

Title II: Of Property

544. Property is the right of enjoying and disposing of things in the most absolute manner, provided they are not used in a way prohibited by the laws or statutes.

545. No one can be compelled to give up his property, except for the public good, and for a just and previous indemnity.

[. . .]

Book III: Of the Different Modes of Acquiring Property

General Dispositions

711. Ownership in goods is acquired and transmitted by succession, by donation between living parties, or by will and by the effect of obligation.

Section III: Of successions devolving upon Descendants

745. Children or their descendants succeed to their father and mother, grandfathers, grandmothers, or other ancestors, without distinction of sex or primogeniture, and although they be the issue of different marriages.

They succeed by equal portions and by heads . . .

[. . .]

Chapter IV: Of Irregular Successions

Section I: Of the Rights of Natural Children . . .

756. Natural children are not heirs; the law does not grant to such any rights over the property of their father or mother deceased, except where they have been legally recognised.

[. . .]

5.4

The Riga Memorandum, September 1807

J. Breuilly (2002) *Austria, Prussia and Germany 1806–1871*, Harlow: Longman, pp. 113–16.

Karl August von Hardenberg (1750–1822) was a Prussian diplomat who drafted this memorandum following Prussia's defeat by France in 1806 and his own forced resignation. In the document, he outlined the reforms that he considered necessary in the wake of military disaster. In September 1810, Frederick William II (reigned 1758–97) recalled Hardenberg to his government as *Staatskanzler* (effectively prime minister).

I. GENERAL CONSIDERATIONS

[. . .] The French Revolution, of which the present war is a continuation, gave to the French, despite all the casualties and upheaval, a completely new vitality. All slumbering forces were awakened, misery and weakness, antiquated prejudices and crimes – admittedly with some good things – were destroyed . . .

The illusion that one can best combat revolution by holding fast to the old ways . . . has actually promoted revolution. . . . The power of the basic principles [underpinning revolution] is so great . . . that the state which does not accept them will either perish or be forced to adopt them.

Therefore, revolution in the good sense of the word . . . that is our aim, our watchword. Democratic principles in a monarchical state seem to me to be the appropriate form for the spirit of the age. Pure democracy we must put off until the year 2440.

[. . .]

II. EXTERNAL RELATIONS

Independence is now an empty word.

How can we get it back? How can we avoid complete dependence?

As I see it Prussia must adopt the following principles.

Above all we must gather together forces to enable good organisation and effective planning of our internal affairs. Without delay we must arm again for struggle, insofar as we have the means, especially for our defence. Such a struggle could – probably will – come about quickly and it is urgently necessary to be ready. . . .

We must not delude ourselves that we can remain neutral. . . . It does not suit Prussia's circumstances and is completely impossible in the present situation. Only large and powerful states with a favourable situation can assert neutrality and avoid the entanglements which bring it to an end.

Above all we must show character. . . . We have started to do this. Through its conduct in misfortune and true fortitude Prussia has won back something of the esteem it had lost and washed itself clean of the old political sins.

[. . .]

Avoid all conflicts so far as possible and give no grounds for conflict, so that we can win time during which we can strengthen ourselves.

Especially we must be extremely cautious in our dealings with Napoleon where there are still many issues to be resolved and he still holds the sword over us. Above all we must strive to get French soldiers off our land and be prepared for new sacrifices to achieve this.

III. INTERNAL ARRANGEMENTS

We must not flinch from granting the greatest possible freedom and equality. By this is not meant the anarchic and bloody horrors of the

French revolution ... but rather the wise laws of a monarchical state which will not restrict the natural freedom and equality of its citizens any more than is required by their level of culture and for their own good.

[...]

The Nobility

Every position in the state, without exception, is not restricted to this or that caste but must be open to all classes on the basis of merit and ability ...

The exclusive privilege of the nobility to own noble manors ... is so damaging and so unsuited to our current time and condition that it must be abolished along with all other associated privileges.

The Bourgeois Estate

The bourgeois estate will gain much by having opened up to them access to all places, trades and employments and in turn must give up any practices which excluded members of other estates.

The Peasants

This is the most numerous and important but also the most neglected and oppressed of classes and must now be the principal object of great care. We need a short and effective law as soon as possible abolishing serfdom. We also need to repeal all laws which prevent peasants from moving out of their own class. .... They must have the right to acquire property. .... It is not necessary to abolish compulsory labour services. They are often less onerous than money payments, according to local circumstances. Changes must be by agreement and only promoted by law to the extent of permitting peasants to buy out services in kind or labour.

Uniting the nation with the government

[...] The idea of national representation ... is fine and appropriate. Amalgamating representatives with branches of the administration will be useful.

[...]

Creating the greatest possible freedom of action to subjects of all classes

There should be freedom to practice every trade or craft and the same taxation in town and country. .... We must also get rid of monopolies over such matters as milling and brewing.

[...]

IV. MILITARY MATTERS

It is necessary to assemble again as much military force as possible. ....

We must completely change the system of conscription, abolishing all existing exemptions. We must turn military service into an honourable calling. . . .

Everyone must have the same chance of promotion. . . . Non-commissioned officers should be chosen by the rank and file; the lowest officers by the NCOs.

[. . .]

5.5
Letters of Napoleon Bonaparte

J.M. Thompson (ed.) (1998) *Napoleon's Letters*, London: Prion, pp. 166–7, 311.

(a) Napoleon to Joseph Fouché, Minister of Police, 21 April 1807

Britain had to contend with rebellion in Ireland on two occasions during the wars against Revolutionary and Napoleonic France (in 1798 and 1801). On the first occasion the rebellion was assisted by a small French force. The 1798 rebellion was fought with appalling brutality on both sides and was harshly suppressed.

I want you to get up a great agitation, especially in the provincial press of Brittany, Vendée, Piedmont, and Belgium, against the persecutions which the Irish Catholics are suffering at the hands of the Anglican church. For this purpose you must collect all the features that represent the persecution in its strongest colours. I will get M. Portalis[1] to make private arrangements with some of the bishop, so that, when these newspaper articles have had time to produce their effect, intercessions may be offered for the stoppage of the persecutions. But the whole affair must be managed very tactfully, from the government side. You must make use of the papers without their suspecting the end we have in view. The editors of the *Journal de l'Empire* are the

---

[1] Jean-Etienne-Marie Portalis was a jurist who had drawn up the provision of the Concordat signed by Napoleon (when First Consul) and the Pope in 1801. In 1804 Portalis became Minister of Ecclesiastical Affairs.

very people for the job. You must make people realise the cruelties and indignities committed by England against the Irish Catholics, whom they have been massacring in St. Bartholemew's Eve[2] fashion for the last hundred years. Don't talk of 'Protestants'; say 'the Anglican Church': for there are Protestants in France, but there are no Anglicans.

(b) Napoleon to General Caulaincourt, Minister for Foreign Affairs, 28 March 1815

In April 1814 Napoleon abdicated. The victorious allies, meeting at the Congress of Vienna, sent him to the Mediterranean island of Elba as its monarch. In March 1815 he returned to France and marched on Paris winning popular support on the way. He reached Paris on 20 March, as the 'restored' Bourbon monarch, Louis XVIII (b. 1755; reigned 1814–24), fled to Ghent.

I want you to instruct Bignon to write a history of the Congress of Vienna. One could print an Appendix of all the documents, with appropriate extracts from Talleyrand's despatches.[3] Such a work would be useful, as showing foreign greed and injustice. But until it is written we can't tell whether it is suitable for publication.

I think it very important to have a history written of all the treaties during my reign. . . . This work seems to me to be of essential importance for the history of the nation, and for its glory and mine, since these events need to be presented in their proper light [. . .].

Find me a competent man, who could be entrusted with this work.

It is necessary that you should send daily articles to the *Moniteur*,[4] dated from different countries, to let people know what is happening; for instance, the dispute between Sweden and Denmark over Pomerania; the differences between Saxony, Bavaria, and the Prince of Orange, who refuses to give up his family estates in Germany; and

[2] Infamous massacre of French Protestants that began in Paris on 24 August 1572, on the orders of the queen-mother, Catherine de Médici, after an attempted assassination of the Protestant leader, Admiral Coligny, had failed. An estimated 3,000 Protestants died in Paris, 70,000 in all of France over the following two months.

[3] Charles Maurice Talleyrand (1754–1838), former bishop of Autun, had served as Foreign Minister from 1799 until 1807. In 1814 he was deeply involved in the restoration of the Bourbons and he served as the French representative at the Congress of Vienna throughout 1814 and 1815.

[4] *Le Moniteur* was the official newspaper of the French government.

so on. Public curiosity can thus be fed upon articles edited from a proper point of view, so as to bring to light the greediness of the powers.

5.6

Reflections of a Romantic

C. Emsley (2003) *Napoleon: Conquest, Reform and Reorganisation*, Harlow: Longman, pp. 114–15

Alfred de Musset (1810–57) was a French Romantic poet, playwright and novelist. The following extract from his *La confession d'un enfant du siècle* (1835) contains one of the most striking of the literary reflections on the Napoleonic adventure by a Romantic.

There was then but one man alive in Europe; all the rest sought to fill their lungs with the air that he had breathed. Each year France made a gift to this man of three hundred thousand young men; it was a tax paid to Caesar, and without this troop behind him, he could not follow his fortune. It was the escort he needed to be able to traverse the world, and then to fall in a little valley on a deserted island beneath a weeping willow.

Never were there so many sleepless nights, as in the time of this man; never have you seen so many desolate mothers leaning over town ramparts; never was there such a silence around those who spoke of death. Yet never was there so much joy, so much life, so many warlike fanfares in every heart. Never were there suns as pure as those that dried all this blood. It is said that God made them for this man, and they are called the suns of Austerlitz.[1] But he made them well enough himself with his ever thundering cannon that left clouds only the day after his battles.

It was the air of this unsullied sky, where so much glory shone, where so much steel gleamed, that the children would breathe. They knew well enough that they were destined for the hecatombs; but they

---

[1] Austerlitz was one of Napoleon's greatest victories, fought on 2 December 1805 against the combined armies of Austria and Russia.

325

believed Murat[2] invulnerable, and the Emperor had been seen to cross a bridge in a hail of bullets, and it seemed he could not die. And even when you had to die, so what? Death itself was then so beautiful, so magnificent in its smoking crimson! . . . All the cradles of France were shields, and so were all the coffins; truly, there were no longer any old men, there were only corpses and demi-gods.

[. . .]

Now, seated on a ruined world is a frustrated generation. All these children were drops of a burning blood that has flooded the ground; they were born in the bosom of war, for war. For fifteen years they have dreamed of the snows of Moscow and the sun of the Pyramids. They have never left their towns, but they have been told that through each town gates is the route to a European capital. They had a whole world in their heads; they looked at the ground, the sky, the streets and the roads; everything was empty, and the bells of their parishes rang alone in the distance.

5.7

The king of Prussia to his people, 17 March 1813

J. Breuilly (2002) *Austria, Prussia and Germany 1806–1871*, London: Longman, pp. 118–19.

Frederick William III (b. 1770; reigned 1797–1840) made this celebrated call to arms at the beginning of the *Befreiungskrieg*.[1] Prussia had been humiliated following the battles of Jena and Auerstadt in 1806. She had been reduced in size, forced to pay reparations and compelled to become a French ally. Napoleon's disastrous campaign in Russia appeared to offer an opportunity for turning the tables.

---

[2] Joachim Murat (1767–1815) was Napoleon's dashing cavalry commander who specialised in flamboyant uniforms. Murat married Napoleon's youngest sister, Caroline, and was made King of Naples in 1808.

---

[1] This translates as the 'War of Liberation', the term used in Germany to describe the campaign to defeat Napoleon in 1813–14.

It is not necessary for my true people, as for Germans, to provide an account of the reasons for the war which is just beginning. The reasons are obvious to all in Europe who are not blind.

We suffer under the over-mighty power of France. The peace which tore away half of my subjects from me brought no blessings. Instead it inflicted further wounds upon us, even that of war itself. The marrow was sucked out of the land. The main fortresses remained occupied by the enemy. Agriculture was ruined as was the prosperity of our towns. Free trade was strangled and thus the sources of wealth and welfare dried up. The country has fallen victim to poverty.

By means of the strictest fulfilment of the agreements we have made, I hoped to make things easier for my people and to convince the French Emperor that it was in his own interest to let Prussia have her independence. But my purest intentions were undermined by arrogance and faithlessness. We see clearly that the Emperor [Napoleon]'s agreements will slowly ruin us even more surely than his wars. Now the time has come when all misunderstanding of our situation must cease.

Brandenburgers, Prussians, Silesians, Pomeranians, Lithuanians! You know what you have suffered for seven years and what will be your tragic fate if we do not bring this new war to an honourable end. Think back to earlier times, to the great Electors, to the great Frederick. Keep in your minds the things for which your forefathers fought – freedom of conscience, honour, independence, trade, the arts and sciences. Think of the great example of our powerful ally, the Russians. Think of the Spanish and the Portugese, also small nations who have fought successfully for these same goals against a more powerful enemy. Think of the heroic Swiss and Dutch.

Great sacrifices are demanded from all classes, for we make a great start and equally great are the numbers and resources of our enemies. You will give that more willingly for your fatherland, for your own king, than for a foreign despot who has given countless examples that he will sacrifice your sons and all that is yours for ends which are utterly alien to you. Trust in God, endurance, effort, and solidarity with our allies will reward our virtuous efforts with success.

Whatever sacrifices are demanded of individuals, they are outweighed by the holy cause for which we make them, for which we fight and must win, if we do not wish to cease being Prussian and German.

This is the last and decisive struggle, for our existence, our independence, our welfare. The only choice is between an honourable peace or noble destruction. Even that can be faced with equanimity if it preserves our honour, for without honour no Prussian or German wishes to live. But let us trust that God and our firm resolve will bring our just cause to victory, with a secure and glorious peace and the return of a happier time.

5.8

British volunteer forces called to arms

During the Revolutionary and Napoleonic Wars large numbers of men came forward to join volunteer military units to counter any French invasion. The following represent a typical call for a volunteer company and a patriotic song dedicated to the volunteers.

(a) Appeal for a volunteer company

Chelmsford, Essex County Record Office, D/DGg [L/U] 3/2.

Chelmsford, 2nd April, 1798

It is a serious truth that the people in general of this Commercial Country, can with difficulty be brought to turn their minds seriously on the necessity of forming themselves into Military Corps. Is it possible that any young and active Briton *can at such a period as the present*, think that he is discharging that duty he owes to himself – his Country – his aged Parent – his female Connections and Acquaintance – and to Posterity, if he at this moment finds himself unattached to some Regiment or Volunteer Corps, panting with a virtuous ardour to distinguish himself in the glorious defence of his Country and its Constitution? Surely there is not an Englishman so base as unresistingly to submit to be a Slave of France; to have its Requisitions laid upon his Country, at the pleasure of the Military Officers of the Tyrant Directory. Is there an Englishman who does not clearly foresee that, should France succeed, the Youth of Briton will be dragged into their Armies, to extend their destructive and plundering depredations to any part of the Globe, that these Tyrants of Europe may think it worth while to spoil?

Gallant Youths of this happy Isle, rouse yourselves from this apparent state of insensibility of your present arduous situation! If you let pass in inactivity the present moment, which calls aloud for exertion, it will be – in vain will you begin military organization when once the Enemy have landed: the forming a Company or regiment fit to meet an Enemy with any hope of success, is not the business of one week, no, nor one month! – Read with a proper impression, of the incapability of the Swiss the other day to resist, from not knowing the use of arms!* – Imitate their prowess, but take warning from their tardiness in preparation.

* The Loyal Inhabitants of this Town, being desirous, in the present critical State of the Country, of forming a *Volunteer Corps,* a Meeting has been convened, by Notice given in the Church, to be held in the Vestry to-morrow, at Twelve o'Clock, for the purpose of taking the measure into consideration.

(b) Volunteer song

The York Herald, 15 October 1803.

Of love, of wine, it were treason to sing
When, like locusts, the robbers of France are on wing:
Our green island to ravage, in myriads they throng:
Then swell the full chorus, brave friends of my song:
O'er the wave let them come,
They but rush to their doom;
To our shores should they fly, they shall never fly home.

Hark! Your sires from their tombs in . . . accents implore,
That you'd crush the fierce foe, as they crush'd him before;
That you'd gild with fresh glories proud History's page,
And grace with new Cressys and Blenheims your age.[1]
    O'er the wave, etc.

Their Edwards and Henrys were lions in fight,
But we have our Nelson and Acre's dread knight:[2]

[1] Reference to the battles of Crécy (26 August 1346) and Blenheim (13 August 1704), celebrated English/British victories over the French.

[2] Sir Sidney Smith (1764–1840), a British naval officer who organised the successful defence of Acre against the army of Citizen-General Bonaparte when it moved north out of Egypt in 1799.

Its broom let the house of Plantagenet boast,
Our Navy's the broom to sweep clean yon foul coast.
    O'er the wave, etc.

Then away to the field! 'tis your country invites
Remember your homes, and your fireside delights!
Yet, if France but one spot in that country should crave,
Indulge her; and, oh! let that spot be her grave.
    O'er the wave let them come,
They but rush to their doom;
To our shores should they fly, they shall never fly home.

5.9

Prince Metternich's political confession of faith, sent to Tsar Alexander I, December 1820

Prince Metternich (1882) *Memoirs of Prince Metternich*, ed.
Prince Richard Metternich, trans. Mrs Alexander Napier,
5 vols., London: Charles Scribner & Sons, vol. 3, pp. 453,
453–76.

Clemens von Metternich (1773–1859) was born into the Rhineland nobility. He moved to Vienna in 1794 and entered the Austrian diplomatic service. He became foreign minister in 1809 and while initially nervous of breaking with Napoleon, he eventually presided over the Congress of Vienna that reorganised Europe after Napoleon's fall. In the aftermath of Waterloo he was regarded as the principal architect of a system that sought to maintain stability by stifling reform. He was instrumental in organising a series of international congresses and actions designed to maintain what he considered to be a balance of power in Europe. Following the Congress of Troppau in 1820 he drafted the following secret document to Tsar Alexander I (1777–1825) outlining what he believed to be the threats to stability in Europe. The document is commonly described as his 'Confession of Faith'. During the Revolutions of 1848, when he became the focus for much popular anger, he was forced from power and took refuge in England.

'*L'Europe*', a celebrated writer has recently said, '*fait aujourd' hui pittier à l'homme d'esprit et horreur a l'homme verteuex*'[1]

It would be difficult to comprise in a few words a more exact picture of the situation at the time which we are writing these lines!

[. . .]

[I]t is necessary to point out in a more particular manner the evil which threatens to deprive it, at one blow, of the real blessings, the fruits of genuine civilization, and to disturb it in the midst of its enjoyment. This evil may be described in one word – presumption; the natural effect of the rapid progress of the human mind towards the perfecting of so many things. This is it which at the present day leads so many individuals astray, for it has become an almost universal sentiment.

Religion, morality, legislation, economy, politics, administration, all have become common and accessible to everyone. Knowledge seems to come by inspiration; experience has no value for the presumptuous man; faith is nothing to him; he substitutes for it a pretended individual conviction, and to arrive at this conviction dispenses with all enquiry and with all study; for these men appear too trivial to a mind which believes itself strong enough to embrace at one glance all questions and all facts. Laws have no value for him, because he has not contributed to make them, and it would be beneath a man of his parts to recognise the limits traced by rude and ignorant generations. Power resides in himself; why should he submit himself to that which was only useful to the man deprived of light and knowledge? That which, according to him, was required in an age of weakness cannot be suitable in an age of reason and vigour, amounting to universal perfection, which the German innovators designate by the idea, absurd in itself, of the Emancipation of the People! Morality itself he does not attack openly, for without it he could not be sure for a single instant of his own existence; but he interprets its essence after his own fashion, and allows every other person to do so likewise, provided that other persons neither kill nor rob him. . . . Presumption makes every man the guide of his own belief, the arbiter of laws according to which he is pleased to govern himself, or to allow someone else to govern him and his neighbours; it makes him, in short, the sole judge of his own faith, his own actions, and the principles according to which he guides them.

[. . .]

---

[1] 'Europe today arouses pity in a man of intelligence, and horror in a man of virtue.'

It is principally the middle classes of society which this moral gangrene has affected, and it is only among them that the real heads of the party are found.

For the great mass of the people it has no attraction and can have none. The labours to which this class – the real people – are obliged to devote themselves, are too continuous and too positive to allow them to throw themselves into vague abstractions and ambitions. The people know what is the happiest thing for them: namely to be able to count on the morrow, for it is the morrow which will repay them for the cares and sorrows of today. The laws which afford a just protection to individuals, to families, and to property, are quite simple in their essence. The people dread any movement which injures industry and brings new burdens in its train.

[. . .]

In all four countries [Germany, Spain, Italy and France] the agitated classes are principally composed of wealthy men – real cosmopolitans, securing their personal advantage at the expense of any order of things whatever – paid State officials, men of letters, lawyers, and the individuals charged with the public education.

To these classes may be added that of the falsely ambitious, whose number is never considerable among the lower orders, but is large in the higher ranks of society.

There is besides scarcely any epoch which does not offer a rallying cry to some particular faction. This cry, since 1815, has been *constitution*. But do not let us deceive ourselves; this word, susceptible of great latitude of interpretation, would be but imperfectly understood if we supposed that the factions attached quite the same meaning to it under the different *régimes*. Such is certainly not the case. In pure monarchies it is qualified by the name of 'National representation'. In countries which have lately been brought under the representative *régime* it is called 'development' and promises charters and fundamental laws. In the only state [England] which possesses an ancient national representation it takes 'reform' as its object. Everywhere it means change and trouble.

In pure monarchies it may be paraphrased thus: 'the level of equality shall pass over your heads; your fortunes shall pass into other hands; your ambitions, which have been satisfied for centuries, shall now give place to our ambitions, which have been hitherto repressed'.

In the states under a new *régime* they say: 'the ambitions satisfied yesterday must give place to those of the morrow, and this is the morrow for us'.

Lastly, in England, the only place in the third class, the rallying cry – that of reform – combines the two meanings.

[. . .]

We see this intermediary class abandon itself with a blind fury and animosity which proves much more its own fears than any confidence in the success of its enterprises, to all the means which seem proper to assuage its thirst for power, applying itself to the task of persuading kings that their rights are confined to sitting upon a throne, while those of the people are to govern, and to attack all that centuries have bequeathed as holy and worthy of man's respect – denying, in fact, the value of the past and declaring themselves the masters of the future. We see this class take all sorts of disguises, uniting and sub-dividing as occasion offers, helping each other in the hour of danger, and the next day depriving each other of their conquests. It takes possession of the press, and employs it to promote impiety, disobedience to the laws of religion and the state, and goes so far as to preach murder as a duty for those who desire what is good.

[. . .]

We are convinced that society can no longer be saved without strong and vigorous resolutions on the part of the Governments still free in their opinions and actions.

We are also convinced that this may yet be, if the Governments face the truth, if they free themselves from all illusion, if they join their ranks and take their stand on a line of correct, unambiguous, and frankly announced principles.

[. . .]

Governments, in establishing the principle of *stability*, will in nowise exclude the development of what is good, for stability is not immobility. But it is for those who are burdened with the heavy task of government to augment the well-being of their people! It is for Governments to regulate it according to necessity and to suit the times. It is not by concessions, which the factions try to force from legitimate power, and which they have neither the right to claim nor the faculty of keeping within just bounds, that wise reforms can be carried out. . . . Respect for all that is; liberty for every Government to watch over the well-being of its own people; a league between all Governments against factions in all States; contempt for the meaningless words which have become the rallying cry of the factious; respect for the progressive development of institutions in lawful ways; refusal on the part of every monarch to aid or succour partisans under any mask whatever – such are happily the ideas of the great monarchs: the world will be saved if they bring them into action – it is lost if they do not.

Union between the monarchs is the basis of the policy which must now be followed to save society from total ruin.

[. . .]

If the same elements of destruction which are now throwing society into convulsion have existed in all ages – for every age has seen immoral and ambitious men, hypocrites, men of heated imaginations, wrong motives, and wild projects – yet ours, by the single fact of the liberty of the press, possesses more than any preceding age the means of contact, seduction, and attraction whereby to act on these different classes of men.

We are certainly not alone in questioning if society can exist with the liberty of the press, a scourge unknown to the world before the latter half of the seventeenth century, and restrained until the end of the eighteenth, with scarcely any exceptions but England – a part of Europe separated from the Continent by the sea, as well as by her language and by her peculiar manners. . . .

Let them [the monarchs] in these troublous times be more than usually cautious in attempting real ameliorations, not imperatively claimed by the needs of the moment, to the end that good itself may not turn against them – which is the case whenever a Government measure seems to be inspired by fear.

Let them not confound concessions made to parties with the good they ought to do for their people, in modifying, according to their recognised needs, such branches of the administration as require it.

Let them give minute attention to the financial state of their kingdoms, so that their people might enjoy, by the reduction of public burdens, the real, not imaginary, benefits of a state of peace.

Let them be just, but strong; beneficent but strict.

Let them maintain religious principles in all their purity, and not allow the faith to be attacked and morality interpreted according to the *social contract* or the visions of foolish sectarians.

Let them suppress Secret Societies, that gangrene of society.

In short, let the great monarchs strengthen their union, and prove to the world that if it exists, it is beneficent, and ensures a political peace of Europe: that it is powerful only for the maintenance of tranquillity at a time when so many attacks are directed against it; that's the principles which they profess are paternal and protective, menacing only the disturbers of public tranquillity.

[. . .]

5.10

A soldier and a citizen

W. Cobbett (1830) *Advice to Young Men, and (incidentally)*
to Young Women, in the middle and higher ranks of life:
in a series of letters addressed to a youth, a bachelor, a
lover, a husband, a father, a citizen, or a subject, London:
Ward Lock, paragraph 338.

William Cobbett (1763–1835) served in the army before becoming
a self-taught journalist. Politically he started as a Tory shifting
to radicalism during the period of the French Revolution. His
radical *Political Register* began publication in 1802 with articles
highly critical of privilege, corruption and what he saw as the
destruction of a traditional way of life. He is best-known for his
Rural Rides, describing his travels through the English countryside in the early 1820s and highly critical of his usual targets,
especially the 'Great Wen' of London. In this document, he echoes
some of the arguments made by radicals in the wars against
Napoleon.

All men are equal by nature; nobody denies that they all ought to be
equal in the eye of the law; but, how are they to be thus equal if the
law begins by suffering some to enjoy this right and refusing the enjoyment to others? It is the duty of every man to defend his country
against an enemy, a duty imposed by the law of nature as well as by
that of civil society, and without the recognition of this duty, there
could exist no independent nation, and no civil society. Yet, how are
you to maintain that this is the duty of every man, if you deny to some
men the enjoyment of a share in making laws? Upon what principle
are you to contend for equality here, while you deny its existence as
to the right of sharing in the making of the laws? The poor man has a
body and a soul as well as the rich man; like the latter, he has parents,
wife and children; a bullet or a sword is as deadly to him as to the rich
man; there are hearts to ache and tears to flow for him as well as for
the squire or the lord or the loan-monger: yet, notwithstanding this
equality, he is to risk all, and, if he escape, he is still to be denied an
equality of rights! If, in such a state of things, the artisan, or labourer,
when called out to fight in defence of his country, were to answer:
'Why should I risk my life? I have no possession but my labour; no

enemy will take that from me; you, the rich, possess all the land and all its products; and you make what laws you please without my participation or assent; you punish me at your pleasure; you say that my want of property excludes me from the right of having a share in the making of the laws; you say that the property have in my labour is nothing worth; on what ground, then, do you call on me to risk my life?' If, in such a case, such questions were put, the answer is very difficult to be imagined.

5.11
The Silesian Weavers' rising, June 1844

F. Eyck (ed.) (1972) *The Revolutions of 1848*, Edinburgh: Oliver and Boyd, pp. 19–23.

This account of the Silesian Weavers' rising was written and published by Wilhelm Wolff (1809–64) immediately after the incidents that it described. Wolff was a language and writing teacher living in Breslau, the capital of Silesia. He had already spent several years in prison for his radical political activities when he wrote this account. He served as an extreme-left deputy in the Frankfurt Parliament of 1848. He was a member of Karl Marx's circle and Marx dedicated the first volume of *Das Kapital* to his memory. He died in exile in Manchester.

Here in the great villages Langenbielau (13,000 inhabitants) and Peterswaldau (5,000 inhabitants) and in the other villages such as Arnsdorf, Peilau, etc., cotton weaving particularly is done at home. The distress of the workers was and is here not less important, perhaps even more so than in other areas, although one might think that misery could not reach a higher degree than can be found in the Landshut, Hirschberg, Bolkenhain and other districts. In the winter already, at the beginning of February, a small rising took place in Bielau. A crowd used signals to call together the weavers of the village. A comrade who had been arrested was freed. The crowd was appeased by some gifts. An inquiry into the incident followed but owing to the secrecy of our procedure this event remained almost unknown even in Breslau, that is among the non-governmental public. In the meantime the distress and the urge to obtain work was used by the individual manufacturers to the greatest possible extent in order to obtain a great quantity of goods for little pay. Among these the brothers Zwanziger in Peterswaldau were preeminent. For a web of cotton of 140 ells, on which a weaver had to work for nine days and for which other employers paid 32 silver *groschen*[1] they paid only 15. For 160 ells of fustian which required eight full days of strenuous work, they paid a wage of 121 and 12 silver *groschen*. Indeed, they declared themselves ready to give work to another three hundred weavers prepared to work as much for 10 silver *groschen*. Bitter misery forced the poor to work even under these conditions. From his 12 or 10 silver *groschen* respectively the weaver had to give up 2 to 3 silver *groschen* to the bobbin winder, bear all state, communal and seignorial dues and – live. Oh! If only someone would explain to me why . . . the major, colonel, general . . . retires after a bloodless game of war during a long period of peace with a pension of 1,000, 1,500, 2,000 *taler* and the industrial worker becomes brutalised and grows dull, deprived of all moral and intellectual development, [and] gains for his daily laborious work of 14 to 16 hours not even so much that he can satisfy at least the needs of an animal, the demands of the stomach!

[. . .]

The fortune of the Zwanzigers, which was not initially too large, had in a short time grown into great wealth. . . . I can guarantee the following short report which I repeat from the accounts of eye witnesses, and indeed trustworthy men. A poem composed to the popular melody 'There is a Castle in Austria' [*Es liegt ein Schloss in Österreich*] and sung by the weavers was, as it were, the Marseillaise of the needy. They sang it several times particularly in front of the house of the Zwanzigers. One of them was seized, taken into the house, flogged and handed over to the local police. Finally, at two o'clock in the afternoon of 4 June, the stream overflowed its banks. A crowd of weavers appeared in Nieder-Peterswaldau and on its march attracted all weavers from their dwellings on the left and right. Then they went to the not far distant Kapellenberg and formed up into pairs and moved towards the new residence of the Zwanzigers. They demanded higher pay and a present! With ridicule and threats this was refused to them. Now it was not long before the crowd stormed into the house, broke into all chambers, vaults, lofts and cellars and smashed everything, from splendid mirror windows, trumeaus, chandeliers, tiled stoves,

---

[1] One silver *groschen* was one-thirteenth of a *taler*, the standard silver currency of much of central and eastern Europe in this period. The English word 'dollar' derives from *taler*.

porcelain, furniture, to the staircases, tore up the books, bills of exchange and papers, penetrated into the second residence, into the coach houses, into the drying house, to the mangling machine, into the baggage warehouse and threw the goods and stock out of the windows where they were torn up, cut into little pieces and trodden under foot, or – in imitation of the Leipzig mess business – distributed to those standing around. In fear of death Zwanziger fled with his family to Reichenbach. The citizens there, who did not want to tolerate a guest like that who could draw the weavers towards them, made him travel on to Schweidnitz. But there, too, the authorities signified to him that he should leave the city because they could become exposed to danger by his presence; and so he finally found safety here in Breslau.

The police official Christ and a policeman carried out an arrest in Peterswaldau, but the weavers soon freed the prisoner. The manufacturer Wagenknecht lived next to Zwanziger. He had treated the weavers more humanely, he was spared. As he also gave them a small present, they cheered him. Soon weavers from Arnsdorf and Bielau arrived. Whatever had been left at the Zwanzigers was now finally smashed. Night interrupted the work of revenge. I may not omit because it is too characteristic – the proposal of some weavers to set fire to the houses and its rejection for the reason that those thus damaged would then receive fire insurance money [*Brandgelder*] and that the main thing was for once to make them poor so that they would experience the effect of hunger. On the following day, 5 June, was the third turn for the establishments of the Zwanzigers. A stock of ham in the loft of the house had not been discovered on 4 June; therefore it was destroyed today. In the end even the roofs were partially destroyed. After all this had been completed, the mob went to the manufacturer F.W. Fellman Jun. Fellman appeased the men by paying them 5 *groschen* each and gave them bread and butter as well as some sides of bacon. A piece of bread and a coin of 5 *groschen* sufficed to keep in check the fury of men driven by hunger and revenge! Then they went on to E.G. Hofrichters Witwe and Söhne. The weavers now already numbered nearly 3,000. Hofrichter, too, paid a present of 5 *groschen* to each individual but only the first ones received this, the last ones less.

From here the crowd moved to the 'Sechsgröschel Hilbert'. Hilbert and Andretzky live in Bielau. The destruction in this place began with their house. At first it was the turn of the Gebrüder Dierig. The pastor Seiffert, son-in-law of Dierig, to whom his wife had brought a dowry of 20,000 *taler*, and who now, comfortable in the calm resignation of the true Christian in his fate, wanted to speak of the joys which beckon to the sufferer on this earth, up there, and admonish the crowd to calm and peace, is reported to have been thrown into the water. In the meantime the clerks had assembled the factory servants and other people, armed them with clubs and whatever else came to hand, and now attacked the weavers under the leadership of the farmer Werner. After a heavy battle the weavers fled out of the building with battered heads and leaving behind manifold traces of blood. However, those who had escaped turned up with new arrivals in front of the second house of Dierig. These included in particular many weavers who worked for Dierig. The latter had promised all who protected his property – and thus preserved their opportunity of continuing to work – a present of 5 silver *groschen*. Several strangers who wanted to break in were repelled by those ready to provide this protection. In the meantime the military who had already been requisitioned twenty-four hours before from Schweidnitz, moved into Bielau.

I do not guarantee that Pastor Seiffert said to his father-in-law that now he need not have to pay any more, as the military were there! Suffice it to say that this has been almost universally reported. What is certain is that the crowd had just arranged itself in an orderly fashion in order to accept the 5 silver *groschen* promised by Dierig on a piece of paper which had been pasted on to the house, when the military arrived. The troops secured themselves some space by moving back; weavers spoke to them close by and the commander may rightly have considered such conversation dangerous. Therefore the major moved from his first place in order to choose a more advantageous position behind the house and on either side. A lieutenant with ten men was ordered into the garden in front of the house. The weavers formed two rows so that each could receive his 5 silver *groschen*. The distribution was supposed to take place by Dierig's house and everybody was to retire into the open through the house soon after receiving it. The entries and exits were occupied by soldiers. But it took so long and the payment was delayed so much that the crowd became impatient and, furthermore, nervous at the sight of soldiers, roughly called to order by some noncommissioned officers and soon convinced that they would receive no money, it pressed increasingly against the troops. The major, who saw Dierig's house and his troops increasingly threatened, ordered his men to open fire.

As a consequence of three rifle volleys, eleven people were killed instantly. Blood and brains gushed forth all over the place. The brain of one man protruded above his eye. A woman who stood two hundred steps away at the door of her house sank down motionless. One side of a man's head was torn away. The bloody brain and skull was at some distance from him. A mother of six children died on the same evening of several shot wounds. A girl who was going to her knitting lesson sank to the ground, hit by bullets. A woman who saw her husband fall went to the loft of her home and hanged herself. A boy of eight years was shot through the knee. So far it has become known that twenty-four people were severely or mortally wounded in addition to the eleven dead mentioned above. Perhaps one may learn later how many kept their wounds secret. After the first volleys there was for a few seconds a mortal silence. But the sight of blood around and next to them, the sighs . . . of the dying, the moaning of the wounded, drove the most courageous among the weavers to resistance. They replied with stones which they snatched up from the stone heaps in the streets. When some more shots had been fired and some weavers were again wounded by them, while the weavers escaped on the one side and returned from the other and continued under the most terrible oaths and curses to throw stones, and advanced with clubs and axes, etc., Major von Rosenberger effected his retreat. If he had delayed any longer it might have been too late for ever. At ten o'clock in the evening Major von Schlichting arrived in Peterswaldau with four companies. Four guns also arrived from Schweidnitz.

On 6 June, early in the morning, this infantry and artillery moved to Bielau, but one company remained in Peterswaldau which yet on the same day, because there was again a violent ferment, received support from a second. The guns drove up into Bielau, the artillerymen with burning slow matches marching beside them. On the night of 5 and 6 June, after the departure of von Rosenberger's troops, one of Dierig's houses, as well as an annexe, had been demolished. A part of his soldiers was posted by Major von Schlichting near Dierig's houses, the others at the manor house. It is true that on this morning clusters of people were to be seen moving up and down the alleys; it is true that the blood which had congealed thickly in front of Dierig's house, mixed on posts, planks and steps with parts of brains, attracted the fixed gaze of the crowds of weavers standing about, and that all this seemed bound to unleash once more the inwardly raging fury of revenge. It was solely the strength of the military power, of the infantry and artillery and later even of the cavalry that prevented the weavers from trying any further resistance.

5.12
Memoirs of a young journeyman

M. Traugott (ed.) (1993) *The French Worker:*
Autobiographies from the Early Industrial Era, Berkeley:
University of California Press, pp. 130–2.

Agricol Perdiguier (1805–75) was born near Avignon in the south
of France. His father was a joiner and Agricol followed in his
father's footsteps. His memoir was drafted in 1852 while he was
in exile in Antwerp following the coup by which Louis Napoleon
Bonaparte made himself Emperor Napoleon III. It first appeared
in serial form in Switzerland before being published as a book in
1854. In 1855 Perdiguier was allowed to return to France. The
memoirs were reprinted several times before his death and are
generally regarded as one of the best accounts of a young journeyman's 'tour of France' in the early nineteenth century.
Perdiguer's 'tour' lasted four and a half years.

Every brotherhood [*compagnonnage*][1] would hold a general assembly
on the first Sunday of every month. . . .
   At the agreed Sunday, [the roller] first had all the compagnons, then
the affiliates, go upstairs to the meeting chamber. I was left all alone
in the room below. Then the roller[2] came down, took my hand, and led
me upstairs, giving a special knock at the door, which immediately
opened. He took me into the meeting room, where I was surrounded
by a circle of men, standing calm, silent, and neatly dressed, their
outfits decorated with blue and white ribbons. I was dazzled, astonished, and perplexed. He had me cross the length of the room to meet
the First Fellow, who was presiding, telling him, 'Here is a young man
who asks to become part of the brotherhood.' The First Fellow asked
me, 'Do you wish to become a member of the brotherhood?'
   'Yes.'
   'Do you know which brotherhood this is?'
   'It's the Society of Compagnons.'

---

[1] *Compagnonnage* refers to both a specific brotherhood and to the system of worker
brotherhoods. Artisans in training belonged to such associations of journeymen; though
it was also possible to be a journeyman who was not attached to such a body.
   [2] A 'roller' (*rouler*), among other things, arranged for the employment of newly arrived
journeymen in a town.

'That's true, but there are several brotherhoods: the Compagnons du Devoir, or *devoirants*; then there's the Compagnons du Devoir de Liberté, or *gavots*. Which of the two do you wish to affiliate with?'

'The Compagnons du Devoir de Liberté.'

'They're both good, and if you've come to the wrong place, you're free to withdraw.'

'It's definitely this one I want to join.'

When he had finished reading me the regulations the First Fellow asked me, 'Can you abide by these rules?'

'Yes' I answered. He added that if I did not feel capable of observing them, I was free to leave.

I approved of what I had just heard and I promised to comply. The First Fellow proclaimed me an affiliate [*affilié*]. The roller led me to the place reserved for me. Since I was the newest member of the brotherhood, I was lowest in rank . . .

I attended all meetings and paid my dues promptly. Everything I had seen, except for the hatred and violence, pleased me. After a while I was ready to undertake my Tour of France.

[. . .]

In those days, compagnons often fought among themselves, and leaving to do one's Tour of France was almost like leaving for war. For that reason, my mother experienced a certain anxiety and advised me to make my confession before beginning so perilous an expedition.

Until then, all I had ever worn was a plain jacket. My father had a coat made for me, and a few shirts and some other clothes, and he bought me a trunk to hold them all. He gave me thirty francs, in six five-franc pieces, the largest sum that I had ever possessed. On the third day of Easter, [Tuesday,] 20 April 1824, having sent my trunk ahead by carriage and carrying a small bundle hung from a stick on my shoulder, I left Avignon on foot with a friend named Jargea. He was nicknamed Vivarais the Palm-of-Glory and, like me, was going to Marseille. The other compagnons saw us on our way with songs, as was the custom. Then, fraternal embraces were exchanged, and they left us to continue our journey alone.

[. . .]

At Saint-Andiol, we entered an inn to drink a glass of wine and have a bite to eat. A gendarme followed us in and asked for our passports.[3] When he saw that we were joiners, he sat down beside us and offered

---

[3] Since the Old Regime internal travel in France required an internal passport and, in addition, every workman had to carry a worker's passport (*livret ouvrier*) that held details of a man's trade and was signed by previous employers.

to serve as roller by finding us jobs, for there was a shortage of workers in that region. We could not accept his offer as we were in a hurry to reach Marseille, but the gendarme had been kind to us, and we returned the favour by offering him a drink. We clinked glasses, and then went on our way, as delighted with him as he with us.

5.13
Food riots

There was a common belief among plebeian members of European societies, at least from the early modern period, that they had a right to the necessities of life at a fair price. Food riots, particularly in the seventeenth and eighteenth centuries, were usually about settling and paying that fair price in markets at times of dearth. A key problem for the historian researching food riots, as manifested here, is that most of the descriptions of such behaviour tended to be written by men in authority rather than the participants.

(a) Cornish letter, 1795[1]

London, National Archives, H.O. 42.34.19.

The Stream Tinners have begun again to be riotous upon account of the Scarcity of Corn. They assembled and came over to Padstow last Saturday to the number of four hundred and took from a cellar forty Bushels of Wheat which nobody would own, (suppos'd to be Baseley's) and then quietly dispers'd; the soldiers did not molest them. . . . The Dennibole Quarry men assembled at Port Isaac last Thursday and took as much Barley from Traer as they wanted, but paid eleven shillings a Bushel for it, and told him if he offer'd to ship the remainder they would come and take it without making him any recompense. They are in daily expectation of a visit from the Tinners at Wadebridge. Corn is very scarce, and at a great Price, Wheat four and twenty shillings a Bushel and Barley fourteen in the Market, and not sufficient

---

[1] This is an extract of a letter from Cornwall forwarded to the Home Office by Sir William Lemon, 29 March 1795.

for the buyers, and many Farmers refuse to sell it in small quantities to the Poor, which causes a great murmuring.

(b) Revd A.B. Haden to the Home Secretary,[2] 1800

London, National Archives, H.O. 42.50.

I agree with your Grace that Persons and Property ought to stand secure, and that it is the Duty of a Magistrate to give ... that protection; but, my Lord, I have too high a respect for a British Parliament even to suspect that it was ever intended that Protection should extend to the withholding of Corn at the Discretion of the Farmer, 'till it is out of the power of the labouring Poor (of which there are I presume 50,000 at least in this Neighbourhood) to purchase a reasonable supply: consequently their Inability must bring them into the utmost distress. As to a real scarcity, I have not the least distant idea of it, and am fully persuaded that where the money is ready for the purchase, any quantity may be had in the Market at Wolverhampton. As a proof that we have sufficient to carry us to (I hope) a more favourable harvest, more than forty Wheat Ricks were conveyed into the Barns in the Parish of Worfield in Shropshire during the three Days of the late Riots, when the Farmers expected a visit from those depredators.

[...]

I fully agree with your Grace that every Tendency to Tumult and Insurrection ought to be suppressed: but, my Lord, I fear it would be a difficult matter to persuade any Man to protect the Person or Property of another under the conviction that the person he was protecting was starving his own Family, by withholding that Corn which is indispensably necessary for their support and comfort. There is not a [Volunteer] Corps in the Kingdom more attached to their King and Country than the Bilston Loyal Association, but I fear, the situation of wives and families of some of them would induce them to confirm the above observation.

---

[2] William Cavendish-Bentinck, 3rd duke of Portland (1738–1809), British statesman, Prime Minister (1783, 1807–9) and Home Secretary (1794–1801). The letter is dated 16 May 1800.

(c) French Minister of the Interior to Louis XVIII, 1817[3]

Le Moniteur, 7 February 1818. Translation from French by
Clive Emsley.

Sire,

Your Majesty has desired me to submit a general report on the administration of food supplies in France during the years 1816 and 1817 . . .

At the beginning of the harvest of 1816, the earliest signs seemed most favourable.

[. . .]

Then the rain came. At first it was confined to certain localities, but it soon spread generally, not only across France but also the whole of Europe. . . . The hay harvest was spoilt in all areas, and this early misfortune, which reduced the stocks normally used for feeding the animals, had an adverse effect on the consumption of grain. The rain, which prevented the corn from ripening and caused a deterioration in quality, was followed by several days of good weather, and farmers had high hopes for the more important crops that remained to be got in.

[. . .]

These hopes were nowhere fulfilled. Already some mountainous departments[4] such as Lozère and Aveyron had lost the chance of harvesting various kinds of corn because they were buried under the September snows.

[. . .]

As soon as the Commission for Food Supplies received confirmation of this disaster, and before the full extent was known, orders were given for quantities of corn to be bought in the home market and above all from abroad.

[. . .]

On 15 October 1816 the average price of corn throughout the kingdom was 28 francs 50 centimes a hectolitre, and on 15 November it was 31

---

[3] The letter, of 24 December 1817, was sent from Joseph, vicomte de Lâiné (1767–1835) Minister of the Interior [Home Secretary] from 1816–18 to Louis XVIII (1755–1824; reigned 1814–24).

[4] *Départements* are the administrative districts of France, roughly comparable to British counties.

francs 51 centimes. [. . .] This made a difference of more than 1 franc 71 centimes between the average price in 1816 and the highest price reached during the previous fifteen years. This high price of corn was the cause of the unrest which spread among the people and of the disturbances which broke out at the beginning of the winter.

During the first few days of November there was a serious insurrection at Toulouse; people refused to buy corn at the fixed price and tried to steal it from the markets. Order was only restored with difficulty and the unrest continued for several days.

On 1 November the inhabitants of some of the communes of Vendôme (department of Loir-et-Cher) assembled in groups to stop the grain convoys, and the gendarmes who tried to disperse the mobs were repulsed. Troops had to be sent to protect sales in the markets and the departure of wagons loaded with produce.

In the departments of Loire-Inférieure and the Vendée on several occasions people tried to stop the loading of grain into boats for transit elsewhere.

[. . .]

In the department of Cher, although this was an area which produced plenty of corn, the canton and town of Vierzon rioted continually against its removal. The arrondissements of Yvetot and Dieppe, some markets at Le Havre and Neufchâtel (Seine-Inférieure), and some in the department of Eure were the scene of trouble and pillaging. Peasants and unemployed workers roamed about the countryside stealing grain or demanding money from isolated farmhouses. It was necessary to organize patrols along the main roads to put down these disorders and protect navigation along the Seine.

5.14

The first national Chartist petition, July 1839

R.W. Postgate (ed.) (1962) *Revolution, from 1789 to 1906*, New York: Harper Torchbooks, pp. 127–9.

In 1837 the radical London Working-Men's Association drafted a petition to parliament requesting: equal electoral districts; the vote for all men aged 21 years; annual parliaments; no property qualifications for MPs; vote by ballot; and payment for MPs. This

5.2 The so-called 'Battle of the Westgate Hotel', Newport, 1839, in which several Chartist protesters were killed.

programme was subsequently drafted into a bill and became known as the People's Charter. In the following year the Chartist movement, aiming to bring about the six points of the Charter, was formally constituted. The petition of 1839, with nearly 1.3

347

million signatures, was the first attempt of the Chartists (there were others in 1842 and 1848) to persuade parliament to accept the Charter. Like the two subsequent petitions, this was rejected.

Unto the Honourable Commons of the United Kingdom of Great Britain and Ireland in Parliament assembled, the Petition of the undersigned, their suffering countrymen,

HUMBLY SHEWETH,

That we, your petitioners, dwell in a land where merchants are noted for enterprize, whose manufacturers are very skilful, and whose workmen are proverbial for their industry.

The land itself is goodly, the soil rich, and the temperature wholesome; it is abundantly furnished with the materials of commerce and trade; it has numerous and convenient harbours; in facility of communication it exceeds all others.

For three-and-twenty years we have enjoyed a profound peace.

Yet, with all these elements of national prosperity, and with every disposition and capacity to take advantage of them, we find ourselves overwhelmed with public and private suffering.

We are bowed down under a load of taxes; which, notwithstanding, fall greatly short of the wants of our rulers; our traders are trembling on the verge of bankruptcy; our workmen are starving; capital brings no profit and labour or remuneration; the home of the artificer is desolate, and the warehouse of the pawnbroker is full; the workhouse is crowded and the manufactury is deserted.

We have looked on every side, we have searched diligently in order to find out the causes of a distress so sore and so long continued.

We can find none in nature, or in Providence.

Heaven has dealt graciously by the people; but the foolishness of our rulers has made the goodness of God of none effect.

The energies of a mighty kingdom have been wasted in building up the power of selfish and ignorant men, and its resources squandered for their aggrandisement.

The good of a party has been advanced to the sacrifice of the good of the nation; the few have governed for the interests of the few, while the interest of the many has been neglected or insolently and tyrannously trampled upon.

It was the fond expectation of the people that a remedy for the greater part, if not the whole, of their grievances, would be found in the Reform Act of 1832.

didn't bring about prosperity.

They were taught to regard that Act as a wise means to a worthy end; as the machinery of an improved legislation, when the will of the masses would be at length potential.

They have been bitterly deceived.

The fruit which looked so fair to the eye has turned to dust and ashes when gathered.

The Reform Act has effected a transfer of power from one dominating faction to another, and left the people helpless as before.

Our slavery has been exchanged for an apprenticeship to liberty, which has aggravated the painful feeling of our social degradation, by adding to it the sickening of still deferred hope.

We come before your Honourable House to tell you, with all humility, that this state of things must not be permitted to continue; that it cannot long continue without very seriously endangering the stability of the throne and the peace of the kingdom; and that if by God's help and all lawful and constitutional appliances, an end can be put to it, we are fully resolved that it shall speedily come to an end.

We tell your Honourable House that the capital of the master must no longer be deprived of its due reward; that the laws which make food dear, and those which, by making money scarce, make labour cheap, must be abolished; that taxation must be made to fall on property, not on industry; that the good of the many, as it is the only legitimate end, so it must be the sole study of the government.

As a preliminary essential to these and other requisite changes, as means by which alone the interests of the people can be effectually vindicated and secured we demand that those interests be confided to the keeping of the people.

When the state calls for defenders, when it calls for money, no consideration of poverty or ignorance can be pleaded in refusal or delay of the call.

Required as we are, universally, to support and obey the laws, nature and reason entitle us to demand, that in the making of the laws, the universal voice shall be implicitly listened to.

We perform the duties of freemen; we must have the privileges of freemen.

[. . .]

[There follows the demand for the six points of the People's Charter.]

Finally, we would most earnestly impress on your Honourable House, that this petition has not been dictated by any idle love of

349

change; that it springs out of no inconsiderate attachment to fanciful theories; but that it is the result of much and long deliberation, and of convictions, which the events of each succeeding year tend more and more to strengthen.

The management of this mighty kingdom has hitherto been a subject for contending factions to try their selfish experiments upon.

We have felt the consequences in our sorrowful experience – short glimmerings of uncertain enjoyment swallowed up by long and dark seasons of suffering.

If the self-government of the people should not remove their distresses, it will at least remove their repinings.

Universal suffrage will, and it alone can, bring true and lasting peace to the nation; we firmly believe that it will also bring prosperity.

5.15

The prospectus for *L'Artisan, Journal de la Classe Ouvrière*, 1830

A. Faure & J. Rancière (eds.) (1976) *La parole ouvrière, 1830–1851*, Paris: Union Générale d'Editions, pp. 214–19. Translation from French by Clive Emsley.

L'Artisan (The Artisan, Journal of the Working Class) was one of three newspapers founded, written and edited by workers in Paris around September 1830. This particular paper was founded by printing workers. These men had played a significant role in the beginning of the three-day Revolution of July 1830 that overthrew Charles X[1] and the restored Bourbon monarchy. They were rapidly disillusioned by the replacement – the 'bourgeois monarchy' of Louis Philippe.[2]

---

[1] Charles X (1757–1836) reigned from 1824 until 1830 when he abdicated rather than become a constitutional monarch.

[2] Louis Philippe (1773–1850) reigned from 1830 until the revolution of 1848. He was the last king of France.

The most numerous and the most useful class in society, without contradiction, is the working class. Without it capital has no value; without it there would be no machines, no industry, no commerce. All classes that rest on it, that profit from its work, know this well; it alone seems to ignore this or take no care of it. It lives in misery, enslaved by monopoly without seeing it, suffering all kinds of humiliation from those whose fortune it makes and, without astonishment, seeing itself comfortably decimated by the police.

[. . .]

Certain journalists shut inside their petty bourgeois aristocracy insist on seeing the working class only as machines to produce their needs alone. . . . But we are no longer in the times when workers were serfs and a master could sell or kill at his pleasure; we are no longer in the distant epoch when our class counted only in society as the arm of the social body. Three days have sufficed to change our function in the economy of society, and we are now the principal part of this society, the stomach, which spreads life into the superior classes, now restored to their true function as servants.

Cease then, oh noble bourgeois, from repulsing us from your heart, for we are also men and not machines. Our industry, which you have exploited for so long, belongs to us alone, and the illumination of instruction, the blood that we have shed for liberty have given us the means and the right to free ourselves from the servitude in which you hold us.

[. . .]

It is in vain that the middle class tries to repress the momentum of the working class towards the amelioration of its lot, the moment has come when every means of coercion can become fatal for those who would use it. Presiding over the emancipation of the workers, guiding their endeavours, these are the roles that this middle class, so proud and so tyrannical, should take.

[. . .]

But one of the most effective means to aid the work of the working classes, to improve their lot, will be to publish a special journal focussed on their needs and interests. Without such a tribune where they can expose their grievances and their complaints, how can workers make the government understand?

[. . .]

Who can raise this tribune for the working class, if not men taken from its bosom? We have had journals for the use of workers; but they spoke to us in a foreign language, since they were made by men who knew nothing of our needs.

5.16

The Communist Manifesto, 1848

K. Marx ([1850] 1973) 'The Manifesto of the Communist
Party', in *Political Writings,* vol. 1: *The Revolutions of 1848,*
ed. D. Fernbach, Harmondsworth: Penguin, pp. 67–77.[1]

The *Communist Manifesto* was written by Karl Marx (1818–83)
and Frederick Engels (1820–95). Marx was the university-
educated son of a Jewish lawyer practising in the Rhineland.
Engels was the son of a well-to-do Rhenish cotton manufacturer.
By the mid-1840s, both young men were active in radical politics.
The Communist Manifesto was written at the behest of the
Communist League, a secret organisation of German radicals
founded in Paris but based principally in London. Communism
(*Kommunismus*), at this time in German, was virtually
interchangeable with Socialism (*Sozialismus*). The aim of the
Manifesto was to spell out the League's principles based on the
'scientific socialism' that Marx and Engels espoused.

A spectre is haunting Europe – the spectre of Communism.

[. . .]

The history of all hitherto existing society is the history of class
struggles. Freeman and slave, patrician and plebeian, lord and serf,
guildmaster and journeyman, in a word, oppressor and oppressed,
stood in constant opposition to one another, carried on an uninterrupted, now hidden, now open fight, a fight that each time ended, either
in a revolutionary reconstitution of society at large, or in the common
ruin of the contending classes.

[. . .]

The modern bourgeois society that has sprouted from the ruins of
feudal society has not done away with class antagonisms. It has established new classes, new conditions of oppression, new forms of struggle in place of the old ones.

Our epoch, the epoch of the bourgeoisie, possesses, however, this
distinctive feature: it has simplified the class antagonisms. Society as

---

[1] *The Communist Manifesto* was published in English for the first time in 1850. This
translation was first published in 1888.

a whole is splitting up into two great hostile camps, into two great classes directly facing each other: bourgeoisie and proletariat.

From the serfs of the Middle Ages sprang the chartered burghers of the earliest towns. From these burgesses the first elements of the bourgeoisie were developed.

The discovery of America, the rounding of the Cape, opened up fresh ground for the rising bourgeoisie. The East Indian and Chinese markets, the colonization of America, trade with the colonies, the increase in the means of exchange and in commodities generally, gave to commerce, to navigation, to industry, an impulse never before known, and thereby, to the revolutionary element in the tottering feudal society, a rapid development.

The feudal system of industry, under which industrial production was monopolized by the closed guilds, now no longer sufficed for the growing wants of the new markets. The manufacturing system took its place.

[. . .]

Meantime the markets kept ever growing, the demand ever rising. Even manufacture no longer sufficed. Thereupon, steam and machinery revolutionized industrial production. The place of manufacture was taken by the giant modern industry, the place of the industrial middle class, by industrial millionaires, the leaders of whole industrial armies, the modern bourgeois.

[. . .]

The bourgeoisie, wherever it has got the upper hand, has put an end to all feudal, patriarchal, idyllic relations. It has pitilessly torn asunder the motley feudal ties that bound man to his 'natural superiors', and has left remaining no other nexus between man and man than naked self-interest, the callous 'cash payment'. It has drowned the most heavenly ecstasies of religious fervour, or chivalrous enthusiasm, of philistine sentimentalism, in the icy water of egotistical calculation. It has resolved personal worth into exchange value, and in place of the numberless indefeasible chartered freedoms, has set up that single unconscionable freedom – free trade. In one word, for exploitation, veiled by religious and political illusions, it has substituted naked, shameless, direct, brutal exploitation.

[. . .]

The bourgeoisie cannot exist without constantly revolutionizing the instruments of production, and thereby the relations of production, and with them the whole relations of society. Conservation of the old modes of production in unaltered form, was, on the contrary, the first condition of existence for all earlier industrial classes. Constant revolutionizing of production, uninterrupted disturbance of all social conditions, everlasting uncertainty and agitation distinguish the bourgeois epoch from all earlier ones. All fixed, fast-frozen relations, with their train of ancient and venerable prejudices and opinions, are swept away, all new-formed ones become antiquated before they can ossify. All that is solid melts into air, all that is holy is profaned, and man is at last compelled to face with sober senses, his real conditions of life, and his relations with his kind.

The need of a constantly expanding market for its products chases the bourgeoisie over the whole surface of the globe. It must nestle everywhere, settle everywhere, establish connections everywhere.

The bourgeoisie has through its exploitation of the world market given a cosmopolitan character to production and consumption in every country. To the great chagrin of reactionists, it has drawn from under the feet of industry the national ground on which it stood. All old-established national industries have been destroyed or are daily being destroyed. They are dislodged by new industries, whose introduction becomes a life and death question for all civilized nations, by industries that no longer work up indigenous raw material, but raw material drawn from the remotest zones; industries whose products are consumed, not only at home, but in every quarter of the globe. In place of the old wants, satisfied by the production of the country, we find new wants, requiring for their satisfaction the products of distant lands and climes. In place of the old local and national seclusion and self-sufficiency, we have intercourse in every direction, universal interdependence of nations. And as in materials, so also in intellectual production. The intellectual creations of individual nations become common property. National one-sidedness and narrow-mindedness become more and more impossible, and from the numerous national and local literatures, there arises a world literature.

[. . .]

The bourgeoisie keeps more and more doing away with the scattered state of the population, of the means of production, and of property. It has agglomerated population, centralized means of production, and has concentrated property in a few hands. The necessary consequence of this was political centralization. Independent, or but loosely connected, provinces with separate interests, laws, governments and systems of taxation, became lumped together into one nation, with one government, one code of laws, one national class-interest, one frontier and one customs-tariff.

In proportion as the bourgeoisie, i.e., capital, is developed, in the same proportion is the proletariat, the modern working class, developed – a class of labourers, who live only so long as they find work, and who find work only so long as their labour increases capital. These labourers, who must sell themselves piecemeal, are a commodity, like every other article of commerce, and are consequently exposed to all the vicissitudes of competition, to all the fluctuations of the market.

Owing to the extensive use of machinery and to division of labour, the work of the proletarians has lost all individual character, and, consequently, all charm for the workman. He becomes an appendage of the machine, and it is only the most simple, most monotonous, and most easily acquired knack, that is required of him. Hence, the cost of production of a workman is restricted, almost entirely to the means of subsistence that he requires for his maintenance, and for the propagation of his race. But the price of a commodity, and therefore also of labour, is equal to its cost of production. In proportion, therefore, as the repulsiveness of the work increases, the wage decreases. Nay more, in proportion as the use of machinery and division of labour increases, in the same proportion the burden of toil also increases, whether by prolongation of the working hours, by increase of the work exacted in a given time or by increased speed of the machinery, etc.

[. . .]

No sooner is the exploitation of the labourer by the manufacturer so far at an end that he receives his wages in cash, than he is set upon by the other portions of the bourgeoisie, the landlord, the shopkeeper, the pawnbroker, etc.

The lower strata of the middle class – the small tradespeople, shopkeepers and *rentiers* [persons making a living from rental property], the handcraftsmen and peasants – all these sink gradually into the proletariat, partly because their diminutive capital does not suffice for the scale on which modern industry is carried on, and is swamped in the competition with the large capitalists, partly because their specialized skill is rendered worthless by new methods of production. Thus the proletariat is recruited from all classes of the population.

The proletariat goes through various stages of development. With its birth begins its struggle with the bourgeoisie.

[. . .]

At this stage the labourers still form an incoherent mass scattered over the whole country, and broken up by their mutual competition. If anywhere they unite to form more compact bodies, this is not yet the consequence of their own active union, but of the union of the bourgeoisie, which class, in order to attain its own political ends, is compelled to set the whole proletariat in motion, and is moreover yet, for a time, able to do so. At this stage, therefore, the proletarians do not fight their enemies, but the enemies of their enemies, the remnants of absolute monarchy, the landowners, the non-industrial bourgeois, the petty bourgeoisie. Thus the whole historical movement is concentrated in the hands of the bourgeoisie; every victory so obtained is a victory for the bourgeoisie.

But with the development of industry the proletariat not only increases in number; it becomes concentrated in greater masses, its strength grows, and it feels that strength more. . . .

Of all the classes that stand face to face with the bourgeoisie today, the proletariat alone is a really revolutionary class. The other classes decay and finally disappear in the face of modern industry; the proletariat is its special and essential product.

[. . .]

In the conditions of the proletariat, those of old society at large are already virtually swamped. The proletarian is without property; his relation to his wife and children has no longer anything in common with the bourgeois family relations; modern industrial labour, modern subjection to capital, the same in England as in France, in America as in Germany, has stripped him of every trace of national character. Law, morality, religion, are to him so many bourgeois prejudices, behind which lurk in ambush just as many bourgeois interests.

[. . .] Though not in substance, yet in form, the struggle of the proletariat with the bourgeoisie is at first a national struggle. The proletariat of each country must, of course, first of all settle matters with its own bourgeoisie.

[. . .] What the bourgeoisie, therefore, produces, above all, is its own grave-diggers. Its fall and the victory of the proletariat are equally inevitable.

5.17
Decrees of the French provisional government, 25 February 1848

R.W. Postgate (ed.) (1962) *Revolution, from 1789 to 1906*, New York: Harper Torchbooks, p. 191.

Revolutionary action in Paris from 22 to 24 February 1848 brought about the abdication of the king, Louis Philippe, and the creation of a provisional government. The three following decrees were written by a socialist journalist, Louis Blanc (1811–82). In 1839, Blanc had published *L' organisation du travail (The Organisation of Work)* that was highly critical of the idea of competition and that urged *à chacun selon ses besoins, de chacun selon ses facultés* ('to each according to his needs; from each according to his abilities'). In February 1848, he became a member of the Provisional Government. That government found itself under pressure from the Parisian workers and charged Blanc with writing a decree that would guarantee 'the right to work'.

(a) The right to work

The Government of the French Republic pledges itself to guarantee the livelihood of the worker by labour;

It pledges itself to guarantee work for all citizens;

It recognises that the workers should form associations among themselves to enjoy the legitimate profit of their labour;

The Provisional Government returns to workers, to whom it belongs, the Million [francs] which falls into its hands from the Civil List.

(b) Goods pawned

The Provisional Government of the French Republic decrees:

The objects in pawn at the *Mont de Piété*[1] since 1 February, consisting of linen, garments, clothes, etc., in the value of less than ten francs, shall be returned to the depositors. The Minister of Finance is instructed to provide for the expense thus incurred.

(c) Injured workers

The Provisional Government of the French Republic decrees:

Henceforth the Tuileries [Palace] will serve as a hospital for workers injured in industry.

(d) National workshops

The Provisional Government decrees the immediate establishment of national workshops.

---

[1] Name given to state pawnshops.

The Minister of Public Works is entrusted with the execution of this decree.

5.18

Manifesto of the Delegates of the Corporations (Seated at the Luxembourg) to the Workers of the Department of the Seine, 8 June 1848

A. Faure & J. Rancière (eds.) (1976) *La parole ouvrière, 1830–1851*, Paris: Union Générale d'Editions, pp. 303, 305–6. Translation from French by Clive Emsley.

This Manifesto was produced by elected representatives of the Luxembourg Commission, appointed by the Provisional Government to investigate the problems of labour and propose solutions for a new National Assembly. It was so-called because it met in the Luxembourg Palace in Paris, the former seat of the Chamber of Peers under the July Monarchy.

[. . .] Our aim, brothers, is the emancipation of the proletariat, the achievement of our social rights . . .

The people, this multitude of producers for whom misery is the appanage, the people has existed until today only to procure for its exploiters those enjoyments that it, the pariah of society, has never known.

Yes, it is by its labour that the people makes the bourgeois, the proprietors, the capitalists; yes, it is the people that makes all the happy individuals on earth.

The State, in other words the men that govern the people, only exists because of the taxes paid by everyone, taxes, the evident source of which, is the producer.

Suppress the producer, and with a single blow you will obliterate the bourgeois, the proprietors, the capitalists, and you will drive the state to bankruptcy.

Thus the State is the people, it is the producer.

[. . .]

No more intermediaries between the people and the government!

The people, without more ado, should organise itself! Is it not sovereign, the producer of all riches?

5.19

Peasants in the mid-nineteenth century

Peasants were commonly illiterate and the historian is dependent on what others wrote about them to seek to assess their ideas, beliefs and behaviour. The following documents range widely across peasant Europe to give an idea of these issues. They show peasant violence in Italy during the Revolution of 1848 in extract (a), and what looks like a relatively peaceful end to feudal authority in one of the German states in extract (b) – again during the 1848 upheavals. The Russian documents, extracts (d) and (e), reveal concerns about the peasantry and what it was thinking, and provide an argument in favour of emancipation. The comments by a British traveller in Hungary, extract (c), echo the latter – but does this demonstrate the commentator's commitment to the new gospel of work rather than any seriously humanitarian perspective?

(a) Riots at Venosa in Basilicata, 23–25 April 1848

A. Basile (1962) 'Moti sociali in Basilicata nel 1848', *Archivio storico di Calabria e Lucania*, vol. 31, pp. 444–5.
Translation from Italian by Tim Benton.

In the city of Venosa on the morning of last Easter Sunday, the 23rd, a large number of people presented themselves to the mayor asking for the distribution of certain demesne lands, which were said to have been usurped by certain landowners. The mayor, in order to calm down the popular excitement, gave good assurances, promising everyone that their wishes would be fulfilled. Despite this the mob did not disperse but continued to make a disturbance throughout the day. That evening toward midnight they presented themselves at the palace of Don Carlo Buccino, one of the owners of the land that they wanted to redistribute, and in a fury threw stones at the windows, breaking several; and a certain Nicola Tamburrino let off a gun shot which caused no damage at all.

359

On the next day, the 24th, there was much ferment for the same reason, and accordingly Signor Buccino, to escape the tempest which menaced him, took the people to one of his properties, called Boreano, on the morning of the next day, Tuesday the 25th, where there were portions of the land being claimed, and by showing himself ready to cede them made the multitude believe that it could be admitted to possession of the property.

The mob was satisfied by this act of generosity and took Signor Buccino back in triumph to Venosa to the sound of the drum. They happened to pass by the house of the doctor, Don Giuseppe Gasparrini, and it happened that he, presenting himself at the window, was unwise enough to disapprove of the work of Signor Buccino and said at the top of his voice how ill-advised he had been to placate that rabble. This insult so maddened the people that they quickly broke down the door to enter the house and take revenge on the imprudent doctor who had brought it on himself. Then he, wishing to intimidate the tumultuous mob, fired several gun shots at them, wounding one of the people in the thigh. At this development the deputy [*supplente*] arrived who, due to the illness of the judge, was deputy in charge; anxious to save Signor Gasparrini from the popular fury, he suggested to him to give in and be arrested. But he instead, condemned by his act, had taken the decision to flee by a secret door. However as he crossed the square he was discovered by the rioters and with blows from axes and other lethal weapons, was cruelly killed. After the spilling of this citizen's blood the crowd became more daring and took over the power of the public authority, stopping any person from entering or leaving Venosa.

(b) Demands of a peasant deputation in the German Grand Duchy of Hesse, 1848

K. Obermann (1970) (ed.) *Flugblätter der Revolution. Eine Flugblättsammlung zur Geschichte der Revolution von 1848/49 in Deutschland,* Berlin: Deutscher Verlag der Wissenschaften, pp. 75–6. Translated from German by John Breuilly.

Demands put to the *Standesherrn*[1] of the district of Breuberg (Grand Duchy of Hesse).

[1] *Standesherrn.* Princes who, in 1806, were placed under the sovereignty of other princes, but had special legal rights which distinguished them from the rest of the nobility.

(a) Abolition of all privileges, whatever their name, such as rights of presentation to legal, church, school or communal office.

(b) Ending of all rights of hunting and pasture on other people's property.

(c) Ending of fishing rights.

(d) Freedom from all feudal burdens, tithes, ground rents . . .

(e) Ending of monopoly of milling and all other economic monopolies whatsoever.

(f) Ending of all inheritance payments.[2]

(g) Abolition of the lien of lordship, and equal rights for all citizens in taking legal action.

(h) Return of all land in wrongful ownership, concerning which no property titles of the *Standesherrn* can be produced without application of the rights of limitation and donation.

(i) Privileges of the *Standesherrn* which have not been included in those above recommended for abolition shall be treated in the same way.

(j) Freedom from all obligations imposed by church and monastic funds of any sort.

(k) Freeing the community of all debts contracted to redeem such burdens.

(l) The forests, capital, and such-like property of the monastery Hochst shall be divided up amongst those communities with a rightful claim.

(m) Judgements in disputes over property and compensation in the future will be left to committees elected by majority vote.

(n) An end to all trials pending, and surrender of claims upon all rent-, interest-, fine-, and tithe-payments in arrears.

(o) Concessions of the *Standesherrn* to these demands cannot be retracted.

(p) Having carefully considered them, the *Standesherrnschaft* freely concede the above demands.

(q) For any disadvantages, pecuniary or official, affecting individuals or whole communities, which occur as a result of carrying out these demands, there is a responsibility of one for all, and all for one.

---

[2] Peasants had to pay a sum of money to the lord when land was passed on by inheritance.

In the situation as described to me by the deputation which has appeared here I concede and permit all the demands (a) to (q), for all those who wish to avail themselves of this permission.

Schönberg, 10 March 1848 LUDWIG GRAF ZE ERLACH

(c) Commentary on the condition of the Hungarian peasantry

J. Paget (1839) *Hungary and Transylvania, with remarks on their condition, social, political and economical*, London: J. Murray, 2 vols., vol. 1, pp. 298–300, 305–7, 316.

. . . The holder of an entire fief was bound to labour for his landlord, in every year, one hundred and four days, or, if he brought a team of oxen or horses, fifty-two, from sun-rise to sun-set . . . Of all the productions of the soil, one ninth belonged to the landlord . . . of cattle, lambs and kids, a ninth was also the lord's due. The Manor Court, in which the Lord or his representatives appointed the judges, was declared the legal tribunal for the settlement of differences between the peasant and his lord, as well as those that might arise among the peasants themselves.

. . . I believe that many of these laws have an injurious effect on the peasantry. The system of rent by *robot* or forced labour – that is, so many days' labour without any specification of the quantity of work to be performed – is a direct premium on idleness. A landlord wishes a field of corn to be cut; his steward sends out, by means of his Haiduks,[1] information to the peasants to meet at such a field at such an hour with their sickles. Some time after the hour appointed a great part of them arrive, the rest finding some excuse by which they hope to escape a day's work; while others send their children or their wives, declaring some reason for their own absence. After much arranging they at last get to work; a Haiduk stands over them to see that they do not go to sleep, and between talking, laughing, and resting, they do get something done. Where horses are employed, they are still less inclined to hurry; lest they should tire them for the next day, when they use them for their own purposes.

Now how much does the reader suppose such workmen perform in one day? Count S__says, just one-third of what the same men can

---

[1] A village officer, appointed by the landowner.

do easily when working by the piece; and he has accordingly compounded his peasants' one hundred and four days' robot for a certain amount of labour, which they generally get through in about thirty-four days.

Another evil of the robot is the ill-will it begets between the masters and the workmen: their whole lives seem to be a constant effort, on the one hand, to see how much can be pressed out of the reluctant peasant; and, on the other, how little can be done to satisfy the terms of agreement, and escape punishment. Mutual injury becomes a mutual profit; suspicion and ill-will are the natural results.

Let the nobles gradually yield the vexatious rights of seigneury, which bring little profit to them, but do much injury to others; let them enable the peasant to purchase his freedom from service; grant him independent justice; as he acquires property, let him acquire consideration and rights; leave men and things to act as circumstances show to be best, untrammelled by restrictions, unaided by privilege; and the peasant of Hungary will soon occupy a position which may justly be envied by his fellows of any other part of Europe.

(d) Secret Memorandum by Andrei Zablotskii-Desyatovskii, Assistant Minister, to the Minister of State Domains, Count Paul Kiselev, Russia, 1841

D. Moon (2002) *The Abolition of Serfdom in Russia,*
1762–1907, London: Longman, p. 141.

[Following a survey of relations between noble estate owners and the peasants on their land in central Russia, Zablotskii-Desyatovskii concluded 'serf labour is less productive than freely-hired' labour]. This conviction is shared by the peasants, who have created a saying about a lazy labourer: 'you are working as if for the estate owner', and by the estate owners themselves. 'There is no doubt', Titov, the marshal of the nobility of Zaraisk [district, Ryazan province] told us, 'that free labour is better. It is wrong to think that our peasant, once free, will become even lazier. It is not true! A free person knows that without work there will be nothing to eat, and that is why he will work diligently. Here is my own experience: 20 *versty* [about 12 miles] from my Zimenki (the estate we were visiting) I own unsettled land, which is cultivated by my own peasants, but not as labour services, but for hire on the basis of voluntary agreement. The same peasants who idle while working labour services, are uncommonly diligent there, [they are] prepared to work on a holiday, as long as they are not driven to, and they take care of the place so [well], that they are even afraid to anger the elder.'

(e) Annual Report of the Chief of Third Section (the Secret Police) to Nicholas I for 1839

D. Moon (2002) *The Abolition of Serfdom in Russia, 1762–1907*, London: Longman, pp. 139–41.

With every new reign and with every major event in the court or in the affairs of the state . . . news spreads around the common people of an impending change in the internal administration, and the idea of freedom for the peasants is aroused; as a consequence of this, disorders, murmurs and dissatisfaction occur, and [in fact] took place last year. [Such events] pose a danger that, although distant, is terrible. Thus, on the occasion of the wedding of the Grand Duchess Maria Nikolaevna [daughter of Tsar Nicholas I (reigned 1825–55)], news has spread that the peasants will be freed. The rumours are always the same: the tsar wants it [freedom for the peasants], but the boyars are resisting. This is a dangerous matter, and to conceal this danger would be a crime. The simple people now are not as they were 25 years ago. Clerks, thousands of petty officials, merchants and retired soldiers, who have a common interest with the people, have spread many new ideas to them, and have blown a spark into their heart which may one day flare up.

The people constantly talk about how all the non-Russians in Russia . . . are free, but only the Russians, the Orthodox, are unfree, in spite of the Holy Scripture. That the cause of this whole evil is the masters, i.e., the nobles! On them is heaped the whole misfortune! That the masters deceive the tsar and slander the Orthodox people in his presence etc. They even bring in texts from the Holy Scripture and prophesies based on interpretations of the Bible that foreshadow the emancipation of the peasants, [and] vengeance on the boyars, whom they compare with Aman and Pharaoh. In general, the whole spirit of the people is directed towards one aim, towards freedom, and meanwhile, in all parts of Russia, there are idle people, who stir up this idea, and in recent years the persecution of the Old Believers has turned them against the government so that their retreats have become centres of this evil. . . . In general serfdom is a powder keg beneath the state, and it is all the more dangerous because the army is made up of these same peasants, and that now a large mass of landless nobles has emerged from officials who are inflamed with ambition and, having nothing to lose, welcome any disorder. The reforms of the appanage peasants [peasants on the estates of members of the imperial family] and the protection that has been granted them have had the effect of arousing even greater loathing for serfdom. In this regard, soldiers released on indefinite leave draw attention to themselves. The best of them remain in the capital cities and towns, while men who are lazy or of bad behaviour have dispersed around the villages. Having lost the habit of peasant labour, without any property, [and] alien to their home villages, they provoke hatred against the landowners with their tales of Poland, the Baltic provinces and, in general, could have a harmful influence on the mind of the people. The best of the soldiers on indefinite leave will not be able to counteract this harmful influence, because opinions which stir up passions are readily accepted.

[. . .]

The opinion of sensible people is that, without announcing freedom for the peasants, which could lead to disorders by its suddenness, it would be possible to start to act in this spirit. Now the serfs are not even considered members of the state, and do not even swear allegiance to the sovereign. They stand outside the law, for the landowner can banish them to Siberia without trial. It would be possible to start by ratifying by law all the arrangements that already exist on well organised estates. This would not be anything new. Thus, for example, it would be possible to establish township administrations, selection of recruits by lot or by a general court of township elders, and not according to the whim of landowners. It would be possible to determine measures of punishment for faults and subject serfs to the protection of general laws; and most importantly of all, to divide Russia into zones, according to the quality of the soil, the climate and the state of industry . . . and then set the number of working days for the master according to the land occupied by the peasants, and set dues in the same way.

It is necessary to start some time and with something, and it is better to start gradually, carefully, than to wait until it starts from below, from the people. A measure [of reform] will be successful only if it is undertaken by the government itself, quietly, without noise, without loud words, and if a prudent gradual approach is followed. But, that it is necessary and that the peasantry is a powder keg, is agreed by all.

5.20
Letter by Richard Oastler to the *Leeds Mercury*, 1830

Leeds Mercury, 16 October 1830.

Richard Oastler (1789–1861) was the steward of an estate on the outskirts of Huddersfield in the West Riding of Yorkshire. He was a Tory and a social reformer. He opposed universal suffrage and the New Poor Law, but supported the Established Church (to the extent of opposing Catholic emancipation) and the existing social order.

Let truth speak out . . . Thousands of our fellow creatures and fellow subjects both male and female, the miserable inhabitants of a Yorkshire town (Yorkshire now represented in this parliament by the giant of anti-slavery principles) are at this very moment existing in a state of slavery, *more horrid* than are the victims of that hellish system *'colonial slavery'*. These innocent creatures drawl out, unpitied their short but miserable existence, in a place famed for its profession of religious zeal, whose inhabitants are ever foremost in professing 'temperance' and 'reformation' and are striving to outrun their neighbours in missionary exertions, and would fain send the Bible to the farthest corner of the globe – aye in the very place where the anti-slavery fever rages her charity is not more admired on earth. [. . .] The very streets which receive the droppings of the 'Anti-Slavery Society' are every morning wet with the tears of victims at the accursed shrine of avarice, who are *compelled* (not by the cart-whip of the negro slave-driver) but by the dread of the equally appalling thong or strap of the over-looker, to hasten half-dressed *but not half fed*, to those magazines of British infantile slavery – *the worsted mills in the town and neighbourhood of Bradford!!!*

[. . .]

Thousands of little children, both male and female, *but principally female*, from seven to fourteen years of age, are daily *compelled to labour* from six o'clock in the morning to seven in the evening, with only – Britons, blush while you read it! – *with only thirty minutes allowed for eating and recreation*. Poor infants! Ye are indeed sacrificed at the shrine of avarice, *without even the solace of the negro slave*. . . . He knows it is his sordid, mercenary master's interest that he should *live*, be *strong* and *healthy*. Not so with you. Ye are doomed to labour from morning to night for one who cares not how soon your weak and tender frames are stretched to breaking! . . . When your joints can act no longer, your emaciated frames are cast aside, the boards on which you lately toiled and wasted life away, are instantly supplied with other victims, who in this boasted land of liberty are HIRED – not sold – as slaves and daily forced to hear that they are free.

5.21
Ernest Renan's 'Qu'est-ce qu'une Nation?' [What is a Nation?]

E. Renan (1996) 'Qu'est ce qu'une nation / What is a nation?',
introd. C. Taylor; trans. W.R. Taylor, Toronto:
Tapir Press, pp. 21–49. Section and paragraph
numbers added.

Although a noted theologian, the name of Ernest Renan (1823–92) is now routinely associated with the title of a famous lecture delivered at the Sorbonne on 11 March 1882 – Qu'est-ce qu'une Nation? [What is a Nation?]. Reprinted countless times, this essay was written in the wake of the Franco-Prussian war, as the tensions and contradictions between the concept and reality of nationalist doctrine were becoming clear in the light of ongoing territorial disputes over the annexation of Alsace and Lorraine.

1. The modern nation is therefore the historic consequence of a series of convergent facts. Sometimes, unity was brought about by a dynasty, as was the case with France; sometimes by the direct will of provinces, as with Holland, Switzerland, Belgium; sometimes by a general consciousness, the belated conqueror of the vagaries of feudalism, as with Italy and Germany.

[. . .]

It is to France's glory to have proclaimed, through the French Revolution, that a nation exists of itself. We should not take it ill that others imitate us. The principle of nations is ours. But what then is a

Why . indeed

Why ?

nation? Why is Holland a nation, when Hanover or the Grand Duchy of Parma are not? How does France continue to be a nation, when the principle that created it has disappeared? How is it that Switzerland, with three languages, two religions and three or four races, is a nation, when a homogeneous region such as Tuscany, for instance, is not? Why is the Austrian Empire a state and not a nation? In what way does the principle of nationality differ from the principle of race? These are all questions that thoughtful people, for their own peace of mind, would wish to answer. The affairs of the world are rarely resolved by such argumentation. But diligent minds wish to bring reason to bear on these matters, to disentangle the confusion in which superficial minds are easily ensnared.

2. Certain political theorists would have us believe that a nation is above all a dynasty, the embodiment of a former conquest, first accepted and then forgotten by the masses. [. . .] It is quite true that most modern nations were made by families of feudal origin, who contracted marriages with the soil and provided some sort of central-izing nucleus. [. . .] Is such a law absolute, however? Undoubtedly not. Switzerland and the United States, formed as conglomerates, through successive additions, have no dynastic basis. [. . .] It must be admitted therefore that a nation can exist without a dynastic principle, and even that nations formed by dynasties can be separated from them without thereby ceasing to exist. The old principle that takes into account only the right of princes is no longer sustainable. Aside from the right of dynasties, there is also the right of nations. Upon what criterion should this national right be based? By what sign should it be known? From what tangible fact does it derive?

i. From one's race, many confidently reply. [. . .] This is what constitutes a right, a legitimate title. According to this theory, the German race, for instance, has the right to reclaim the scattered members of its family, even if these members do not ask to be reclaimed. [. . .] In the tribes and cities of antiquity, the fact of race was, we acknowledge, of absolute primacy. [. . .] However, the Roman Empire . . . this vast agglomerate of entirely different towns and prov-inces dealt the notion of race the gravest of blows. Christianity, in its capacity as universal and absolute, worked even more effectively to the same end. In intimate alliance, these two incomparable agents of unification eliminated the ethnographic principle from the govern-ment of human affairs for centuries. [. . .] The truth is that there is no such thing as a pure race and that to found politics on ethnographic analysis is to base it on a chimera. The most noble countries, England,

France and Italy are those whose blood is most mixed. Is Germany an exception to this rule? Is it a purely Germanic country? What an illusion!

[. . .]

3.   ii. What we have just said about race should also be said of language. Language invites unity, without, however, compelling it. The United States and England, Latin America and Spain share the same languages, but do not form single nations. Conversely, Switzerland, so solid because based on the consent of its various parties, has three or four languages [. . .] To France's honour, it never sought to obtain linguistic unity through coercive measures. Can we not have the same sentiments, the same thoughts and love the same things in different languages?

[. . .]

iii. Religion can no more offer a sufficient basis for the constitution of modern nationality than can language or race. In its origins, religion stemmed from the very existence of the social group, itself an extension of the family. [. . .] In our day, the situation is perfectly clear. There are no longer masses of people uniformly professing a single belief. Each believes and practises in his or her own way, as he or she can and wishes. There is no longer a state religion. [. . .] We no longer divide nations into Catholic and Protestant.

[. . .]

iv. Common interests are surely powerful bonds between human beings. But do interests suffice in creating a nation? I do not believe so. Common interests bring about trade agreements. But nationality is also partly a matter of conscious feeling; it is simultaneously body and soul; a customs union is not a homeland.

4.   v. Geography, or what we term natural frontiers, has certainly played a considerable part in the division of nations. [. . .] Can we say, however, as some do, that the borders of a nation are inscribed on the map and that this nation has the right to seize what is necessary to round off certain contours, to reach a particular mountain, a particular river, which landmarks are thereby granted a kind of *a priori* limiting power? I know of no doctrine more arbitrary nor more grievous. [. . .] A nation is a spiritual principle, originating in the profound complexities of history; it is a spiritual family, not a group determined by the configuration of the soil.

We have now examined those things that do not suffice to create this spiritual principle. They are race, language, common interests, religious affinity, geography, military necessity. What more is then required?

[. . .]

A nation is a soul, a spiritual principle. Two things, which in truth are but one, constitute this soul or spiritual principle. One lies in the past, one in the present. One is the possession in common of a rich legacy of memories; the other is present-day consent, the desire to live together, the will to perpetuate the value of the heritage that one has received in an undivided form. Human beings, I tell you, are not made overnight. The nation, like the individual, is the culmination of a long past of endeavours, sacrifice, and devotion. Of all cults, that of the ancestors is the most legitimate, for our ancestors have made us what we are. A heroic past, great men, glory (by which I understand genuine glory), this is the social capital upon which one bases a national idea. To have common glories in the past and to have a common will in the present; to have performed great deeds together, to wish to perform still more – these are the essential conditions for being a people. We love in proportion to the sacrifices to which we have consented, and in proportion to the ills we have suffered. We love the house we have built and handed down. The Spartan song – 'We are what you were; we will be what you are' – is, in its simplicity, the abridged hymn of every *patrie.*

5. More valuable by far than common customs posts and frontiers conforming to strategic interests is the fact of sharing, in the past, a glorious heritage and regrets, and of having, in the future, a shared plan of action, or the fact of having suffered, enjoyed, and hoped together. These are the kinds of things that can be understood in spite of differences of race and language. I spoke just now of 'having suffered together' and, indeed, suffering in common unifies more than joy does. Where national memories are concerned, griefs are of more value than triumphs, for they impose duties, and require a common effort.

A nation is therefore a vast solidarity, constituted by the feeling of the sacrifices that one has made in the past and of those that one is prepared to make in the future. It presupposes a past; it is summarized, however, in the present by a tangible fact, namely, consent, the clearly expressed desire to pursue a common life. A nation's existence is, if you will pardon the metaphor, a daily plebiscite, just as an individual's existence is a perpetual affirmation of life.

5.22
French ministerial circular, 14 August 1925

C. Hayes (1930) *France – A Nation of Patriots*, New York:
Columbia University Press, pp. 311–12.

This circular was written by the Minister of Public Instruction,
Anatole de Monzie (1876–1947) in response to a petition from a
number of dignitaries from Provence (a region in the south of
France), requesting that primary school teachers should be able
to teach in the Provençal dialect, rather than in French. The petition, and the resulting circular, produced an extensive discussion
of the subject in the French press.

Since the time when Francis I effected in 1539 the monarchy of letters
by ordering that all pieces of justice and administration should be
written in French, all our Governments have professed a common
and constant doctrine of linguistic unification. 'As it is of importance
to accustom the peoples of ceded provinces to our manners and
usages, there is nothing which can contribute more thereto than the
assurance that children learn the French language, in order that they
may be as familiar with it as with German and that in the course of
time the inhabitants of the provinces may even abandon the use of the
latter and at any rate have a preference for French'. This policy, defined
in a letter of Colbert[1] to his brother, March 12, 1666, has always been
ours, not only in respect of the Alsatian population,[2] but also in respect
of all French subjects in the interior of the country. Indeed . . . the text
of 5 Brumaire, Year II, [26 October 1793] stated: 'public instruction is
directed so that one of its primary benefits will be that the French
language shall become in a short time the family language of all parts
of the Republic. In all parts of the Republic, instruction should be only
in the French language. Neither class in Latin, nor school in dialect:
unification through public instruction in French'. In spite of the vicissitudes which public instruction experienced under the Directory and
the Consulate, the essentials of those Revolutionary prescriptions
were reaffirmed in the instructions issued by Napoleon to his prefects

---

[1] Jean-Baptiste Colbert (1619–83), the powerful minister of finance under Louis XIV.
[2] People of Alsace in north-eastern France, a border region disputed over between
France and Germany.

and bishops. The investigation of dialects which he carried on from 1806 to 1812 redounded to the advantage of the single official language. The same continuity of linguistic policy has been reaffirmed during the years of Republic secularization: M. Fallières,[3] by a circular of October 30, 1890 and M. Waldeck-Rousseau,[4] by a dispatch of January 26, 1901, prohibited the employment of dialects in sermons and in catechism-lessons. On January 16, 1903, by 339 votes against 185, the Chamber of Deputies approved the action of M. Emile Combes,[5] President of the Council and Minister of Worship, in having renewed those prohibitions – and after a prolonged debate in the course of which the Prime Minister had reaffirmed the continuous and traditional doctrine the history of which I have too rapidly sketched.

I attach my instructions to this doctrine. [. . .] I may observe, furthermore, that there remain too many illiterates among us to allow us to distract, in favour of the most respectable local or regional tongues, any portion of the effort necessary for the propagation of good French. 'He alone is truly French in heart, from head to foot, who knows, speaks, and reads the French language'. Until this definition . . . is applicable to the totality of adult citizens, instructions in the dialects must be deemed a luxury, and I beg you to believe that our era is scarcely favourable to expenditures for luxury at the cost of collectivity.

5.23

Materials for the Philosophy of the History of Mankind, 1784

Internet Modern History Sourcebook – http://www.fordham.
edu/halsall/mod/modsbook.html

In this work, Johann Gottfried von Herder (1744–1803) laid the intellectual foundations for the claims of romantic philosophy that the nation was a fundamental part of human nature. Although

---

[3] C. Armand Fallières (1841–1931) was a representative of Lot-and-Garonne in 1890 but eventually President of the Republic between 1906 and 1913.

[4] René Waldeck-Rousseau (1846–1904) was prime minister from 1898–1901.

[5] Emile Combes (1835–1921) was prime minister between 1902–5.

his theories were soon picked up by German political activists, he was inspired to consider these issues because, as a resident of a German city in Latvia (many cities of Eastern Europe were German speaking, even as the local rural population spoke a Slavic or Baltic language), he reflected on the value of local Lettish culture, and the problems of its suppression by international cosmopolitan culture.

Nature has sketched with mountain ranges which she fashioned and with streams which she caused to flow from them the rough but substantial outline of the whole history of man . . . One height produced nations of hunters, thus supporting and rendering necessary a savage state; another, more extended and mild, afforded a field to shepherd peoples and supplied them with tame animals; a third made agriculture easy and needful; while a fourth led to fishing and navigation and at length to trade. The structure of the earth, in its natural variety and diversity, rendered all such distinguishing conditions inescapable. [. . .] Seas, mountain ranges and rivers are the most natural boundaries not only of lands but also of peoples, customs, languages and empires, and they have been, even in the greatest revolutions in human affairs, the directing lines or limits of world history. If otherwise mountains had arisen, rivers flowed, or coasts trended, then how very different would mankind have scattered over this tilting place of nations.

[. . .]

Nature brings forth families; the most natural state therefore is also one people, with a national character of its own. For thousands of years this character preserves itself within the people and, if the native princes concern themselves with it, it can be cultivated in the most natural way: for a people is as much a plant of nature as is a family, except that it has more branches. Nothing therefore seems more contradictory to the true end of governments than the endless expansion of states, the wild confusion of races and nations under one sceptre. An empire made up of a hundred peoples and a 120 provinces which have been forced together is a monstrosity, not a state-body.

[. . .]

Has a people anything dearer than the speech of its fathers? In its speech resides its whole thought-domain, its tradition, history, religion, and basis of life, all its heart and soul. To deprive a people of its speech is to deprive it of its one eternal good. [. . .] As God tolerates all the different languages in the world, so also should a ruler not only

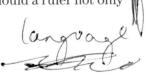

tolerate but honour the various languages of his peoples. [. . .] The best culture of a people cannot be expressed through a foreign language; it thrives on the soil of a nation most beautifully, and, I may say, it thrives only by means of the nation's inherited and inheritable dialect. With language is created the heart of a people; and is it not a high concern, amongst so many peoples – Hungarians, Slavs, Rumanians, etc. – to plant seeds of well-being for the far future and in the way that is dearest and most appropriate to them?

[. . .]

The savage who loves himself, his wife, and his child with quiet joy and glows with limited activity for his tribe as for his own life is, it seems to me, a more genuine being than that cultured shade who is enchanted by the shadow of his whole species. . . . In his poor hut, the former finds room for every stranger, receives him as a brother with impartial good humour and never asks whence he came. The inundated heart of the idle cosmopolitan is a home for no one.

[. . .]

No greater injury can be inflicted on a nation than to be robbed of her national character, the peculiarity of her spirit and her language. Reflect on this and you will perceive our irreparable loss. Look about you in Germany for the character of the nation, for their own particular cast of thought, for their own peculiar vein of speech; where are they?

5.24

Extracts from a range of Third Republic primary and secondary school textbooks

C. Hayes (1930) *France – A Nation of Patriots*, New York: Columbia University Press, pp. 343, 354–5, 392.

During the early 1880s the French Third Republic abolished all fees and tuition charges in public primary schools and required all French children to attend school between the ages of 6 and 13. These extracts give a flavour of the patriotic nature of many of the publications used for teaching during the period between 1880 and 1920.

(a) For use of children aged 6–7 during their 'preparatory' year in primary school

France has not always been as educated, as rich, and as prosperous as to-day. She was formed slowly, she has grown little by little, and she has ended by becoming one of the greatest states in the world. In studying history you will learn to know all those who have made the French fatherland: the generals who have won battles, the men who have governed our country, the writers and artists who have immortalized the genius of our race. You will see that if France is powerful and respected it is because she has never despaired after the most trying experiences. The glory of France has been slowly and dearly acquired: you have the right to be proud of it, but you have the duty to be worthy of it. And that is why you should learn none too soon, by examples of history, to acquire love of work and devotion to the fatherland.

(b) For use with children aged 9–11 during primary schooling

In civilized humanity, the French nation is the only one which strives to give an example of a society aspiring to govern itself by reason, only by reason, without invoking the aid of a superhuman authority. The French have the duty of defending France by arms, if, unfortunately, foreigners make war on us [. . .] We must love ourselves and aid each other and let every individual live not only for himself, but for France, for the nation, for the Republic. That is what we mean by patriotism.

The *role* of France in the world, as the French Revolution has defined it, is to proclaim the right of people to govern themselves, to give the example of fraternity among peoples by the pacific diffusion of the *principles of 1789* [. . .] There is the *historic rôle*, the true grandeur of France among all the nations. Therefore, let us love France and let us not hate other nations.

(c) For use in the first years of secondary schools

Without denying the political and commercial role of England and the philosophical role of Germany, we must recognize that France has occupied a great place in the history of this century. She has had the glory of seeking to realize the ideas of humanity, liberty and justice preached by the philosophy of the eighteenth century. With the armies of the Republic, even with the conquering armies of Napoleon, it is French ideas which have spread everywhere.

[. . .] The civilizing mission of France is not achieved. She has not yet succeeded in effecting the complete triumph in Europe of the idea of justice which she carries within herself. Outside of Europe she has painfully reconstructed a colonial empire, in which now lives a population greater than ours. These peoples she has the duty of governing with mildness and equity, of transmitting progressively to them her ideas. After having been the preceptress of Europe, it remains to her, for her part, to teach the world.

5.25

David Hume, 'Of National Characters'

L.L. Snyder (ed.) (1964) *The Dynamics of Nationalism,*
New York: Van Nostrand, pp. 56–8.

The Scottish philosopher and historian, David Hume (1711–76), an innovator in the history of modern metaphysical thinking, pondered the question of national character just prior to the rapid changes of the Industrial Revolution. In his *Essays and Treatises on Several Subjects* (1753), Hume wrote the following passage.

The vulgar are apt to carry all *national characters* to extremes; and having once established it as a principle, that any people are knavish, or cowardly, or ignorant, they will admit of no exception, but comprehend every individual under the same censure. Men of sense condemn these undistinguishing judgments: Though at the same time, they allow, that each nation has a peculiar set of manners, and that some particular qualities are more frequently to be met with among one people than among their neighbours. The common people in Switzerland have probably more honesty than those of the same rank in Ireland; and every prudent man will, from that circumstance alone, make a difference in the trust which he reposes in each. We have reason to expect greater wit and gaiety in a Frenchman than in a Spaniard; though Cervantes[1] was born in Spain. An Englishman will naturally be supposed to have more knowledge than a Dane; though Tycho Brahe[2] was a native of Denmark.

[. . .]

---

[1] Miguel de Cervantes (1547–1616), Spanish novelist, playwright and poet, and author of *Don Quixote.*

[2] Tycho Brahe (1546–1601), a noted astronomer, astrologer and alchemist.

The human mind is of a very imitative nature; nor is it possible for any set of men to converse often together, without acquiring a similitude of manners, and communicating to each other their vices as well as virtues. The propensity to company and society is strong in all rational creatures; and the same disposition, which gives us this propensity, makes us enter deeply into each other's sentiments, and causes like passions and inclinations to run, as it were, by contagion, through the whole club or knot of companions. Where a number of men are united into one political body, the occasions of their intercourse must be so frequent, for defence, commerce, and government, that, together with the same speech or language, they must acquire a resemblance in their manners, and have a common or national character, as well as a personal one, peculiar to each individual.

[...]

If we run over the globe, or revolve the annals of history, we shall discover every where signs of a sympathy or contagion of manners, none of the influence of air or climate.

First. We may observe, that, where a very extensive government has been established for many centuries, it spreads a national character over the whole empire, and communicates to every part a similarity of manners. Thus the Chinese have the greatest uniformity of character imaginable: though the air and climate, in different parts of those vast dominions, admit of very considerable variations.

Secondly. In small governments, which are contiguous, the people have notwithstanding a different character, and are often as distinguishable in their manners as the most distant nations. Athens and Thebes were but a short day's journey from each other; though the Athenians were as remarkable for ingenuity, politeness, and gaiety, as the Thebans for dullness, rusticity, and a phlegmatic temper.

Thirdly. The same national character commonly follows the authority of government to a precise boundary; and upon crossing a river or passing a mountain, one finds a new set of manners, with a new government. The Languedocians and Gascons are the gayest [merriest] people in France; but whenever you pass the Pyrenees, you are among Spaniards.

Fourthly. Where any set of men, scattered over distant nations, maintain a close society or communication together, they acquire a similitude of manners, and have but little in common with the nations amongst whom they live. Thus the Jews in Europe, and the Armenians in the east, have a peculiar character; and the former are as much noted for fraud, as the latter for probity.

[...]

377

Sixthly. The same set of manners will follow a nation, and adhere to them over the whole globe, as well as the same laws and language. The Spanish, English, French and Dutch colonies are all distinguishable even between the tropics.

[. . .]

Ninthly. We may often remark a wonderful mixture of manners and characters in the same nation, speaking the same language, and subject to the same government: And in this particular the English are the most remarkable of any people, that perhaps ever were in the world. Nor is this to be ascribed to the mutability and uncertainty of their climate, or to any other *physical* causes; since all these causes take place in the neighbouring country of Scotland, without having the same effect. Where the government of a nation is altogether republican, it is apt to beget a peculiar set of manners. Where it is altogether monarchical, it is more apt to have the same effect; the imitation of superiors spreading the national manners faster among the people. If the governing part of a state consist altogether of merchants, as in Holland, their uniform way of life will fix their character. If it consists chiefly of nobles and landed gentry, like Germany, France, and Spain, the same effect follows. The genius of a particular sect or religion is also apt to mould the manners of a people. But the English government is a mixture of monarchy, aristocracy, and democracy. The people in authority are composed of gentry and merchants. All sects of religion are to be found among them. And the great liberty and independency, which every man enjoys, allows him to display the manners peculiar to him. Hence the English, of any people in the universe, have the least of a national character; unless this very singularity may pass for such.

5.26

William Shakespeare's *Henry V*

S. Greenblatt, W. Cohen, J.E. Howard, C. Eisaman Maus (eds.) (1997) *The Norton Shakespeare*, New York: W.W. Norton, pp. 1476–7.

In this famous passage from the play *Henry V* (Act 3, Scene 1), the king is addressing his troops during battle with the French at the siege of Harfleur. While Shakespeare probably wrote the play in 1599, the events which it dramatises took place, in the main, in 1415.

Once more unto the breach, dear friends, once more;
Or close the wall up with our English dead.
In peace there's nothing so becomes a man
As modest stillness and humility:
But when the blast of war blows in our ears,
Then imitate the action of the tiger.
Stiffen the sinews, conjure up the blood,
Disguise fair nature with hard-favoured rage.
Then lend the eye a terrible aspect,
Let it pry through the portage of the head
Like the brass cannon; let the brow o'erwhelm it
As fearfully as doth a gallèd rock
O'erhang and jutty his confounded base,
Swilled with the wild and wasteful ocean.
Now set the teeth and stretch the nostril wide,
Hold hard the breath and bend up every spirit
To his full height. On, on, you noblest English.
Whose blood is fet from fathers of war-proof,
Fathers, that, like so many Alexanders
Have in these parts from morn till even fought
And sheathed their swords for lack of argument.
Dishonour not your mothers; now attest
That those whom you called fathers did beget you.
Be copy now to men of grosser blood,
And teach them how to war! And you, good yeomen,
Whose limbs were made in England, show us here
The mettle of your pasture; let us swear
That you are worth your breeding – which I doubt not,
For there is none of you so mean and base
That hath not noble lustre in your eyes.
I see you stand like greyhounds in the slips,
Straining upon the start. The game's afoot.
Follow your spirit, and upon this charge
Cry 'God for Harry! England and Saint George!'

5.27

Introduction to Macaulay's
History of England

*Whig
England
of
History*

T.B. Macaulay ([1848–61] 1966) *History of England from
the Accession of James II*, London: Dent, 5 vols., vol. 1,
pp. 1–2.

Published in five volumes, Macaulay's *History of England* was
one of the most acclaimed and popular English history books
ever, selling over 140,000 sets. To Thomas Babington Macaulay
(1800–59), as to most others of his class and generation, the
Glorious Revolution in 1688 was the final triumph over the influence of the Pope and absolute monarchy, was the start of an era
of brilliant progress which had reached its culmination in the
political reforms of the nineteenth century, reforms in which he
himself had participated as a member of parliament.

I purpose to write the history of England from the accession of King
James the Second down to a time which is within the memory of men
still living. I shall recount . . . how, from the auspicious union of order
and freedom, sprang a prosperity of which the annals of human affairs
had furnished no example; how our country, from a state of ignomini-
ous vassalage, rapidly rose to the place of umpire among European
powers; how her opulence and her martial glory grew together; how,
by wise and resolute good faith, was gradually established a public
credit fruitful of marvels which to the statesmen of any former age
would have seemed incredible; how a gigantic commerce gave birth
to a maritime power, compared with which every other maritime
power, ancient or modern, sinks into insignificance; how Scotland,
after ages of enmity, was at length united to England, not merely by
legal bonds, but by indissoluble ties of interest and affection; how, in
America, the British colonies rapidly became far mightier and wealth-
ier than the realms of which Cortes and Pizzaro had added to the
[Spanish Hapsburg] dominions of Charles the Fifth; how, in Asia,
British adventurers founded an empire not less splendid and more
durable than that of Alexander [the Great].
[. . .]
Unless I greatly deceive myself, the general effect of this chequered
narrative will be to excite thankfulness in all religious minds, and

hope in the breasts of all patriots. For the history of our country during the last hundred and sixty years is eminently the history of physical, of moral, and of intellectual improvement. Those who compare the age on which their lot has fallen with a golden age which exists only in their imagination may talk of degeneracy and decay: but no man who is correctly informed as to the past will be disposed to take a morose or desponding view of the present.

5.28
Guizot's *History of Civilization in Europe*

F. Guizot ([1828] 1997) *The History of Civilization in Europe*, trans. W. Hazlitt (1846), London: Penguin, pp. 9–11.

François Guizot (1787–1874) was well-known (both within France and abroad) as a provocative and politically committed historian. A series of lectures on civilization, quickly published as books, caused comment and excitement among enthusiasts of liberal reform in the early nineteenth century. After writing these lectures, Guizot was involved in the July Revolution of 1830, and subsequently became a deputy and minister in the new regime – the July Monarchy – remaining as chief minister until the 1848 Revolution put an end to the regime.

We of France occupy a favourable position for pursuing the study of European civilization. Flattery of individuals, even of our country, should be at all times avoided: it is without vanity, I think, we may say that France has been the centre, the focus of European civilization. I do not pretend, it were monstrous to do so, that she has always, and in every direction, arched at the head of nations. At different epochs, Italy has taken the lead of her, in the arts; England, in political institutions; and there may be other respects under which, at particular periods, other European nations have manifested a superiority to her; but it is impossible to deny, that whenever France has seen herself thus outstripped in the career of civilization, she has called up fresh vigour, has sprung forward with a new impulse, and has soon found herself abreast with, or in advance of, all the rest. And not only has

381

this been the peculiar fortune of France, but we have seen that when ideas and institutions which have taken their rise in other lands, have sought to extend their sphere, to become fertile and general, to operate for the common benefit of European civilization, they have been necessitated to undergo, to a certain extent, a new preparation in France; and it has been France, as from a second native country, that they have gone forth to the conquest of Europe. There is scarcely any great idea, any great principle of civilization, which, prior to its diffusion, has not passed in this way through France.

And for this reason: there is in the French character something sociable, something sympathetic, something which makes its way with greater facility and effect than does the national genius of any other people; whether from our language, whether from the turn of our mind, of our manners, it is certain that our ideas are more popular than those of other people, present themselves more clearly and intelligibly to the masses, and penetrate among them more readily; in a word, perspicuity, sociability, sympathy, are the peculiar characteristics of France, of her civilization, and it is these qualities which rendered her eminently fit to march at the very head of European civilization.

In entering, therefore, upon the study of this great fact, it is no arbitrary or conventional choice to take France as the centre of this study; we must needs do so if we would place ourselves, as it were, in the very heart of civilization, in the very heart of the fact that we are about to consider.

5.29

Michelet, *History of the French Revolution*

J. Michelet ([1847–53] 1967) *History of the French Revolution*, trans. C. Cocks, Chicago: University of Chicago Press, 7 vols., vol., 1, pp. 12–13.

Born in Paris less than a decade after the French Revolution, Jules Michelet (1798–1874) was one of France's foremost nineteenth-century historians. Michelet came to believe that the study of world history revealed a progressive movement from enslave-

5.3 'La Republique triomphante'. Marianne (France personified) presiding over the first national day celebrations, 14 July 1880.

ment to liberty, and that France had a crucial role to play in the next phase of world history – the unification of humanity. Michelet eventually came to see the French Revolution as the moment when nations (and France in particular) attained the final stage of self-consciousness. His glowing patriotism and intense sense of what it meant to be 'French', combined with a strong current of enlightenment universalism, meant that he came to view France as 'the brilliant culmination of universal history'.

A thing to be told to everybody, and which it is but too easy to prove, is, that the humane and benevolent period of our Revolution had for its actors the very people, the whole people, – everybody. And the period of violence, the period of sanguinary deeds, into which danger afterwards thrust it, had for actors, but an inconsiderable, an extremely small number of men.

That is what I have found established and verified, either by written testimony, or by such as I have gathered from the lips of old men.

The remarkable exclamation of a man who belonged to the Faubourg Saint-Antoine will never die: 'We were all of us at the 10th of August, and not one at the 2nd of September'.[1]

Another thing which this history will render most conspicuous, and which is true of every party, is, that the people were generally much better than their leaders. The further I have searched, the more generally have I found that the more deserving class was ever underneath, buried among the utterly obscure. I have also found that those brilliant, powerful speakers, who expressed the thoughts of the masses, are usually but wrongfully considered as the sole actors. The fact is, that they rather received than communicated the impulse. The chief actor is the people. In order to find and restore the latter to its proper position, I have been obliged to reduce to their proportions those ambitious puppets whom they had set in motion, and in whom, till now, people fancied they saw, and have sought for, the secret transactions of history.

This sight, I must confess, struck me with astonishment. In proportion as I entered more deeply into this study, I observed that the mere party leaders, those heroes of the prepared scene, neither foresaw nor prepared anything, that they were never the first proposers of any grand measure, – more particularly of those which were the unanimous work of the people at the outset of the Revolution.

Left to themselves, at those decisive moments, by their pretended leaders, they found out what was necessary to be done, and did it.

Great, astonishing results! But how much greater was the heart which conceived them! The deeds themselves are as nothing in comparison. So astonishing, indeed, was that greatness of heart, that the future may draw upon it for ever, without fearing to exhaust its resources. No one can approach its contemplation, without retiring a better man. Every soul dejected, or crushed with grief, every human or national heart has but to look there in order to find comfort: it is a mirror wherein humanity, in beholding itself, becomes once more heroic, magnanimous, disinterested; a singular purity, shrinking from the contamination of lucre as from filth, appears to be the characteristic glory of all.

---

[1] On 10 August 1792 a mob, backed by the new government of Paris, the Commune, besieged the royal family in the Tuileries Palace. The armed insurgents divided into columns named after the districts of Paris where they lived, including the Faubourg Saint-Antoine in the Right Bank; September refers to the September Massacres, three days in which over 1,200 Royalist and suspected 'counter-revolutionary' prisoners were murdered by the mob, fearful of an advancing Prussian army that was intent on restoring the monarchy.

I am endeavouring to describe to-day that epoch of unanimity, that holy period, when a whole nation, free from all party distinction, as yet a comparative stranger to the opposition of classes, marched together under a flag of brotherly love. Nobody can behold that marvellous unanimity, in which the self-same heart beat together in the breasts of twenty millions of men, without returning thanks to God. These are the sacred days of the world – thrice happy days for history. For my part, I have had my reward, in the mere narration of them.

5.30
Nationality and representative government

J.S. Mill ([1861] 1991) *Considerations on Representative Government*, New York: Prometheus Books, pp. 308–19.

One of the foremost English philosophers of the nineteenth century, John Stuart Mill (1806–73) wrote a series of influential philosophical and political works of which the most well-known was probably *On Liberty* (1859), which made him famous as a defender of human rights. In this extract from his *Considerations on Representative Government* (1861), Mill turned his mind to the way in which nationality was linked to politics and liberty.

A PORTION of mankind may be said to constitute a nationality if they are united among themselves by common sympathies which do not exist between them and any others – which make them co-operate with each other more willingly than with other people, desire to be under the same government, and desire that it should be government by themselves, or a portion of themselves, exclusively. This feeling of nationality may have been generated by various causes. Sometimes it is the effect of identity of race and descent. Community of language and community of religion greatly contribute to it. Geographical limits are one of its causes. But the strongest of all is identity of political antecedents, the possession of a national history, and consequent community of recollections; collective pride and humiliation, pleasure and regret, connected with the same incidents in the past. None of these circumstances, however, are either indispensable or necessarily sufficient by themselves. Switzerland has a strong sentiment of nationality, though the cantons are of different races, different languages, and different religions. Sicily has hitherto felt itself quite distinct in nationality from Naples, notwithstanding identity of religion, almost identity of language, and a considerable amount of common historical antecedents. The Flemish and the Walloon provinces of Belgium, notwithstanding diversity of race and language, have a much greater feeling of common nationality than the former have with Holland, or the latter with France. Yet in general, the national feeling is proportionally weakened by the failure of any of the causes which contribute to it. Identity of language, literature, and, to some extent, of race and recollections, have maintained the feeling of nationality in considerable strength among the different portions of the German name, though they have at no time been really united under the same government; but the feeling has never reached to making the separate states desire to get rid of their autonomy. Among Italians, an identity far from complete of language and literature, combined with a geographical position which separates them by a distinct line from other countries, and, perhaps more than every thing else, the possession of a common name, which makes them all glory in the past achievements in arts, arms, politics, religious primacy, science, and literature, of any who share the same designation, give rise to an amount of national feeling in the population which, though still imperfect, has been sufficient to produce the great events now passing before us, notwithstanding a great mixture of races, and although they have never, in either ancient or modern history, been under the same government, except while that government extended or was extending itself over the greater part of the known world.

Where the sentiment of nationality exists in any force, there is a *prima facie* case for uniting all the members of the nationality under the same government, and a government to themselves apart. This is merely saying that the question of government ought to be decided by the governed. One hardly knows what any division of the human race should be free to do if not to determine with which of the various collective bodies of human beings they choose to associate themselves. But, when a people are ripe for free institutions, there is still a more vital consideration. Free institutions are next to impossible in a country made up of different nationalities. Among a people without fellow-feeling, especially if they read and speak different languages, the united public opinion necessary to the working of representative government can not exist. The influences which form opinions and decide political acts are different in the different sections of the country. An altogether different set of leaders have the confidence of one part of the country and of another. The same books, newspapers, pamphlets, speeches, do not reach them. One section does not know what opinions or what instigations are circulating in another. The same incidents, the same acts, the same system of government, affect them in different ways, and each fears more injury to itself from the other nationalities than from the common arbiter, the state. Their mutual antipathies are generally much stronger than dislike of the government. That any one of them feels aggrieved by the policy of the common ruler is sufficient to determine another to support that policy. Even if all are aggrieved, none feel that they can rely on the others for fidelity in a joint resistance; the strength of none is sufficient to resist alone, and each may reasonably think that it consults its own advantage most by bidding for the favor of the government against the rest. Above all, the grand and only reliable security in the last resort against the despotism of the government is in that case wanting the sympathy of the army with the people. The military are the part of every community in whom, from the nature of the case, the distinction between their fellow countrymen and foreigners is the deepest and strongest. To the rest of the people foreigners are merely strangers; to the soldier, they are men against whom he may be called, at a week's notice, to fight for life or death. The difference to him is that between friends and enemies we may almost say between fellow-men and another kind of animals; for, as respects the enemy, the only law is that of force, and the only mitigation the same as in the case of other animals – that of simple humanity. Soldiers to whose feelings half or three-fourths of the subjects of the same government are foreigners, will have no more scruple in mowing them down, and no more desire to ask the reason why, than they would have in doing the same thing against declared enemies. An army composed of various nationalities has no other patriotism than devotion to the flag. Such armies have been the executioners of liberty through the whole duration of modern history. The sole bond which holds them together is their officers and the government which they serve, and their only idea, if they have any, of public duty, is obedience to orders.

[. . .]

For the preceding reasons, it is in general a necessary condition of free institutions that the boundaries of governments should coincide in the main with those of nationalities. But several considerations are liable to conflict in practice with this general principle. In the first place, its application is often precluded by geographical hindrances. There are parts even of Europe in which different nationalities are so

387

locally intermingled that it is not practicable for them to be under separate governments. The population of Hungary is composed of Magyars, Slovacks, Croats, Serbs, Roumans, and in some districts Germans, so mixed up as to be incapable of local separation; and there is no course open to them but to make a virtue of necessity, and reconcile themselves to living together under equal rights and laws. Their community of servitude, which dates only from the destruction of Hungarian independence in 1849, seems to be ripening and disposing them for such an equal union. The German colony of East Prussia is cut off from Germany by part of the ancient Poland, and being too weak to maintain separate independence, must, if geographical continuity is to be maintained, be either under a non-German government, or the intervening Polish territory must be under a German one. Another considerable region in which the dominant element of the population is German, the provinces of Courland, Esthonia, and Livonia,[1] is condemned by its local situation to form part of a Slavonian state. In Eastern Germany itself, there is a large Slavonic population; Bohemia is principally Slavonic, Silesia and other districts partially so. The most united country in Europe, France, is far from being homogeneous: independently of the fragments of foreign nationalities at its remote extremities, it consists, as language and history prove, of two portions, one occupied almost exclusively by a Gallo-Roman population, while in the other the Frankish, Burgundian, and other Teutonic races form a considerable ingredient. When proper allowance has been made for geographical exigencies, another more purely moral and social consideration offers itself. Experience proves that it is possible for one nationality to merge and be absorbed in another; and when it was originally an inferior and more backward portion of the human race, the absorption is greatly to its advantage. Nobody can suppose that it is not more beneficial to a Breton, or a Basque of French Navarre, to be brought into the current of the ideas and feelings of a highly civilized and cultivated people – to be a member of the French nationality, admitted on equal terms to all the privileges of French citizenship, sharing the advantages of French protection, and the dignity and prestige of French power – than to sulk on his own rocks, the half-savage relic of past times, revolving in his own little mental orbit, without participation or interest in the general movement of the world. The same remark applies to the Welshman or the Scottish Highlander as members of the British nation.

---

[1] Provinces now forming the Balkan states of Estonia, Latvia and Lithuania.

5.31

Max Weber, 'The Nation', 1921

J. Hutchinson & A.D. Smith (1994) *Nationalism*, Oxford:
Oxford University Press, pp. 21–5.

Renowned for his breadth of scholarship and erudition, Maximilian
Weber (1864–1920) became one of the founders of sociology. His
'interpretive method' was allied to a strong commitment to causal
analysis and value neutrality. A convinced German nationalist,
his main intellectual interest was in analysing the role of various
factors – religious, economic and political – which came to shape
the unique civilisation of the West. Although he never wrote the
promised book on the formation of national states, Weber adopted
a 'political' approach to ethnicity and national identity which has
been highly influential.

The fervor of this emotional influence does not, in the main, have an
economic origin. It is based upon sentiments of prestige, which often
extend deep down to the petty bourgeois masses of political structures rich in the historical attainment of power-positions. The attachment to all this political prestige may fuse with a specific belief in
responsibility towards succeeding generations. The great power structures *per se* are then held to have a responsibility of their own for the
way in which power and prestige are distributed between their own
and foreign polities. It goes without saying that all those groups who
hold the power to steer common conduct within a polity will most
strongly instill themselves with this ideal fervor of power prestige.
They remain the specific and most reliable bearers of the idea of
the state as an imperialist power structure demanding unqualified
devotion.

In addition to the direct and material imperialist interests, discussed above, there are partly indirect and material and partly ideological interests of strata that are in various ways intellectually
privileged within a polity and, indeed, privileged by its very existence.
They comprise especially all those who think of themselves as being
the specific 'partners' of a specific 'culture' diffused among the
members of the polity. Under the influence of these circles, the naked
prestige of 'power' is unavoidably transformed into other special forms
of prestige and especially into the idea of the 'nation'.

If the concept of 'nation' can in any way be defined unambiguously, it certainly cannot be stated in terms of empirical qualities common to those who count as members of the nation. In the sense of those using the term at a given time, the concept undoubtedly means, above all, that one may exact from certain groups of men a specific sentiment of solidarity in the face of other groups. Thus, the concept belongs in the sphere of values. Yet, there is no agreement on how these groups should be delimited or about what concerted action should result from such solidarity.

In ordinary language, 'nation' is, first of all, not identical with the 'people of a state', that is, with the membership of a given polity. Numerous polities comprise groups among whom the independence of their 'nation' is emphatically asserted in the face of the other groups; or, on the other hand, they comprise parts of a group whose members declare this group to be one homogeneous 'nation' (Austria before 1918, for example). Furthermore, a 'nation' is not identical with a community speaking the same language; that this by no means always suffices is indicated by the Serbs and Croats, the North Americans, the Irish, and the English. On the contrary, a common language does not seem to be absolutely necessary to a 'nation'. In official documents, besides 'Swiss People' one also finds the phrase 'Swiss Nation'. And some language groups do not think of themselves as a separate 'nation', for example, at least until recently, the white Russians. The pretension, however, to be considered a special 'nation' is regularly associated with a common language as a culture value of the masses; this is predominantly the case in the classic country of language conflicts, Austria, and equally so in Russia and in eastern Prussia. But this linkage of the common language and 'nation' is of varying intensity; for instance, it is very low in the United States as well as in Canada.

'National' solidarity among men speaking the same language may be just as well rejected as accepted. Solidarity, instead, may be linked with differences in the other great 'culture value of the masses', namely, a religious creed, as is the case with the Serbs and Croats. National solidarity may be connected with differing social structure and mores and hence with 'ethnic' elements, as is the case with the German Swiss and the Alsatians in the face of the Germans of the Reich, or with the Irish facing the British. Yet above all, national solidarity may be linked to memories of a common political destiny with other nations, among the Alsatians with the French since the revolutionary war which represents their common heroic age, just as among the Baltic Barons with the Russians whose political destiny they helped to steer.

It goes without saying that 'national' affiliation need not be based upon common blood. Indeed, everywhere the especially radical 'nationalists' are often of foreign descent. Furthermore, although a specific common anthropological type is not irrelevant to nationality, it is neither sufficient nor a prerequisite to found a nation. Nevertheless, the idea of the 'nation' is apt to include the notions of common descent and of an essential, though frequently indefinite, homogeneity. The nation has these notions in common with the sentiment of solidarity of ethnic communities, which is also nourished from various sources. But the sentiment of ethnic solidarity does not by itself make a 'nation'. Undoubtedly, even the white Russians in the face of the Great Russians have always had a sentiment of ethnic solidarity, yet even at the present time they would hardly claim to qualify as a separate 'nation'. The Poles of Upper Silesia, until recently, had hardly any feeling of solidarity with the 'Polish Nation'. They felt themselves to be a separate ethnic group in the face of the Germans, but for the rest they were Prussian subjects and nothing else.

Whether the Jews may be called a 'nation' is an old problem. The mass of the Russian Jews, the assimilating West-European-American Jews, the Zionists – these would in the main give a negative answer. In any case, their answers would vary in nature and extent. In particular, the question would be answered very differently by the peoples of their environment, for example, by the Russians on the one side and by the Americans on the other – or at least by those Americans who at the present time still maintain American and Jewish nature to be essentially similar, as an American President has asserted in an official document.

Those German-speaking Alsatians who refuse to belong to the German 'nation' and who cultivate the memory of political union with France do not thereby consider themselves simply as members of the French 'nation'. The Negroes of the United States, at least at present, consider themselves members of the American 'nation', but they will hardly ever be so considered by the Southern Whites.

Only fifteen years ago, men knowing the Far East still denied that the Chinese qualified as a 'nation'; they held them to be only a 'race'. Yet today, not only the Chinese political leaders but also the very same observers would judge differently. Thus it seems that a group of people under certain conditions may attain the quality of a nation through specific behavior, or they may claim this quality as an 'attainment' – and within short spans of time at that.

There are, on the other hand, social groups that profess indifference to, and even directly relinquish, any evaluational adherence to a single

nation. At the present time, certain leading strata of the class movement of the modern proletariat consider such indifference and relin-
quishment to be an accomplishment. Their argument meets with
varying success, depending upon political and linguistic affiliations
and also upon different strata of the proletariat; on the whole, their
success is rather diminishing at the present time.

An unbroken scale of quite varied and highly changeable attitudes
toward the idea of the 'nation' is to be found among social strata
and also within single groups to whom language usage ascribes the
quality of 'nations'. The scale extends from emphatic affirmation to
emphatic negation and finally complete indifference, as may be characteristic of the citizens of Luxembourg and of nationally 'unawak-
ened' peoples. Feudal strata, strata of officials, entrepreneurial
bourgeois strata of various categories, strata of 'intellectuals' do
not have homogeneous or historically constant attitudes towards
the idea.

The reasons for the belief that one represents a nation vary greatly,
just as does the empirical conduct that actually results from affiliation
or lack of it with a nation. The 'national sentiments' of the German,
the Englishman, the North American, the Spaniard, the Frenchman,
or the Russian do not function in an identical manner. Thus, to take
only the simplest illustration, national sentiment is variously related
to political associations, and the 'idea' of the nation may become
antagonistic to the empirical scope of given political associations.
This antagonism may lead to quite different results.

Certainly the Italians in the Austrian state-association would fight
Italian troops only if coerced into doing so. Large portions of the
German Austrians would today fight against Germany only with the
greatest reluctance; they could not be relied upon. The German
Americans, however, even those valuing their 'nationality' most highly,
would fight against Germany, not gladly, yet, given the occasion,
unconditionally. The Poles in the German State would fight readily
against a Russian Polish army but hardly against an autonomous
Polish army. The Austrian Serbs would fight against Serbia with very
mixed feelings and only in the hope of attaining common autonomy.
The Russian Poles would fight more reliably against a German than
against an Austrian army.

It is a well-known historical fact that within the same nation the
intensity of solidarity felt toward the outside is changeable and
varies greatly in strength. On the whole, this sentiment has grown
even where internal conflicts of interest have not diminished. Only

sixty years ago the *Kreuzzeitung*[1] still appealed to the intervention of the emperor of Russia in internal German affairs; today, in spite of increased class antagonism, this would be difficult to imagine.

In any case, the differences in national sentiment are both significant and fluid and, as is the case in all other fields, fundamentally different answers are given to the question: What conclusions are a group of people willing to draw from the 'national sentiment' found among them? No matter how emphatic and subjectively sincere a pathos may be formed among them, what sort of specific joint action are they ready to develop? The extent to which in the diaspora a convention is adhered to as a 'national' trait varies just as much as does the importance of common conventions for the belief in the existence of a separate 'nation'. In the face of these value concepts of the 'idea of the nation', which empirically are entirely ambiguous, a sociological typology would have to analyse all sorts of community sentiments of solidarity in their genetic conditions and in their consequences for the concerted action of the participants. This cannot here be attempted.

Instead, we shall have to look a little closer into the fact that the idea of the nation for its advocates stands in very intimate relation to 'prestige' interests. The earliest and most energetic manifestations of the idea, in some form, even though it may have been veiled, have contained the legend of a providential 'mission'. Those to whom the representatives of the idea zealously turned were expected to shoulder this mission. Another element of the early idea was the notion that this mission was facilitated solely through the very cultivation of the peculiarity of the group set off as a nation. Therewith, in so far as its self-justification is sought in the value of its content, this mission can consistently be thought of only as a specific 'culture' mission. The significance of the 'nation' is usually anchored in the superiority, or at least the irreplaceability, of the culture values that are to be preserved and developed only through the cultivation of the peculiarity of the group. It therefore goes without saying that the intellectuals, as we have in a preliminary fashion called them, are to a specific degree predestined to propagate the 'national idea', just as those who wield power in the polity provoke the idea of the state.

---

[1] A German conservative newspaper.

By 'intellectuals' we understand a group of men who by virtue of their peculiarity have special access to certain achievements considered to be 'culture values', and who therefore usurp the leadership of a 'culture community'.

In so far as there is at all a common object lying behind the obviously ambiguous term 'nation', it is apparently located in the field of politics. One might well define the concept of nation in the following way: a nation is a community of sentiment which would adequately manifest itself in a state of its own; hence, a nation is a community which normally tends to produce a state of its own.

The causal components that lead to the emergence of a national sentiment in this sense may vary greatly. If we for once disregard religious belief – which has not yet played its last role in this matter, especially among Serbs and Croats – then common purely political destinies have first to be considered. Under certain conditions, otherwise heterogeneous peoples can be melted together through common destinies. The reason for the Alsatians' not feeling themselves as belonging to the German nation has to be sought in their memories. Their political destiny has taken its course outside the German sphere for too long; their heroes are the heroes of French history. If the custodian of the Kolmar museum wants to show you which among his treasures he cherishes most, he takes you away from Grunewald's altar[2] to a room filled with tricolors, *pompier*,[3] and other helmets and souvenirs of a seemingly most cant nature; they are from a time that to him is a heroic age.

[. . .]

If one believes that it is at all expedient to distinguish national sentiment as something homogeneous and specifically set apart, one can do so only by referring to a tendency toward an autonomous state. And one must be clearly aware of the fact that sentiments of solidarity, very heterogeneous in both their nature and their origin, are comprised within national sentiments.

[2] The altarpiece by Matthias Grunewald (c. 1470–1528) is considered one of the greatest works of the northern Renaissance. It was originally painted for the hospital chapel of St Anthony's monastery in Isenheim, Alsace but is now housed in the Musee d'Unterlinden in Colmar.

[3] Here, 'kitsch'.

5.32

Lord Acton, 'Nationality', 1862

Lord Acton (1922) *The History of Freedom and Other Essays*, eds. J.N. Figgis & R.V. Laurence, London: Macmillan, pp. 290–300. The essay on 'Nationality' first appeared in *Home and Foreign Review* (July, 1862).

John Emerich Edward Dalberg-Acton (1834–1902), English historian, was Regius Professor of Modern History at Cambridge University, original editor of the great *Cambridge Modern History*, and cofounder of *English Historical Review*. In 1862, he became editor of the *Home and Foreign Review*, in which his essay on 'Nationality' first appeared. In this essay, Lord Acton intimated that a state which identifies itself with any single object, either one class or a nationality, may well become absolutistic. In a multinational state, however, a nationality could become 'a limit to the excessive power of the state as well as a bulwark of self-government'. A nationality inside a multinational state, he believed, when the state was based on freedom, could counteract the worst effects of absolutism. This excerpt is from the concluding section to Lord Acton's essay.

The combination of different nations in one State is as necessary a condition of civilized life as the combination of men in society. Inferior races are raised by living in political union with races intellectually superior. Exhausted and decaying nations are revived by the contact of a younger vitality. Nations in which the elements of organization and the capacity for government have been lost, either through the demoralizing influence of despotism, or the disintegrating action of democracy, are restored and educated anew under the discipline of a stronger and less corrupted race. This fertilizing and regenerating process can only be obtained by living under one government. It is in the cauldron of the State that the fusion takes place by which the vigour, the knowledge, and the capacity of one portion of mankind may be communicated to another. Where political and national boundaries coincide, society ceases to advance, and nations relapse into a condition corresponding to that of men who renounce intercourse with their fellow-men. The difference between the two unites mankind not only by the benefits it confers on those who live together, but because it connects society either by a political or a national bond, gives to every people an interest in its neighbours, either because they are under the same government or because they are of the same race, and thus promotes the interests of humanity, of civilization, and of religion.

Christianity rejoices at the mixture of races, as paganism identifies itself with their differences, because truth is universal, and errors various and particular. In the ancient world idolatry and nationality went together, and the same term is applied in Scripture to both. It was the mission of the Church to overcome national differences. The period of her undisputed supremacy was that in which all Western Europe obeyed the same laws, all literature was contained in one language, and the political unity of Christendom was personified in a single potentate, while its intellectual unity was represented in one university. As the ancient Romans concluded their conquests by carrying away the gods of the conquered people, Charlemagne[1] overcame the national resistance of the Saxons only by the forcible destruction of their pagan rites. Out of the mediaeval period, and the combined action of the German race and the Church, came forth a new system of nations and a new conception of nationality. Nature was overcome in the nation as well as in the individual. In pagan and uncultivated times, nations were distinguished from each other by the widest diversity, not only in religion, but in customs, language, and character. Under the new law they had many things in common; the old barriers which separated them were removed, and the new principle of self-government, which Christianity imposed, enabled them to live together under the same authority, without necessarily losing their cherished habits, their customs, or their laws. The new idea of freedom made room for different races in one State. A nation was no longer what it had been to the ancient world, – the progeny of a common ancestor, or the aboriginal product of a particular region, – a result of merely physical and material causes, – but a moral and political being; not the creation of geographical or physiological unity, but developed in the course of history by the action of the State. It is derived from the State, not supreme over it. A State may in course of time produce a nationality; but that a nationality should constitute a State is contrary

---

[1] Charlemagne (742–814 CE) (French for *Carolus Magnus* or Charles the Great) was king of the Franks and the first sovereign of the Holy Roman Empire of the West, crowned in Rome by the pope on Christmas Day 800. He undertook a thirty-year campaign to conquer and forcibly Christianise the pagan Saxons (772–804), in which around a quarter of the Saxon population died, either in battle or by being executed for refusing to convert.

to the nature of modern civilization. The nation derives its rights and its power from the memory of a former independence.

[. . .]

The difference between nationality and the State is exhibited in the nature of patriotic attachment. Our connection with the race is merely natural or physical, whilst our duties to the political nation are ethical. One is a community of affections and instincts infinitely important and powerful in savage life, but pertaining more to the animal than to the civilized man; the other is an authority governing by laws, imposing obligations, and giving a moral sanction and character to the natural relations of society. Patriotism is in political life what faith is in religion, and it stands to the domestic feelings and to home-sickness as faith to fanaticism and to superstition. It has one aspect derived from private life and nature, for it is an extension of the family affections, as the tribe is an extension of the family. But in its real political character, patriotism consists in the development of the instinct of self-preservation into a moral duty which may involve self-sacrifice. Self-preservation is both an instinct and a duty, natural and involuntary in one respect, and at the same time a moral obligation. By the first it produces the family; by the last the State. If the nation could exist without the State, subject only to the instinct of self-preservation, it would be incapable of denying, controlling, or sacrificing itself; it would be an end and a rule to itself. But in the political order moral purposes are realized and public ends are pursued to which private interests and even existence must be sacrificed. The great sign of true patriotism, the development of selfishness into sacrifice, is the product of political life. That sense of duty which is supplied by race is not entirely separated from its selfish and instinctive basis; and the love of country, like married love, stands at the same time on a material and a moral foundation. The patriot must distinguish between the two causes or objects of his devotion. The attachment which is given only to the country is like obedience given only to the State – a submission to physical influences. The man who prefers his country before every other duty shows the same spirit as the man who surrenders every right to the State. They both deny that right is superior to authority.

[. . .]

The nationality formed by the State is the only one to which we owe political duties, and it is, therefore, the only one which has political rights. The Swiss are ethnologically either French, Italian, or German; but no nationality has the slightest claim upon them, except the purely political nationality of Switzerland. The Tuscan or the Neapolitan

State has formed a nationality, but the citizens of Florence and of Naples have no political community with each other. There are other States which have neither succeeded in absorbing distinct races in a political nationality, nor in separating a particular district from a larger nation. Austria and Mexico are instances on the one hand, Parma and Baden on the other. The progress of civilization deals hardly with the last description of States. In order to maintain their integrity they must attach themselves by confederations, or family alliances, to greater Powers, and thus lose something of their independence. Their tendency is to isolate and shut off their inhabitants, to narrow the horizon of their views, and to dwarf in some degree the proportions of their ideas. Public opinion cannot maintain its liberty and purity in such small dimensions, and the currents that come from larger communities sweep over a contracted territory. In a small and homogeneous population there is hardly room for a natural classification of society, or for inner groups of interests that set bounds to sovereign power.

[. . .]

The great importance of nationality in the State consists in the fact that it is the basis of political capacity. The character of a nation determines in great measure the form and vitality of the State. Certain political habits and ideas belong to particular nations, and they vary with the course of the national history. A people just emerging from barbarism, a people effete from the excesses of a luxurious civilization, cannot possess the means of governing itself; a people devoted to equality, or to absolute monarchy, is incapable of producing an aristocracy; a people averse to the institution of private property is without the first element of freedom. Each of these can be converted into efficient members of a free community only by the contact of a superior race, in whose power will lie the future prospects of the State. A system which ignores these things, and does not rely for its support on the character and aptitude of the people, does not intend that they should administer their own affairs, but that they should simply be obedient to the supreme command. The denial of nationality, therefore, implies the denial of political liberty.

The greatest adversary of the rights of nationality is the modern theory of nationality. By making the State and the nation commensurate with each other in theory, it reduces practically to a subject condition all other nationalities that may be within the boundary. It cannot admit them to an equality with the ruling nation which constitutes the State, because the State would then cease to be national, which would be a contradiction of the principle of its existence. According, therefore, to the degree of humanity and civilization in that dominant body which claims all the rights of the community, the inferior races are exterminated, or reduced to servitude, or outlawed, or put in a condition of dependence.

If we take the establishment of liberty for the realization of moral duties to be the end of civil society, we must conclude that those states are substantially the most perfect which, like the British and Austrian Empires, include various distinct nationalities without oppressing them. Those in which no mixture of races has occurred are imperfect; and those in which its effects have disappeared are decrepit.

A State which is incompetent to satisfy different races condemns itself; a State which labours to neutralize, to absorb, or to expel them, destroys its own vitality; a State which does not include them is destitute of the chief basis of self-government. The theory of nationality, therefore, is a retrograde step in history.

Chapter 6
Nations and Empire, 1870–1914

Introduction

The final chapter of this Anthology contains extracts from sources related to imperialism in the late nineteenth and early twentieth century. All the texts are intended to introduce some European perspectives on imperialism and, as such, they are all written by European authors. They mostly relate to European expansion in Africa, as this was the focus of the more aggressive expansion of the late nineteenth century that has become associated with 'new imperialism'. In other respects the texts are more varied. Some of them are by rulers or politicians advocating specific policies, others are by contemporary writers reflecting on or analysing empire and imperialism, others again are by individuals caught up in the process of conquest and expansion. They are drawn from a wide range of sources: political speeches, newspapers, government reports, partisan pamphlets and eye-witness accounts.

We start with two extracts that have become central to any discussion of imperialism in this period. John Atkinson Hobson was one of the first writers to consider empire from a critical perspective and his analysis of British imperialism is a text to which historians continually return. His work greatly influenced that of Lenin, who argued forcefully that the 'new imperialism' was the product of the drive for spheres of influence for financial capital which was supported by governments. Extracts from Joseph Chamberlain and Earl Cromer show some of the ways politics and economics were combined in the forging of imperial policy.

The second group of texts is rather different, focusing on the economics of empire. All the texts in this section relate to a single example of an imperial industry, the jute industry of Dundee. You

6.1 'The Rhodes Colossus'. Cartoon in *Punch*, 10 December 1892, depicting Cecil Rhodes (1853–1902), the leading colonialist in southern Africa who championed the building of a railway linking British possessions from Cairo to Cape Town.

will find analyses of the ups and downs of the trade and several sources discussing the issues of free trade or tariffs, which was one of the great imperial controversies that divided Britain in the first decades of the twentieth century. There are also a number of sources that describe the impact of the jute industry on the economic and social life of Dundee.

The third group of texts relate to a particular episode in the European conquest of Africa: the Congo Free State. This unusual state was effectively the private empire of the Belgian King, Leopold II. The texts include extracts from a number of his speeches and papers and also two highly critical accounts of the Free State, an extract from a pamphlet by E.D. Morel (6.13) and a report by the British consul, Roger Casement (6.14).

The final set of texts concern the German empire in Africa. Again, you will find extracts from political speeches on empire, both for and against. There are also several long extracts from a fascinating account by a German woman, Else Sonnenberg, who witnessed the Herero uprising in South-West Africa (now Namibia), a text not previously printed in English (6.16). Also included are extracts from the memoirs of an officer who participated in the war against the Herero.

Together these texts are intended to give an insight into some of the ways that ideas about empire were formed and articulated by Europeans. As they show, late nineteenth-century imperialism was motivated by a complex web of economic, political and cultural factors. Understanding imperialism involves investigating economics, state policy at home and abroad and the ideologies that made the pursuit of these policies possible.

Donna Loftus and Robin Mackie

6.1
Theories of imperialism

J.A. Hobson ([1902] 1988) *Imperialism: A Study*, 3rd edn., introd. J. Townshend, London: Unwin Hyman, pp. 23, 26–7, 80–1, 200–2.

John Atkinson Hobson (1858–1940) was an English economist who became well known for his critique of imperialism written in 1902 from which the extracts below are taken. His work is known for suggesting a link between capitalism and imperialism. His writings reveal that he was a believer in the ability of a laissez-faire political economy to lead to a genuine internationalism of self-governing states trading fairly. But, as the extracts show, Hobson was anti the 'new imperialism', a term he helped to popularise, as an anti-democratic impulse to colonise as an outlet for surplus capital. As the final extract illustrates, Hobson developed his argument into a critique of the way finance capital manipulated popular patriotic sentiments to gain support for imperialistic ventures.

The new Imperialism established no single British colony endowed with responsible self-government. Nor, with the exception of the three new States in South Africa, where white settlers lived in some numbers, is it seriously pretended that any of these annexed territories was being prepared and educated for representative, responsible self-government; and even in these South African States there is no serious intention, either on the part of the Home Government or of the colonists, that the majority of the inhabitants shall control the government.

It is true that some of these areas enjoy a measure of self-government, as protectorates or as feudatory States, under their own native princes. But all these in major matters of policy are subject to the absolute rule of the British Government, or of some British official, while the general tendency is towards drawing the reins of arbitrary control more tightly over protectorates, converting them into States which are in substance, though not always in name, Crown colonies. With the exception of a couple of experiments in India, the tendency everywhere has been towards a closer and more drastic imperial control over the territories that have been annexed, transforming protectorates, company rule, and spheres of influence into definite British States of the Crown colony order.

This is attributable, not to any greed of tyranny on the part of the Imperial Government, but to the conditions imposed upon our rule by considerations of climate and native population. Almost the whole of this new territory is tropical, or so near to the tropics as to preclude genuine colonisation of British settlers, while in those few districts where Europeans can work and breed, as in parts of South Africa and Egypt, the preoccupation of the country by large native populations of 'lower races' precludes any considerable settlement of British workers and the safe bestowal of the full self-government which prevails in Australasia and Canada.

The same is true to an even more complete extent of the Imperialism of other continental countries. The new Imperialism nowhere extended the political and civil liberties of the mother country to any part of the vast territories which, after 1870, fell under the government of Western civilized Powers. Politically, the new Imperialism was an expansion of autocracy.

[. . .]

Over-production in the sense of an excessive manufacturing plant, and surplus capital which could not find sound investments within the country, forced Great Britain, Germany, Holland, France to place larger and larger portions of their economic resources outside the area of their present political domain, and then stimulate a policy of political expansion so as to take in the new areas. The economic sources of this movement are laid bare by periodic trade-depressions due to an inability of producers to find adequate and profitable markets for what they can produce. The Majority Report of the Commission upon the Depression of Trade in 1885 put the matter in a nutshell. 'That, owing to the nature of the times, the demand for our commodities does not increase at the same rate as formerly; that our capacity for production is consequently in excess of our requirements, and could be considerably increased at short notice; that this is due partly to the competition of the capital which is being steadily accumulated in the country.' The Minority Report straightly imputed the condition of affairs to 'over-production.' Germany was in the early 1900s suffering severely from what is called a glut of capital and of manufacturing power: she had to have new markets; her Consuls all over the world were 'hustling' for trade; trading settlements were forced upon Asia Minor; in East and West Africa, in China and elsewhere the German Empire was impelled to a policy of colonization and protectorates as outlets for German commercial energy.

GERMANY

Every improvement of methods of production, every concentration of ownership and control, seems to accentuate the tendency. As one nation after another enters the machine economy and adopts advanced industrial methods, it becomes more difficult for its manufacturers, merchants, and financiers to dispose profitably of their economic resources, and they are tempted more and more to use their Governments in order to secure for their particular use some distant undeveloped country by annexation and protection.

The process, we may be told, is inevitable, and so it seems upon a superficial inspection. Everywhere appear excessive powers of production, excessive capital in search of investment. It is admitted by all business men that the growth of the powers of production in their country exceeds the growth in consumption, that more goods can be produced than can be sold at a profit, and that more capital exists than can find remunerative investment.

It is this economic condition of affairs that forms the taproot of Imperialism. If the consuming public in this country raised its standard of consumption to keep pace with every rise of productive powers, there could be no excess of goods or capital clamorous to use Imperialism in order to find markets: foreign trade would indeed exist, but there would be no difficulty in exchanging a small surplus of our manufactures for the food and raw material we annually absorbed, and all the savings that we made could find employment, if we chose, in home industries.

[. . .]

Aggressive Imperialism, as our investigation has shown, is virtually confined to the coercion by stronger or better-armed nations of nations which are, or seem to be, weaker and incapable of effective resistance; everywhere some definite economic or political gain is sought by the imperial aggressor. The chivalrous spirit of Imperialism leads neither Great Britain nor any other Western nation to assail a powerful State, however tyrannous, or to assist a weak State reputed to be poor.

The blending of strong interested with weak disinterested forces is indeed characteristic of the age. It is the homage which Imperialism pays to humanity. But just as the mixture known as 'philanthropy and 5 per cent.' is distrusted in the ordinary business world, so in the larger policy of nations the same combination is by right suspect. When business is harnessed with benevolence the former is commonly allowed to determine the direction and to set the pace. Doubtless it says something for the moral sensibility of a nation that a gainful course is rendered more attractive by a tincture of disinterestedness. But the theory and the practice in modern history often border so closely on hypocrisy that we cannot feel surprise that unfriendly foreigners apply the term to them. What, for example, can we say of the following frank description of Imperialism by Sir George now Lord Baden-Powell? 'The ultimate unit, the taxpayer – whether home or colonial – looks for two groups of results as his reward. On the one hand, he hopes to see Christianity and civilization *pro tanto* extended; and, on the other, to see some compensating development of industry and trade. Unless he, or "his servants the Government," secure either or both

405

these results, the question must be plainly asked, Has he the right, and is he right, to wage such wars?'[1]

What is the mode of equating the two groups of results? how much Christianity and civilization balance how much industry and trade? are curious questions which seem to need an answer. Is not the ultimate unit in his capacity of taxpayer liable to lay more stress upon the asset which admits of monetary measurement, and to undervalue the one that evades arithmetic?

'To combine the commercial with the imaginative' was the aim which Mr. Rhodes ascribed to himself as the key of his policy. The conjunction is commonly described by the word 'speculation,' a word whose meaning becomes more sinister when politics and private business are so inextricably interwoven as they were in the career of Mr. Rhodes, who used the legislature of Cape Colony to support and strengthen the diamond monopoly of De Beers, while from De Beers he financed the Raid, debauched the constituencies of Cape Colony, and bought the public press, in order to engineer the war, which was to win him full possession of his great 'thought' the North.

6.2
Imperialism and capitalism

N. [Vladimir Illyich] Lenin (1926 edn.) *Imperialism.
The State and Revolution,* New York: Vanguard, pp. 103–6.
This preface was first published under the title 'Imperialism and Capitalism' in *Communist International,* no. 18,
dated October 1921.

Vladimir Illyich Lenin (1870–1924) was a Russian Marxist revolutionary. He wrote *Imperialism* in 1915–16. In a preface written in 1917, after the Russian Revolution, Lenin argued that he wrote the pamphlet with limited access to literature and subject to the

---

[1] Sir George S. Baden-Powell (1896) 'Policy and Wealth in Ashanti'. Addendum to R.S.S. Baden-Powell (1896) *The Downfall of Prempeh: A Diary of Life with the Native Levy in Ashanti 1895–96,* London: Methuen and Co. The book was an account by the then Major Robert Baden Powell (1857–1941), future founder of the Scout Movement, of his campaigns in the Gold Coast colony (now Ghana) against King Prempeh of Asante. The reference to George Baden-Powell as Lord Baden-Powell is incorrect.

censorship of the Tsarist regime. Lenin openly declared his work to be influenced by Hobson and others such as the Austrian Marxist Rudolf Hilferding. In the extract below, Lenin summarises his argument that imperialism is caused by the competitive drive to find outlets for the profits of monopoly capitalism, a stage of capitalism he saw as final. In the preface to the French and German edition, written in 1920, Lenin argued that the war of 1914 to 1918 was imperialist, caused by a desire to carve out spheres for the 'influence of financial capital'. Lenin's concept of monopoly capitalism does not accurately describe the British economy of the late nineteenth and early twentieth century. Nevertheless his treatise has had a considerable influence on historiography in the twentieth century, leading many historians to consider the economic costs and benefits of imperialism.

We have seen that imperialism is, in its economic essence, monopolist capitalism. Its historic place is determined by this fact, for monopoly born out of free competition, and precisely out of *free* competition, is the transition of the capitalist social order to a higher order. We must notice especially four chief aspects of monopolies, or four chief manifestations of capitalist monopoly, which are characteristic of the period under review.

(1) Monopoly has grown up out of the concentration of production at a very advanced stage of the latter's development. This is illustrated in the case of monopolist capitalist unions: combines, syndicates and trusts. We have seen the large part that it plays in modern economic life. At the beginning of the 20th century, monopolies have acquired complete supremacy in the advanced countries. And if the first steps towards the formation of the combines were earlier made by countries enjoying the protection of high tariffs (Germany, America), Britain, with her system of free trade, has shown, only a little later, the same fact, namely, the birth of monopoly out of the concentration of production.

(2) Monopolies have led to the intensive seizure of the most important sources of raw materials, especially for the coal and iron industry, which is the principal industry of capitalist society and that over which the trusts have the greatest control. The exercise of monopoly over the most important sources of raw materials has terribly increased the power of big capital, and has sharpened the antagonism between production which is in the hands of the trusts, and production which is not.

(3) Monopoly has sprung from the banks. These have developed into the monopolists of finance-capital out of modest intermediaries. Some three or five of the biggest banks in each of the foremost capitalist countries have achieved the 'personal union' of industrial and banking capital, and concentrated in their hands the disposal of thousands upon thousands of millions which form the greater part of the capital and revenue of entire countries. A financial oligarchy, imposing an infinite number of financial ties of dependence upon all the economic and political institutions of contemporary capitalist society without exception – such is the most striking manifestation of this monopoly.

(4) Monopoly has grown out of colonial policy. To the numerous 'old' motives of colonial policy the capitalist financier has added the struggle for the sources of raw materials, for the exportation of capital, for 'spheres of influence,' *i.e.*, for spheres of good business, concessions, monopolist profits, and so on; in fine, for economic territory in general. When the European powers did not as yet occupy with their colonies a tenth part of Africa (as was the case in 1876), colonial policy was able to develop otherwise than by the methods of monopoly – by 'free grabbing' of territories, so to speak. But when nine-tenths of Africa had been seized (towards 1900), when the whole world had been shared out, the period of colonial monopoly opened and as a result the period of bitterest struggle for the partition and the repartition of the world.

It is known in general how much monopolist capital has deepened all the inherent contradictions of capitalism. It is enough to mention the high cost of living and the yoke of the trusts. This deepening of contradictions constitutes the most powerful driving force of the transitional period of history, which began from the time of the definite victory of finance-capital.

Monopolies, oligarchy, the tendency towards domination instead of the tendency towards liberty, the exploitation of an increasing number of small or weak nations by an extremely small minority of the richest or most powerful nations – all these have given birth to those distinctive characteristics of imperialism which oblige us to define it as parasitic or decaying capitalism. More and more there emerges, as one of the tendencies of imperialism, the creation of the 'Bond-holding (Rentier) State,' the usurer State, in which the bourgeoisie lives on the exportation of capital and on the 'clipping of interest coupons.' It would be a mistake to believe that this tendency to decay excludes the possibility of the rapid growth of capitalism. It does not. Separate branches of production, different strata of the bourgeoisie, and individual countries display with more or less strength in the imperialist period one or other of these tendencies. In a general way capitalism is growing far more rapidly than before, but this growth is becoming more and more irregular, and the irregularity is showing itself, in particular, in the decay of the countries which are richest in capital (such as England).

[. . .]

The receipt of high monopoly profits by the capitalists of one of the numerous branches of industry, of one of the numerous countries, etc., gives them the economic possibility of corrupting individual sections of the working class and sometimes a fairly considerable minority, attracting them on to the side of the capitalists of a given industry or nation against all the others. The deepening of antagonisms between imperialist nations for the partition of the world, increases the importance of this fact. And so there is created the bond between imperialism and opportunism, which has revealed itself first and most clearly in England, thanks to the fact that certain characteristics of imperialist development have been observable much sooner than in other countries.

6.3

Joseph Chamberlain, speech on 'The True Conception of Empire', 1897

C.W. Boyd (ed.) (1914) *Mr Chamberlain's Speeches*, introd. A. Chamberlain, London: Constable & Co., 2 vols., vol. 2, pp. 3–4.

Joseph Chamberlain (1836–1914) first entered Parliament as a Radical Liberal MP, serving in Gladstone's government. However, he later split with the Liberals over Home Rule for Ireland. When the Conservative Lord Salisbury formed a Unionist government in 1895, Chamberlain was made Colonial Secretary, a position he held during the Boer War (1899–1902). As the extract shows, Chamberlain believed that Britain was a superior nation that could bring prosperity through imperialist expansion. In the first few years of the twentieth century he campaigned for a united empire and tariff reform to establish a preferable market for the goods from Britain and the empire. He withdrew from political life after suffering a stroke in 1906 without realising his aims.

In carrying out this work of civilisation we are fulfilling what I believe to be our national mission, and we are finding scope for the exercise of those faculties and qualities which have made of us a great governing race. I do not say that our success has been perfect in every case, I do not say that all our methods have been beyond reproach; but I do say that in almost every instance in which the rule of the Queen has been established and the great *Pax Britannica*[1] has been enforced, there has come with it greater security to life and property, and a material improvement in the condition of the bulk of the population. No doubt, in the first instance, when these conquests have been made, there has been bloodshed, there has been loss of life among the native populations, loss of still more precious lives among those who have been sent out to bring these countries into some kind of disciplined order, but it must be remembered that that is the condition of the mission we have to fulfil. There are, of course, among us – there always are among us, I think – a very small minority of men who are ready to be the advocates of the most detestable tyrants, provided their skin is black – men who sympathise with the sorrows of Prempeh and Lobengula,[2] and who denounce as murderers those of their countrymen who have gone forth at the command of the Queen, and who have redeemed districts as large as Europe from the barbarism and the superstition in which they had been steeped for centuries. I remember a picture by Mr. Selous[3] of a philanthropist – an imaginary philanthropist, I will hope – sitting cosily by his fireside and denouncing the methods by which British civilisation was promoted. This philanthropist complained of the use of Maxim guns and other instruments of warfare, and asked why we could not proceed by more conciliatory methods, and why the impis of Lobengula could not be brought before a magistrate, and fined five shillings and bound over to keep the peace.

[1] Latin for the 'British Peace'. Like the *Pax Romana* (the 'Roman Peace') it refers to the period when the empire was in its prime. The *Pax Britannica* is seen as beginning after the battle of Waterloo (1815) and declining from the 1870s with the industrialisation of the United States and Germany. It was a period when the British empire controlled key trade routes and overseas markets. This in turn led to the spread of the English language and parliamentary democracy.

[2] Lobengula Kumalo (d. 1894), last king of the Ndebele people, who dominated a large area of what is now Zimbabwe before their defeat in the 1890s by the forces of the British South Africa Company.

[3] Henry Courteney Selous (1803–90), British painter and illustrator.

No doubt there is a humorous exaggeration in this picture, but there is gross exaggeration in the frame of mind against which it was directed. You cannot have omelettes without breaking eggs; you cannot destroy the practices of barbarism, of slavery, of superstition, which for centuries have desolated the interior of Africa, without the use of force; but if you will fairly contrast the gain to humanity with the price which we are bound to pay for it, I think you may well rejoice in the result of such expeditions as those which have been recently conducted with such signal success in Nyassaland, Ashanti, Benin, and Nupé[4] – expeditions which may have, and indeed have, cost valuable lives, but as to which we may rest assured that for one life lost a hundred will be gained, and the cause of civilisation and the prosperity of the people will in the long run be eminently advanced. But no doubt such a state of things, such a mission as I have described, involves heavy responsibility. In the wide dominions of the Queen the doors of the temple of Janus are never closed,[5] and it is a gigantic task that we have undertaken when we have determined to wield the sceptre of empire. Great is the task, great is the responsibility, but great is the honour; and I am convinced that the conscience and the spirit of the country will rise to the height of its obligations, and that we shall have the strength to fulfil the mission which our history and our national character have imposed upon us. ??

6.4

Britain's acquisition of Egypt in 1882

Earl of Cromer (1908), *Modern Egypt*, New York: Macmillan, 2 vols., vol. 1, pp. xvii–xviii.

The Earl of Cromer, Sir Evelyn Baring (1841–1917), served as the first British Viceroy of Egypt (1883–1907). In this extract from his account of his time there, he gives the reasons why, in his opinion,

[4] British protectorates and territories in West and Central Africa. Nyassaland forms part of modern-day Malawi. The Ashanti empire was annexed in to the Gold Coast colony (now Ghana). The kingdom of Benin then was in Southern Nigeria. Nupé covered northern and central Nigeria.

[5] The temple of Janus stood in the Roman Forum. The temple contained a statue of Janus, the Roman god of boundaries. It had doors at both ends which were usually open. They were closed, rarely, in times of peace.

the British had to occupy Egypt in 1882. The Egyptian ruler, Ismail Pasha (ruled 1863–79), borrowed considerable sums of money from Britain and France that he was unable to pay back, leading the European powers to take control of Egyptian finances in 1879 to ensure the debts were repaid. A rebellion led by Ahmed Bey Arabi, a colonel in the Egyptian army who was angry at corruption and foreign interference in the Egyptian government, was put down when the British bombarded the port of Alexandria and occupied Egypt in 1882. Although not formally annexed, Egypt was administered by the British for over seventy years.

Egypt may now almost be said to form part of Europe. It is on the high road to the Far East. It can never cease to be an object of interest to all the powers of Europe, and especially to England. A numerous and intelligent body of Europeans and of non-Egyptian orientals have made Egypt their home. European capital to a large extent has been sunk in the country. The rights and privileges of Europeans are jealously guarded, and, moreover, give rise to complicated questions, which it requires no small amount of ingenuity and technical knowledge to solve. Exotic institutions have sprung up and have taken root in the country. The capitulations impair those rights of internal sovereignty which are enjoyed by the rulers or legislatures of most states. The population is heterogeneous and cosmopolitan to a degree almost unknown elsewhere. Although the prevailing faith is that of Islam, in no country in the world is a greater variety of religious creeds to be found amongst important sections of the community.

In addition to these peculiarities, which are of a normal character, it has to be borne in mind that in 1882 the [Egyptian] army was in a state of mutiny; the treasury was bankrupt; every branch of the administration had been dislocated; the ancient and arbitrary method, under which the country had for centuries been governed, had received a severe blow, whilst, at the same time, no more orderly and law-abiding form of government had been inaugurated to take its place. Is it probable that a government composed of the rude elements described above, and led by men of such poor ability as Arabi and his coadjutators, would have been able to control a complicated machine of this nature? Were the sheikhs of the El-Azhar mosque likely to succeed where Tewfik Pasha[1] and his ministers, who were men of comparative

---

[1] Tewfik Pasha (1852–92) succeeded his father Ismail as Khedive of Egypt in 1879 when Britain and France put pressure on the Sultan of Turkey to remove him. Until the occupation, Tewfik worked with the European powers.

education and enlightenment, acting under the guidance and inspiration of a first-class European power, only met with a modified success after years of patient labor? There can be but one answer to these questions. Nor is it in the nature of things that any similar movement should, under the present conditions of Egyptian society, meet with any better success. The full and immediate execution of a policy of 'Egypt for the Egyptians', as it was conceived by the Arabists in 1882, was, and still is, impossible.

[. . .]

By the process of exhausting all other expedients, we arrive at the conclusion that armed British intervention was, under the special circumstances of the case, the only possible solution of the difficulties which existed in 1882. Probably also it was the best solution. The arguments against British intervention, indeed, were sufficiently obvious. It was easy to foresee that, with a British garrison in Egypt, it would be difficult that the relations of England either with France or Turkey should be cordial. With France, especially, there would be a danger that our relations might become seriously strained. Moreover, we lost the advantages of our insular position. The occupation of Egypt necessarily dragged England to a certain extent within the arena of Continental politics. In the event of war, the presence of a British garrison in Egypt would possibly be a source of weakness rather than of strength. Our position in Egypt placed us in a disadvantageous diplomatic position, for any power, with whom we had a difference of opinion about some non-Egyptian question, was at one time able to retaliate by opposing our Egyptian policy. The complicated rights and privileges possessed by the various powers of Europe in Egypt facilitated action of this nature.

There can be no doubt of the force of these arguments. The answer to them is that it was impossible for Great Britain to allow the troops of any other power to occupy Egypt. When it became apparent that some foreign occupation was necessary, that the Sultan would not act save under conditions which were impossible of acceptance, and that neither French nor Italian cooperation could be secured, the British government acted with promptitude and vigor. A great nation cannot throw off the responsibilities which its past history and its position in the world have imposed upon it. English history affords other examples of the government and people of England drifting by accident into doing what was not only right, but was also most in accordance with British interests.

similar sentiments to Chamberlain

413

6.5

Booms and slumps in the Dundee textile industry

A.J. Warden (1864) *The Linen Trade, Ancient and Modern*,
London: Longman, Green, Longman, Roberts & Green,
pp. 614, 618–19, 632.

Alexander J. Warden (1810–92) was recognised by contemporaries as one of the authorities on the Dundee linen trade in which he worked for over 60 years. He ran his own business from 1833 to 1852 until his factory burnt down. Later he turned to writing. As well as *The Linen Trade*, he wrote a five-volume history of Forfarshire. In the following passage, Warden describes the dramatic ups and downs in the Dundee linen and jute industries of the preceding decade.

Within the last few years a new era has dawned on the trade. Many power-loom works have been put up; others are in course of erection, and others contemplated, some of them of great magnitude. Judging from the changes which have taken place within the last ten years, a very few years more will see handlooms almost entirely supplanted, as they cannot compete successfully with power-looms, excepting for a few fabrics for which they seem to be best suited.

[. . .]

During the Crimean War an immense demand sprang up for coarse Linens, and the manufactures of Dundee were largely consumed by both belligerents during the siege of Sebastopol.[1] The profits then realised stimulated enterprise, and led to the erection of extensive new works for spinning and weaving by power, and to great additions to previous ones. In this way the production was extended greatly beyond the legitimate wants of consumers, and much money was locked up in buildings and machinery which ought to have been conserved and retained in the trade. In 1857 the report of the failure of a Trust Company in America, followed by a panic there, reached this country. Suddenly the storm burst over the kingdom; merchant

---

[1] Sebastapol was one of the chief battles of the Crimean War (1854–6) which pitted Turkey, Britain and France against Russia. The war years were good for business but were followed by a slump in 1857.

princes succumbed to the tornado, and banks of good repute gave way before it.

[. . .]

In Dundee the prices of goods fell seriously, in some cases 50 per cent., many failures occurred, and much distress was endured by the working-classes. After that period trade went on regularly, but quietly, until the second year of the war in America. Cottons, which had risen to five times their cost before the war, could not be got in quantity, and the void was in many cases supplied by Linen, which increased the demand throughout the world.[2] The extensive requirements of the armies in America, both Federal and Confederate, have absorbed an immense quantity of coarse and heavy Linens, and caused the pressing demand for them which has kept the mills and factories in full operation for the last two years. The immediate effect of this unparalleled activity has been to add greatly to the wealth of almost every house engaged in the Linen trade here, and to the prosperity and importance of the whole town. Part of the wealth thus acquired has been laid out in extending old works or in building new ones.

[. . .]

It was a fortunate circumstance for Dundee that Jute was introduced into its manufactures. Since then the extension of the town has been in some measure dependent on the progress made in incorporating this fibre into its staple trade. During the last two years, in consequence of the cotton famine and the American war, the demand for Linen, as already mentioned, has increased amazingly. Flax has been an important article, as genuine Linens have been largely consumed, and this branch of the trade has enjoyed universal prosperity. Its Oriental sister, Jute, has, however, been a more important fibre here, as its products are cheap yet sightly, and they have afforded a ready means for supplying the extraordinary demand for low class Linens. The consumption of this article has therefore increased enormously, and is still extending, and it may now be called the great staple of Dundee. Notwithstanding the high price of Jute for the past two years, this trade has been very remunerative, and some parties have realized handsome fortunes in it. The superstructure of the prosperity of Dundee may therefore be said to be founded on Jute. May the building be as stable as it is stately! May the halo which surrounds the Linen trade of Dundee long continue to shine with undiminished lustre!

---

[2] This is a reference to the American Civil War (1861–5). The Northern blockage of the South cut Britain off from Southern cotton with devastating effects for the cotton industry.

6.6

Summary of evidence presented to the Tariff Commission, 1905

Tariff Commission (1905) *Report of the Tariff Commission*,
vol. 2. Part 7: *The Textiles Trades. Evidence on the Flax,
Jute and Hemp Industries*, London, paras. 3640 to 3641:
'Summary of Oral and Written Evidence'.

The Tariff Commission was set up by the Tariff Reform League, a political pressure group which campaigned for an imperial tariff (a tariff on goods coming in to the British Empire). The Tariff Commission collected evidence from manufacturers and other businessmen on the damage that they believed free trade was doing to Britain. The following passage is ascribed to 'a Dundee merchant'.

We have lost since 1860 all the Continental markets . . . Then there was practically no foreign competition. Dundee supplied the whole world, even San Francisco and the Cape and all the South African and Australian markets. Of course, the demand was not so great; it has developed over the course of time. Foreign competition began in Germany. The first factory was erected in Brunswick in about 1862 by an agent of our own who was also the means of bringing about the tariff of 1879. . . . I am perfectly sure that large manufacturing industries would not have sprung up in the competing countries without the tariffs. These countries have also taken a large share of our foreign trade in other countries, and that has developed during these last three years through the Kartells; in fact they even compete with the Dundee manufacturers in our own trade here. The occasional trade that is left is when Calcutta does not supply, or the Argentine countries require a quick delivery when they find all of a sudden they have a very great harvest, and cannot wait for shipment from Calcutta, which takes between three or four months, and they want to have the goods in three or four weeks. Then they must buy them in Dundee. Such a demand as that springs up, and even that is supplied now very often by the Germans.

6.7

The Protectionist Revival:
letters by Dundee merchants

The *Dundee Yearbook* was an annual round-up of local news published by the local newspaper, the *Dundee Advertiser*. In July 1903, following Joseph Chamberlain's speech in Birmingham advocating tariff reform, the Editor of the *Advertiser* wrote to 'leading merchants in the city, asking them to give opinions as to the effect of such a Policy on local trade' (*Dundee Yearbook, 1903*, p. 160). Extracts (a), (b) and (c) are from answers they received. Victor Fraenkl, of Jaffé Brothers, was a leading merchant in the city; George Thom was a manufacturer. Extract (d) is from a debate held at the Dundee Chamber of Commerce in January 1904. The local MP, Sir John Leng (who was also the editor of the *Dundee Advertiser*), spoke seconding a motion in favour of free trade.

Dundee Advertiser (1904) *The Dundee Yearbook: facts and figures for 1903*, Dundee: John Leng & Co., pp. 162–76.

(a)

Having lost the Continental markets of France, Germany, Austria-Hungary, and Italy for the sale of jute goods and yarns, the merchants were restricted in Europe to those countries which for reasons of their own did not yet spin or manufacture all their requirements. These markets were until recently entirely supplied by us, but overproduction in Austria, Italy, and Germany brings us face to face with a competition which threatens to rob us of the last outlet we had for jute goods in Europe. [. . .] It is a fact well known that these countries export at a great loss to themselves. [. . .] It is bad enough if these Continental countries decide to shut us out from their own markets, but it is calamitous if they interfere with legitimate trade by most unnatural and artificial means.

[. . .]

One remedy is certainly visible if all others fail – viz., an export duty on jute to all parts of the world where spinning or weaving are done. . . . [W]e have surely some right to a certain amount of consideration from India, and we believe we should meet with no objection from our Calcutta competitors. Jute is practically a monopoly, and, as far as one can see, will never be grown anywhere else. [. . .] India being part of our Empire, is it not natural enough to expect that we should be treated by it on special terms?

[. . .]

Your second query relates to Calcutta competition. There is no denying that Calcutta has taken all the most important markets from us, and is likely to make further inroads into the remaining ones as time goes on. I don't see that this can be prevented, and, being an industry of our own country, it must continue to enjoy its full liberty. But it should have no more liberty than we have ourselves, and all we can ask for is that it should be placed under the same Factory Act.[1] This should help us a little, and we should then feel that we have to deal with a legitimate competition. More we cannot expect.

[. . .]

VICTOR FRAENKL.

(b)

Tariffs have certainly deprived us of the bulk of our continental trade, which in the earlier days formed such a large proportion of our exports. . . . For a good period now our export trade has been chiefly with the United States, South America, and other markets, all of which have developed so enormously that without Calcutta competition instead of Dundee marking time the trade would have been steady and largely expanding. It is not the foreigner we have got to fear, but the children of our own household in India, who are throttling our trade in conditions that are absolutely unfair, and against which the Factory Acts of our high civilisation at home as compared with the lax law in India will prohibit any possibility of much further development of our industry here. . . . The lynx-eyed factory inspector of our high civilisation does not exist in the East where under a Factory Act more fitted to the 17th century the conditions are such that we are being killed by inches by the children of our great Empire – not respectable foreigners at whom we are so ready to point the finger of scorn. We could survive all the foreign competition there is, or ever may be, but it is beyond the wit of man to fight aggressively successful against the jute industry

---

[1] The Factory Acts referred to here and in subsequent texts were a series of Acts of Parliament that restricted the number of hours that women and children could be employed. Restrictions did not apply to adult male workers.

in India as it exists under the British Empire. . . . Nor would the plausible idea of an export duty on raw jute in India with a rebate to British possessions save us from Indian competition. It would only give us cheaper fibre than the foreigner, who, of course, has retaliation open to him.

GEO. R. THOM.

Craigolea, Stonehaven, 31st July 1903

(c)

It is a perfect marvel to me, when there has been so much intercourse between Dundee and Calcutta, and when everything is known that can be known about the jute industry and environing conditions in India amongst the merchants and manufacturers at home, that there should be so much that is unintelligent yet spoken on the subject in Dundee.

Some seem to think that the British Government ought to compel India to put an export duty on all jute save that which goes to Britain, and thereby involve us in a war of tariffs with all our Continental and American customers for the sake of enabling some 50 or 60 manufacturers in a Scotch town to make a little more money than they are now doing.

[. . .]

Then some of your spinners still seem to be under the impression that if they could get a Factory Act imposed on India cutting down our working hours to somewhere about the same number that you have in Dundee, then what they are pleased to call 'unfair competition' would cease. A very little reflection will show them the utter absurdity of the position they have taken up.

Just here, and by way of parenthesis, I may state that the women and children are better cared for under our Factory Act than yours are at home. Our women and children work fewer hours per week, are better and more sanitarily housed, can save a greater percentage of their wages, and enjoy more holidays than the Dundee mill-workers do.

Supposing, then, that the British Government were foolish enough, at the unintelligent cry of Dundee, to order the Indian Government to pass an Act curtailing our working hours to, say, 60 per week, what would happen? Certainly not a sudden curtailment of production equal to 25 per cent. – . . . If a mill had to increase its production so that it could turn out as much production during 60 hours as it now does in

80, the increased cost of production would not be more than R[upee]s 6 (equal to 8 s[hillings]) per ton.

[. . .]

There are some mill men here who think (and I fully agree with them) . . . that even the Rs.6 would be saved in the increased output per loom per hour under a 60 hours week than is obtained now under the very long day. But how any possible manipulation of our Factory Act such as competitors in Dundee are continually crying for would weaken our competition with home manufacturers it is impossible to see. Dundee has her own share of the jute manufacturing industry, and the enterprise of her manufacturers and merchants has sought out new markets for jute specialities, while we have gone in for the common run of easily made fabrics. This kind of work will suit Calcutta for a long time to come. Somehow or other, also, Dundee spinners can buy their jute better, and (even freight included) can lay down their batch in their mills as cheap as most of the mills do out here, and they are abler yet to take more money out of inferior fibre than Calcutta has tried to do up to the present. Dundee is able to hold her own. Let her go on and prosper along her own lines, but let her never think that she can do any good to herself or anybody else by crying out for protective duties and impossible Factory Acts for India. Her commercial salvation lies altogether in another direction. – I am &c.,

A CALCUTTA DUNDONIAN.

Calcutta, 3rd September 1903

(d) 'The Fiscal Question. Debate in the Dundee Chamber of Commerce'

Dundee Advertiser (1905) *The Dundee Yearbook: facts and figures for 1904*, Dundee: John Leng & Co., p. 97.

[Sir John Leng starts by reviewing the history of the town and reminding the audience of trades now gone]:

It may be admitted that a few particular trades in this country are not as prosperous as they once were. [. . .] There are changes in trades and changes in the localities of trades. One fails and another prospers. One rises and another decays. The Sugar House Wynd, the Bucklemaker Wynd, and the Bonnet Hill either exist no longer or are not known by those names; nevertheless the trade of the town as a whole, the number of people employed, and their wages have greatly increased.

Taking the jute trade as a whole – What is the great complaint? What competition has it chiefly suffered from? The answer is Calcutta. The mills on the Hooghly, several of which have been built by Dundee capital, and most of them planned, engined, spindled, and loomed by Dundee engineers; financed and directed from Panmure Street, within a few yards of this Exchange – these Dundee-owned and managed Calcutta mills have been the chief invaders of Dundee markets, and in a sense the most formidable dumpers of cheap jute goods in competition with those made in Dundee mills.

Having visited Calcutta, and seen a number of the mills on the Hooghly between Calcutta and Barnagore, I confess it seems to me their situation in the country where jute grows, with native labour so much cheaper than ours, with such facilities both of land and water carriage, and without the restrictions of our factory legislation, give them advantages which make it exceedingly difficult for our local manufacturers to meet their competition. Is there any responsible statesman prepared to propose that the Mother Country shall be protected against the competition of its own great dependencies?

6.8

Textile manufacturers in Dundee, 1864

A.J. Warden (1864) *The Linen Trade, Ancient and Modern,*
London: Longman, Green, Longman, Roberts & Green,
pp. 656–7.

The following tables are taken from the same book as Document 6.5. Warden included this list of all flax and jute works in Dundee as an Appendix.

Statement of the Spinning & Power-Loom Works in Dundee & Lochee, with Proprietors' Names, Horse-Power, Spindles, Power-Looms, and Numbers Employed, May 1864, Compiled from Information Derived, Excepting in a Very Few Instances, from the Proprietors.

	Proprietors' Names.	Designation of Works.	Engines.	Horse Power.	Spindles.	Power Looms.	Hands Employed.
1	A. and J. Adie,	South Anchor Works,	1	40	1,512	44	250
2	Peter Balfour's Creditors,	Rose Factory,	1	6	...	19	30
3	Baxter Brothers and Co.,	Dens Works,	16	615	19,744	1,200	4,000
4	Alexander Berrie,	West Dudhope Mill,	2	30	1,386	...	120
5	H. and T. Blyth,	Bank Mill,	1	35	1,500	67	350
6	Andrew Brown and Co.,	Bell Mill,	2	65	2,200	100	450
7	Alexander J. Buist,	Ward Mill,	2	55	2,500	...	240
8	Thomas Brough,	Taybank Works,	1	12	...	68	200
9	Edward Caird,	Ashton Works,	1	30	...	208	350
10	T. and J. Cargill,	Lower Pleasance Mill,	1	20	1,220	...	120
11	Cherles Chalmers and Co.,	Tay Street Works,	3	65	3,338	...	330
12	Cox Brothers,	Camperdown Linen Works, Lochee,	17	404	10,018	560	3,220
13	J. L. Cunningham,	Cotton Road Factory,	2	6	...	6	80
14	James Donald and Donald Brothers,	Pitalpine Works, Lochee,	2	70	1,802	85	300
15	A. and D. Edward and Co.,	Logie Works,	5	260	17,000	600	2,500
16	John Ewan,	Verdant Mill,	3	82	2,800	70	500
17	William Fergusson and Sons,	Dudhope Works,	1	35	...	260	330
18	D. H. Fleming,	Rosebank Factory,	1	8	...	20	150
19	W. and R. H. Fleming,	Hillside Works,	1	6	...	20	200
20	Gibson, Farquharson, and Co.,	Craigie Mill,	2	80	2,800	20	450
21	Gilroy Brothers and Co.,	Tay Works,	5	240	10,096	300	2,000
22	John Gordon and Co.,	Anchor and Douglas Mills,	5	170	7,610	...	700
23	J. and A. D. Grimond,	Bowbridge Works and Maxwelltown Works,	5	132	3,600	136	1,600
24	J. and A. Guthrie,	Sea Braes Mill,	1	35	1,816	...	190
25	William Halley and Sons,	Wallace Craigie Mill,	2	80	3,000	100	700
26	Alexander Henderson,	South Dudhope Works,	2	50	2,000	85	460
27	John Henderson and Sons,	Lindsay Street Works,	1	40	1,790	45	480
28	J. Hoile and Co.,	Ramsay Works,	1	20	...	120	150
29	George Ireland, Jun.,	Barrack Street Mill,	2	35	960	22	200
30	James Irons,	Park Mill,	2	30	1,200	50	260
31	Kennedy and Co.,	Wellington Street Works,	1	10	...	35	120
		Carry Forward,.......	91	2,766	99,892	4,240	21,030

422

STATEMENT OF THE SPINNING & POWER-LOOM WORKS IN DUNDEE & LOCHEE, WITH PROPRIETORS' NAMES, HORSE-POWER, SPINDLES, POWER-LOOMS, AND NUMBERS EMPLOYED, MAY 1864, COMPILED FROM INFORMATION DERIVED, EXCEPTING IN A VERY FEW INSTANCES, FROM THE PROPRIETORS. – *contd.*

	PROPRIETORS' NAMES.	DESIGNATION OF WORKS.	Engines.	Horse Power.	Spindles.	Power. Looms.	Hands Employed.
		Brought Forward,	91	2,766	99,892	4,240	21,030
32	Kinmond, Luke, and Co.,	Pleasance Mill,	2	110	6,500	140	1,000
33	Laing and Ewan,	Dens Road Factory,	1	40	...	283	400
34	Lornie and Robertson,	Westfield Factory,	1	10	...	36	50
35	Alexander Low,	Hillbank Works,	2	50	2,100	120	420
36	Charles Lucas and Co.,	Clepington Works,	1	12	...	85	100
37	Malcolm, Ogilvie, and Co.,	Constable Works,	3	140	4,000	220	1,000
38	James Malcolm and Sons,	Chapelshade Works,	3	65	2,412	136	430
39	Mathers and Chalmers,	Scouringburn Mill,	1	30	1,500	...	160
40	O. G. Miller,	North, East, South, Column, and Arch Mills,	10	260	16,970	...	1,600
41	John Moir and Son,	Cottage Factory,	1	20	...	140	200
42	Alexander Moncur and Son,	Ure Street Works,	1	20	...	96	150
43	W. R. Morison and Co.,	Wallace Mill, and Wallace Works,	6	192	4,000	510	1,700
44	A. and J. Nicoll,	Ward Mills,	3	50	940	32	230
45	Edward Parker,	West Mills, Lochee,	2	40	1,124	12	170
46	James Paterson,	Law Mill, and Heathfield Factory,	3	75	3,080	...	770
47	James Prain,	Larch Street Factory,	1	8	...	40	100
48	H. P. Ree and Co.,	Blackness Road Factory,	2	24	...	140	300
49	Ritchie and Simpson,	Ward Road Mill,	1	30	1,124	24	600
50	H. Samson and Son,	Jamaica Street Factory,	1	10	...	28	150
51	George Schleselman,	Lochee Road Factory,	1	10	...	51	100
52	J. and W. Scott,	Hawkhill,	1	15	...	60	200
53	Shaw, Baxter, and Co.,	Annfield Factory,	1	12	...	24	200
54	John Sharp,	Milne Street Mill,	3	80	3,200	80	500
55	Smiths, Mitchell, and Co.,	Pole Park Mill,	1	80	4,500	...	750
56	Soutar and Nicoll,	Ladybank Mill,	2	40	880	12	150
57	Swan Brothers,	Hillbank Mill,	2	120	5,200	...	460
58	William Taylor and Co.,	Temple Mills,	2	52	2,400	...	300
59	Thomson, Shepherd, and Briggs,	Seafield Works,	7	165	6,000	120	2,000
60	J. and H. Walker,	Dura Mill,	2	60	3,230	80	600
61	Wybrants Brothers,	North Dudhope Mill,	2	35	1,500	...	200
		Total,	160	4,621	170,552	6,709	36,020

423

6.9

The Dundee local trade in 1892

Dundee Advertiser (1893) *The Dundee Yearbook: facts and figures for 1892,* Dundee: John Leng & Co., pp. 35–6.

The following passage is again taken from the *Dundee Yearbook* and looks back on the main developments in Dundee's principal trade in 1892.

Not within recent times has our leading local industry passed through such startling vicissitudes as those of 1892; and seldom, we are glad to think, has a twelvemonth's trading culminated so unsatisfactorily to all concerned. There has been a succession of rapid changes, with violent fluctuations in values and demand, occasioned by rash speculation and reckless overtrading, with the nett result that the year closes amidst distrust and depression.

[. . .]

The year opened, as it will be remembered, with a very excited market for raw material, values having been advanced greatly beyond their normal ratio owing to adverse reports from Calcutta as to available supplies. It was almost anticipated that the advance had reached the highest limit at the beginning of the year; but further adverse reports, supported by parties dealing in the article at full rates, led to a further advance, which was unfortunately followed to too great an extent by spinners and others here, the ultimate price being fully 100 per cent. over the average value of jute for the past ten years. Counsels of moderation were thrown to the winds. The 'bulls' had full possession of the situation, and spinners were convinced against their own better judgement. Statistics, estimates, &c., were freely current predicting the total collapse of the jute industry here and the stoppage of works from pure lack of material by the time that July should arrive and stocks had been worked up. The effect on yarns and cloth was not sufficient for those chiefly interested, and as the advance in these branches did not come quick enough speculative transactions were entered into also in those productions to continue 'the boom'. With jute at £21 to £22 for first marks[1] as against an average of £10 5s to

---

[1] The jute arriving in Dundee was graded. Prices were often quoted in first marks, the top grade for standard qualities of jute.

£10 10s, holders began to estimate their profits, and to act on them, their fortunes being as good as secured. Unfortunately everybody could not get out in time, and just when the works were to be stopped for want of jute, and holders expected a further advance, the whole thing had collapsed, and there was a scramble for a quittance. The estimates had proved false, the stocks here were larger than supposed, the amount required for current consumption less, and the new crop promised to be the largest on record.

[. . .]

Competition is becoming year by year more keen and close, and producers will have to use every effort to keep in close touch with consumers as directly as possible. The speculative element in the jute trade so largely predominant, and to which we have so often referred, is very unwholesome.

6.10
A tourist description of Dundee

Scott Moncrieff Penney (ed.) (1903) *Murray's Handbook for Travellers in Scotland*, London: Edward Stanford, pp. 276–7.

The following is the description of Dundee that appeared in a popular tourist guide to Scotland.

DUNDEE occupies a favourable position on the N. side of the Firth of Tay, not far from its mouth, on two hills, sloping gently to the water. It is a flourishing seaport and parl. burgh, ranking third in all Scotland for population and shipping, and is second only to Glasgow in respect of its manufactures. It was made a Royal Burgh by William the Lion, *circa* 1160, and was created a City by Royal Charter, dated 26th Jan. 1889. Its Chief Magistrate is styled Lord Provost by virtue of a Royal Warrant, dated 10th Feb. 1892. Dundee returns 2 Members of Parliament, and is the only town in Scotland which does so undivided into electoral areas.

It bristles with tall chimneys and abounds in great steam-loom mills. In these the spinning and weaving of *jute* and *flax* is carried on. Jute – from which the town has been nicknamed *Juteopolis* – is the fibre of a Bengal annual plant (*Corchorus capsularis*), 8–10 ft. high, with the stem no thicker than a finger. It is imported direct from

Calcutta, and is made into carpets and sacking. It was first introduced about 1840, but the trade received a great impetus when, owing to the American Civil War, cotton became scarce and dear. Now about 1,250,000 bales, each weighing 400 lbs., are imported annually at about £14 a ton. The *Camperdown Jute Works* of Cox Bros., Lim., at *Lochee*, N. W. of the town, occupying 28 acres, containing 20,000 spindles and 1000 power looms, producing 30–40 million yds. of cloth annually and employing 5500 hands, are the largest in the world, while those of Messrs. Gilroy in Lochee Road are also very large. The value of the annual export of linen from Dundee is about £3,000,000. The *Flax Mills* of Baxter Bros. and Co., Lim., alone employ about 4000 hands.

6.11

Report of the Committee of the Dundee Social Union

Dundee Social Union (1905) *Report on the Housing and Industrial Conditions in Dundee*, Dundee: John Leng & Co., pp. vii, xi–xii.

The Dundee Social Union was a philanthropic organisation which campaigned for social reform in Dundee. It was founded in 1888 by academics at Dundee's new university and other members of Dundee's middle class who were shocked by the appalling conditions in Dundee's slums. In the early years of the twentieth century, they organised a major investigation of social conditions in Dundee. This passage is taken from the Introduction to their report, describing the situation in 1904.

Preface by the Social Enquiry Committee

Except incidentally, and only in a minor degree, the Reports do not deal with remedies for the evils disclosed. This reticence may possibly be held to detract from the value of the results presented, but in the view of the Committee it is better that the larger reforms required should spring from a public opinion enlightened by data gathered from many enquiries prosecuted along similar lines. The weight of such opinion will be more effective in finding and applying remedies to certain social evils, which may be described fittingly and without exaggeration as a disgrace and national peril.

[. . .]

The enquiry into the conditions of women's labour and infant mortality touches upon a subject which has a special claim for consideration by the community of Dundee. Without women's labour the city would sink to the level of a small burgh: as a manufacturing centre it would possibly cease to exist. No other community, therefore, has a more vital interest in everything pertaining to the welfare of women.

Economic conditions beyond the control of employers have settled that labour in jute mills and factories must be cheap labour. The jute brought from India to be spun and woven in Dundee has to compete in the world's markets with the product of the native labour of Calcutta. The unequal fight has gone on for the past thirty years or more, with the advantage always in favour of Calcutta, which has grown from small beginnings in the manufacture of jute until to-day its production is double that of Dundee. It is true that efficient labour and cheap labour are not interchangeable terms, but it is an open question whether in the ordinary processes of jute manufacture the white workers have any special advantage in brain or skill in a contest with the Indian workers. If they have not, they must, in time, yield place to the cheaper workers unless a way is found to develop aptitudes in the white workers for more specialised forms of production. The problem is a difficult and anxious one.

It is chiefly because labour must be cheap in the jute works that women's labour is employed. Could men's labour be substituted in some substantial part of the work now done by women, some grave social evils would be mitigated. Between the ages of 20 and 45, Dundee has three women for two men, and around this significant fact hang some of the most serious problems.

Juvenile male labour is also in demand and is well paid, but the youth who has passed some years in the mill often finds himself at 17 or 18 without occupation, and with no trade or other skilled employment available. He either leaves the city, becomes an unskilled labourer, or develops into a loafer. The crying need of Dundee is more occupation for men and if employers of women's labour would accept the responsibility of finding a remedy, even if partial, they would do more for the city's welfare than can be effected front any other quarter.

Under such conditions women's labour is naturally to no inconsiderable extent also married women's labour. The married woman is often the principal, sometimes the sole, wage-earner, and in many works she is preferred for her experience and steadiness. The obligation to support a family and also to bring it up is an unnatural condition of life, which leads to the usual consequences – broken-down mothers in early life, and ill-nourished, rickety children, who develop into weedy, unhealthy men and women.

The Report upon Infant Mortality shows that Dundee in 1904 headed the list of 15 principal towns in Scotland with an infant mortality rate of 174 per 1000 births, Aberdeen being second with a rate of 151, Glasgow 146, Paisley 136, and Edinburgh 130. For the ten years 1893–1902 the rate for Dundee was 176, Glasgow being next with 149. Working mothers being most numerous in Dundee, owing to its special industrial life, and the conditions of textile employment unfavourable to the healthy nourishment of children before and after birth, this pre-eminence in mortality is what might be expected.

[. . .]

6.12

Speeches and documents of Leopold II, king of the Belgians[1]

Comte Louis de Lichtervelde (1929) *Léopold of the Belgians*,
trans. T.H. Reed, London: Stanley Paul & Co
(French original, 1926), pp. 33–4, 124–5, 193–5, 229.

The comte de Lichtervelde was private secretary to Charles de Broqueville, chief minister of Belgium from 1911 to 1918. As such, he had close links to the royal family and monarchist circles in Belgium. His book was written 'to establish in the eyes of the Belgians, first of all, the title to glory of this great King whose genius has been recognised at last, twenty years after his death, and to express the immortal gratitude which Belgium owes him for the creation of the rich Congo colony' (p. vi). The book includes extensive quotes from Leopold II's speeches and papers, including the four extracts below. (All were, of course, originally in French, and the de Lichtervelde translation varies slightly from other versions).

---

[1] Leopold II (1835–1909) was king of the Belgians from 1865.

6.2 African women in the Congolese village at the 1897 International Exposition in Brussels. Many World Fairs in this period included recreated 'African' villages as a means of bringing the Empire to a curious public: note the onlookers in the background. Photo by René Schoentjes.

(a) Speech to the Belgian Senate, 31 March 1861

> As heir to the throne, Leopold was automatically a member of the Senate, the upper house of the Belgian parliament. He used this position to make a number of speeches on foreign policy issues.

If the country should consult its best friend, the one from which it has received the greatest proofs of affection and devotion, if it asked, 'What must we do to raise to its highest degree the material and spiritual prosperity of the kingdom?' this friend would reply: 'Imitate your neighbors, reach across the seas each time the opportunity presents itself[']. You will find there precious outlets for your products, food for your commerce, occupation for all the activities from which we cannot draw a profit at the present time, a useful place for our surplus population, new revenues for the treasury which will perhaps, some day, permit the Government, after the example of the Netherlands, to lower the tax rates in the mother country, [and] finally, a certain increase in power and a still better position in the center of the great European family. The realization of all that can be useful to the country will always be regarded by us, from father to son, as a family duty.

[. . .]

(b) Speech opening the International Geographical Conference on Africa, in Brussels, 12 September 1876

In 1876 an international conference of explorers and geographers was held in Brussels under the patronage of Leopold II. The purpose of the conference was to discuss the exploration of Africa and the suppression of the slave trade. This was Leopold II's first direct involvement with Africa.

The subject which calls us together to-day is one which deserves to interest in the highest degree the friends of humanity. To open to civilization the sole part of our globe which it has not yet penetrated, to pierce the darkness which envelops whole populations is, I dare say, a crusade worthy of this century of progress, and I am happy to affirm how favorable public sentiment is to its accomplishment. The current is with us.

[. . .]

Do I need to tell you that in calling you together at Brussels, I have not been guided by egotistical motives? No, gentlemen, if Belgium is small, it is happy and satisfied with its lot. I have no other ambition than to serve it well. But I do not go so far as to claim that I would be insensible to the honor which would result for my country if an important advance in a matter which will be of note in our epoch was dated from Brussels. I would be very happy if Brussels became, in a way, the headquarters of this civilizing movement.

(c) Letter to M. Beernaert, First Minister of Belgium, 22 September 1889

Auguste Beernaert (1829–1912), a moderate Catholic, became First Minister in 1884 with Leopold II's backing. By 1889, the Congo adventure was proving very expensive and Leopold II desperately needed financial support from the Belgian Parliament. This letter was written to Beernaert at a time when Leopold II was trying to persuade him and his Cabinet colleagues to support a scheme to bail out the Congo's finances.

A country must grow or decline. Convinced for a long time of this truth, I have devoted my efforts to extending the horizon open to my compatriots. This road is the only one over which I can lead them, for the other leads to misery and to the political and social disorders to which all nations, incapable of supporting the responsibilities of their existence and development, are exposed.

For thirteen years as senator, for twenty-four years as constitutional chief of state, I have been constantly preoccupied with saving the country from choking in its narrow limits and with finding an outlet for her surplus production of men, things and ideas. Belgium has been justly compared to a boiler without a safety valve. During these thirty-seven years, not a day, not an hour has passed in which I have not striven personally to direct its excess activity to a wider sphere of enterprise and to prepare it a future worthy of its glorious past. The country has supported me and I now have the means of being very useful to it in the direction of its most pressing interests. Having worked solely for my country, my heart desires that it profit by my labor and my sacrifices, not only during my short existence, but for many years after me.

[. . .]

I ask nothing except to be able usefully to continue to devote all my available personal resources to the expansion of our exterior interests.

The Congo, if it were ceded to a great power or to a sovereign company, would march to a rapid and certain development. Henceforth it has an immense market value. In writing you, it is not of my personal interests that I am thinking.

My aspirations are higher. I would like, without sacrifice on the part of the taxpayers, to have helped in enlarging to-day's sphere of our national activity with another forty-six times as large as Belgium where our manufacturers shall never be excluded. What I have sought in Africa, what I shall find there more and more if I am followed is, with the progress of civilization, work for our industrial establishments and, as a consequence, for their numerous workers.

(d) Memorial by Leopold II in the last edition of the *Official Bulletin of the Congo Free State*, 1908

The Congo Free State was taken over by the Belgian state in 1908, the year before Leopold II died. This memorial from the king was published in the last edition of the official journal of the Free State.

The sovereign . . . , having constituted the private domain of the State and having, by ordering the creation of forests in accordance with the most modern methods of rational exploitation, assured its maximum productivity, having authorized numerous investigations of its mineral resources and secured to the State a notable part of the eventual profits from mining, nevertheless did not choose to dispose of the revenues of the foundation for his personal benefit. He divided these revenues into two parts. He believed, in the first place, that the wealth created by the efforts of both whites and blacks could, and in all justice should, be useful to both. He wished that a part of the property which he took over in the general interest be utilized to ameliorate the material and moral lot of the natives, and notably to develop Belgian missions; [. . .] Finally he wished that a large part be given to the arts and sciences and to the beautifying of Belgium in order to make it shine with a more brilliant luster, augment its prestige in the world, and increase its prosperity and wealth. A program equally favorable to all those, of color or not, who were destined to depend on the future Belgian administration, assuring wages to a multitude of workers, stimulating national exertion and assigning to Belgium and its future colony a worthy rank among the nations.

6.13
Protest against atrocities in the Congo

E.D. Morel (1903) *The Congo Slave State. A Protest against the new African Slavery; And an Appeal to the Public of Great Britain, of the United States, and of the Continent of Europe*, Liverpool: John Richardson & Sons, pp. 14–17.

Edmund Morel (1873–1924) was one of the sharpest critics of the Congo Free State. The following extract is from one of his earlier pamphlets on the subject. In it, he examines the economic implications of the legal framework created by Leopold's decrees. Morel was both very well informed about the Congo and precise in his analysis of how the State worked.

No sooner, however, had the Sovereign of the Congo State entered, on paper, into possession of the territories assigned to him by the Powers, than he issued a decree, as we have seen, claiming that all 'vacant lands' belonged to the State; the term 'vacant lands' meaning – as was explained in that decree and successive decrees – all land throughout the territories assigned to him, with the exception of the land built upon, or in actual cultivation by the natives. Now as neither the land upon which native villages are built, nor land upon which the natives cultivate food-stuffs for their consumption contain products of commercial value, this decree was not only calculated to hinder trade, actual or potential, but positively debarred the native from trading at all.

This decree was represented as a measure really framed in the interests of the natives themselves to prevent their being taken in by unscrupulous European merchants. In the years that followed, the international position of the Congo State strengthened considerably.

[. . .]

When he felt himself sufficiently strong, the Sovereign of the Congo State showed clearly the true significance he attached to the decree of July, 1885, by issuing in 1891 a decree . . . claiming that all the products of the land belonged to the *Domaine Privé* – that is to say to the State (which is himself), forbidding natives to collect these products, and forbidding European merchants to purchase such products under threat of being denounced to the Judicial – mark the Judicial – Authorities.

By this decree and by the circulars which followed it, coupled with the decree of July, 1885, which preceded it, trade was not only hindered, natives were not merely debarred in theory from trading at all, **but Trade, actual and potential, was swept out of existence throughout one million square miles of territory in Africa in which the Powers had expressly declared trade should be free and unrestricted.**

The right of the native to collect the products of commercial value which his land produces; the right of the native to sell those products to European merchants in exchange for goods; the right of the European to purchase those products, had disappeared because **one man sitting in Brussels, thousands of miles away, had decreed that it should be so.**

[. . .]

To frame such a **Policy** was one thing. To give effect to it was another; but what was its motive?

433

It was given effect to in this wise, and its motive has never been one instant in doubt.

All land not built upon or cultivated, having been 'juridically' declared 'vacant,' all the products of the land having been 'juridically' declared State property; the theory that the native owned the products of commercial value yielded by the soil having been 'juridically' disposed of, and such a thing as trade having therefore, 'juridically' disappeared; all that remained to be done was to gather in as great a quantity as possible of those products of commercial value. As the native of Equatorial Africa is not a brute, but a man, the expectation that he would bring in the produce of the land, which he no doubt persists in continuing to believe to be his, for a trifling payment, or for no payment at all, was not to be entertained, and was not in point of fact entertained in Brussels. So a system of taxation was started and applied. The native would be called upon to pay taxes, and he would pay those taxes in kind: that is to say, in the products of commercial value, growing in that 'vacant land' which used to be his, but which had now been 'juridically' acquired by somebody else. That 'vacant' land should contain inhabitants whom it was decided ought to pay taxes, might be a contradiction in terms – but what matter? The land had been 'juridically' declared vacant.

[. . .]

6.14

Roger Casement's *Congo Report,* 11 December 1903

B. Harlow & M. Carter (eds.) (2003) *Archives of Empire.*
Vol II: *The Scramble for Africa*, Durham, NC:
Duke University Press, pp. 716–17, 723–4.

The following is an extract from the official report by the British Consul, Roger Casement (1864–1916), on his journey to the Upper Congo. Henry Petty-FitzMaurice, 5th marquess of Landsdowne (1845–1927) was the British Foreign Secretary.

Mr Casement to the Marquess of Landsdowne
My Lord,
I have the honour to submit my Report on my recent journey to the Upper Congo.

[. . .]

Although my visit was of such short duration, and the points touched at nowhere lay far off the beaten tracks of communication, the region visited was one of the most central in the Congo State, and the district in which most of my time was spent, that of the Equator, is probably the most productive. Moreover, I was enabled, by visiting this district, to contrast its present day state with the condition in which I had known it some sixteen years ago. Then (in 1887) I had visited most of the places I now revisited, and I was thus able to institute a comparison between a state of affairs I had myself seen when the natives lived their own savage lives in anarchic and disorderly communities uncontrolled by Europeans, and that created by more than a decade of very energetic European intervention. That very much of this intervention has been called for no one who formerly knew the Upper Congo could doubt, and there are widespread proofs of the great energy displayed by Belgian officials in introducing their methods of rule over one of the most savage regions of Africa.

[. . .]

This region is, I believe, the home, or birthplace of the sleeping sickness – a terrible disease, which is, all too rapidly, eating its way into the heart of Africa, and has traversed the entire continent to well-nigh the shores of the Indian Ocean. The population of the Lower Congo has been gradually reduced by the unchecked ravages of this, as yet, undiagnosed and incurable disease, and as one cause of the seemingly wholesale diminution of human life which I everywhere observed in the regions visited, a prominent place must be assigned to this malady. The natives certainly attribute their alarming death rate to this as one of the inducing causes, although they attribute, and I think principally, their rapid decrease in numbers to other causes as well. Perhaps the most striking change observed during my journey into the interior was the great reduction observable everywhere in native life. Communities I had formerly known as large and flourishing centres of population are today entirely gone, or now exist in such diminished numbers as to be no longer recognizable. The southern shores of Stanley Pool had formerly a population of fully

5,000 Batekes,[1] distributed through the three townships of Ngaliema's (Leopoldville), Kinchasa and Ndolo, lying within a few miles of each other. These people, some two years ago, decided to abandon their homes, and in one night the great majority of them crossed over into the French territory on the north shores of Stanley Pool. Where formerly had stretched these populous native African villages, I saw today a few scattered European houses, belonging either to Government officials or local traders. In Leopoldville today there are not, I should estimate, 100 of the original natives or their descendants now residing.

[. . .]

[The following extract is taken from an enclosure with transcript reports of his meetings with local inhabitants:]

'I am N.N. These two beside me are O.O. and P.P. all of us from Y . . . From our country each village had to take twenty loads of rubber. These loads were big; they were as big as this . . .' (producing an empty basket which came nearly up to the handle of my walking stick). 'That was the first size. We had to fill that up but as the rubber got scarcer the white man reduced the amount. We had to take these loads in four times a month.'

Question: 'How much did you get paid for this?'

Answer (entire audience): 'We got no pay. We got nothing.'

And then, N.N., whom I asked again said:

'Our village got cloth and a little salt, but not the people who did the work. Our Chief ate up the cloth; the workers got nothing. The pay was a fathom of cloth and a little salt for every basket full, but it was given to the Chief, never to the men. It used to take ten days to get the twenty baskets of rubber – we were always in the forest to find the rubber vines, to go without food, and our women had to give up cultivating the fields and gardens. Then we starved. Wild beasts – the leopards killed some of us while we were working away in the forest and others got lost or died from exposure and starvation and we begged the white man to leave us alone, saying we could get no more rubber, but the white men and their soldiers said: "Go. You are only beasts yourselves, you are only nyama (meat)". We tried, always going further into the forest, and when we failed and our rubber was short, the soldiers came to our towns and killed us. Many were shot, some had their ears cut off; others were tied up with ropes round their necks and bodies and taken away. The white men sometimes at the post did

---

[1] One of the tribes of the Bantu ethnic group in West Africa, settled in the Congo river basin.

not know of the bad things the soldiers did to us, but it was the white man who sent the soldiers to punish us for not bringing in enough rubber.'

6.15

The 'Hun-Speech'

J. Penzler (ed.) (1904) *Die Reden Kaiser Wilhelms II. in den Jahren 1896 bis 1900,* Leipzig, vol. 2, pp. 209–11. Translation from German by Annika Mombauer.

On 27 July 1900, Wilhelm II, emperor of Germany (1859–1941), addressed the volunteers of the First East Asia infantry regiment who were due to leave for China. The exact wording of the speech is not known; various different accounts were taken by the journalists present. The significance of the speech however is widely recognised. Wilhelm was determined to avenge the deaths of Germans in the Boxer Rebellion, particularly that of German envoy Clemens von Ketteler (1853–1900). In bellicose and belligerent terms he roused the troops to what he saw as a crusade against an 'evil' oppressor.

A great task awaits you: you are to avenge the large injustice that has occurred. The Chinese have overthrown international law, they have made a mockery of the holiness of the envoy and of the duties of hosts in a way that has not previously been seen in world history. . . . You know well that you are to fight against a cunning, brave, well armed, cruel enemy. When you meet him, then know: Pardon will not be granted [to you], prisoners will not be taken. Wield your weapons in such a way that for a thousand years no Chinese person will ever dare so much as to look askance at a German. Preserve manly order! God's blessing be with you, the prayers of an entire nation, and my wishes, accompany you, every single one. Open a path for culture once and for all! Now you may travel. Adieu, comrades!

6.3 French political cartoon, *Le Petit Journal*, 1890. Outside powers (left to right): Great Britain, Germany, Russia, France and Japan carve up China into 'spheres of influence'. This cartoon well represents the situation in China in the 1890s prior to the Boxer Rebellion.

6.16

German settlers and the Herero uprising, 1904

E. Sonnenberg (1905) *Wie es damals am Waterberg zuging.*
Ein Beitrag zur Geschichte des Hereroaufstandes, Berlin:
Wilhelm Süsserott Verlagsbuchhandlung, pp. 34–6, 49–50,
69–72. Translation from German by Annika Mombauer.

Else Sonnenberg was married to a German trader and joined him
in German South-West Africa in March 1903. They set up their
home in the town of Waterberg, where they would be caught up
in the uprising of the Herero in January 1904. Gustav Sonnenberg
was murdered by the Herero on 14 January 1904, while his wife
and baby son survived the brutal attacks on the settlers that took
place in Waterberg that day. On her return to Germany, Else
Sonnenberg wrote her account 'What it was like at the Waterberg',
which was published in 1905. The book is a unique account of the
German settlers' life in the region and of the uprising as the
Germans experienced it. In addition, it is of course unusual
because it was written by a female settler.

(a) How the Herero lived

It is now time to say something about the traditions and customs of
the natives, as far as I had opportunity to observe these. Sometimes
I went with my husband to the heathens' large wharf[1] of old 'Beibei',
which is what the Herero called their Chief Kambasembi. This wharf
was a large place with many pontoks,[2] fenced by some thorn-bushes
that were tightly laid on top of and next to each other. In the evenings,
hundreds of cows came into the pens where the women, all in their
brown foul-smelling fur clothing, waited with their milk receptacles
(ehorro). In front of each pontok stood at least one onjuppa,[3] and from
each the old blind Kambasembi took the first drink. Thus demanded
the heathen tradition. Kambasembi's hut was not round like a mole-
hill, like the others, but rather square and was located in the middle
of the wharf, where the holy fire burnt which never went out.

[. . .]

---

[1] Herero settlements were known as wharfs or, in German, 'Werften'.
[2] The name of a Herero hut.
[3] Another Herero term for a receptacle for milk.

The building of the pontoks was the task of the women, and I watched how this was done. First, strong sticks were driven into the soil in a circle of three-metre circumference; those were then laced as tightly as possible with twigs and reed. Then this leaf-hut was smeared with clay and cow-dung, and soon the entire magnificent building was finished. In the rainy season it received a protective roof of straw. However, it was not rare for these huts to collapse. There were few domestic utensils to be seen in them: an onjuppa plus wooden bowls, an iron sauce-pan and at most one small wooden chair, covered in leather strips, – I rarely saw more than that. In the hut itself a wood fire is lit around which the residents lie and sleep, usually on blankets of fur.

The Herero lives for the day without worry. As far as I know, he has no concept of time. Cattle are his sole riches. Everything is about that; he has little interest in anything else, unless it is tobacco and pipe, and everyone is his master (mohonna), who gives him some tobacco.

Every elder has several wives. Kambasembi had twenty. Marriage is not holy to this people, they take wives or send them away at will, and jealousy does not plague the Herero. The Mission only accepted men with one wife into the baptism classes as a rule . . . The heathen marriage rituals were largely still used even for Christian weddings, as was also the case with our own ancestors. The wedding meal is only eaten by the men, the bride gets nothing at all, so that the marriage will not remain childless. The main meal consists of a horribly strong meat broth which does not agree with our palate.

The Herero are very superstitious; my Sofia, the washer-woman, also gave us some samples of this. She sometimes spoke of the spirit that lives in the roar of the wind, of the meaningful cries of some of the birds, and was one day beside herself with horror when she discovered a chameleon on the back of my husband, for whoever touches this animal will be struck down by a serious illness and must turn very thin, some even die from it.

Sofia also had a little daughter, a pretty, strong child of twelve years, but she was spoiling the child, like so many Herero do with their children. She was also missing the four bottom front teeth, and the two top ones were filed to a point – a tradition that was even still customary among christened Hereros. This is how they marked the tribe of the Herero. Even if the people of the Herero are not strict towards their own children, this does not mean that they are considerate towards their tribal children in general. We took in a small, very thin boy in order to strengthen him with better food. He was calm and would perhaps make a good servant later. Nobody in the whole of Waterberg, apart from the family of the missionary, had looked after the little thing, but he had scarcely been with us a few weeks when several Herero presented themselves who maintained that he was their boy and demanded payment for him. They were envious that the boy became increasingly stronger at our house, and begged him for his milk. It seemed in any case as if the lower people were rather kept in poverty and servitude, for it occurred that one of them took our dogs' bones off them or drank the rest of the milk out of the dogs' bowl; incidentally, rich and poor Herero alike stole and did not see any guilt in that, particularly if it was for the benefit of their stomachs.

[. . .]

A particularly nasty little rascal once wreaked havoc in the missionary's henhouse. Little by little 11 chickens went missing without the culprit being found. People thought it was a wild animal. Finally the thief, about twelve years old, was caught in the garden under an orange tree. He had tucked into oranges and fried chickens; as a punishment, he was buried to his neck in clay at the [military] station. . . . However, he escaped, taking half a mutton which had hung outside the veranda of the station. After that he was put in chains.

Although I had daily dealings with the people and hundreds of them came to us, I never really got to know them so thoroughly that I had complete understanding for their ways. I tried to be friendly, charitable, reserved or even unfriendly, depending on my impression of what was required. The Christians among them were on the whole less proud and more easy to convince. Several spoke highly of me to the missionary's wife. My husband managed to deal very well with the natives, and I simply copied his way of treating them.

However, as transpired later, none of all the Hereros was worthy of his mild treatment, and only a few were influenced by their 'Christian beliefs' regarding their way of life.

(b) Relations between the German settlers and the Herero[4]

On the heathen wharf, busy life did not stop. Strangers were now seen more often, who seemed to have no reason for coming, but who claimed to be distant relatives. Kamoreropo from Gaub was there for months,

[4] This excerpt from the book follows Sonnenberg's description of the death of the Herero chief Kambasembi in the autumn of 1903.

as was Samuel Maharero. Great meetings were held. When, following hour-long debates, when elders that we knew, such as Timotheus, David, Josef Katwesembana, passed our farm on their way home or even occasionally bought some wares, my husband enquired as to the reason for their endless deliberations. We were then always told: 'We are deciding who will be Kambasembi's successor, David or Salatiel'. This seemed credible, because both brothers were hostile towards each other, particularly following their father's death. 'By right' Salatiel was the successor, however David was the more talented of the two and favoured by the government. Both had many supporters, and neither wanted to budge.

[. . .]

But one never received any kind of hint regarding a decision which the assembly might have come to, and it is thus more than likely that the elders were even then brought together with the secret aim of shaking off German rule. Every now and then, some resentment also came through. Some people on the wharf complained that their land was taken away from them, that all places belonged to the whites and that they were being sold without their agreement. They also thought that [the whites] now wanted to take everything away from them, because a law[5] had been passed regarding the expiration of debts of the natives to the whites. This law necessitated that the traders and debtors to the natives attempted to recoup their debts quickly because they ran the danger of expiring after a year. There was also the occasional talk of ruthless recovery of demands. I remember that a trader came who was owed 5 Marks by a Herero. The Herero asked his debtor to wait one to two days, so that he could have his cattle brought back from the cattle-post. The trader charged him 100 Marks for the delay, that is to say he took a whole cow off him. Several elders were in our store to tell my husband this story, and their rage seemed huge. My husband and the other whites in the village were also of the opinion that such things could end up causing resentment.

Other such incidents may have occurred here and there, like the following, which I experienced myself and in which alcohol probably was the cause of the injustice that was done to a Herero. Near to our house a trader had unharnessed his cart with his wares. Katwesembana and Katjaka went to him to buy, or perhaps only to chat. The former had not taken off his hat and therefore the trader did not reply to his

---

[5] The *Kreditverordnung* (Credit Law) of 1899, which, in an effort to regulate the indebtedness of the Herero people to German traders, made instalment credit void after one year had elapsed.

address, but indicated to him that he should take his hat off before talking to him. Katwesembana laughed and continued talking without following the order. The trader then jumped at him, slapped the hat off his hat and throttled him. Several Herero hurried to the scene and parted the fighters. I stood outside the house and saw how Katwesembana, whom I did not like at all on account of his cheeky character, related this event, which Ludwig had to report to my husband about, to his fellow tribesmen. His eyes were rolling horribly and passionate hatred flashed in them; approaching me with an imperious tone, he demanded a cup of coffee, which I quickly gave him in order to be rid of him. It is to be assumed that Katwesembana did not speak in favour of the whites in the discussions of the elders. In any case I do not think that all these little events provided sufficient reason for the terrible uprising of the blacks which was no doubt being discussed back then at the Waterberg.

(c) Else Sonnenberg's account of the attack of the Herero on her family, 14 January 1904

[In the days preceding the attack, the local Herero were behaving strangely, attempting to buy everything in the Sonnenberg store on credit, and displaying increasingly threatening behaviour towards the whites in the village.]

When I stepped out of the house, my husband was sitting in a comfortable chair and in front of which were many Hereros who were waiting for him to go to the store with them. 'Ongoaye?' ('What do you want?'), he asked everyone who approached, and replied to the long answer which he was usually given: 'Kako' ('Nothing there'). . . .

I went back into the room when I heard that Herr Watermeyer arrived, who complained about the obtrusive nature of the Hereros, and that they now took everything that pleased them without asking. This used to be different before. The conversation lasted a long time. Again I became very worried, particularly when two old heathen Hereros, still with shells in their hair, armed with thick kirris (sticks), peered curiously into the room where the guns seemed to take their particular fancy.

[. . .]

Finally Herr Watermeyer left; . . . He asked my husband to sell him something. They went to the store and then I saw that immediately all the Hereros followed them. Gripped by great worry I also went to the store. . . . I called out to my husband that I wanted to help him. 'Stand in front of the box of bullets', he called out to me, 'old Tjomeva seems to be particularly keen on that'. Indeed, some sought to push closer while others were purchasing. . . . They wanted to buy everything, without enquiring after price or quality, and what they were not given they took, and my husband had to add it to the tab.

[. . .]

[A while later, Gustav Sonnenberg and his wife managed to close the store, and returned to their house for some rest. Gustav was asleep while Else did housework.]

Suddenly some people approached. Oh, it was only Perenna and two or three Hereros. He positioned himself in the door and asked as calmly as always – I hardly looked up – 'Mister iripi?' ('Where is the master?'). Lowering my head I replied: 'Mister rara, kurama' ('He is asleep, wait').

'Etjo', Perenna said very slowly, and turning around with a gesture he made room for Ludwig and Kamugenju (Judas) who entered quickly and immediately disappeared down the corridor which led to the bedroom.

That was really something, to want to wake up my husband, and I shouted: 'What do you think you're doing, come back at once!' and, repeating this, I jumped up. Then Perenna rushed towards me, held me back, ripped the guns off the wall and gave them to one of the many who were suddenly in the room. Loudly I shouted the name of my husband.

Then – three dull, terrible strokes sounded from the bedroom – a short murmuring – I staggered – Perenna let go of me. Rushing towards the corridor I saw Ludwig. He held a heavy stone hammer in his hand, his face was terribly distorted and, shouting 'Otjurumbu kackoka' ('The white is dead'), he rushed out of the house.

[. . .]

From the annexe a loud commotion could be heard. The nurse jumped up, but I pushed my way back through the threatening men who were hitting at me with their kirris, towards the bed of my husband. Only now did I realise the horror of what I had called out in search for help: 'He has been murdered'. The right temple was shattered and a small trickle of blood ran down the cheek onto the white pillow. . . .

Then they charged in, the horde of thieves, and threw themselves onto boxes and suitcases, dragging out linen and clothes. One smashed the window. How quickly this was done! . . . Loud screams could be heard outside. Oh God, there was the nurse with the child in her arms. Men approached and grabbed hold of her. Loud and shrill she called my name. In terrible fear over the child I jumped out of the window.

444

How they were raging! It sounded like the howling of wild animals. Can humans shout so terribly?! Where was I? I looked around for help, and my eye was caught by women in heathen costume who dragged away what the men passed to them, in receptacles whose contents were poured away and into which they hastily stuffed things. Where did the men get all those guns from? Where to seek refuge?

<hr>

6.17
Retribution against the Herero

L. von Estorff (1968) *Wanderungen und Kämpfe in Südwestafrika, Ostafrika und Südafrika 1904–1910*, Wiesbaden: private publication, p. 117. Translation from German by Annika Mombauer.

Ludwig von Estorff (1859–1943) took part in the war against the Herero, and recorded his impressions after the event. This is his account of his experience of the treatment of the Herero after the Battle of Waterberg in 1904.

I followed their footprints and reached several wells just after them, which were a terrible sight. Cattle that had died of thirst lay in heaps around the wells after they had reached them with their last strength but had not been able to drink in time. The Herero continued to flee in front of us into the desert. Again and again the terrible spectacle repeated itself. The men had worked with feverish haste at digging wells, but water became increasingly sparse, the watering holes less frequent. They fled from one to the next and lost almost all cattle and very many people. The tribe shrank to some minimal remains who gradually fell into our hands, parts escaped then and later through the desert into English territory. To shatter this people in this way was a policy that was both stupid and cruel, we could have saved many of them and their cattle. I suggested this to General von Trotha,[1] but he wanted their entire destruction.

---

[1] General A.D. Lothar von Trotha (1848–1920), commander-in-chief of the German armies in South-West Africa whose ruthless policy of pursuit of the Herero people into the desert after Waterberg was condemned at the time and, in 2004, was admitted by the German Government as equivalent to genocide.

6.18
German colonial policy: speeches at the Reichstag

H. Melber (2002) '". . . dass die Kultur der Neger gehoben werde!" – Kolonialdebatten im deutschen Reichstag', in U. van der Heyden & J. Zeller (eds.), *Kolonialmetropole Berlin. Eine Spurensuche*, Berlin: Berlin Edition, p. 69. Translation from German by Annika Mombauer.

Of the following three extracts, the first two are taken from speeches delivered by members of the Reichstag in 1906, almost three years after the Herero Rebellion. They represent different perspectives on German colonial policy but both illustrate the way ideas about German superiority were used to promote and justify expansion overseas. The Chancellor, Bernhard von Bülow (1849–1929), sets out what he sees as Germany's colonial destiny based on the superior qualities of the German nation. August Bebel (1840–1914), as a leading Social Democrat, was a critic of the German government's colonial policy, which he saw as brutal and cruel. But, as his speech makes clear, he was no anti-imperialist. Instead, he sets out his own vision of a colonial policy which, despite being more benevolent, was still based on the superiority of Germany. The final extract is from a speech by Dr Wilhelm Heinrich Solf (1862–1936) the State Secretary of the Colonial Office, to Parliament in 1913 shortly before the First World War. It outlines a highly radical view of the colonised as childlike, thus requiring the authority and direction of a German superior power.

(a) Chancellor Bernhard von Bülow, 28 November 1906

The question is not: whether we want to colonise or not; rather we have to colonise, whether we want to or not. The drive to colonisation, towards the spread of one's own culture, exists in every people which benefits from healthy growth and a forceful energy of life. That is why the German people has been a colonising people since its entry into

446

world history, for 2000 years, and we will remain a colonising people as long as we have healthy marrow in our bones.

(b) August Bebel, 1 November 1906

Gentlemen, the fact that colonial policy is undertaken is not in itself a crime. Colonial policy can, in certain circumstances, be an act of culture; it just depends on how colonial policy is practised. There is a big difference between how colonial policy should be, and how it is. If the representatives of cultivated and civilized peoples, like the European and North American nations are, for example, come to foreign peoples as liberators, as friends and educators, as helpers in need, in order to bring them the fruits of culture and civilization, in order to educate them to be cultured people, if it happens in this honourable and correct way, then us Social Democrats are the first who are willing to support such colonisation as a big cultural mission.

(c) Wilhelm Solf, State Secretary of the Colonial Office, 6 March 1913

The peoples with which our colonial work brings us into contact are culturally lower than us civilizing whites, in some cases far below us. It is not only our legal duty as protective masters that obliges us – no, gentlemen, our position as a cultured state forces us to help these peoples with the obvious arguments of a civilizing view of the world and to try to give them better living conditions than they have been able to create for themselves owing to their limited capacities. Colonising is missionary, that is a mission in the higher sense of education towards culture. . . . The natives are ignorant – they must be taught. They are lazy – they must learn to work. They are dirty – they must be washed. They are wild, cruel and superstitious – they must be calmed and enlightened. All in all, gentlemen: they are big children who need education and leadership.

Index

Note: 'n.' after a page number indicates the number of a note on that page; numbers in *italic* refer to illustrations.

464